Irene L. Borrett. 1987.

Gazania 'Sunbeam'

AN ILLUSTRATED GUIDE TO

Garden FLOWERS

Chrysanthemum 'Southway Suave'

AN ILLUSTRATED GUIDE TO *Garden* FLOWERS

Packed with practical advice on how to grow over 450 exciting and colourful plants to enhance your garden

David Papworth • Bob Legge • Noël Prockter

a Salamander book

Published by Salamander Books Limited
LONDON • NEW YORK

A Salamander Book

Published by Salamander Books Ltd.,
52 Bedford Row,
London WC1R 4LR,
England.

ISBN 0 86101 340 9

Distributed by
Hodder and Stoughton Services,
PO Box 6, Mill Road, Dunton Green,
Sevenoaks, Kent TN13 2XX.

Credits

Authors: David Papworth, Bob Legge and Noël Prockter. Special contributions by David Squire

Editor: Geoffrey Rogers

Designer: Roger Hyde

Filmset: SX Composing Ltd., England

Colour reproductions: Rodney Howe Ltd., Melbourne Graphics and Bantam Litho Ltd.

Photographs and line drawings: A full list of credits appears on page 488

Printed in Belgium by Proost International Book Production, Turnhout, Belgium

CONTENTS

Part One:

Annuals page 9

Part Two

Perennials page 169

Part Three

Bulbs page 329

Zinnia elegans 'Thumbelina'

INTRODUCTION

Flower borders ablaze with colour from spring to the frosts of autumn are the aim of every gardener. However large or small your garden, there are many plants to choose from to help you to achieve this goal.

This colourful book is packed with detailed and readily accessible information about flowers to brighten and beautify your garden. Each plant is accompanied by a clear line drawing, together with information about the soil type and amount of sun it requires, propagation and, of course, when it blooms.

Few gardeners can resist early-flowering bulbs that cheekily peer out of the soil in spring, creating splashes of colour when most parts of the garden are still drab and bare. But bulbs are not just for spring – many flower right through summer and into autumn. For instance, the Autumn Crocus (*Colchicum autumnale*) produces rosy-mauve flowers from August to October. Because the flowers are bare of leaves, this bulb is also known as 'Naked Boys'.

Annual plants are also included in this powerhouse of gardening knowledge. These are usually the first plants most of us are aware of as children. Youthful enthusiasm and a packet of Sunflower seeds soon capture the interest of inquisitive minds. Few young gardeners are not excited by the immense, bright-faced flowers that peer down from 1.8m (6ft) high.

Herbaceous perennials are the traditional brighteners of borders, creating dominant splashes of colour from mid- to late summer. A few, however, will even flower in late spring. The Leopard's Bane (*Doronicum* 'Miss Mason') develops large, bright yellow, daisy-like flowers, sometimes amid late daffodils.

The traditional flower borders, packed solely with herbaceous perennials, are now seldom seen. They need a large garden, a vast number of plants, and a great deal of time to keep them looking at their best. Nowadays, these plants are either grown mixed-in with shrubs, annuals and bulbous plants, or in small beds that form islands of colour amid a lawn. These beds need not be large, but 1.5m (5ft) is about the minimum width. To keep the widths of the beds in proportion to their heights, the tallest plant should be about half the width of the border. Only those herbaceous perennials that do not need staking are used, and this cuts down enormously on the amount of labour and time needed to look after them.

You don't have to have a large garden to grow bulbs, annuals and perennials. Patio gardens, packed with tubs and troughs can look charming, even in the smallest area. Spring-flowering bulbs planted in combination with biennials such as Wallflowers, Forget-me-nots and Daisies in window-boxes or tubs will soon brighten dull spots. In summer, hanging-baskets are eye-catching when trailing with colourful annuals, while a few perennials can be a dominant feast of colour in large containers. *Agapanthus*, with their umbrella-like heads in blue or white, look especially attractive when planted in a large, square-sided wooden tub.

Part One

ANNUALS

Venidium fastuosum

Author

Until his recent death, Bob Legge was Superintendent of the Central Royal Parks, London. His career in horticulture spanned over 30 years, from training at Bicton and the RHS Garden at Wisley to radio and TV broadcasts. He was a member of the RHS Floral Committee and regularly exhibited at the Chelsea Flower Show. This book communicates his enthusiasm for growing plants and serves as a tribute to his dedication.

Tagetes erecta 'Orange Jubilee' F1

Index of Scientific Names

The plants are arranged in alphabetical order of Latin name.
Page numbers in **bold** refer to text entries; those in *italics* refer to photographs.

Adonis aestivalis **25**
Ageratum houstonianum **25** *20*
Alonsoa warscewiczii **26** *20*
Althaea rosea **26** *21*
Alyssum maritimum **27** *23*
Amaranthus caudatus **27** *22*
Anagallis caerulea **28**
Anchusa capensis 'Blue Angel' **28**
Angelica archangelica **29** *23*
Antirrhinum majus 'Guardsman' **29**
Antirrhinum majus 'Trumpet Serenade' **30** *24*
Antirrhinum nanum 'Floral Carpet' F1 **30**
Callistephus chinensis 'Milady Dark Rose **36** *43*
Callistephus chinensis 'Milady Mixed' **36**
Callistephus chinensis 'Ostrich Plume Mixed' **37**
Callistephus chinensis 'Single Mixed' **37**
Campanula medium **38** *44*
Celosia argentea 'Cristata' **38**
Celosia argentea 'Pyramidalis' Apricot Brandy' **39** *45*
Celosia argentea 'Pyramidalis' 'Pampas Plume Mixture' **39**

Arctotis x hybrida **31**
Argemone mexicana **31** *24*
Asperula orientalis **32**
Begonia semperflorens **32**
Borago officinalis **33** *41*
Brachycombe iberidifolia **33** *42*
Brassica oleracea acephala **34**
Calandrinia umbellata **34**
Calendula officinalis 'Fiesta Gitana' **35**
Calendula officinalis 'Lemon Gem' **35** *42-3*
Centaurea cyanus 'Blue Ball' **40** *45*
Centaurea cyanus 'Red Ball' **40** *45*
Centaurea moschata **57** *46*
Cheiranthus x allionii 'Orange Queen' **57**
Cheiranthus cheiri **58** *46-7*
Chrysanthemum carinatum 'Court Jesters' **58** *47*
Chrysanthemum parthenium 'Golden Ball' **59** *48*
Chrysanthemum parthenium 'Snow Ball' **59**

Cineraria maritima 'Silver Dust' **60** *48*
Cladanthus arabicus **60** *49*
Clarkia elegans 'Bouquet Mixed' **61** *50*
Cleome spinosa 'Colour Fountain' **61** *51*
Cobaea scandens **62** *50*
Coix lacryma-jobi **62**
Coleus blumei 'Monarch Mixed' **63** *52*
Collinsia bicolor **63** *53*
Convolvulus major **64**
Convulvulus tricolor 'Rainbow Flash' **64** *52*
Coreopsis tinctoria 'Dwarf Dazzler' **65** *54*
Cosmos bipinnatus 'Candy Stripe' **65**
Cosmos sulphureus 'Sunny Gold' **66**
Crepis rubra **66**
Cuphea miniata 'Firefly' **67** *54-5*
Cynoglossum amabile **67**
Dahlia 'Dandy' **68**
Dahlia 'Gypsy Dance' **68** *55*
Delphinium consolida **69** *56*
Dianthus barbatus **69** *73*
Dianthus caryophyllus **70**
Dianthus chinensis 'Queen of Hearts **70**
Dianthus chinensis 'Telstar' **71** *74*
Didiscus caeruleus **71** *74*
Digitalis purpurea **72** *75*
Dimorphotheca aurantiaca 'Dwarf Salmon' **72** *76*
Echium plantagineum 'Monarch Dwarf Hybrids' **89** *76-7*
Eschscholzia californica **89** *77*
Euphorbia marginata **90** *79*
Exacum affine **90** *78*
Felicia bergeriana **91** *79*
Foeniculum vulgare **91** *80*
Gazania 'Chansonette' **92** *80*
Godetia grandiflora 'Amoena' types **92** *81, 82*
Godetia grandiflora 'Azalea-flowered **93**
Helianthus annuus 'Autumn Beauty' **93**
Helianthus annuus 'Sungold' **94** *82*
Helichrysum bracteatum **94** *83*
Helipterum manglesii **95** *83*
Hibsicus trionum **95** *84*
Iberis amara **96**
Iberis umbellata **96** *84-5*
Impatiens 'Novette' F1 Mixed **97** *85*
Kochia trichophylla childsii **97** *86*
Lagurus ovatus **98** *86*
Lathyrus odoratus 'Jet Set Mixed' **98**
Lathyrus odoratus 'Leamington' **99**
Lathyrus odoratus 'Red Arrow' **99**
Lathyrus odoratus 'Sheila McQueen' **100** *87*
Lavatera trimestris 'Alba' **100**
Lavatera trimestris 'Silver Cup' **101** *88*
Limnanthes douglasii **101** *88*
Limonium sinuatum 'Gold Coast **102** *105*
Linaria maroccana **102** *106*
Linaria reticulata 'Crimson and Gold' **103** *107*
Linum grandiflorum 'Rubrum' **103** *106-7*
Lobelia erinus 'Colour Cascade' **104** *108*
Lunaria annua **104** *108*
Lupinus hartwegii 'Pixie Delight' **121** *109*
Malope trifida 'Grandiflora' **121** *110*

Index of Common Names

African daisy 31
African marigold 157
Angelica 29
Annual aster 37
Annual border carnation 70
Annual woodruff 32
Apple of Peru 127

Baby blue eyes 126
Black-eyed Susan 136, 159
Bladder ketmia 95
Blazing star 123
Bluebottle 40
Blue lace flower 71
Borage 33
Bugloss 89
Burning bush 97
Busy Lizzie 97
Butterfly flower 156

Californian poppy 89
Canary creeper 160
Candytuft 96
Canterbury bell 38
Castor oil plant 135
Cathedral bells 62
Chinese aster 36
Chinese forget-me-not 67
Clary 153, 154
Clock vine 159
Cockscomb 38
Cone flower 136
Cornflower 40
Corn poppy 130
Creeping zinnia 155

Dwarf French marigold 158

Everlasting flower 94, 102

Fennel 91
Fibrous-rooted begonia 32
Flame nettle plant 63
Forget-me-not 125
Foxglove 72
French marigold 157

Geranium 131
Giant candytuft 96

Hare's tail grass 98
Hollyhock 26
Honesty 104
Hound's tongue 67

Indian pink 70, 71

Job's tears 62

Kingfisher daisy 91

Larkspur 69
Livingstone daisy 123, 124

Matthiola incana Dwarf Ten Week Stock **122**
Matthiola incana 'Giant Imperial Mixed' **122** *110-111*
Mentzelia lindleyi **123** *111*
Mesembryanthemum criniflorum **123** *112*
Mesembryanthemum oculatus 'Lunette' **124** *112*
Mimulus guttatus **124**
Mimulus variegatus **125** *113*
Myosotis alpestris 'Ultramarine' **125** *113*
Nemesia strumosa **126** *114-5*
Nemophila menziesii **126** *114*
Nicandra physaloides **127** *115*
Nicotiana 'Crimson Rock F1' **127** *116*
Nicotiana 'Nicki F1 Hybrids' **128** *116-7*
Nicotiana tabacum **128**
Nigella damascena **129** *117*
Papaver glaucum **129**
Papaver rhoeas **130**
Papaver somniferum 'Paeony-flowered Mixed' **130** *118-9*
Pelargonium zonale **131**
Perilla nankinensis **131** *119*
Petunia hybrids **132** *118*
Phacelia campanularia **132** *120*
Phlox drummondii 'Carnival' **133** *137*
Portulaca grandiflora **133** *137*
Pyrethrum ptarmicaeflorum 'Silver Feathers' **134** *138*
Ranunculus gramineus **134** *138*
Reseda odorata **135** *139*
Ricinus communis **135** *140*
Rudbeckia hirta 'Marmalade' **136** *140*
Salpiglossis sinuata 'Grandiflora' **136** *141*
Salvia coccinea **153**
Salvia horminum **153** *142*
Salvia patens **154**
Salvia sclarea **154** *143*
Salvia splendens 'Flarepath' **155** *143*
Sanvitalia procumbens **155** *144*
Schizanthus pinnatus 'Angel Wings' **156** *145*
Silybum marianum **156** *144*
Tagetes erecta 'Orange Jubilee' **157** *146-7*
Tagetes patula 'Yellow Jacket' **157**
Tagetes patula 'Florence' **158**
Tagetes patula 'Silvia' **158**
Tagetes signata pumila 'Starfire' **159**
Thunbergia alata **159** *146*
Tropaeolum majus 'Whirlybird' **160**
Tropaeolum peregrinum **160** *147*
Ursinia anethoides 'Sunshine' **161** *148*
Venidium fastuosum **161** *148*
Verbascum bombyciferum **162** *149*
Verbena x hybrida 'Dwarf Compact Blaze' **162**
Verbena 'Florist Mixed' **163** *150*
Viola cornuta **163** *151*
Viola x wittrockiana **164** *151*
Viscaria elegans 'Love' **164** *152*
Zea japonica 'Harlequin Mixed' **165**
Zinnia elegans 'Chippendale Daisy' **165**
Zinnia elegans 'Hobglobin Mixed' **166** *152*
Zinnia elegans 'Ruffles Hybrids' **166**

Love-in-a-mist 129
Love-lies-bleeding 27
Lupin 121

Mallow 101
Mallow wort 121
Mask flower 26
Mexican aster 65
Mignonette 135
Monarch of the veldt 161
Monkey flower 125
Moonwort 104
Morning glory 64
Mullein 162

Nasturtium 160

Opium poppy 130
Ornamental cabbage 34
Ornamental maize 165
Our Lady's milk thistle 156

Pansy 164
Pheasant's eye 25
Pimpernel 28
Poached egg flower 101
Portuguese toadflax 103
Pot marigold 35
Prickly poppy 31
Prince of Wales' feathers 39

Rock purslane 34

Scarlet flax 103
Scarlet sage 155
Shoo fly plant 127
Siberian wallflower 57
Snapdragon 29, 30
Snow on the mountain 90
Spider plant 61
Star of the veldt 72
Sunflower 93, 94
Sun plant 133
Swan River daisy 33
Sweet pea 98, 99, 100
Sweet-scented tobacco plant 127, 128
Sweet sultan 57
Sweet William 59

Toadflax 102
Tobacco plant 128
Treasure flowers 92
Tulip poppy 129

Vervain 162, 163

Wallflower 58
White mallow 100

Introduction

Annuals are those plants that create bursts of bright colour in gardens from mid-summer to the frosts of autumn. They are increased from seeds sown in spring or early summer, which germinate, grow, flower and produce seeds all in one season. There are two types of annuals, the hardy annuals (often known as HA) and half-hardy annuals (frequently known as HHA). The hardy annuals are sown where they are to flower, whereas the half-hardy annuals are sown in a greenhouse and planted out into the garden when all risk of frost has passed.

Biennials are also raised from seeds. These are sown during mid to late summer of one year, to produce flowers early during the following season.

Not all plants raised each year as annuals are proper annuals, but to produce a better display of colour they are treated in that way. For instance, both Lobelia and *Salvia splendens* are half-hardy perennials usually grown as half-hardy annuals. Sweet Williams and Common Daisies are perennials grown as biennials.

F1 hybrids

In recent years much research has gone into the production of many new F1 hybrid flowers. Gardeners now enjoy a much wider choice of variety than ever before. Although the seed of F1 hybrids is generally more expensive than that of older kinds, their advantages in colour, flower size, plant habit and general performance are well worth the extra cost of the seed.

F2 hybrids result from first and second generation crosses made between two parent lines specially bred and selected for their ability

Left: **Lavatera trimestris**
This elegant species brings colour to the garden in midsummer. The blooms are 10cm (4in) across and borne on stems up to 1m (39in) tall. Lovely varieties are available.

Below: **Brassica oleracea acephala**
Ornamental cabbages can be used to great effect as spot plants near the front of the border. Sow the seeds in spring and check for caterpillars.

Above:
Tagetes patula 'Yellow Jacket'
A beautifully compact French marigold ideal for edging a border.

Right:
Tropaeolum majus 'Whirlybird'
This colourful nasturtium variety will thrive on the poorest of soils.

to produce the desirable qualities that the breeder has in mind, and which go to make a good garden plant. In some instances, such as petunias, the introduction of F1 hybrids has almost completely superseded the older cultivars within the space of a few years. The range of species that are bred by this method is gradually extending to further enrich our homes and gardens.

Propagation
All the kinds listed in this section are grown from seed. Many of these will not require a greenhouse or frame but can be sown directly where they are to flower. In fact a number of annuals with small roots or tap-rooted systems do not transplant readily and can best be sown where they are to flower when soil conditions are suitable. Some species that have seeds large enough to handle may be sown direct into small peat pots or other containers; this avoids both pricking off and the risk of root disturbance that may occur when transplanting seedlings.

When seedlings are being pricked off or transplanted into trays from the containers in which the seed was broadcast, they are best planted with sufficient space to allow development of the planting-out stage. Thin sowings enable this task to be carried out as early as possible, before much root development has taken place.

Outdoor sowings may be either broadcast in patches or put into shallow drills or grooves drawn at intervals to allow for the full development of plants. The drills should be drawn in different directions if more than one kind of seed is sown in a border, so that the groups or patches will look less formal.

Drills will be easier to thin and weed, particularly when seedling weeds are likely to be troublesome. Thinning should be gradual and done in stages as seedlings develop. On some soils, if difficulty is experienced in making a good seed bed, it may be an advantage to cover seeds with some moistened peat.

As noted under certain species that are hardy, there is usually much to be gained, in strength and in earlier flowering, if plants are sown in the autumn. In the event of a severe winter killing them, this does give another opportunity to sow in the spring.

Many hardy annuals are admirable for filling in bare places in the garden after early spring flowering bulbs and plants are finished. Direct sowings usually start in early spring, as soon as the soil is suitably dry and crumbly.

Position

Because many species need to complete their growth in one season it is essential to give them the most suitable position possible and to allow room for their full development. A sunny site will suit most but many will tolerate partial shade and a few full shade.

Since heights vary, the taller varieties are best planted towards the back of one-sided borders, or centrally in a more formal area or where the plants may be viewed from various aspects. Those plants of intermediate height should be grown nearer the front, and the shortest or most compact kinds are the most suitable for edging.

Annual climbers may effectively be used as a background, on trellis or wire mesh, or even as groups grown wigwam fashion; there are many excellent kinds of plastic mesh suited to this purpose. Some kinds of climbers could be used to scramble over a hedge, or old tree stumps, or a bank where little else will grow. The tall climbing nasturtiums, for example, are very effective when used in this way.

Culture

Failures in all stages of development, from seedling through to flowering, can often be attributed to such causes as over- or under-watering, or seeds may have been sown too deeply or in unsuitable temperatures; pests and diseases can also take their toll if precautions are not observed.

Keep the soil just moist throughout their growing life and if possible water seedlings early in the day so that they do not remain wet overnight, which encourages the growth of diseases such as those causing damping-off and root rots.

Watering from above in full sunshine may result in leaf scorch, and drying-out of seeds during germination may kill them. Some shading at this stage is usually beneficial but should be removed before seedlings become drawn or elongated.

A number of excellent seed and growing-on mediums are now readily obtainable, and suitable for growing most kinds of annuals.

The use of suitable greenhouse sprays and smokes as soon as any pests or diseases are observed should ensure healthy plants.

The recommendations for thin sowing, whether indoors or out, must be noted; overcrowded and starved seedlings rarely develop into vigorous plants, and in any case are usually difficult to handle.

Hardening off

This stage of a seedling's life may be critical if sudden changes of temperature occur. Those plants raised in heat and intended for outdoor planting need to be gradually accustomed to lower temperatures and more airy conditions a week or two before planting out. This will depend on the species and the locality.

Tender or half-hardy kinds should be protected from frost or cold winds until very late spring. A short period during which plants stand in a sheltered position outdoors will help the hardening-off process and avoid any check in growth that might occur.

Planting out

The planting area should be prepared well beforehand, working in any necessary addition of compost or fertilizer. Seedlings should be watered a few hours before planting out and also afterwards if the soil is dry. Spacing must be sufficient to allow the full development of the species. Of course, cultivation and weeding should be carried out at suitable intervals.

Remove dead flowerheads where possible, to promote continued flowering, and destroy any plants that become affected by disease.

Above:
Eschscholzia 'Harlequin Hybrids'
A stunning variety of the Californian poppy that will revel in a sunny and dry location. Flowers all summer.

Left:
Begonia semperflorens 'Venus'
A compact cultivar of fibrous-rooted begonia with relatively large deep rose flowers. Grow in light moist soil.

Above: **Alonsoa warscewiczii**
Slender stems of dainty scarlet flowers appear in succession for many weeks in the summer. 26▸

Below: **Ageratum houstonianum 'Adriatic Blue' F1**
Neat cushions of fluffy blue flowers for carpeting and border edgings. 25▸

Above: **Althaea rosea**
The showy upstanding hollyhocks put on a splendid show in summer. They look especially effective when planted against a wall. Avoid windy areas or stake plants. 26▶

Above: **Amaranthus caudatus**
This vigorous plant produces lovely crimson tassels during midsummer. Grow them in groups in a mixed border or singly in containers. The leaves bronze with age. 27▸

Above: **Alyssum maritimum 'Violet Queen'**
These scented plants are ideal for ground cover and edgings. 27▸

Below: **Angelica archangelica**
A double bonus of aromatic feathery foliage and greenish yellow flowers. Striking as an architectural plant. 29▸

Above:
Antirrhinum 'Trumpet Serenade'
An unusual, tubular-flowered mixture of bicoloured blooms. 30◆

Below: **Argemone mexicana**
Large, light golden blooms appear against spiny, silvery green leaves. Grow in a light soil in the sun. 31◆

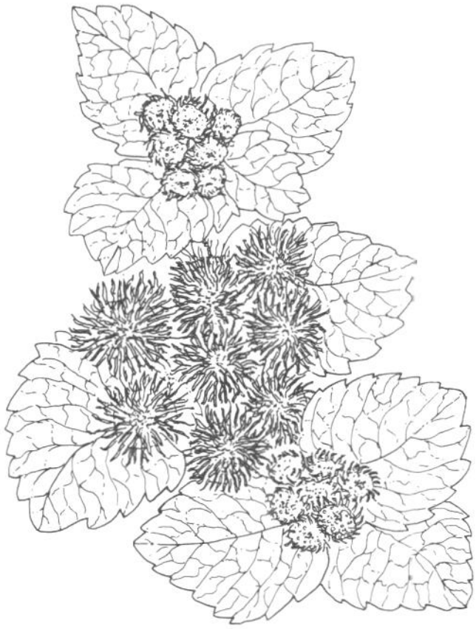

Adonis aestivalis

(Pheasant's eye)

- **Sow in spring**
- **Ordinary soil, with added peat**
- **Partly shaded or sunny position**

This hardy annual is of outstanding beauty; the deep crimson petals of the flower contrast vividly with the near-black stamens in the centre of the cup-shaped flowers. Growing on stems 30cm (12in) high, the leaves are fine, deeply cut, and almost fern-like. It is a beautiful plant for all.

Sow seed in any good growing medium in spring, prick off and grow on in the usual way. Plant out into final positions in late spring at 30cm (12in) apart. Alternatively sow seeds where they are to flower in the autumn. Once germinated make the first thinning at 15cm (6in) spacings. The following early spring complete spacing to 30cm (12in). Germination may be slow, so be patient.

Ideally suited to the front of a border, they combine very well with other annuals and biennials. When designing an area for these plants make sure you plan for bold drifts to get maximum effect. They can also be used in containers.

Take care

Watch for slug damage.

Ageratum houstonianum

- **Sow in spring**
- **Most ordinary types of soil**
- **Tolerates all positions except heavy shade**

Flowering from early summer onwards these beautiful plants resemble small powder puffs from a distance. Shown to their best when edging a formal bedding scheme, they are also good subjects for window boxes and containers.

Try to use the F1 hybrids now available; these give larger and longer trusses of blooms. The cultivar 'Adriatic' is in this class: its height is 20cm (8in), and the mid-blue flower is produced above light green hairy leaves. Although most cultivars are in the blue range there are a few whites now available.

Sow seed in boxes of growing medium in spring, under glass When large enough to handle, prick out in the usual way. Plant out in final positions at the end of spring or when the risk of frost has disappeared. Until planting out try to maintain a temperature of 10-16°C (50-60°F); lower than this will tend to check the growth of young plants.

Take care

Avoid planting out too early. 20▶

Alonsoa warscewiczi

(Mask flower)

- **Sow in late winter or early spring**
- **Rich and well-drained soil**
- **Sunny location**

Introduced from Peru this splendid plant grows to a height of 30-60cm (12-24in). Striking saucer-shaped red flowers are produced on reddish branched stems from summer to late autumn, 2-3cm (0.8-1.25in) in diameter. Leaves are ovate and a rich dark green.

Annual in habit, it requires a heated greenhouse for propagation; a temperature of 16°C (60°F), maintained up to planting-out time, will suffice. Sow the seeds in pots of a good growing medium in late winter or early spring. Prick out into boxes or individual pots when the seedlings are large enough. Grow on in gentle heat until late spring. Harden off in the usual way and plant out into permanent positions, approximately 30-40cm (12-15in) apart. Choose a sunny position for the best results and make sure the soil is free-draining, otherwise flowers will be disappointing. Stake with bushy twigs if necessary.

Take care

Do not overwater. **20▸**

Althaea rosea

(Hollyhock)

- **Sow in spring**
- **Heavy and rich soil**
- **Sheltered position but not shade**

Hollyhocks are probably the tallest plants you are likely to deal with in an ordinary garden. There are many varieties to choose from but *A. rosea* and its cultivars are by far the easiest. Flowers are produced on short stalks directly from the main stem; they range in colour from pink and red to white and light yellow. Up to 10cm (4in) in diameter, they can be single or double.

Treat as a biennial to obtain the tallest plants, by sowing where they are to flower in early summer. Take out shallow drills 23cm (9in) apart. Thin out seedlings in summer to 60cm (24in) apart. Such plants will attain a height of 2.7m (9ft) the following summer.

For annual treatment, sow on site in spring in the same way, and thin out to 38cm (15in) apart. Plants treated in this way will flower in the same year, reaching a height of about 1.8m (6ft).

Take care

Mulch in spring, and water freely in dry weather. **21▸**

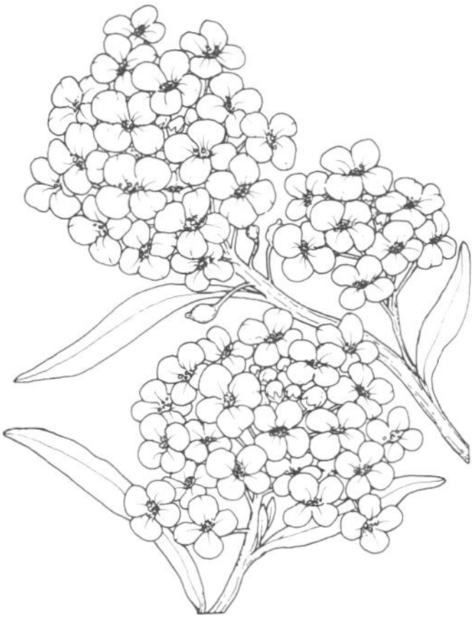

Alyssum maritimum

(Lobularia maritima)
- **Sow in early spring**
- **Ordinary soil**
- **Full sun**

An annual of extraordinary resilience, mainly because of its ability to self-seed in great quantities. Some gardeners have difficulty in eradicating it from the garden. Mats of tiny flowers are produced on short stems 7.5-10cm (3-4in) from early summer onwards if plants are sown directly where they are to flower in spring.

Plants can be raised by sowing seeds in boxes of seed-growing medium a month earlier. Prick out the seedlings into a free-draining potting medium when large enough to handle. Plant out in final positions in mid-spring. To prolong the flowering period make a further sowing in late spring.

Commonly used for edging formal beds and borders, this species can also be used effectively with other annuals in window boxes and containers. Other colours include rose pink, mauve, purple and lilac.

Take care

Use slug bait in spring. 23▶

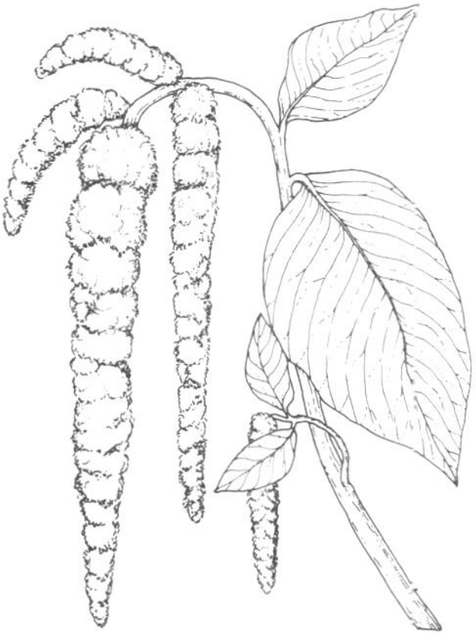

Amaranthus caudatus

(Love-lies-bleeding)
- **Sow in spring**
- **Well-cultivated soil**
- **Sunny location**

The long tail-like racemes of crimson flowers of this plant can reach 45cm (18in) in length. The flowers are produced on stems up to 105cm (3.5ft) tall. Leaves are ovate in shape and green in colour, the latter changing to bronze as the season progresses. *A. caudatus* is used mainly in formal beds as a 'spot' plant to give height. Try them as individual specimens in largish containers or in groups on a mixed border. The flowers appear in summer.

For borders sow the seed directly into the open ground in spring in a sunny position. When thinning out seedlings give plenty of room for development, about 60cm (24in) apart.

Raise plants for containers and formal borders by sowing in boxes of good seed-growing medium in early spring, prick off into individual pots under glass, and plant out into final positions in late spring.

Take care

Keep well watered in dry periods. 22▶

Anagallis caerulea

(Pimpernel)

- **Sow from spring onwards**
- **Ordinary well-drained soil**
- **Sunny location**

The hybrids and species related to the common scarlet pimpernel have now become many gardeners' favourites for planting in various parts of the garden. This beautiful blue species is low growing. Not much taller than 10cm (4in), the flowers are borne on semi-prostrate stems about 1.25cm (0.5in) in diameter and saucer-shaped. These appear from early summer onwards.

Easily grown on light soils, they can be directly sown where they are to flower. Take out shallow drills 1.25cm (0.5in) deep in spring, sow in the drills, and cover. Thin out the subsequent seedlings to 15cm (6in) apart. If soil conditions remain dry, water once a week until a good germination can be seen, then ease off the watering. Use near the edge of borders, containers and window boxes, and try a few plants in small pockets on the rock garden.

Take care

Do not overwater plants.

Anchusa capensis 'Blue Angel'

- **Sow in spring or autumn**
- **Ordinary well-drained soil**
- **Open sunny position**

This improved compact form of the wild tall species, originating from the Cape, grows only about 23cm (9in) high. The plants form neat clumps covered with ultramarine blue flowers for a considerable period. The many branching stems arise from a basal rosette of neat dark green leaves.

For early flowering, sow seed in heat in winter in seed mixture. Prick out seedlings in trays, or singly in small pots. They should be grown cool and hardened off ready for planting out in spring. Sow also outdoors in spring or in early autumn where they are to flower. Seedlings should finally be thinned to about 20cm (8in) apart. Remove dead blooms to encourage a further display. A few autumn-sown seedlings make an early indoor show if grown in 10cm (4in) pots in a cold greenhouse. Keep well watered in dry spells.

Take care

Spray against mildew in dry conditions.

Angelica archangelica

(Angelica)

- **Sow in spring**
- **Rich easily worked soil**
- **Partial shade**

A large hardy biennial, usually grown for two purposes: as a culinary herb for glazing, and as an architectural plant for the back of a large border. Umbels of yellow-green flowers open in summer; these are carried on thick hollow stems, 2-3m (6.5-10ft) in height. For the average garden three or four plants should be adequate to cover both purposes.

Sow the seed outdoors in mid-spring to flower the following year. Shallow drills deep enough to take the flat seed can be taken out in a spare part of the vegetable garden. Thin out seedlings to 30cm (12in). Plant out into final positions the following spring. Plants will die once seed has been set, but by keeping the flowers cut off a further useful year's growth can be obtained. Others left to seed will produce more than enough young plants for ordinary purposes in ensuing years. Stems should be cut young in early summer for culinary uses.

Take care

Give plants plenty of room. 23▸

Antirrhinum majus 'Guardsman'

(Snapdragon)

- **Sow late winter/early spring**
- **Light to medium soil**
- **Sunny position**

An intermediate antirrhinum of great merit, 'Guardsman' is brilliant scarlet with a white throat and yellow lips to the open parts of the central petals. Growing to a height of 38-45cm (15-18in) this cultivar is very free flowering.

As this is a half-hardy annual, sow seeds in late winter under glass or in early spring in a temperature of 16-18°C (60-65°F). Use a good peat-based growing medium or make up your own (without nutrients) of equal parts of peat and sand. Sow seed thinly and cover only lightly. Seedlings are prone to damping off disease and this is often caused by a too rich growing medium so beware. Prick off into boxes when large enough to handle. Harden off and plant out in early summer at 23cm (9in) apart.

Take care

Pinch out the central growing point when the young plants are 10cm (4in) high; this makes bushier plants.

Antirrhinum majus 'Trumpet Serenade'

(Snapdragon)

- **Sow in winter to spring**
- **Light to medium soil**
- **Sunny location**

Because of the introduction of rust-resistant cultivars the snapdragons have now returned to favour. There are many to choose from, either for planting in beds or borders or – the tall types – for use as cut flowers. The range of colours available makes it difficult to choose, but for ordinary garden purposes try the mixture 'Trumpet Serenade'. Having a dwarf bushy habit they are ideal for bedding out from the end of spring onwards. Trumpet-shaped flowers in red, pink, yellow and shades of orange are carried on 30cm (12in) stems. Leaves are a shiny dark green and ovate.

Sow seed on a peat-based growing medium in late winter or early spring, and lightly cover the seed. Keep in a temperature of 16-21°C (60-70°F). Prick off seedlings in the usual way, grow on until the end of spring, then gradually harden off.

Take care

Be sure to use a good quality medium for sowing seeds. 24▸

Antirrhinum nanum 'Floral Carpet'

(Snapdragon)

- **Sow late winter/early spring**
- **Light to medium soil**
- **Sunny site**

This is an excellent mixture of dwarf bushy uniform plants bearing many stems of bright blooms about 20cm (8in) high.

Sow from late winter to early spring in heat, or in late summer to overwinter under cold glass for earlier flowering. Sow seed very thinly in seed-growing mixture and germinate in a temperature of 16-18°C (60-65°F). Barely cover seed with mixture and shade from bright sun until germination. Prick out seedlings into trays and grow on in a lower temperature until ready to harden off. Antirrhinums may be planted out in late spring or early summer, about 23cm (9in) apart. The dwarf strains need no pinching out because they branch naturally. Remove dead flower spikes as soon as possible to prevent seed formation and encourage flowering.

Take care

Although antirrhinums are perennials best results are obtained from vigorous seedlings.

Arctotis × hybrida

(African daisy)

- **Sow in mid-spring**
- **Ordinary soil**
- **Sunny position**

Perennial in habit, this daisy is better treated as an annual for its very fine large blooms in the first year. Many plants can be lost through the winter months. Large flowers up to 10cm (4in) across can be produced from spring sowings, on stems up to 60cm (24in) tall. The narrow grey-green leaves are a lovely foil for the apricot, yellow, white or red blooms.

Choose the middle part of a sunny border to get the best from these plants. In spring make direct sowings where they are to flower. Rake the ground down to a fine tilth, take out drills 30cm (12in) apart, sow the seed thinly and cover. When germination is complete thin the seedlings in the drills to 30cm (12in) apart. Flowers will appear from early summer and keep blooming until the first frosts. As growth continues, use shortened peasticks around the plants to give a little support.

Take care

Keep plants well weeded in the early stages of growth.

Argemone mexicana

(Prickly poppy)

- **Sow in mid-spring**
- **Light and dry soil**
- **Sunny position**

This unusual annual, introduced from the semi- and tropical areas of America, is as the name implies prickly. Extremely majestic orange or yellow flowers will appear from early summer onwards and some protection is given to them by the prickly stems and leaves, the latter being pinnate and glaucous. Some individual flowers can be up to 9cm (3.5in) in diameter and being scented they will attract a number of flying insects. Reaching a height of 60cm (24in) the stems are straggly; do not however try to support them, or you will probably do more harm than good.

Sow seeds in boxes of ordinary seed-growing medium in spring at a temperature of 16°C (60°F), prick out into boxes in the usual way and plant into final positions at 30cm (12in) apart in late spring. Alternatively sow directly into the border in a sunny position during mid-spring, and later thin out to correct spacings.

Take care

Dead-head to prolong flowering 24▸

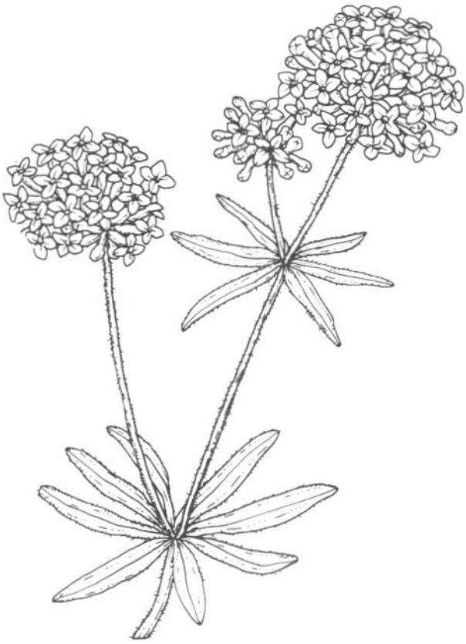

Asperula orientalis

(Annual woodruff)

- **Sow in mid-spring**
- **Ordinary but moist soil**
- **Partial shade**

The pale blue flowers of this semi-dwarf annual are strongly aromatic, and this species has a long flowering period. The tubular flowers are borne in bunches at the end of 30cm (12in) stems on which are whorls of narrow lanceolate hairy leaves.

Because of its ability to tolerate partial shade it can be used in some of the more difficult parts of the garden, and it is also valuable for ground cover purposes.

Sow in mid-spring on prepared ground where the plants are to flower. Rake the ground down to a fine tilth, broadcast the seed over the given area, and lightly rake in the seed. When germination has taken place thin out to 10cm (4in) apart.

For very early flowering in pots for the patio or windowsill, sow seed in the autumn; plant five or six seedlings to a 13cm (5in) pot, grow on through the winter in a cool position, and these will flower in spring.

Take care

Keep soil moist.

Begonia semperflorens

(Fibrous-rooted begonia)

- **Sow in late winter**
- **Light, slightly moist soil**
- **Semi-shade, or some sun**

Of all the summer annuals the begonia must rank high on the list of most gardeners. A very wide range of this group of plants is available: short, tall or medium in height, green or copper foliage, red, pink or white flowers. However they are tender and therefore some heat will be necessary at propagating time if good results are expected. Try a batch of the cultivar 'Venus'; this plant grows to a height of 15cm (6in) and has deep rose flowers large for its type. Plants spread to about 15cm (6in) across.

Sow seeds on a peat-based growing medium in late winter. Mix the seed with a little fine sand before sowing, to enable it to be sown more evenly. Do not cover the seed. Place in a temperature of 21°C (70°F). When they are large enough to handle, prick off the seedlings in the usual way. Plant out into final positions in early summer, after the danger of frost.

Take care

Do not plant out too early. 18▸

Borago officinalis

(Borage)

- **Sow in mid-spring**
- **Ordinary soil**
- **Sunny location**

This annual native herb is grown for its foliage and flowers and as a valuable addition to summer salads. Usually attaining a height of 1m (39in), the plants are better suited to the middle or back of a large border; group them together in fours or fives for a bold effect. Larger plants will need staking. The large leaves are obovate, tending to narrow at the base, covered with hairs (as are the long stems), and a good green in colour. Flowers are generally blue, but purple and white forms occur. About 2cm (0.8in) across, they resemble five-pointed stars.

This species is very easy to grow. Sow the seeds where the plants are to flower, in mid-spring. Take out small drills and cover the seed. Later thin them out to 30cm (12in) apart. Flowering begins in early summer.

Dried flowers of borage can be used to enhance the ever-popular pot-pourri; blooms are collected before they fully open.

Take care

Clear unwanted seedlings. 41▸

Brachycome iberidifolia

(Swan River daisy)

- **Sow in mid-spring**
- **Rich soil**
- **Sunny but sheltered site**

The daisy flowers of this half-hardy annual may be lilac, blue-purple, pink or white. Very free-flowering and fragrant, the blooms are produced on compact plants from early summer onwards. It is very striking when sited towards the front of a border, and can also be planted in containers on a sunny sheltered patio or yard. Wiry stems reach a height of 45cm (18in) and carry light green leaves that are deeply cut. The scented flowers, when fully open, are about 4cm (1.6in) across.

Sow the seed under glass in spring. Use a good ordinary seed-growing medium, and keep in a temperature of 16°C (60°F). When seedlings are ready, prick off in the usual way. Set plants out at 35cm (14in) intervals in late spring. Alternatively, sow seed directly into the border during mid-spring and thin out later. Some support may be necessary.

Take care

Avoid windy sites. 42▸

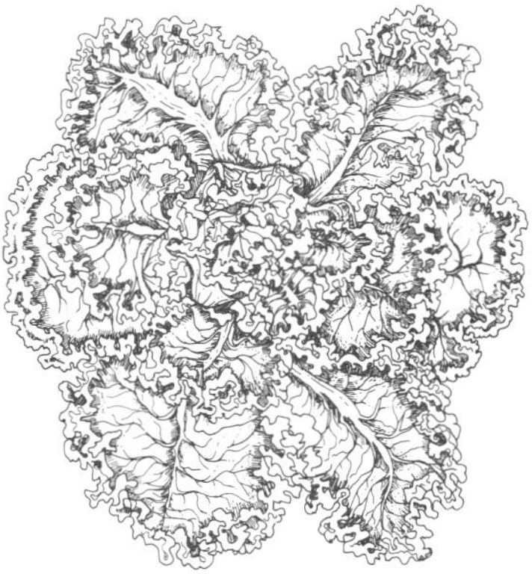

Brassica oleracea acephala

(Ornamental cabbage)

- **Sow in mid-spring**
- **Ordinary but not too acid soil**
- **Moist, not too shady position**

Grown with great panache by the Victorians, today's cultivars vary in size, shape and colour and can be safely planted with other annuals to add interest. Of the brassica (cabbage) family the two main types are the open Savoy cabbages and the somewhat taller kales. Colours range from pure white to pale yellow, pink, purple and light red. Use the Savoy types near the front of a border, and the kales towards the centre or back. The latter can be effective 'spot' plants.

Sow seed thinly in drills, in early spring. Cover the seed to a depth of 2cm (0.8in). When they are large enough plant the seedlings into permanent positions. Spacing will depend on the cultivar so read the growing instructions on the seed packet carefully. Remember that all brassicas are prone to various pests and diseases, but in particular pigeons, which can decimate them.

Take care

Spray against caterpillars in early summer.

Calandrinia umbellata

(Rock purslane)

- **Sow in spring**
- **Light, sandy soil**
- **Full sun, but sheltered site**

This dwarf plant, grown as an annual in milder areas or as a biennial elsewhere, is best suited to a sunny sheltered spot in the garden. As it grows to only 15cm (6in), put it in small pockets on the rock garden or at the front of a border. The crimson to purple flowers, 2cm (0.8in) across, are bowl-shaped, and open from early summer onwards. Mats of short stems carry linear, grey-green leaves.

For annual propagation sow seed under glass in spring in any good seed-growing medium; keep in a temperature of 16°C (60°F), prick out in the usual way, and grow on at a temperature of 10-16°C (50-60°F). Harden off and plant out in late spring at 23-30cm (9-12in) intervals.

As a biennial sow the seed during early summer where the plants are to flower the following year. Thin out the seedlings before the end of the summer, and complete final spacing the following spring.

Take care

Do not overwater.

Calendula officinalis 'Fiesta Gitana'

(Pot marigold)

- **Sow in early spring or autumn**
- **Ordinary free-draining soil**
- **Sunny spot**

The newer marigolds, in particular 'Fiesta Gitana', have large double flowers up to 10cm (4in) across. Cream, yellow, gold or orange flowers are formed on compact plants 30cm (12in) high. Stems bear light green leaves, which are long and narrow, and these set off the bright blooms admirably. Apart from their usefulness in the annual border, preferably towards the front, try them in window boxes and other containers. They thrive on poor soil; use them in conditions where other plants may not survive, but make sure such soils are free-draining.

Sow the seeds where they are to flower in early spring, lightly covering them with soil; thin out subsequent seedlings to 15cm (6in) apart. Alternatively sow seed in the usual way during the autumn; such sowings will provide earlier flowers on stronger plants. At the end of each season get rid of any unwanted self-sown seedlings.

Take care
Dead-head to prolong flowering.

Calendula officinalis 'Lemon Gem'

(Pot marigold)

- **Sow in early spring or autumn**
- **Ordinary free-draining soil**
- **Sunny spot**

The very reliable calendulas never cease to delight. The beautiful yellow, orange or gold shades of the flowers are a cheerful sight throughout the season. 'Lemon Gem' has striking double yellow flowers that are formed on compact plants 30cm (12in) high. The long light green leaves are a perfect foil for the bright flowers. Very free-flowering and highly pungent they can be used almost anywhere in the garden.

As this is a hardy annual, seeds can be sown where they are to flower during the autumn or early spring. Take out shallow drills and then lightly cover the seed. Thin out to 15cm (6in) apart. Alternatively, they can be raised under glass to give uniformity for the formal planting areas. Raise during early spring in a frost-free temperature. Autumn-sown plants will be stronger, and flower earlier.

Take care
Dead-head to prolong flowering. 42▶

Callistephus chinensis 'Milady Dark Rose'

(China aster)

- **Sow in early spring**
- **Ordinary well-drained soil**
- **Sunny and open site**

China asters are useful plants for the bed or border, or in containers including window boxes. Recent developments have led to a number of useful additions of the dwarf bedding types, and the cultivar 'Milady Dark Rose' is recommended. The rose-coloured double flowers are borne above the dark green foliage. Plants are about 23cm (9in) high, making them ideal bedding plants especially in areas where wind may cause damage to taller types.

Asters can be affected by various wilt disorders so avoid planting them in the same spot more than once. Sow seed under glass in early spring at a temperature of 16°C (60°F). Use any good growing medium for this purpose, and the subsequent pricking out into boxes. Harden them off in the usual way and plant out into flowering positions in early summer, 15cm (6in) apart.

Take care

Avoid overwatering at any stage. 43▸

Callistephus chinensis 'Milady Mixed'

(China aster)

- **Sow in early spring**
- **Any soil, but well drained**
- **Sunny and open position**

A half-hardy annual, the aster is useful for almost any purpose. Many forms have been developed, from 15cm (6in) high to 75cm (30in). A wide range of colours is available and the shape of the flowers can be just as varied, from button types to large chrysanthemum forms. As a moderate choice try the 'Milady Mixture'. The blooms are slightly incurving and weather resistant, stems are 25cm (10in) high, and the double flowers are in shades of blue, rose, rose-red and white. They are ideal as bedding plants or as drifts in the annual border.

Early flowering plants should be raised under glass in a temperature of 16°C (60°F) during early spring. Sow the seeds in pots or boxes of any good soil-based growing medium. Prick out into boxes, harden off in the usual way and plant out into final positions, 15cm (6in) apart, in late spring or early summer.

Take care

Dead-head to prolong flowering.

Callistephus chinensis Ostrich Plume Mixed

(Annual aster)

- **Sow in early spring**
- **Any well-drained soil**
- **Sunny and open location**

Probably the best of the double strains, the ostrich plume types are earlier flowering than most. The lovely flowers are formed on branching strong stems up to 45cm (18in) high. Each individual bloom is elegantly plumed and can be 10-15cm (4-6in) in diameter. The violet, pink, red, crimson, lavender-blue or white flowers are fairly weather resistant, but remove damaged or dead blooms. Very popular as cut flowers for the house because of their long-lasting qualities, they are also quite at home as bedding plants in a formal bed.

Raise from seed in early spring under glass, in a temperature of 16°C (60°F). Use any good growing medium. Prick off the seedlings in the usual way. Harden off and plant out into flowering positions in early summer at 23cm (9in) intervals.

Take care

Try not to soak the open flowers when watering.

Callistephus chinensis Single Mixed

(Annual aster)

- **Sow in early spring**
- **Any well-drained soil**
- **Sunny and open situation**

Remarkable for their long-lasting qualities in the garden or when cut for floral decoration, these flowers are worth a place in any garden. Petals of the single large daisy-like flowers are carried in two or three rows in shades of pink, red, mauve, blue or purple. The long branching stems can be up to 60cm (24in). Leaves are coarsely toothed, ovate in shape and a good green. Although relatively tall the strong stems should not require support. Keep removing dead flowers so that further buds can develop into new blooms.

Sow seed of this half-hardy annual in spring under glass, in a temperature of 16°C (60°F). Use any good growing medium. Prick out in the usual way and harden off. Plant out into flowering positions in early summer, 23cm (9in) apart.

Take care

To avoid various aster wilts, use a fresh growing site each year.

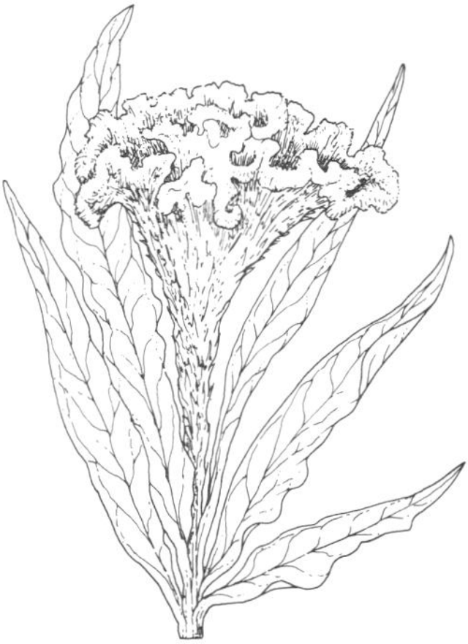

Campanula medium

(Canterbury bell)

- **Sow in early summer**
- **Rich and fertile soil**
- **Sunny location or partial shade**

This is a biennial of very great merit. If you can afford the space and time to wait it is worthy of a place in any garden.

Flowering in late spring to mid-summer from the previous year's sowing, the upturned bell-shaped flowers are produced in profusion on sturdy plants up to 90cm (3ft) in height. The contrasting foliage is fairly long, wavy edged, hairy and a striking green that sets off the blue, pink, white or violet flowers.

Sow seed in boxes in early summer, prick off the seedlings into individual pots, grow on until the autumn and then plant out into permanent positions; give at least 30cm (12in) space around each plant. Alternatively keep plants growing in pots through the winter and plant out in spring.

This species is very successful in partial shade, but ideally suited to a sunny position.

Take care

Watch for slug damage in winter.

Celosia argentea cristata

(Cockscomb)

- **Sow in early spring**
- **Rich and well-drained soil**
- **Sunny but sheltered position**

As the common name implies the flowers are unusual in being crested in shape. Colours are red, orange, yellow or pink. Stems are up to 30cm (12in) in height and carry light green ovate leaves. These plants can be successfully grown outdoors in the summer. Flowers are at their best from early summer onwards, with crests 7-13cm (2.75-5in) across.

This tender annual requires heat for good germination. Sow under glass in early spring at a temperature of 16-18°C (60-65°F). Use a reliable seed-growing medium. Prick off seedlings into individual small pots for better results. Harden off carefully about two weeks before required for planting. (Should plants look a little starved in the pots, give a weak liquid feed once a week up to hardening off.) Plant out into flowering positions in early summer, or late spring in milder areas. Space at 30cm (12in) intervals.

Take care

Overwatering causes collar rot. 44▸

Celosia argentea pyramidalis 'Apricot Brandy'

(Prince of Wales' feathers)

- **Sow in early spring**
- **Well-drained, fertile soil**
- **Sunny, sheltered location**

Outdoor cultural requirements and propagation are the same as for all celosias. 'Apricot Brandy' was introduced for its dwarf effect: the height at most will be 40cm (16in). A handsome shade of apricot, the plumes are an aggregate of both central and basal side shoots. The plants may have plumes up to 50cm (20in) across, and the light green foliage can be overwhelmed by the bloom.

This cultivar makes an excellent bedding subject for formal plantings, but is also invaluable for displays in window boxes, troughs or containers for the patio or yard. Group together in large pots and place near the front door, to make a pleasant feature for visitors to admire.

Take care

Do not overwater at any stage or plant out too early. 45▶

Celosia argentea pyramidalis 'Pampas Plume Mixture'

(Prince of Wales' feathers)

- **Sow in early spring**
- **Well-drained, fertile soil**
- **Sunny and sheltered spot**

'Pampas Plume Mixture' is worth trying. It has an ideal colour range for the average garden and includes shades of red, yellow, pink and orange. This strain will yield plants up to 75cm (30in), and secondary side shoots will provide a continuing wealth of colour. The feather plumes will themselves measure 10-20cm (4-8in).

As this is a very tender annual, it will require some heat for propagation purposes. Sow seed under glass during early spring in a proprietary peat-based growing medium. Temperatures of 16-18°C (60-65°F) should be maintained. Prick out seedlings into individual pots, and grow on in a warm part of the greenhouse. Harden off about two weeks before planting out into final positions in early summer, 30cm (12in) apart, in a sunny position.

Take care

Do not overwater at any stage.

Centaurea cyanus 'Blue Ball'

(Cornflower; Bluebottle)

- **Sow in autumn or spring**
- **Ordinary well-drained soil**
- **Sunny position**

The common native cornflower is a great favourite, but selection and breeding over many years has led to improved strains for the garden. If you decide to grow this plant, try 'Blue Ball', which is very true to type and free from the purple tinge often found in the blues. Strong 90cm (36in) stems carry the ball-like flowers well above the leaves, which are narrow and lanceolate in shape. Grow in bold groups near godetias and you will have a beautiful contrast of colour during the summer. They are often grown as cut flowers either in the border or in rows in another part of the garden.

Sow seeds in either autumn or spring; those sown in autumn will make larger plants. Take out drills where the plants are to flower, sow the seed and cover. Thin out subsequent seedlings to 45cm (18in). In very cold areas protect autumn-sown seedlings from frost.

Take care
Give support to very tall types. 45▸

Centaurea cyanus 'Red Ball'

(Cornflower)

- **Sow in spring**
- **Ordinary well-drained soil**
- **Sunny site**

This very useful cultivar is an attractive partner to 'Blue Ball' especially if grown for flower arrangements. The individual blooms can be up to 5cm (2in) across, deep red and double. The cultivar has been selected and bred for earliness, and is more suited to springtime sowing, either directly where it is to flower or under glass.

Make first sowings in the greenhouse in early spring in any good growing medium, prick out into boxes and grow on in reduced temperature; harden off and plant out in late spring. Space out to 30-45cm (12-18in).

'Red Ball' is worth a place in the annual border, in combination with plants of similar height.

Take care
Cut off dead flowers to encourage new buds and growth. 45▸

Above: **Borago officinalis**
This tall decorative herb has delightful blue flowers in summer. Young leaves can be used in summer salads and the flowers can be dried for use in potpourris. 33◆

Left: **Brachycome iberidifolia**
Myriads of fragrant daisy flowers cover these compact bushy plants during the summer months. They thrive in the sun but must be sheltered from strong winds. Plant towards the front of the border. 33▸

Right: **Callistephus chinensis 'Milady Dark Rose'**
This dwarf type of China aster bears large, long-lasting blooms. An ideal bedding plant, particularly in windy areas. Good for window boxes. 36▸

Below: **Calendula officinalis 'Lemon Gem'**
Double flowers of a beautiful yellow adorn this compact plant throughout the summer. The calendulas are very reliable annuals and can be used in any sunny area of the garden. 35▸

Left: **Campanula medium**
This old favourite biennial produces large bell-shaped flowers on sturdy plants. Grow in a rich fertile soil for best results and position where it receives some sunshine. This is a single-flowered plant. 38▸

Right: **Centaurea cyanus**
The cultivars 'Blue Ball' and 'Red Ball' are shown here growing together. Excellent for cutting, these are dependable plants for a sunny spot. They thrive in ordinary soil. 40▸

Below: **Celosia argentea pyramidalis 'Apricot Brandy'**
These fine plants revel in a warm and sunny position. Their plume-like flowers last for weeks during the summer, showing up elegantly against the light green foliage. 39▸

Left: **Centaurea moschata 'Dobies Giant'**
Large fragrant flowers in pastel shades adorn this oriental plant in summer. Sow in the border. 57▸

Right: **Chrysanthemum carinatum 'Court Jesters'**
These brightly coloured flowers will last well in water when cut. A very reliable annual for most soils. 58▸

Below: **Cheiranthus cheiri**
Plant these near the house to enjoy their beautiful fragrance on spring evenings. There are many cultivars to choose from, varying in height and colour. Sow the previous summer and protect tall types in winter. 58▸

Above: **Chrysanthemum parthenium 'Golden Ball'**
This compact plant is smothered with bright, button-like blooms for many weeks during the summer. Ideal for borders, tubs and window boxes. 59▶

Below **Cineraria maritima 'Silver Dust'**
The fine silvery foliage provides an excellent foil for summer bedding flowers. Remove the yellow blooms to encourage a neat shape. 60▶

Above: **Cladanthus arabicus**
Orange buds open to golden yellow flowers in endless succession well into the autumn. The plant will thrive in a light soil and a sunny position. The flowers are fragrant. 60▸

Above: **Cobaea scandens**
A vigorous climber for a sheltered sunny spot. The large bell flowers change from green to purple as they mature. Provide support. 62▶

Right: **Cleome spinosa 'Colour Fountain'**
This spectacular plant produces clusters of spidery flowers on tall strong stems. Delicately scented. 61▶

Below: **Clarkia elegans 'Bouquet Mixed'**
These frilly double flowers are long lasting when cut and superb for flower arranging. Grow in sun. 61▶

Above: **Coleus blumei 'Monarch Mixed'**
A large-leaved mixture of rich colour combinations that will thrive in a sheltered sunny position. Pinch out the flowers for compact plants. 63▸

Below: **Convolvulus tricolor 'Rainbow Flash'**
This dwarf hybrid produces bright new flowers each morning; they will fade during the afternoon. Excellent in tubs and window boxes. 64▸

Above: **Collinsia bicolor**
A pretty annual with tiered sprays of dainty bicoloured flowers. It will grow in a damp, partially shaded position. Be sure to provide support for the slender 60cm (24in) stems. 63▸

Above: **Cuphea miniata 'Firefly'**
This bushy, highly branched plant produces clouds of bright scarlet blooms from early summer onwards. Plant in the centre of the border, where it will require no staking. 67▶

Left: **Coreopsis tinctoria 'Dwarf Dazzler'**
A reliable dwarf cultivar with masses of crimson and gold flowers in summer. Will tolerate the polluted atmosphere of towns and cities. 65▶

Right: **Dahlia 'Gypsy Dance'**
A dwarf semi-double strain of bedding dahlia with many new colours on bushy plants. Grow from seed sown under glass in early spring and plant out in early summer. Plants will grow to 60cm (24in). 68▶

Above: **Delphinium consolida 'Tall Double Mixed'**
Tall branching sprays of lovely flowers in many shades for cutting and border display. These are very vigorous plants and need support. 69▸

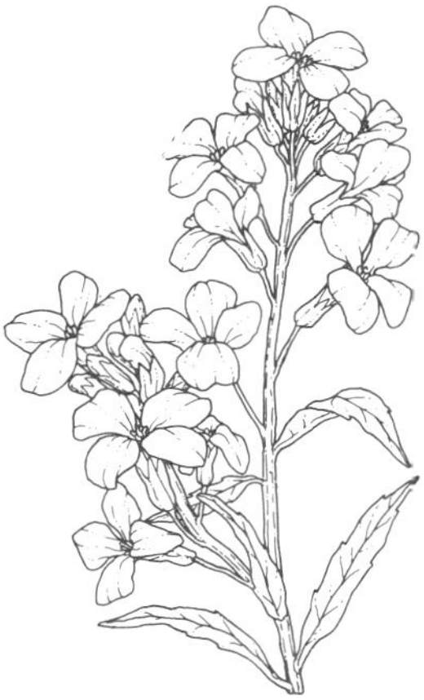

Centaurea moschata

(Sweet sultan)

- **Sow in mid-spring**
- **Fertile, well-drained soil**
- **Sunny position**

From the Orient, this annual has sweetly scented yellow, purple, pink or white flowers up to 7.5cm (3in) across. Carried on thin stems 45cm (18in) high, the leaves are narrow and their margins tend to be toothed. This species is ideal for the middle of the border, planted in groups.

Plants come into flower in early summer and from this period keep dead blooms picked off, to encourage lower lateral shoots to develop and produce further flowers.

Wherever possible, make sowings directly where plants are to flower, as disturbance can result in considerable losses. To avoid such disappointments sow in drills in mid-spring in a well-drained border, and thin out the germinated seedlings to 23cm (9in) apart. If possible, make a further sowing a month later to ensure a longer period of bloom. The giant strain is well recommended, and has finely fringed petals.

Take care

Avoid replanting seedlings. 46▸

Cheiranthus × allionii 'Orange Queen'

(Siberian wallflower)

- **Sow in late spring or early summer**
- **Almost any soil**
- **Sunny location**

Although it is really a shrubby perennial, the wallflower is short-lived and is better treated as a biennial. The hybrid described here is a beautiful orange. Flowers form in clusters at the end of 38cm (15in) stems on which lanceolate leaves of a good green develop to form a nicely shaped plant.

If your soil tends to be on the acid side, do not despair that the wallflower prefers an alkaline soil; dress the ground with hydrated lime at the rate of 115g per sq metre (4oz per sq yard).

Sow seeds in drills during late spring or early summer. Plant the seedlings in nursery rows 23-30cm (9-12in) apart; put them in their final positions in late autumn. Keep plants watered and hoed throughout the summer.

Take care

Remove damaged stems after winter storms.

Cheiranthus cheiri

(Wallflower)

- **Sow in late spring or early summer**
- **Almost any soil**
- **Sunny position**

This is by far the most popular of spring or early summer bedding plants. Within the wallflower group you can select from many cultivars for both height and colour. All are fairly strongly scented and they give added pleasure if planted near doorways or under windows. The aroma is usually at its best early in the morning or in the late evening. They are quite hardy and come through the worst of winter weather, although heavy snowfall can cause some damage. Ranging in height from 23-60cm (9-24in), the flowers come in a vast range of colours including white, red, yellow and purple. Flowers will appear from mid-spring onwards.

Propagation time and method is the same as that of *C.* × *allionii*; but when planting out in final positions, give taller types slightly wider spacing.

Take care

In exposed areas give protection to the tall cultivars during winter.

Chrysanthemum carinatum 'Court Jesters'

(C. tricolor)

- **Sow in early spring**
- **Ordinary soil**
- **Sunny position**

This member of the daisy family is one of a number of annual species originating from the Mediterranean area. The plants will grow about 60cm (24in) tall and branch freely under good conditions. The daisy-shaped multicoloured flowers, 5-6cm (2-2.4in) across, open from midsummer onwards and last well when cut. Their varied markings are attractive in an annual border. They will continue to flower until autumn frosts.

Sowings may be direct into flowering position when soil conditions are suitable, in early spring. Thin out seedlings to about 20cm (8in) apart to allow for development. This annual will succeed on most soils given good drainage. The young growths are sometimes attacked by aphids; spray as soon as seen.

Take care

Remove dead flowerheads. 47▸

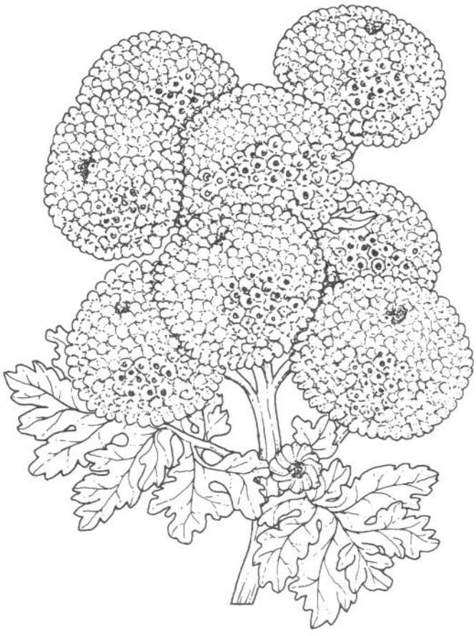

Chrysanthemum parthenium 'Golden Ball'

(Matricaria eximia)
- **Sow in autumn or spring**
- **Ordinary soil**
- **Sunny position**

'Golden Ball' has similar traits to 'Snow Ball'; it has pungent foliage but is usually grown for the bright colour of its flowers. It is 25cm (10in), slightly shorter than its relative, but it produces a wealth of golden yellow flowers, 2cm (0.8in) across, on firm stems. Avoid very confined or humid conditions, or diseases may occur.

Propagation is the same as for its white counterpart, or alternatively sow seed under glass in spring in a temperature of 13°C (55°F). A good soil-based growing medium will give better results. Prick out in the usual way, harden off in a sheltered frost-free area, and plant out in late spring. This method will ensure an evenly grown batch of plants, essential for formal plantings. Those grown as pot plants should be pricked out singly into individual pots, gradually moving them into larger pots as growth progresses. Spacing in the garden should be 25-30cm (10-12in).

Take care
Spray against pests or disease. 48▶

Chrysanthemum parthenium 'Snow Ball'

(Matricaria eximia)
- **Sow in autumn or spring**
- **Ordinary soil**
- **Sunny position**

This fairly hardy chrysanthemum produces a mass of ivory white flowers with cushion centres, on stems 30cm (12in) tall. Usually flowering from early summer to autumn, the individual blooms are 2cm (0.8in) across. Leaves are very aromatic and light green, making a pleasant foil to the bright flowers. It is suitable for formal bedding, drifts in a border, or containers.

For informal sites sow directly where they are to flower, in spring. Take out shallow drills and just cover the seed lightly. Thin out the seedlings to 30cm (12in). In mild areas sowing can take place in autumn; plants grown in this way will be larger and will flower earlier. Resistance to pests and diseases will also be greater. Because larger plants can be expected, space a little further apart.

Take care
In severe weather protect autumn sowings with polythene tents or cloches.

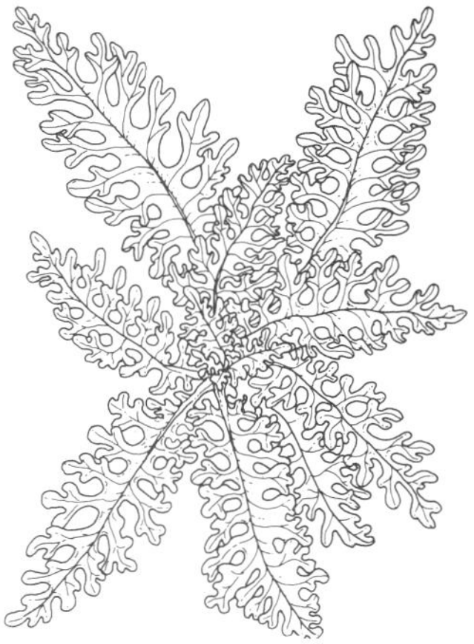

Cineraria maritima 'Silver Dust'

(Senecio maritimus)
- **Sow in early spring**
- **Ordinary soil**
- **Sunny location**

This plant is grown almost exclusively for its foliage effect in bedding and border arrangements. It is a very fine strain, with intense silver-white foliage deeply dissected, looking like a piece of lace. About 15cm (6in) tall, it makes a pleasing edge to a formal bed.

Only in the mildest areas will this cultivar survive the winter, and therefore propagation is carried out annually. Sow seed during early spring under glass, in a temperature of 16-18°C (60-65°F). Use a good proprietary growing medium for sowing and subsequent pricking out. Grow on in slight heat. Harden off in the usual way before planting out into permanent positions in late spring. Early removal of any flower stems and buds that appear will encourage a finer foliage effect and a better habit of growth.

Take care

Spray against leaf miner. 48▶

Cladanthus arabicus

- **Sow in spring**
- **Light and open soil**
- **Sunny site**

A native of Spain, this lovely annual herb is similar to *Anthemis* but it has the habit of branching just below the flowerheads. It starts to bloom in early summer and will continue well into the autumn; individual flowers are 5cm (2in) across and a deep golden yellow colour. Plants develop into mounds as the season progresses, reaching a height of 75cm (30in). Light green leaves, linear and almost feather-like in shape, make a good foil for the profusion of flowers. Nearly always grown as border plants they are an ideal subject for the centre or rear, adding height and interest to the annual border.

Sow seeds during spring where they are to flower; make sure that ground conditions are fit for this by lightly raking down the soil. Thin out the seedlings when they are large enough to handle, to 30cm (12in) apart.

Take care

Dead-head to prolong flowering. 49▶

Clarkia elegans 'Bouquet Mixed'

(C. unguiculata)

- **Sow in spring**
- **Light to medium soil, slightly acid**
- **Sunny location**

This strain will give a galaxy of double pink, red, white, lavender, purple and light orange flowers. Ovate leaves are carried on branching erect stems of 60cm (24in). The blooms, about 5cm (2in) across, are produced along almost the whole length of the stems, appearing from early summer onwards. Use towards the centre of a border in bold drifts.

Given good weather conditions, sow seed in flowering positions in spring; take out shallow drills, sow thinly and cover. Thin out germinated seedlings to 30cm (12in). Alternatively sow during autumn in mild districts; these will flower the following year from the end of spring onwards. Correct spacing is essential for good growth, and to ensure that disease is kept to a minimum. Grey mould is a particular disease to watch for.

Take care

Avoid over-rich soils, or less flowers will be produced. 50▸

Cleome spinosa 'Colour Fountain'

(Spider plant)

- **Sow in spring**
- **Light, ordinary soil**
- **In full sun**

This is a very exotic, unusual-looking annual; the flowers are spider-shaped and scented. 'Colour Fountain' mixture will include shades of rose, carmine, purple, lilac and pink. Stems reach 60-90cm (24-36in) and carry digitate leaves of five to seven lobes. Some spines may be evident on the undersides of these leaves. This is extremely useful as a 'spot' plant to give height to formal bedding schemes. As a border plant its height will add character, but care should be taken to position it towards the rear in a sunny place.

To flower in summer, seed will need to be sown under glass in spring; use a well-recommended growing medium, and keep at a temperature of 18°C (65°F). Prick out the seedlings into individual pots, 9cm (3.5in) in diameter. Harden off gradually and plant out in late spring. The delicately scented flowers will give great pleasure.

Take care

Check for aphids on young plants. 51▸

Cobaea scandens

(Cathedral bells)

- **Sow in very early spring**
- **Ordinary well-drained soil**
- **Sunny, sheltered location**

Climbers are few among the annuals and biennials, but this glorious flowering climber is quite spectacular. It can be a little temperamental to get into flower, but given good conditions it is worth persevering with. Individual blooms are up to 7.5cm (3in) long, and bell-shaped. Young flowers are a light green, soon changing to violet-purple. The calyx at the base of the bell usually remains green. This vigorous climber can reach a height of 7m (23ft) and is therefore suitable on a wall that has some supports in the way of wires or a trellis.

Grow in a sunny sheltered position for the finest results. Sow seed under glass in early spring, using fresh seed if possible for better germination. Temperature should be maintained at 18°C (65°F). Sow individually in small pots of a good loam-based growing medium. Harden off gradually, and plant out in early summer.

Take care

Water freely in dry weather. 50▸

Coix lacryma-jobi

(Job's tears)

- **Sow in early spring**
- **Any well-drained soil**
- **Sunny, south-facing site**

This is one of a number of annual grasses suitable for beds or borders. The tear-like seeds are grey-green in colour, tiny and pearl-shaped, growing on stems 60-90cm (2-3ft) tall. Similar in habit to sweet corn (*Zea*), they are very vigorous. Once plants are established they will tend to become pendulous before flowering in summer, after which the pearl-like seeds will be formed. If grouped together these plants lend an air of strength to an annual border, and can be accommodated quite happily near very colourful subjects. When ready for harvesting, the hard seeds can be safely used by children for threading onto strings.

Sow seed in early spring under glass, in a temperature of 13-16°C (55-60°F). Use a loam-based compost and sow directly into individual small pots to save later potting on. Plant out into final positions in early summer.

Take care

Avoid overfeeding, or flowering and seed development will be delayed.

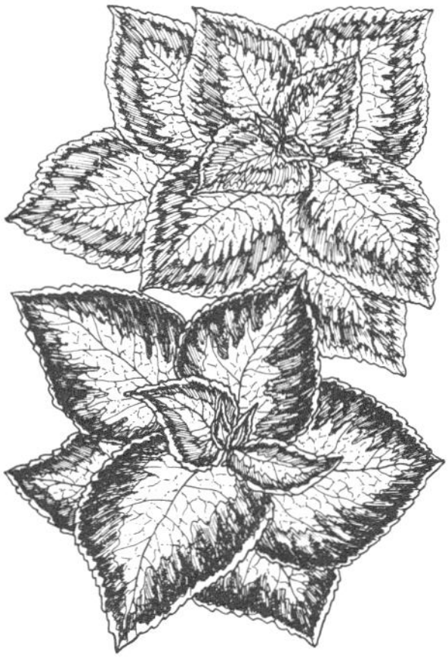

Coleus blumei 'Monarch Mixed'

(Flame nettle plant)

- **Sow in late winter**
- **Ordinary but well-drained soil**
- **Sunny location**

The 'Monarch Mixed' strain is appealing for its wide variation of large coloured foliage; rose, pink, crimson and bronze are the main shades. The bushy plants of nettle-like leaves, up to 45cm (18in) tall, can be put to many uses. Apart from growing as a pot plant they can be safely planted out during the summer months as a bedding plant in formal displays. Drifts in a border can be very effective, too. Window boxes are ideal for this mixture.

Plants are easily grown from seed sown in late winter; use a peat-based growing medium for sowing under glass in a temperature of 16-18°C (60-65°F). Plant single seedlings in individual small pots using a good growing medium. Harden off and set out in final positions in early summer, 30cm (12in) apart. Keep the blue flower spikes pinched out to help the development of compact plants.

Take care

Give container-grown coleus plants a weak liquid feed every 10 days. 52▸

Collinsia bicolor

- **Sow in autumn or spring**
- **Ordinary, moist but well-drained soil**
- **Partial shade**

This very appealing hardy annual can be used in most situations as long as they are not too arid. It is a useful plant because it will tolerate partial shade. It is ideal for the border in a damp shady yard.

Flowers, as its name implies, are two-coloured, having an upper and lower lip formation: the upper petals are usually white and the lower ones lilac to purple. One or two named cultivars are available, mainly pink, and they are worth considering for a change. Their blooms are borne on thin squarish stems carrying lanceolate deep green leaves in pairs. Up to 60cm (24in) in height, they should be grown towards the back of an annual border, preferably near a light yellow subject of a similar height.

Sow seeds where they are to flower, in autumn or spring. Shallow drills will suffice; cover the seeds and thin out when large enough, to 15cm (6in) apart.

Take care

Use bushy peasticks for support. 53▸

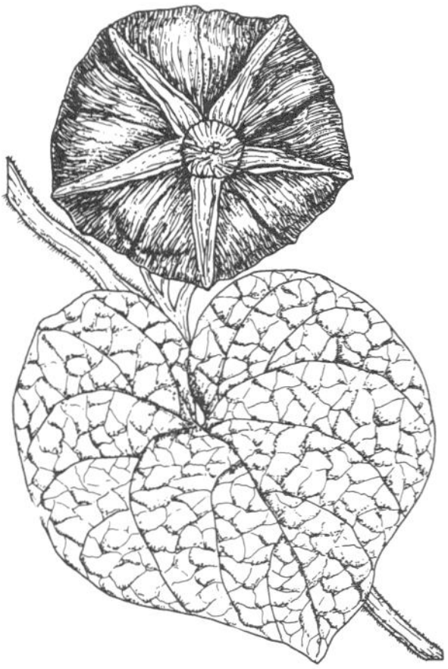

Convolvulus major
(Ipomoea purpurea)
(Morning glory)
- **Sow in spring**
- **Light, rich soil**
- **Sunny but sheltered site**

These annuals will reach a height of 3m (10ft) under normal weather conditions. It is ideal for training on wires or trellis work; use tall peasticks as supports in a border. The lovely flowers, now available in mixed colours, are up to 7.5cm (3in) across and the vine-like stems that twine around the supports are covered with lovely heart-shaped leaves. The trumpet flowers are at their best in the morning and usually close before midday.

Easily grown from seed, this tender annual should be sown in pots of a good growing medium in spring under glass. Maintain a temperature of 18°C (65°F). Use individual pots so that less disturbance is caused at planting time. Place a small cane in each pot when seedlings appear, to support them until setting against permanent supports. Harden off and plant out when the risk of frost has subsided.

Take care
Dead-head to prolong flowering.

Convolvulus tricolor 'Rainbow Flash'
(Morning glory)
- **Sow in spring**
- **Light well-drained soil**
- **Sunny position**

This completely new dwarf hybrid, only 15cm (6in) tall, has a very wide range of colours including blue, purple, pink and rose. The centre of each inflorescence is marked by a star-like form of white or yellow. Because of their dwarf habit, these plants are invaluable for the front of the border or bed, but try them as well in window boxes in a sunny position. If you have a few seedlings left over, pot them into fairly large pots for the patio or conservatory.

Sow seeds under glass in the normal way during spring; it may help germination if you soak the seeds in water for 24 hours before sowing. Keep in a temperature of 18°C (65°F). Harden off and plant out in final positions at the end of spring, 20cm (8in) apart. Water freely during dry weather, especially those plants near the front of a border, where drying out is more likely to occur.

Take care
Keep the temperature constant in the young stages. 52▸

Coreopsis tinctoria 'Dwarf Dazzler'

(Calliopsis)

- **Sow in spring to early summer**
- **Fertile, well-drained soil**
- **Sunny location**

This dwarf cultivar of *Coreopsis* has beautiful daisy-shaped flowers of deep crimson, and each flower is edged with golden yellow, making a vivid contrast. Only 30cm (12in) in height and tending to spread, it is ideally suited to the front of a border or bed in a sunny position. It can also be useful in containers on a patio. An added asset is the remarkable tolerance to smoky environments, and it can therefore be put to good use in industrial towns or cities. Long-lasting and very free-flowering it should be planted in bold groups to get maximum effect.

Wherever you choose to grow these plants, they come readily from seed. Sow in spring to early summer where they are to flower, take out shallow drills and cover seed lightly. If you make later sowings and the weather is dry, then water regularly. Thin out seedlings to 30cm (12in) when large enough to handle.

Take care

Sow only when conditions allow. 54▸

Cosmos bipinnatus 'Candy Stripe'

(Cosmea)

(Mexican aster)

- **Sow in early spring**
- **Light, and also poor soils**
- **Full sun**

The beautiful rose-red and white striped flowers of the cosmos 'Candy Stripe' are very striking, and are a must for any keen gardener. Individual flowers can be almost 7.5cm (3in) across. The intricately cut leaves are formed on branching stems, giving a well-balanced foil to the flowers. Attaining a height of 80cm (32in) and very free flowering, 'Candy Stripe' is most suited to the middle of a border, although it can be used in large pots. It is also excellent as a cut flower.

As it is a half-hardy annual, seed will need to be sown under glass in early spring. Sow in boxes or trays at a temperature of 16°C (60°F). Prick off into small pots, and move on into 13cm (5in) pots of loam-based growing medium when the small pots have filled with roots. Harden off and plant out in late spring, 45cm (18in) apart.

Take care

Stake tall plants before they flower

Cosmos sulphureus 'Sunny Gold'

(Cosmea)

- **Sow in spring**
- **Light to poor soil**
- **Sunny position**

The varieties of *C. sulphureus* include lemon, yellow and orange-red shades. They are compact, with many single or semi-double flowers on slender stems. The light green pinnate leaves are quite decorative. 'Sunny Gold' is a new dwarf variety with many semi-double golden yellow flowers growing only 30cm (12in) high. The plants are very decorative as a group in a sunny border while the flowers are useful for cutting and displaying indoors.

Sow in seed mixture under glass in 16-18°C (60-65°F). To avoid checks in transplanting, prick seedlings direct into small pots or individual containers. Gradually harden off for planting out in early summer after any danger of frost is past. Space plants about 30cm (12in) apart in groups in a sunny sheltered position.

Take care

Dead-head to prolong flowering.

Crepis rubra

- **Sow in autumn or spring**
- **Ordinary soil, also poor soils if well-drained**
- **Sunny location**

Daisy-shaped flowers appear on leafless stalks around midsummer. The compact plant forms a rosette, the main flowering stem arising from its centre. The mid-green leaves are lanceolate and markedly toothed along the edges. Rose-red or white flowers are produced on the ends of the stems, about 2cm (0.8in) across.

Use this plant in the annual border, between the edge and the centre. The whole plant measures only 30cm (12in) in height. Coming from the mountain regions of the Mediterranean, it is an ideal subject for the rock garden.

Time of sowing will depend on whether you have an area of the garden free from summer plants; if you have, then sowings can be made in autumn. Plants produced from this will be stronger and slightly earlier in flowering. Alternatively, make sowings in spring. In both cases sow where they are to flower and thin out to 15cm (6in) apart.

Take care

Remove dead flowers regularly.

Cuphea miniata 'Firefly'

- **Sow in very early spring**
- **Ordinary soil**
- **Sun or partial shade**

Grown as a half-hardy annual this sub-shrub will do well in most gardens. It spreads to 60cm (24in) and the height is similar. The stems carry green lanceolate leaves, which may be covered with very distinct white hairs. Flowers are formed from the axils of the leaves near the terminals of the stems. Tubular 4cm (1.6in) long scarlet blooms will begin to show colour from early summer and it will flower freely throughout that season.

Treat it as a half-hardy annual for propagation purposes. Sow seed under glass in very early spring, using a soil-based growing medium. Cover the seed lightly in boxes or pots and keep in a temperature of 16°C (60°F). Pot off the seedlings into individual small pots and grow on until early summer, when they should be planted out in flowering positions. Give a weak liquid feed once a week in the seedling stages, starting a month after potting on.

Take care

Plant out when frosts are over. 54▸

Cynoglossum amabile

(Hound's tongue; Chinese forget-me-not)

- **Sow in early or late spring**
- **Rich well-drained soil**
- **Sun or partial shade**

This plant has distinctive turquoise blue flowers like large forget-me-nots. About 45cm (18in) high, the stems form a compact plant. Both stems and leaves will be found to have a downy appearance. The flowers usually appear in midsummer. As a biennial it is most useful in a border, especially if you have an odd corner of dappled shape where other plants have difficulty in getting established. If you have, then make sure plenty of humus is added before seed sowing or planting.

Sow the seeds in drills outdoors in late spring to flower the following year, preferably in nursery beds. Plant out seedlings in nursery rows 15cm (6in) apart. Set out in final positions at the end of autumn. Alternatively, sow under glass in a temperature of 16°C (60°F) during early spring, prick off into boxes or trays, harden off and plant out at the end of spring at 30cm (12in) intervals.

Take care

Do not overwater established plants.

Dahlia 'Dandy'

(Dwarf Collarette)
- **Sow in very early spring**
- **Good moisture-holding soil**
- **Open sunny position**

The various strains of bedding dahlias come into flower quickly from seed. The older forms of collarette dahlias are tall, but 'Dandy' is a dwarf mixture of single flowers in many colours, each having an inner collar of narrow petals. Branched plants reach about 50-60cm (20-24in) with well-formed flowers of 7.5-9cm (3-3.5in) in diameter. The plants do not need support and the elegant flowers are excellent for cutting for indoor display.

Sow seed thinly in seed mixture under glass in very early spring at about 16-18°C (60-65°F). Germination is usually rapid; prick out singly into small pots or peat sections to avoid later disturbance. Grow on in a warm greenhouse until ready for hardening off to plant out in late spring after frosts are past; space about 30-35cm (12-14in) apart. Water freely if necessary until well established.

Take care
Dead-head to prolong flowering.

Dahlia 'Gypsy Dance'

- **Sow in early spring**
- **Free-draining and fertile soil**
- **Sun or partial shade**

Although they are really tuberous perennials, many dahlias are now grown from seed on an annual basis.

The cultivar 'Gypsy Dance' is recommended for growing in beds, borders and containers. Plants attain a height of 50-60cm (20-24in). Leaves range from greens through to deep bronze, forming a striking contrast to the wide range of semi-double blooms, some of which will be 9cm (3.5in) across.

Annual production of dahlias from seed will ensure healthier plants, less prone to the many diseases and virus infections to which named cultivars are susceptible. Quite vigorous in growth this 'bedder' should be sown under glass in early spring at a temperature of 16-18°C (60-65°F) in a peat-based growing medium. Prick out seedlings into individual pots, to ensure an even, vigorous batch of plants. Grow on in a warm greenhouse; harden off about two weeks before planting in final positions at the end of spring or early summer, 30cm (12in) apart.

Take care
Tender; do not plant out too early. 55▸

Delphinium consolida

(Larkspur)

- **Sow in autumn or spring**
- **Rich, well-cultivated soil**
- **Sheltered, sunny position**

Enjoying a position in a sunny sheltered border, larkspur will give great pleasure visually; and the innumerable blooms will enable you to cut for arrangements in the house without having any adverse effect on the garden display. Many individual strains and mixtures are available and all are reliable. Colours include blue, purple, pink, white and red. Single or double flowers are produced on erect stems up to 120cm (48in) tall, in long racemes. The plants spread to about 30cm (12in), and need to be planted towards the back of a border. Leaves are mid-green and deeply cut.

As they are very vigorous in growth, make sure you weed through in the early stages on a regular basis. They can be sown in the open ground in spring, but finer results will be obtained if they are planted in the autumn. Take out drills where plants are to flower, about 30cm (12in) apart, sow seed and cover. Thin out to 30cm (12in) intervals.

Take care

Use peasticks to support tall types. 56▶

Dianthus barbatus

(Sweet William)

- **Sow in early summer**
- **Avoid very acid soil**
- **Sunny location**

The fragrant Sweet William is a useful and cheerful biennial. The plant ranges in height from 30-60cm (12-24in); the flowers are produced in a compact head up to 13cm (5in) across. Single or double blooms open from late spring to early summer and many colours are available, but red and white predominate; bicolours are also common, forming concentric rings in each individual floret.

Stocky plants can be obtained by sowing seeds in a prepared seedbed during early summer. Plant out germinated seedlings into nursery rows 15cm (6in) apart. Keep well weeded throughout the summer. Final positioning, 20-25cm (8-10in) apart, should be carried out during in the autumn. Alternatively, sow where they are to flower, in early summer, and thin out to correct spacing when they are large enough to handle. Avoid very acid soils and dress with lime before the final planting if your soil is of this type.

Take care

In exposed positions use bushy twigs to support the plants. 73▶

Dianthus caryophyllus

(Annual border carnation)

- **Sow in late winter**
- **Most soils, but avoid very acid types**
- **Sunny position**

Up to 45cm (18in) tall, the annual border carnation will add grace to any border as long as the soil is not too acid. They are without doubt an ideal subject for anyone gardening on alkaline soils. Single or double flowers 4-5cm (1.6-2in) across will be produced; stems and leaves are greyish green.

Carnations come readily from seed sown in late winter under glass, in a temperature of 16°C (60°F). Use a good loam-based growing medium, and sow the seed thinly. Prick off the seedlings when they are large enough, and lower the temperature to 10°C (50°F). Plant out towards the end of spring, 30cm (12in) apart. Flowering will commence in early summer. In colder districts it is recommended that sowing takes place in the autumn; winter the young plants through in cold frames and plant out in late spring at similar spacings.

Take care

Do not overwater established plants.

Dianthus chinensis 'Queen of Hearts'

(D. sinensis)

(Indian pink)

- **Sow in spring**
- **Alkaline to neutral soil**
- **Sunny site**

Vibrant scarlet flowers appear in early summer and continue to give pleasure until well into the autumn. Pale green leaves on stems 30cm (12in) long will make for bushy plants.

Adopt one of the following methods for producing plants. Sow seed under glass in spring, using a loam-based growing medium; better results will be obtained if peat is left out of the mixture. A temperature of 13°C (55°F) should be maintained. Prick out seedlings in the usual way and plant out in late spring. Alternatively, sow in mid-spring where the plants are to flower; sow thinly and then space out 15cm (6in) apart. Choose a sunny position for best results. When planting in containers, change the soil each season if you suspect that acid conditions prevail; this will avoid disappointment.

Take care

Remove faded flowers to ensure further growth and blooms.

Dianthus chinensis 'Telstar'

(D. sinensis)

(Indian pink)

- **Sow in mid-spring**
- **Alkaline to neutral soil**
- **Sunny spot**

The brilliant colours of the 'Telstar' F1 hybrids are a must for the keen enthusiast of annual pinks. Only 20cm (8in) in height, the flowers are produced on short stems in late spring or early summer, earlier than most other cultivars. Blooms may be scarlet, crimson, pink, white, picotee or variable stripes. This very free-flowering strain has great appeal, and is well recommended. Use it in borders, in window boxes and other containers, or alongside a path.

Sow where they are to flower, in mid-spring. Take out shallow drills, and only lightly cover the seed. Thin out to 15cm (6in) apart. Alternatively, if you have a greenhouse, then – to be sure of a uniform crop of plants – sow seed in a good loam-based growing medium in a temperature of 13°C (55°F) during spring. Prick out the seedlings into boxes, harden off, and plant out in early summer.

Take care

Make sure your soil is alkaline or neutral for best results. 74▸

Didiscus caeruleus

(Blue lace flower)

- **Sow in spring**
- **Ordinary well-cultivated soil**
- **Sheltered and sunny position**

This lovely half-hardy annual from Australia has the appearance of the perennial scabious. Clusters of delicate lavender-blue flowers are carried on stems 45cm (18in) high. The umbel-shaped inflorescence will appear in midsummer and carry on flowering until autumn. Leaves and stems are covered with masses of tiny hairs, and feel rough to the touch. Choose a sheltered position, preferably towards the front of a border near annuals with white or pale yellow flowers.

Sowing should be carried out during spring under glass, in a temperature of 16°C (60°F). Use a loam-based growing medium for both seed and seedlings. When large enough to handle, the latter will respond better if pricked out into small individual pots. After hardening off, plant them out into final positions, 23cm (9in) apart, towards the end of spring.

Take care

Water well in dry periods. 74▸

Digitalis purpurea

(Foxglove)

- **Sow in early summer**
- **Most soils, but slightly acid**
- **Semi-shade**

This hardy biennial has always been a great favourite. Flowering in the year after sowing, it produces the familiar long spikes, 1-1.5m (3-5ft), bearing tubular flowers of maroon or purple, and distinctly spotted in the throat of each bloom. The common foxglove has for a long time been associated with medicine, but careful selection and breeding has resulted in the introduction of beautiful garden forms of variable colour and size. Outstanding in this respect are the Excelsior hybrid strains. Flower spikes up to 30cm (12in) long arise from a rosette of grey-green leaves at the beginning of summer through to the autumn.

Sow seed in well-prepared seed beds in early summer. Sow seed thinly in drills, and plant out seedlings in nursery rows 15-23cm (6-9in) apart. Plant into final flowering positions in autumn, at 60cm (24in) intervals.

Take care

Water well in dry weather. 75▸

Dimorphotheca aurantiaca 'Dwarf Salmon'

(Star of the Veldt)

- **Sow in early or late spring**
- **Light well-drained soil**
- **Sunny site**

Flowering from midsummer, plants of *D. aurantiaca* need the sunniest position you can give, otherwise the blooms will not open, especially in shade or dull weather. The cultivar 'Dwarf Salmon' will make a delightful change from the usual range of colours, and its dwarf habit, 23cm (9in), makes it suitable for edging a border or along the side of a pathway, or for an odd gap in the rock garden in full sun. Daisy-like flowers of apricot-pink, about 5cm (2in) across, are formed on short spreading stems carrying obovate leaves, all of which are scented. If possible, plant next to pale blue or white annuals of a similar height, or in front of taller subjects.

Propagation from seed is relatively easy, either under glass during early spring or directly into the open ground in late spring when ground conditions are favourable. Thin out or plant at intervals of 30cm (12in).

Take care

Remove dead flowers regularly. 76▸

Above: **Dianthus barbatus**
These reliable, sweetly scented flowers are great favourites for cutting and summer bedding. Grow as a biennial and support with bushy peasticks. Red predominates. 69◆

Above:
Dianthus chinensis 'Telstar' F1
A very free-flowering dwarf hybrid in many colours that blooms quickly from seed. For the brightest colours grow in sun. Try it in containers. 71▸

Left: **Didiscus caeruleus**
Clusters of delicate lavender-blue flowers are borne on tall stems from midsummer until autumn. Grow in a sunny sheltered spot and be sure to water well during dry spells. 71▸

Right: **Digitalis purpurea**
Tall and stately spikes of spotted flowers adorn these dependable plants. Grown as a biennial, they will thrive in a moist, shady place in the garden. Can be cut for indoors. 72▸

Left: **Dimorphotheca aurantiaca 'Dwarf Salmon'**
A lovely cultivar with apricot-pink 5cm (2in) flowers suitable for edges or the rock garden. It must have full sun for the flowers to open. 72▸

Right: **Eschscholzia californica**
This original Californian annual has been developed into a wide selection of forms and colours. All will give of their best in dry sunny places. Clear self-sown seedlings. 89▸

Below: **Echium plantagineum 'Monarch Dwarf Hybrids'**
A hardy dwarf mixture with flowers of many pleasing pastel shades. Grown in a sunny spot, they will attract hosts of bees during the summer. 89▸

Above: **Exacum affine**
These beautiful little plants with sweetly scented lavender-blue flowers can be planted out in small beds in mild areas. Otherwise, grow in pots in a cool greenhouse. 90▸

Above: **Euphorbia marginata**
Grown for its striking variegated foliage, this plant is well suited to the centre of the border. Superb for flower arrangements when cut. 90▸

Below: **Felicia bergeriana**
A delightful mat-forming plant with masses of miniature, gold-centred, blue, daisy-like flowers in summer. Grow in a sunny sheltered spot. 91▸

Above: **Foeniculum vulgare**
Grow this well-known herb as an annual in mixed borders; its foliage will set off summer flowers. 91▸

Below: **Gazania 'Chansonette'**
A large-flowered hybrid for a sunny position. It will tolerate salty air so is ideal for seaside gardens. 92▸

Above: **Godetia grandiflora 'Dwarf Vivid'**
One of the many lovely single 'Amoena' types available. These hardy annuals are easy to grow and will provide a dazzling display. 92▶

Above: **Godetia grandiflora 'Sybil Sherwood'**
A beautiful single 'Amoena type' with salmon-pink and white blooms. 92▸

Right: **Helichrysum bracteatum**
These papery textured flowers can be cut and dried for decoration. Plant out after the danger of frosts. 94▸

Below left:
Helianthus annuus 'Sungold'
A low-growing sunflower with double blooms 15cm (6in) across. 94▸

Below right: **Helipterum manglesii**
A pink everlasting flower that can be cut and dried for indoors. Sow seed directly into flowering site. 95▸

Left: **Hibiscus trionum**
Each of these beautiful, creamy, dark-centred flowers lasts for one day only but they appear in succession for many weeks from midsummer until late autumn. Grow in sun in any well-drained soil. 95▸

Right:
Impatiens 'Novette' F1 Mixed
A colourful mixture of glistening flowers for shady or sunny spots in the garden or patio. Plants grow to 10cm (4in) with a wide spread. 97▸

Below: **Iberis umbellata**
Highly fragrant flowers develop quickly on this established favourite. Successive sowings will ensure a long season of colour at the front of the border. Plants will grow and flower well on poor soils. 96▸

Above: **Kochia childsii**
Grown as a half-hardy annual, this is an interesting foliage plant that changes from green during the summer to a rich red as autumn approaches. Use it in borders to add height or as a background. 97▸

Left: **Lagurus ovatus**
An annual grass to add interest to the front of the border. Also suitable for indoor decoration when cut and dried. Do not plant in over-rich soils or in very windy sites. 98▸

Right: **Lathyrus odoratus 'Sheila MacQueen'**
A lovely sweet pea with large waved flowers for exhibition and cutting. Be sure to provide plenty of organic matter in the soil and remove faded flowers regularly. 100▸

Above: **Lavatera trimestris 'Silver Cup'**
A fine hybrid for the garden border or for cutting. Sow in spring or the autumn and space out well. 101▸

Below: **Limnanthes douglasii**
A cheerful hardy annual that will thrive along the edges of a path. The delicately scented flowers will attract bees during the early summer. 101▸

Echium plantagineum 'Monarch Dwarf Hybrids'

(E. violaceum)
(Bugloss)
- **Sow in spring or autumn**
- **Light, dry soil**
- **Open, sunny location**

This member of the borage family produces flowers of an upturned bell shape on the end of light green branching stems. The common species is predominantly blue, but 'Monarch Dwarf Hybrids' have blue, lavender, pink, white and carmine shades, and at only 30cm (12in) tall they require no staking and can be used near the front of a border. The mixture is highly recommended. Choose an open sunny site to ensure free-flowering plants, which will open at the end of spring in mild areas and from early summer onwards elsewhere.

In spring sow seeds where plants are to flower; take out shallow drills and lightly cover the seeds. Thin out to 15cm (6in) apart. Alternatively, sow in autumn in the usual way but wait until spring before thinning out to final distances.

Take care
Do not overwater when plants are established. 76-7▸

Eschscholzia californica

(Californian poppy)
- **Sow in autumn or spring**
- **Most soils, including those considered poor**
- **Sunny and dry position**

In mild areas self-seeding of this annual will produce many plants, but kept under control they are an asset to any garden. Nearly always grown as a border plant, they can be used in the rock garden to good advantage. Choose a sunny position for the best results. Flowers are red, yellow, white, pink and orange. Stems carry deeply cut blue-green leaves. The flower buds have a whorled spike effect and when opened the petals are silky in texture. Double hybrids, listed by many seedsmen, are well worth a try and their frilled blooms are an added attraction. Plants will be 30cm (12in) tall.

Sow in flowering positions in autumn for the best results; the plants that winter through will be stronger and flower earlier. Sow also in spring. In either case thin out the seedlings to 15cm (6in) apart.

Take care
Discard self-sown seedlings at the end of summer.

Euphorbia marginata

(Snow on the mountain)

- **Sow in mid-spring**
- **Ordinary soil, or poor if well-drained**
- **Sun or partial shade**

The annual species *E. marginata* originates from N America and is grown mainly for its splendid foliage effect; the flowers are very small, white and insignificant. Stems reach a height of 60cm (2ft). The leaves are ovate or oblong, and a pleasant green but with white margins – the terminal leaves may be completely white in some cases. Bracts beneath the flowers are papery in appearance, and also white. On starved soils the foliage colours are intensified. Use this species towards the centre of a border.

Sow seed directly where it is to flower, in mid-spring; thin out the seedlings to 30cm (12in) spacings. Avoid damaging plants, as the milky latex can have an irritating effect on the skin. This euphorbia is ideally suited for flower arrangements; when cutting, place the ends of the stems in very hot water, as this will have a cauterizing effect and seal the flow of latex from the stems.

Take care

Give peastick supports. 79▸

Exacum affine

- **Sow in spring**
- **Ordinary well-drained soil**
- **Sunny and sheltered location**

Only in the mildest areas can this annual be considered for outdoor culture; but if you have such conditions, the exacums are worth considering not just to be different but because of the unusual flowers. They are usually grown as pot plants in the cool greenhouse, but during the summer they can be bedded out in a sheltered border or formal bed. Plants are very compact and bushy, with very shiny deep green ovate leaves. They are only 23-30cm (9-12in) in height. The flowers are 1cm (0.4in) across, saucer-shaped and lavender-blue, with a yellow centre of conspicuous stamens. Once open they are fragrant.

Sow seed in pots or boxes in spring using a good growing medium. Keep at a temperature of 16°C (60°F). Prick out the seedlings into medium pots and grow on until midsummer, when they can be planted out. Spacing will depend on the size of individual plants, but put them as close together as possible.

Take care

Avoid full sun on seedlings. 78▸

Felicia bergeriana

(Kingfisher daisy)

- **Sow in very early spring**
- **Ordinary well-drained soil**
- **Sunny and sheltered position**

The kingfisher part of the common name alludes to the beautiful vivid blue of the flowers. Only 15cm (6in) high, the blooms are carried on short branching stems of a glossy green, as are the narrow grass-like leaves. The single daisy flowers are almost like michaelmas daisies at first glance, about 2cm (0.8in) across, the centre part of the disc being clear yellow. Very compact in habit, they are a choice subject for the front part of a border or rock garden; in either case they need to be sited in full sun.

As this species is a half-hardy annual, propagation will need to be carried out under glass. Sow seed very thinly in pots or boxes of a good loam-based growing medium during very early spring, and keep at a temperature of 16°C (60°F). Prick out the seedlings in the usual way. Reduce the growing temperature at this time and harden off towards the end of spring, when they should be planted out 15cm (6in) apart.

Take care

Pick off dead flowers promptly. 79▸

Foeniculum vulgare

(Fennel)

- **Sow in spring**
- **Ordinary well-drained soil**
- **Sunny position**

As most people know, the herb fennel has a very distinct aroma. The leaves are used – fresh or dried – for flavouring dishes, especially fish and pickles. The seeds, when ripe, are also used for flavouring, and they smell strongly of aniseed. Apart from its culinary uses, fennel can be planted in annual or mixed borders for its foliage. Although perennial in habit, fennel plants can be short-lived, and it is wise to treat them as annuals whatever purpose you use them for. The blue-green leaves, very finely cut and feather-like, are carried on smooth shiny stems 90-240cm (3-8ft) in height. The flowers, which appear in late summer, are a powdery yellow, small and shaped into a flattened umbel about 10cm (4in) in diameter.

Sow the seeds outdoors in spring. Take out shallow drills and lightly cover the seeds with soil. Thin out the seedlings to 23-30cm (9-12in) apart.

Take care

Water well in dry spells. 80▸

√89.

Gazania × hybrida 'Chansonette'

(Treasure flowers)

- **Sow in midwinter**
- **Ordinary well-drained soil**
- **Sunny site**

Without doubt this is one of the finest border, bed or rock garden plants, of an almost exotic nature. However only in the mildest parts will they survive winter as a perennial, so they are usually treated as an annual.

Hybrid types carry large daisy flowers, and the 'Chansonette' mixture has a colour range including red, bronze and bicolours. Blooms are carried on short stems 20cm (8in) long and backed by glossy green leaves, but the undersides of white or silver ensure a contrast.

Most useful as a bedder or planted in full sun on the rock garden, they will give an abundance of flower from early summer onwards.

Sow seed under glass in midwinter in a temperature of 16°C (60°F). Use a loam-based compost for sowing, and prick off into individual small pots. Harden off and plant out in early summer, or in late spring in milder districts.

Take care

Make sure ground is free draining to avoid stem and root rots. 80▸

Godetia grandiflora 'Amoena' types

- **Sow in autumn or spring**
- **Light and moist soil**
- **Sunny position**

The 'Amoena' types of godetia are usually taller than the straight 'grandifloras', up to 60cm (24in). Single or double flowers are produced on thin stems, loose in character. Light green lanceolate leaves make an ideal foil for the reddish pink or lilac blooms up to 5cm (2in) across. These are good plants for the centre of a border and they look well in combination with larkspurs. Flowers start to open from early summer onwards. Avoid very rich soils, as these can lead to overproduction of foliage to the detriment of the flowerheads. These plants are worthy of a place in any garden, and the profusion of blooms will enable you to cut flowers for arrangements.

Raise from seed in the same way as for the 'Azalea-flowered' types, but space them at 30cm (12in) intervals. Brushwood supports around the plants will help the slender stems to cope with the weight of the flowers.

Take care

Keep moist in dry periods. 81▸ 82▸

Godetia grandiflora 'Azalea-flowered'

- **Sow in autumn or spring**
- **Light, moist soil**
- **Sunny location**

Of all the hardy annuals godetias are my favourite. The exotically coloured azalea-flowered types are semi-double and have wavy edged petals of pink, salmon, crimson, cerise and white. Almost silky in texture the blooms are produced on branching stems forming a compact plant of about 30cm (12in). The leaves are oblong at the base, narrowing towards the tip; with age they tend to take on a reddish tinge. If these plants are grown next to their near cousins the clarkias, a riot of colour can be expected.

As hardy annuals they are very easy to grow from seed; sow where they are to flower, in either autumn or spring. Plants raised from the autumn sowings will be stronger and will flower slightly earlier, about the end of spring onwards. In either case take out drills, sow seed very thinly, and cover lightly. Thin out the seedlings to 15cm (6in) apart, and water if necessary.

Take care

Keep well watered in dry weather.

Helianthus annuus 'Autumn Beauty'

(Sunflower)

- **Sow in spring**
- **Ordinary soil**
- **Sunny site**

This strain of mixed colours provides an interesting change from the yellow shades of the original types. 'Autumn Beauty' will reach about 180cm (6ft) high and the single flowers include shades of lemon, golden, bronze and mahogany-red; the central brown discs are surrounded by zones of red and brown. Except in exposed positions the plants are sturdy enough to stand without supports.

Seed may be sown direct where the plants are to flower. Sow two or three seeds about 2.5cm (1in) deep, at 30cm (12in) intervals. Thin to one seedling when large enough and protect against slug damage. Choose a position that faces the sun most of the day. Spring sowings should come into flower in late summer and autumn.

Take care

Remove dead heads to encourage further flowering, or leave the nutritious seeds for the birds.

'Dwarf Spangle Mixed'

Helianthus annuus 'Sungold'

(Sunflower)

- **Sow in spring**
- **Ordinary soil**
- **Sunny position**

So many people grow the giant exhibition types of this annual that it is often forgotten that a number of the same sunflowers have dwarf counterparts that are easier to cope with.

'Sungold', only 60cm (24in) tall, can have a worthy place in any border as long as it can benefit from a sunny position. The beautiful double golden-yellow blooms can be up to 15cm (6in) across, and almost ball-shaped. The short stems and longish leaves feel coarse to the touch; the latter have toothed margins. More showy when grown in groups, they are best suited to the front of a bed.

Sow seed directly into the ground where they are to flower, putting three seeds to a station; when germination is complete, discard the two weakest seedlings, leaving only the strongest. Spacing should be 30cm (12in). In mild areas sow in spring; for other districts, late spring.

Take care

Check carefully for slug damage at germination time. 82▸

Helichrysum bracteatum

(Everlasting flower)

- **Sow in very early spring**
- **Light but well-drained soil**
- **Sunny location**

These come in a wide range of colours, and there are both tall and dwarf strains available. Stems may be up to 90cm (36in), fairly stiff and branching, and of a light green colour, as are the lanceolate leaves. Flowers are produced terminally on the stems in shades of red, yellow, pink, orange and white, up to 5cm (2in) across. The centre of each bloom is surrounded by a mass of coloured bracts of a papery texture.

Cut stems for drying before the flower centres are fully open and hang them upside down in a cool airy place away from strong sunlight, which may bleach the colours.

Sow seed under glass in very early spring at a temperature of 18°C (65°F); use a loam-based growing medium for sowing and subsequent pricking off. Harden off carefully and plant out at the end of spring. Blooms appear from early summer onwards.

Take care

Use brushwood supports around the groups of plants. 83▸

Helipterum manglesii

(Rhodanthe manglesii)

- **Sow in spring**
- **Poor or ordinary but free-draining soil**
- **Sunny position**

This is another everlasting flower of merit. Growing 30-60cm (12-24in) high, it is an ideal subject for a single small bed; use a few spot plants through the bed to give extra height. Flowers are mainly pink, white and shades of red, about 2.5cm (1in) in diameter. The dainty bracts supporting the blooms terminate on single glaucous stems. Cut the stems for future use before the bracts are fully open; in this way they will keep their colour longer. Avoid strong sunlight in storage.

Sow directly where they are to flower, during spring, lightly covering the seed. Thin out to 15cm (6in) apart. Alternatively raise under glass in the usual way during early spring at a temperature of 16°C (60°F). Plant out carefully at the end of spring. Losses may occur when transplanting, as helipterums do not take kindly to disturbance, so whenever possible sow directly into flowering position.

Take care

Free-draining soil is essential. 83▸

Hibiscus trionum

(Bladder ketmia)

- **Sow in spring**
- **Ordinary well-drained soil**
- **Sunny location**

This exquisite half-hardy annual from Africa blooms continuously from midsummer through to the end of autumn. The delicate exotic flowers are up to 7.5cm (3in) across, white to pale yellow with a chocolate-maroon centre. Stems bearing these beautiful flowers, up to 75cm (30in) long, are a lovely dark green, with ovate leaves that are toothed along the margins. Individual flowers usually last for only one day, but they are eventually followed by an inflated bladder-shaped calyx that will cause interest.

To obtain early-flowering plants, sow seed in pots or boxes in spring; use any good growing medium. When seeds have germinated, prick off seedlings into individual small pots, harden off in a cold frame and plant out at the end of spring. Plants produced in this way will flower earlier than those directly sown in mid-spring. For both methods space the young plants 30cm (12in) apart.

Take care

Check young plants for aphids. 84▸

Iberis amara

(Giant candytuft)
- **Sow from spring onwards**
- **Ordinary or poor soil**
- **Sunny position**

This is one of a number of candytufts of an annual character, grown for its fragrance and ease of cultivation. At about 38cm (15in) tall, blooms are formed in clusters of pure white flowers 5cm (2in) in diameter.

This is an ideal subject for towns and cities where the atmosphere is smoky, as they tolerate such conditions very well. Try them in window boxes if you have no border; containers are ideal for growing this common but lovely plant. Along the edge of pathways the appealing fragrance will be an added bonus as long as the plant is in full sun.

Raise plants in the same way as for *I. umbellata* and thin out in the border to the same spacing. These easy plants are generally free of disease and will thrive on poor soils.

Take care

Remove dead flowers as soon as possible to extend blooming.

Iberis umbellata

(Candytuft)
- **Sow from spring onwards**
- **Ordinary or poor soil**
- **Sunny situation**

Many gardeners will recall candytuft as among the first plants that they grew in a small plot as children. Still very popular, this strongly aromatic hardy annual looks good along the edge of a well-used pathway where its scent can be appreciated. Use it also in bold drifts towards the front of a border.

Umbel-shaped flowers form in clusters up to 5cm (2in) across, on stems 15-38cm (6-15in) high, from early summer to the autumn. The colours are purple, rose-red and white. Leaves are green, lanceolate and slender-pointed, and may be smothered by the profusion of blooms. As flowering is quick from seed, successive sowings will help to prolong the season of flowering.

Sow thinly where they are to flower, in spring. Seedlings should be thinned to 15cm (6in) spacing. It is essential to carry out this process correctly if overcrowding and losses are to be avoided.

Take care

Keep removing dead flowers. 84▸

Impatiens 'Novette' F1 Mixed

(Busy Lizzie)

- **Sow in mid-spring**
- **Ordinary but fertile soil**
- **Shade, semi-shade or sunshine**

During the last decade, busy Lizzies have been developed to suit almost any position and conditions. They are very versatile, and can be safely used in difficult shady parts of the garden or in full sunshine: not many half-hardy annuals tolerate both.

So many cultivars or hybrids are available that it is difficult to make a choice, but the very dwarf 'Novette' mixture, with plants only 10cm (4in) high, is well worth considering.

As a tender half-hardy annual, it will need to be raised under glass. Sow seed on a peat-based growing medium and lightly cover, in spring. Keep at a temperature of 18°C (65°F); if it falls below this, then germination will be difficult and uneven. When they are large enough to handle, prick out the seedlings into boxes of a peat-based growing medium. Harden off gradually and plant out in final positions in early summer.

Take care

Do not plant out too early. 85▸

Kochia trichophylla childsii

(Burning bush)

- **Sow in spring**
- **Fairly light, open soil**
- **Sunny location**

Fine foliage is always welcomed in the garden and kochias are excellent for providing it. Half hardy in habit, these plants will reach 1m (39in) in height in the one season. Each plant consists of a multitude of fine narrow pointed light green leaves; the flowers are also green, but small and inconspicuous. The whole plant will change its colour to a beautiful deep rich red towards autumn, and hence the common name of this most useful species. Although it is relatively tall, the compactness of its habit makes staking unnecessary.

Propagation is fairly easy and should be carried out in spring. Sow seeds in pots or boxes of a good growing medium, in a temperature of 16°C (60°F). Pot seedlings into individual medium-size pots and grow on at a reduced temperature. Harden off in the usual way and plant out into final positions at the end of spring at 60cm (24in) intervals.

Take care

Remember proportions when planting with other subjects. 86▸

Lagurus ovatus

(Hare's tail grass)

- **Sow in late summer or early autumn**
- **Ordinary well-drained soil**
- **Sunny position**

This beautiful annual grass is of medium height, 30cm (12in), with a very attractive inflorescence. The almost white ovate flowerheads appear from early summer through until autumn. As the common name implies its shape is somewhat like that of a hare's woolly tail. The greenish grey foliage is linear, and gives a good contrast to the fine flowers. Grow near the front of a bed or border where the plants will be admired at their best. As with all grasses, avoid over-rich soils, which can lead to fungal diseases.

Although seed can be sown directly into flowering positions, better results will be obtained if seed is sown into boxes during late summer or early autumn in a cool greenhouse. Prick out the seedlings into clumps in boxes of loam-based growing medium. Grow on through the winter and keep protected only from the severest weather. Plant out in mid-spring 15cm (6in) apart.

Take care

Avoid very windy positions. 86

Lathyrus odoratus 'Jet Set Mixed'

(Sweet pea)

- **Sow in autumn or spring**
- **Ordinary but fertile soil**
- **Sunny sheltered position**

The intermediate types of sweet pea have been bred to provide many of the improved characters of the taller types but with a more compact habit of growth.

The flowers of 'Jet Set Mixed' include a range of bright colours, with 5 or 6 blooms on stems long enough for cutting. The plants are freely branching, but reach only 90cm (3ft) high. Canes may be placed around them for neatness, if desired; otherwise they need no support.

Sow seeds in autumn or spring direct where they are to flower, if conditions are suitable. Alternatively sowing under cold glass would provide some earlier flowers. 'Jet Set' would make an interesting group in a small separate bed or as a feature in a large mixed border. The plants usually break freely without pinching.

Take care

Watch out for aphids and spray with a suitable insecticide.

Lathyrus odoratus 'Leamington'

(Sweet pea)

- **Sow in autumn or spring**
- **Ordinary but fertile soil**
- **Sunny sheltered spot**

Very sweetly scented, the cultivar 'Leamington' has exquisite lavender fairly weatherproof flowers. If you are growing them for exhibition, they should be treated as single cordons; single stems will need to be trained on individual canes or wires. Side shoots formed in the axils of the leaves, together with tendrils, will need to be removed at an early stage so that as much energy as possible is used in the production of high-quality blooms.

Plants are raised from seed (peas) sown in autumn or spring in pots or boxes of a loam-based growing medium. If autumn-sown, they will require no heat for germination. In spring under glass keep in a frost-free temperature until hardening off has been completed. Better results are obtained from the overwintered plants from autumn sowings. Plant out in spring at 15-23cm (6-9in) intervals.

Take care

Remove faded flowers promptly.

Lathyrus odoratus 'Red Arrow'

(Sweet pea)

- **Sow in autumn or spring**
- **Ordinary but fertile soil**
- **Sunny sheltered site**

'Red Arrow' is a recent introduction and has great potential. Very large scarlet flowers are produced on good solid stems. As the petals are quite firm in texture they are reasonably weatherproof. This vigorous cultivar will need space.

For ordinary garden purposes sow seeds in early spring in the area where they are to flower. Sow them 10cm (4in) apart and 2.5cm (1in) deep. Thin out or transplant seedlings to 23cm (9in) apart. Alternatively sow in the autumn into boxes; prick out seedlings into individual small pots. When three pairs of leaves have been developed, pinch out the growing point; this will encourage growth to become bushy later on. Grow on through the winter in a cold frame and protect from the severest weather only. Plant out in early spring. Use peasticks, wires, trellis or canes for support.

Take care

Soak seeds in cold water overnight before sowing, to assist germination.

Lathyrus odoratus 'Sheila McQueen'

(Sweet pea)

- **Sow in autumn or spring**
- **Well-drained, medium loam**
- **Sunny but sheltered location**

'Sheila McQueen' is a lovely shade of salmony orange with a pink tint showing through; a creamy base is also apparent. For ordinary garden purposes let them ramble over trellis work or arches, or provide a wigwam of peasticks in the annual or mixed border.

Dig in plenty of organic matter before planting, to provide for a cool root run by retaining moisture at the hottest times of the year. Sow the seed (peas) in autumn or spring; those sown in autumn will flower earlier. To help the seed to germinate, nick the hard outer casing of the seed or soak it in water for 24 hours before sowing in a loam-based growing medium. Use pots or boxes for sowing and then place the seedlings singly in small pots. Autumn sowings need to be placed in a cold frame; those sown in spring must be kept in a temperature of 16°C (60°F). Plant out in early spring, 15cm (6in) apart.

Take care

Remove faded flowers regularly. 87▸

Lavatera trimestris 'Alba'

(White mallow)

- **Sow in autumn or spring**
- **Ordinary soil**
- **Sunny and sheltered location**

The white mallow has attractive trumpet-shaped flowers up to 10cm (4in) in diameter. The intensely white satiny petals that make up each individual bloom will give lasting pleasure. Self-supporting stems up to 1m (39in) will be covered in a profusion of flowers if given the right growing conditions. Blooms are produced from the axils of the deep green lobed leaves from early summer onwards. Plant breeders have developed a number of strains. Whichever you choose remember that they are vigorous and will need plenty of space to establish themselves. They are ideal for planting in a border, especially against a wall of a contrasting colour.

Produce plants in the same way as for *L. trimestris* 'Silver Cup'. Mallows self-seed very readily and it is wise to weed out those not required at the end of each season; otherwise, unwanted plants could choke other subjects.

Take care

Plant in a sheltered position.

Lavatera trimestris 'Silver Cup' (L. rosea)

(Mallow)

- **Sow in autumn or spring**
- **Ordinary soil**
- **Sunny and sheltered spot**

Mallows have long been grown for their attractive free-flowering effects. The annual cultivar 'Silver Cup' recommended here is one of a number of new hybrids recently developed from *L. rosea*. Glowing pink blooms 7.5-10cm (3-4in) in diameter are freely produced on stems 60-70cm (24-28in) high and spreading to 75cm (30in). This plant is a member of the hollyhock family, and its leaves are a good green, ovate and lobed. Flowers grow from the leaf axils and are trumpet-shaped, almost satin in texture, and very pleasing to the eye. Apart from their use in the perennial border, try them towards the back of an annual border.

Sow seed directly where plants are to flower, in autumn or spring, and cover lightly. Thin out the seedlings of either sowing during late spring to 45cm (18in) intervals. The strong low branching habit of this plant requires no staking.

Take care

Give plants plenty of space. 88▶

Limnanthes douglasii

(Poached egg flower)

- **Sow in spring**
- **Ordinary soil**
- **Sunny position**

This is popularly known as poached egg flower because of its blooms, which have yellow centres surrounded by white. Each flower is saucer-shaped, and the blooms are produced on 15cm (6in) stems with deeply cut light green leaves. The blooms open in early summer, and are 2.5cm (1in) across. Bees have a particular liking for the flowers of this plant, which are delicately scented, and they can nearly swamp the plants. Apart from their outdoor use these plants can give a succession of colour in a cool greenhouse or conservatory during winter or spring; seed for this should be sown in early autumn.

For flowering in the garden, sow seeds where they are to flower, in spring. In milder areas autumn sowings will produce earlier flowering plants. Only just cover the seed with fine soil, and later thin out seedlings in both methods to 10cm (4in) intervals.

Take care

Discard self-sown seedlings. 88▶

Limonium sinuatum 'Gold Coast'

(Statice sinuata)

(Everlasting flower)

- **Sow in very early spring**
- **Ordinary soil**
- **Open, sunny position**

Formerly known as *Statice*, this everlasting flower has long been popular for its papery blooms in white, yellow, rose and blue. The cultivar 'Gold Coast' has excellent bright yellow flowers, which are produced on slightly winged green stems 60cm (24in) high, of erect habit. Formed in clusters up to 10cm (4in) long, the blooms appear in midsummer.

Sow seed under glass in very early spring at a temperature of 16°C (60°F). The seeds will be slightly clustered and will need teasing apart so that individual seeds can be sown; if this task is carried out, patience will be well rewarded by more even germination, and growth will be more rapid. Use a good loam-based growing medium for seeds and pricking out. Harden off in the usual way and plant out at 30cm (12in) intervals in early summer.

Take care

Do not disturb when planted. 105▸

Linaria maroccana

(Toadflax)

- **Sow in mid-spring**
- **Ordinary, preferably gritty soil**
- **Sunny location**

These dainty antirrhinum-like flowers with a short spur will provide a wealth of colour in almost any part of the garden as long as the site is sunny and well-drained. Flowers are produced on shortish stems in the form of a spike; 30cm (12in) is about the average height. They come in a variety of colours; the lower lip of each bloom is usually marked with a white or pale yellow blotch, resulting in a complete contrast to the upper petals. About 1cm (0.4in) long, the flowers are supported by pale green leaves of a linear shape.

Seedlings can be temperamental when moved and it is advisable to sow seeds where they are to flower. Sow in very shallow drills in mid-spring, covering the seeds lightly. If growing on a dry wall then mix the seeds with a little peat and push into the crevices; hold them in place with a little damp moss. Thin out seedlings elsewhere to 15cm (6in).

Take care

Do not overwater mature plants. 106▸

Linaria reticulata 'Crimson and Gold'

(Portuguese toadflax)

- **Sow in mid-spring**
- **Ordinary soil**
- **Sunny position**

This crimson and gold cultivar has been developed from the very tall Portuguese toadflax; its reduced height, 30cm (12in), makes it easier to deal with in the garden. Gold-splashed scarlet-crimson flowers, resembling snapdragons with a short spur, open from late spring and are 2cm (0.8in) long. The compact plants, made up of pale green, linear leaves holding spiky flowerheads, can be put to good use in the annual border. Try also to sow directly into containers on a patio in full sunshine. At the end of each season discard any self-sown seedlings.

As a hardy annual and for ordinary garden purposes, sow the seeds in spring in shallow drills where they are to flower, and only lightly cover the seed. Thin out the seedlings to 15cm (6in) apart. Further sowings at monthly intervals to the end of spring will ensure a succession of flowering over a longer period.

Take care

Keep well weeded when young. 107▸

Linum grandiflorum 'Rubrum'

(Scarlet flax)

- **Sow in autumn or spring**
- **Ordinary well-drained soil**
- **Full sun**

Waving in a light summer breeze this hardy annual is splendid if you can give it the correct cultural conditions. The scarlet saucer-shaped flowers are up to 5cm (2in) across, on wispy 30cm (12in) stems of a light green; the narrow leaves are in sympathy with the light airy feeling of this plant. The slightest air movement will set the flowers in motion. Use in conjunction with a pale contrasting-coloured annual, towards the front of a border.

Sow directly where they are to flower – during spring in most areas, but milder districts can take advantage by sowing in the autumn, which will produce flowers earlier on stronger plants. Broadcast the seed over the chosen area and rake in lightly. Thin out seedlings to 15cm (6in) apart.

Other, usually taller, cultivars of *L. grandiflorum* are available.

Take care

Seeds can rot before germination if the site is not well drained. 106-107▸

Lobelia erinus 'Colour Cascade Mixed'

- **Sow in late winter or early spring**
- **Ordinary well-cultivated soil**
- **Sun or partial shade**

Probably one of the most widely grown half-hardy plants, lobelia has many uses. It includes many shades of blue, rose, red, mauve and white eyed flowers, which continue to appear until cut down by autumn frosts.

Although best results are obtained from planting in sunny positions, lobelias also succeed in partial shade. These tender perennials need to be sown in heat in late winter or early spring to obtain maximum results. Sow the small seeds very thinly on the surface of a moistened peat-based seed mixture and do not cover. Germinate in a temperature of 18-21°C (65-70°F). Water carefully to avoid disturbance. Prick out as soon as the seedlings can be handled, either singly or in small clumps. Grow on in cooler conditions when established and harden off to plant out when risk of frost has passed.

Take care

Keep the plants watered in dry weather, and fed at intervals. 108➧

Lunaria annua

(L. biennis)

(Honesty; Moonwort)

- **Sow in late spring or early summer**
- **Light soil**
- **Partial shade**

This hardy biennial from the cabbage family starts to flower quite early, usually from mid-spring onwards. Individual blooms are made up of four petals in a cross shape, in shades of purple and white; some crimson can appear in mixtures. The flowers are followed by flattened disc-like seedpods highly prized for floral art work. Blooms and seedpods are formed on stems up to 75cm (30in) long, carrying heart-shaped leaves of a dark green. Grow towards the back of a border, but also make use of its tolerance to partial shade.

Sow seeds in nursery rows during late spring. Thin out the seedlings to 15cm (6in) apart, still in nursery rows. Plant out into final positions in the autumn at 30cm (12in) intervals.

If storing the seedpods, cut the stems in late summer when the pods are still slightly green. The clear silver discs are easily damaged by strong winds.

Take care

Keep slugs at bay. 108➧

Above: **Limonium sinuatum 'Gold Coast'**
This yellow-flowered cultivar has papery blooms that will dry well if cut before they are fully open. Many other colours are available. 102▸

Left: **Linaria macroccana 'Fairy Bouquet'**
This dwarf variety grows to about 20cm (8in) in height and produces a most attractive mixture of colours. Grow in sun and in a very well-draining soil for best results. 102▸

Right: **Linaria reticulata 'Crimson and Gold'**
At 30cm (12in) high this is a useful and pretty plant for the annual border. It will also thrive in containers on a sunny patio. 103▸

Below: **Linum grandiflorum 'Rubrum'**
This hardy annual should be sown directly into its flowering position. The bright scarlet flowers are produced throughout the summer. Combine with paler plants. 103▸

Left: **Lunaria annua**
These hardy, early flowering plants grow well in partial shade and poor soils. The cross-shaped blooms give way to flattened seedpods much in demand for indoor decoration; cut in late summer before they ripen. 104▸

Right: **Lupinus hartwegii 'Pixie Delight'**
A dwarf form of annual lupin with pretty mixed flowers that will provide colour well into autumn. These plants will not need support. 121▸

Below:
Lobelia erinus 'Colour Cascade'
A pleasing blend of trailing varieties for hanging baskets, window boxes and low walls. Grow in full sun and give a weak liquid feed every ten days to sustain flowering. 104▸

Above: **Matthiola incana 'Giant Imperial Mixed'**
This is a fine mixture of these sweetly scented garden favourites. The flowering stems will grow to a height of about 50cm (20in). 122▸

Left: **Malope trifida 'Grandiflora'**
This vigorous branching annual will make a bold splash of colour in a large border. It will thrive in a light soil and a sunny location. Also suitable for patio containers. 121▸

Right: **Mentzelia lindleyi**
These lovely golden yellow flowers revel in the sun; they are scented and appear in profusion throughout the summer months. Be sure to water well in dry periods. 123▸

Above left:
Mesembryanthemum criniflorum
These free-flowering plants are ideal for carpeting a dry sunny site. 123▸

Above: **Mimulus variegatus**
In moist situations these compact plants will produce their masked and spotted flowers until autumn. 125▸

Left:
Mesembryanthemum 'Lunette'
A new, early flowering cultivar of this lovely established plant. 124▸

Below:
Myosotis alpestris 'Ultramarine'
The deep blue flowers will blend with spring-flowering bulbs. 125▸

Above: **Nemesia strumosa 'Fiesta'**
A lovely mixture of unusual colours for small beds and containers. Grow nemesias in a sunny place and keep moist in hot dry weather. Make a second sowing for a long display. 126▸

Left: **Nemophila menziesii**
The spreading habit of this hardy annual makes it ideal for planting along the edge of a border. It will tolerate partial shade as well as sun. About 23cm (9in) high. 126▸

Right: **Nicandra physaloides**
This tall, branching annual should be given adequate space to develop. The flowers are produced over many weeks but open only for a few hours during the middle of the day. 127▸

Above: **Nicotiana 'Crimson Rock' F1**
This free-flowering compact variety has beautifully fragrant blooms. 127▸

Right: **Nigella damascena 'Persian Jewels'**
Delicate semi-double blooms in shades of blue, pink and white. 129▸

Below:
Nicotiana 'Nicki F1 Hybrids'
A colourful mixture of fragrant blooms borne on dwarf plants. 128▸

Above: **Papaver somniferum 'Paeony-flowered Mixed'**
These very decorative poppies from the Orient and the Mediterranean provide a short-lived but extremely colourful show in early summer. 130▶

Right: **Perilla nankinensis**
This half-hardy annual provides a rich backdrop of dark foliage. 131▶

Below: **Petunia 'Resisto Rose' F1**
A lovely free-flowering hybrid. 132▶

Above: **Phacelia campanularia 'Blue Bonnet'**
An easily grown, true blue hardy annual for early flowering. The fragrant blooms will attract bees. Ideal for edging a garden path. 132▶

Lupinus hartwegii 'Pixie Delight'

(Lupin)

- **Sow in autumn or spring**
- **Neutral or acid and poor soil**
- **Sun or partial shade**

Handsome spikes of this popular annual will give long-lasting colour in the average garden throughout the summer. 'Pixie Delight' will give shades of pink, purple, blue and red, on stems 45cm (18in) high, from early summer to late autumn. The plants of this mixture do not need staking. Frequently used to fill gaps in mixed or herbaceous borders, they look just as well in a bed or border on their own. Plant them also in containers for the patio or yard. An abundance of seedpods can be produced and it is wise to remove these if you have young children, as tummy upsets may occur if they eat the small peas or pods. To be safe, cut off the flowerhead as soon as the colour has faded.

Plants are easily raised from seeds, sown directly where they are to flower in autumn or spring. Autumn-sown plants will be earlier to flower and somewhat larger. Thin out seedlings to 23cm (9in) apart.

Take care

Fork peat into alkaline soil. 109▶

Malope trifida 'Grandiflora'

(Mallow wort)

- **Sow in mid-spring**
- **Light soil**
- **Sunny position**

This annual of a very distinctive nature comes from Spain. Its richly coloured flowers will enhance any sunny border. Once established the plants, up to 1m (39in) tall, will provide wide trumpet flowers of a light purple with internal veins of a deep almost black-purple, up to 7.5cm (3in) across, borne on erect branching stems with lobed green leaves. They make compact plants, and will require no staking despite their height. In large borders use them near a pale yellow or white annual. Container-grown for the patio they will give height to a somewhat flat area.

As this is a hardy annual it is not necessary to propagate it under glass, but simply sow the seeds where they are to flower. Carry out the usual process in mid-spring and thin out seedlings to 15-23cm (6-9in) apart. The flowers will appear from early summer onwards.

Take care

Discard unwanted self-sown seedlings. 110▶

Matthiola incana Dwarf Ten Week Stock

- **Sow in spring**
- **Most soils, preferably alkaline**
- **Sun or partial shade**

These flowers, on 25cm (10in) stems, and in a splendid range of red, pink, rose, carmine and purple, will be long lasting. Blooms appear about 10 days before other cultivars of the type.

Correct cultural conditions are essential to obtain maximum results. Sow under glass in early spring at a temperature of 18-21°C (65-70°F). Use a sterile growing medium to avoid damping-off disease. When germination has been completed reduce the temperature to 10°C (50°F). If you grow the selectable strains, you can discard the dark types and prick off the light ones; this will ensure that most will be double flowered. When handling young seedlings, hold by the edge of a leaf and not by the sensitive stem, which could be damaged and rot. Plant out after hardening off, at 23cm (9in) intervals.

Take care
Lime the soil before planting, if it is too acid.

Matthiola incana 'Giant Imperial Mixed'

- **Sow in early spring**
- **Most soils, preferably alkaline**
- **Sunny position, but tolerates partial shade**

Stocks must be one of the most popular scented annuals. *En masse* this fragrance can be overpowering, however, so do not overplant. The 'Giant Imperial mixture' always provides reliable flowers with a high percentage of doubles. Stems 38-50cm (15-20in) tall carry a profusion of pink, white, lilac, purple and crimson spikes of flowers from early summer onwards. Grey-green soft narrow leaves are formed under the flowerheads and give a pleasing contrast.

Sow seed for summer flowering during the early spring under glass in a temperature of 13°C (55°F). Use a loam-based mixture for sowing and pricking off seedlings. Grow on in a lower temperature, and harden off before planting out 23cm (9in) apart.

Take care
Kill caterpillars at once. 110-111▸

Mentzelia lindleyi

(Bartonia aurea)

(Blazing star)

- **Sow in early spring**
- **Light and fertile soil**
- **Sunny position**

Known in the past as *Bartonia aurea*, this beautiful annual has lovely golden-yellow flowers resembling the common St John's wort; the masses of stamens in the centre of each bloom are surrounded by five large petals. Fleshy stems carry a profusion of flowers from early summer, up to 45cm (18in) high; the leaves are a lovely foil, and are somewhat narrow and deep green. The choice of site is important as mentzelias love the sun; plant them between the front and the centre of an annual or mixed border. Sweetly scented, they can be used in patio borders, or try them in window boxes, but remember that they may block out some of your indoor light.

As they are hardy annuals sow them directly where they are to flower, in early spring. Take out shallow drills and sow the seed, cover over lightly and water if necessary. The resultant seedlings should be thinned to 23cm (9in).

Take care

Water well in dry periods. 111▸

Mesembryanthemum criniflorum

(Livingstone daisy)

- **Sow in spring**
- **Most soils, including poor ones**
- **Full sun**

This plant originates from S Africa, and a sunny warm position is essential for good flowering. Prostrate in growth but tending to trail, it is an ideal subject for the front of a window box, over a low dry stone wall, or as a drift near the front of a border. Stems are fleshy, green to reddish in colour, with cylindrical leaves. Flowers are up to 4cm (1.5in) across and appear in a multitude of colours including white, orange, red, pink; a number will be bicolours with a white centre.

This tender fleshy annual requires some heat for germination; sow seeds in spring under glass in a temperature of 16°C (60°F). Prick off seedlings into a good growing medium, harden off in the usual way and plant out at the end of spring at intervals of 23-30cm (9-12in). Alternatively sow in flowering positions at the end of spring, and thin out to correct distances apart when plants are large enough.

Take care

Remove faded flowers regularly. 112▸

Mesembryanthemum oculatus 'Lunette'

(Livingstone daisy)

- **Sow in spring**
- **Ordinary or poor soil**
- **Sunny position**

The appealing cultivar 'Lunette' is a clear yellow, 8cm (3.2in) high, flowering much earlier than the crinifolium types. Try to plant it near light blue annuals in the border. For formal designs and in window boxes use it along the front edge, or in hanging baskets in a sunny position; in the latter it should be planted before other subjects are included in the design. As the plants are low in height, remember not to plant them too near overpowering species, or they can become smothered.

Spring sowings are essential if this plant is to flower early. Germination will take two or three weeks if kept at a temperature of 18-21°C (65-70°F). Prick off seedlings into a good growing medium, preferably loam-based. Grow on at a lower temperature and then harden off in the usual way. Plant out at the end of spring at 23cm (9in) intervals.

Keep an eye open for slug damage and bait if necessary.

Take care

Do not plant out too early. 112▸

Mimulus guttatus

(Monkey flower)

- **Sow in spring**
- **Ordinary but moist soil**
- **Sunny location or shade**

The yellow flowers, about 2cm (0.8in) long, are trumpet-shaped, and something like those of the snapdragon; small brown dots or blotches in the throat and on the inside of the yellow petals attract many useful insects. The stems, carrying ovate light green leaves, are about 23cm (9in) long. Flowers appear from early summer in most areas.

Moist conditions will give the finest results and these plants are ideal for bog gardens; but they will be quite happy in the ordinary border as long as it is not too hot or too dry.

Treat this plant as a biennial for propagating purposes. Sow seeds in a cold frame in late spring for flowering the following year. Plant out the seedlings in nursery rows in the garden, a few inches apart. Grow on through the summer and keep well watered and weeded, until setting the plants out where they are to flower in early spring.

Take care

Keep moist at all times.

√89

Mimulus variegatus

(Monkey flower)

- **Sow in late winter**
- **Ordinary but moist soil**
- **Sunny position or shade**

Nearly all mimulus plants like a moist site and this species is no exception. They are very useful in the bog garden or as a marginal plant along the edge of a waterside planting. They are also at home as ground cover plants in the shade, as long as ground conditions remain moist throughout the growing period. Open trumpet-shaped flowers are produced on stems 30cm (12in) high. Individual blooms are 5cm (2in) long and can be yellow, orange or scarlet, and blotched with brown, maroon or purple. The supporting leaves are obovate to oblong. Dwarf strains are available, but flowers tend to be the same size.

Sow seed in late winter or very early spring under glass in a temperature of 13°C (55°F). Use any good growing medium of a loam-based nature. Pot seedlings into individual small pots, and grow on in cool conditions. Plant in late spring or early summer at 30cm (12in).

Take care

Avoid hot, dry situations. 113▶

Myosotis alpestris 'Ultramarine'

(Forget-me-not)

- **Sow in late spring**
- **Most soils**
- **Sun or partial shade**

This is strongly recommended for spring bedding, especially in association with wallflowers and tulips. 'Ultramarine' has flowers of a deep indigo blue, produced on very neat compact plants only 15cm (6in) high; the individual flowers are fairly small but have attractive yellow centres. Stems and leaves feel slightly sticky, due to the mass of small hairs. This to some extent has a repellent effect against birds that devastate other spring-flowering plants.

Treat this species as a hardy biennial by sowing seed in nursery beds in late spring. When seedlings are large enough, plant them in further nursery rows, 15cm (6in) apart; grow on through the summer, and keep well weeded until the autumn when final planting in flowering positions should be undertaken at 15cm (6in) intervals. Water in as necessary so that wilting is kept to a minimum.

Take care

Avoid poorly drained soils. 113▶

Nemesia strumosa

- **Sow in early spring**
- **Most soils, but well cultivated**
- **Sunny and slightly moist location**

Nemesia in the wild is rather untidy, but attractive; continued selection and breeding has led to today's more manageable plants. Many self colours are available but I prefer the mixtures that give a wide variety of colours: usually included are shades of yellow, cream, pink, crimson, blue and purple. Individual blooms are 2.5cm (1in) across and funnel-shaped; these are carried on erect branching stems of up to 45cm (18in). The leaves are pale green and coarsely toothed; some change from green to a pinkish red.

This species is very useful as a bedding plant or in window boxes or other containers. Sow seeds under glass in early spring at a temperature of 16°C (60°F). Only just cover the seed, in boxes or pots of a good loam-based growing medium. Harden off slowly and plant out in flowering positions in early summer, at 15cm (6in) apart.

Take care

Make a second sowing one month after the first, for succession. 114-115▶

Nemophila menziesii

(N. insignis)

(Baby blue eyes)

- **Sow in spring**
- **Ordinary but moist soil**
- **Sun or partial shade**

This is one of the more notable hardy annuals from California; plants grow to a height of 23cms (9in), and have spreading slender stems on which deeply cut feathery light green leaves are carried. Appearing from early summer, the flowers are buttercup-shaped and of a beautiful sky blue with a very striking white centre; each bloom measures 4cm (1.6in) in diameter. This species will tolerate partial shade; use it where a low planting is required.

Before sowing, fork in organic matter if your soil is on the light side; this will ensure that moisture is retained in hot dry spells so that plants can survive. Sow seeds directly where they are to flower, in early spring; take out shallow drills and only lightly cover the seed. Thin out seedlings to 15cm (6in) apart. In mild districts autumn sowings carried out in the same way will provide plants for flowering in late spring of the following year.

Take care

Water freely during dry weather. 114▶

Nicandra physaloides

(Shoo fly plant; Apple of Peru)

- **Sow in early spring**
- **Rich well-cultivated soil**
- **Sunny position**

This is a very strong annual, up to 1m (39in) in height. The pale blue bell-shaped flowers, 4cm (1.6in) long, have a contrasting white throat. The flower is followed by a non-edible green apple-shaped fruit encased in a five-winged purple calyx. Stems tend to be branched and spreading; the finely toothed leaves have wavy edges and are a pleasant green. Because of their ultimate size these plants require plenty of room to develop, and they are best used towards the back of an annual or mixed border, preferably in full sun. Before planting, fork in plenty of organic matter.

This unusual annual is easily grown from seed. Sow under glass in early spring at a temperature of 16°C (60°F). Use a good growing medium for sowing and potting. Put seedlings into individual small pots and grow on in the same temperature. Harden off in the usual way and plant out in early summer, 30cm (12in) apart.

Take care

Support individual specimens. 115▸

Nicotiana × sanderae 'Crimson Rock' F1

(Sweet-scented tobacco plant)

- **Sow in early spring**
- **Fertile and well-drained soil**
- **Sun or partial shade**

One of many hybrids now available, 'Crimson Rock' is a beautiful free-flowering compact variety 45cm (18in) high; the blooms are crimson in colour and sweetly fragrant. It has the added advantage that the flowers stay open throughout the day, when other types tend to close.

As with all nicotianas, stems and leaves are sticky to the touch; these usually attract aphids in the early stages of the plant's growth and it is wise to spray them. Because of the very fragrant flowers, grow in beds or borders towards the centre, beneath windows or on patios.

As a half-hardy annual this species needs to be propagated under glass in early spring. Sow seeds on top of prepared pots or boxes of a peat-based growing medium; do not cover the seeds. Keep in a temperature of 18°C (65°F). Prick off seedlings in the usual way. Harden off and plant out in early summer, 23cm (9in) apart.

Take care

Spray early against insects. 116▸

Nicotiana × sanderae 'Nicki Hybrids' F1

(Sweet-scented tobacco plant)

- **Sow in early spring**
- **Rich, well-drained soil**
- **Sun or partial shade**

The Nicki F1 Hybrids are a lovely mixture of colours including red, pink, rose, lime green and white. Individual blooms are up to 6cm (2.4in) long, formed into loose clusters. Stems bearing the flowers carry large oblong leaves of a light green. This strain is dwarf and reaches only about 25cm (10in) in height. The blooms of this free-flowering cultivar are sweetly fragrant. Use as a bedding plant for formal beds or borders, beneath a window, or on a patio or yard where the scent can be appreciated, especially in the evening.

Sow seeds under glass in early spring, in a temperature of 18°C (65°F). Seeds should be scattered thinly on top of prepared pots or boxes of a peat-based growing medium. Prick out in the usual way. Harden off and plant out in early summer, 23cm (9in) apart.

Take care

Do not plant out too early. 116-117▶

Nicotiana tabacum

(N. gigantea)

(Tobacco plant)

- **Sow in early spring**
- **Rich, well-drained soil**
- **Sunny position**

The true tobacco plant can reach a height of 2m (6.5ft) and therefore if you are considering this plant for an ornamental effect in the garden the choice of site will need to be carefully considered. Large leaves up to 1m long are borne on strong stems. Dull red or pink flowers of a funnel shape usually appear from midsummer until autumn. Use these plants in groups at the back of an annual border as an architectural feature, or in large containers on a patio. The leaves will change from green to a light golden colour towards autumn.

Sow under glass in early spring, in a temperature of 18°C (65°F). Use any good growing medium. Prick off into individual small pots and grow on. Give a weak liquid feed up to hardening-off time, about every 10 days. Plant out in early summer at intervals of 60-90cm (2-3ft). A sheltered sunny site will avoid the necessity for staking, especially if plants are grouped together.

Take care

Spray against aphids.

Nigella damascena

(Love-in-a-mist)

- **Sow in early spring**
- **Well-cultivated ordinary soil**
- **Sunny position**

An old favourite, love in a mist is particularly good for the annual border when planted towards the centre. Growing up to 60cm (24in), the stiff stems carry cornflower-like blooms of blue, mauve, purple, rose-pink or white. Bright green feathery foliage gives a light feeling to the plant. The semi-double blooms are followed by the seedpods, much prized for floral arrangements.

Being hardy annuals, these plants are easy to raise, simply by sowing where they are to flower. Rake down to a fine tilth the area to sow, take out shallow drills in early spring, sow the seeds and lightly cover over. When large enough to handle, thin out the seedlings to 23cm (9in) apart. In mild districts autumn sowings made in the same way will produce earlier flowering plants the following year. Discard any unwanted self-sown seedlings at the end of each season.

Take care

Cut stems for drying when seedpods are a light brown. 117▸

Papaver glaucum

(Tulip poppy)

- **Sow in autumn or spring**
- **Ordinary soil**
- **Sunny location**

An annual in habit, this beautiful poppy from Asia Minor has tulip-shaped flowers of four petals, about 10cm (4in) across. Individual flowers are a shining scarlet-crimson. Before opening in early summer they are preceded by pointed buds, carried on blue-green upright stems 45cm (18in) in height. Leaves are deeply cut and similar in colour to the stems.

Use in the annual or mixed border, in bold groups. If used next to a less showy plant, they will stand out even better. The silky texture of the petals will catch the smallest rays of the sun. Plants can be kept flowering longer if seed heads are removed.

As this is a hardy annual, the seeds can be sown in autumn to flower the following year; plants will be stronger and they stand up well to severe winter weather conditions. Spring sowings will make a useful contribution to the border. Sow in shallow drills and cover lightly. Thin out seedlings to 30cm (12in).

Take care

Water freely during dry weather.

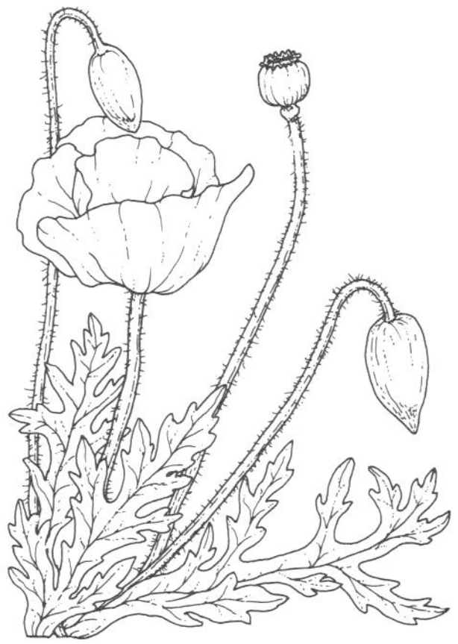

Papaver rhoeas

(Corn poppy)

- **Sow in autumn or spring**
- **Light well-drained soil**
- **Sunny location**

From the common wild scarlet field poppy the Rev. W. Wilks made his famous selections from which, in the 1880s, the world-renowned Shirley poppy strain was introduced. Mainly in the range of pink, red and white, a number will be found to be bicoloured or picotee. Double strains now exist, but the single type are more allied to the original introductions. This very worthy annual is hardy, and can be used in borders and in the odd pocket towards the back of a rock garden, as long as the position is sunny.

Up to 60cm (24in) in height, the stems carry lovely deeply lobed leaves above which the flowers are borne, about 7.5cm (3in) across.

Sow seeds in spring or autumn. Take out shallow drills where the plants are to flower. Sow seeds and lightly cover with soil. Thin out seedlings to 30cm (12in) apart. Flowers appear in early summer.

Take care

Spray against aphids.

Papaver somniferum 'Paeony-flowered Mixed'

(Opium poppy)

- **Sow in spring or autumn**
- **Ordinary soil**
- **Sunny position**

The large paeony-flowered mixture and is well recommended for the garden. Individual double flowers measure up to 10cm (4in) across. Blue-green deeply lobed leaves are carried on smooth stems 75cm (30in) tall. Pink, white, red or purple blooms will appear in early summer and although relatively short-lived they are worth a place in the annual border. The flowers are followed by large bulbous seedpods much prized by flower arrangers.

These poppies are easily grown from seeds sown in the autumn in mild districts, or in the spring elsewhere. Take out drills large enough for the seeds, about 30cm (12in) apart. Cover the seeds lightly with soil; thin out the seedlings to 30cm (12in) apart. Although fairly tall, these plants should not require staking. In severe winters protect autumn-sown seedlings from the weather.

Take care

Spray against mildew disease. 118▸

Pelargonium zonale

(Geranium)

- **Sow in winter or very early spring**
- **Ordinary well-drained soil**
- **Full sun**

Zonal geraniums have become increasingly popular in recent years, and many new seed-raised cultivars have been introduced. F1 hybrids will begin to flower at bedding-out time if sown in heat under glass in early spring. Their well-formed florets of single flowers are borne in large trusses; the few new double kinds are slightly later flowering. Foliage may be plain or with darker zones, and there are several interesting dwarf hybrids.

Geraniums grow in ordinary soil provided they receive sunshine. Sow thinly in seed mixture in a temperature of 21-24°C (70-75°F), just covering the seed. Germination may take three weeks. Prick off singly into small pots when large enough, and grow on in a lower temperature until ready for planting out in a sunny position after frosts are past.

Take care

Remove dead flowerheads to prevent seeding.

Perilla nankinensis

(P. frutescens)

- **Sow in very early spring**
- **Ordinary well-cultivated soil**
- **Sunny site**

Grown for its beautiful bronze-purple foliage, this half-hardy annual is most useful as a spot plant in formal bedding schemes or as an architectural plant in the mixed or annual border. If you have a patio surrounded by a light-coloured wall, large containers of this plant will provide a unique contrast.

The showy leaves are toothed, ovate and pointed. When bruised, these and the insignificant white flowers emit a spice-like fragrance, reminiscent of their Chinese origin. Given good conditions, plants reach a height of 60cm (24in).

Propagate under glass in very early spring. Sow seeds in pots or boxes of a good growing medium. Keep in a temperature of 18°C (65°F). Prick off the seedlings into individual pots. Harden off and plant out in early summer. If growing together in groups allow 30cm (12in) between plants.

Take care

Stake individual specimens. 119▶

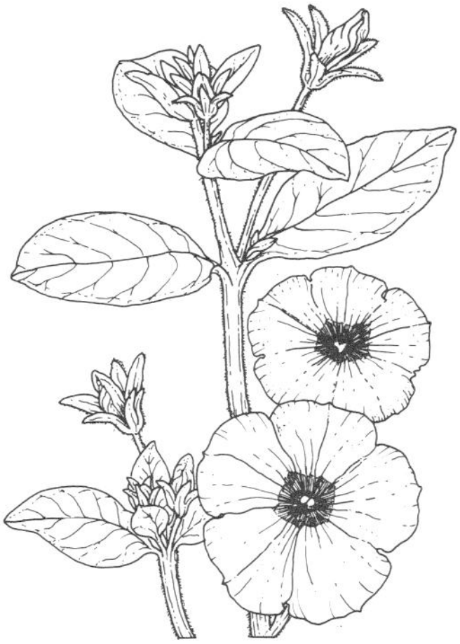

Petunia hybrids

- **Sow in early spring**
- **Ordinary well-cultivated soil**
- **Sunny location**

In a good sunny summer the petunia is second to none for its profusion of colour and versatility of use. Flowers are trumpet-shaped, up to 10cm (4in) across. Leaves and stems will be a mid- to dark green; leaves vary in size but are usually ovate. The whole plant feels sticky to the touch. Use these petunias for a wide range of purposes including formal bedding, borders, containers, window boxes and hanging baskets.

All petunias love a sunny position and benefit from being grown in a well-cultivated soil. Avoid having the soil over-rich, as this can lead to a lot of growth and few flowers. As this is a tender annual, seeds will need to be sown under glass in early spring. Sow thinly on top of a peat-based growing medium in pots or boxes. Prick off the seedlings into boxes, harden off and plant out in early summer. Spacing will depend on the cultivar you choose.

Take care

Remove faded flowers regularly. 118▸

Phacelia campanularia

- **Sow in early spring**
- **Light, sandy, well-drained soil**
- **Sunny site**

This is one of the most striking annuals. The gentian-blue clusters of upturned bell-shaped flowers are worth a place in any annual border. Blooms appear from early summer. Each individual flower has lovely contrasting pale yellow stamens; overall, blooms are about 2.5cm (1in) across. Plants are dwarf and branching in character, about 23cm (9in) high. Stems carry ovate leaves that are cut or toothed along the edge, and dark greyish green in colour. Loved by bees, these plants are ideally suited to the edge of a border or pathway, preferably planted in bold groups to make a greater impact.

In early spring rake down the soil to a fine tilth, sow the seeds thinly in shallow drills where they are to flower and cover lightly. Thin out the subsequent seedlings to 15cm (6in) apart. If your garden is in a relatively mild area, then seeds can be sown in autumn. Plants grown through the winter will flower somewhat earlier.

Take care

Watch out for slugs. 120▸

Phlox drummondii 'Carnival'

- **Sow in spring**
- **Ordinary well-drained soil**
- **Open, sunny site**

Easy-to-grow half-hardy annuals, *P. drummondii* will give a succession of colour throughout the summer. For a really bright display try the cultivar 'Carnival'; this mixture has pink, rose, salmon, scarlet, blue and violet flowers. These are borne on stems 30cm (12in) high, carrying light green lanceolate leaves. Blooms are produced in early summer as dense heads up to 10cm (4in) in diameter; each individual flower is rounded. These plants are ideally suited for low-growing areas of the garden, especially the rock garden, where pockets can be filled to give constant colour.

In spring, sow seeds under glass in a temperature of 16°C (60°F). Use any good growing medium for sowing. Sow the seeds thinly and cover them lightly. Prick off the young seedlings, when large enough to handle, into boxes or trays. Harden off and plant out in flowering positions in early summer at 23cm (9in) intervals.

Take care

Dead-head to prolong flowering. 137▸

Portulaca grandiflora

(Sun plant)

- **Sow in spring**
- **Ordinary well-drained soil**
- **Full sun**

Originating from Brazil, portulacas have now come into their own as worthwhile plants for the annual border or (more especially) for pockets in the rock garden. In some areas they can be temperamental but given a good sunny site they should thrive well on most soils. The flowers of *P. grandiflora* are produced on semi-prostrate stems of a reddish colour, usually up to 23cm (9in) in height. Red, purple, rose, orange-scarlet, yellow and white, the blooms can be over 2.5cm (1in) across. Each centre has pronounced yellow stamens. Leaves are narrow, round and fleshy.

Sow seed in early spring under glass, in a temperature of 18°C (65°F). Use any good growing medium for this purpose and for the subsequent pricking-off of seedlings. Harden off in a cold frame and plant out in early summer, 15cm (6in) apart. Alternatively, sow where they are to flower, in mid-spring.

Take care

Water established plants only in extreme temperatures. 137▸

Pyrethrum ptarmicaeflorum 'Silver Feathers'

(P. roseum)
- **Sow in early spring**
- **Light, well-drained soil**
- **Sunny position**

This is a fine plant used extensively for its silver-grey foliage. The lacy leaves are borne on slender 30cm (12in) stems. The cultivar 'Silver Feathers' is particularly elegant. Although this species is strictly a perennial, plants are raised from seed each year as annuals. Besides using them as an edging plant, group three or five together as spot plants in a small bed with *Begonia semperflorens* as the predominant plant. Make sure that areas to be planted with this plant are very well drained; provide extra drainage by forking in coarse washed sand.

Raise plants by sowing seeds in early spring under glass, in a temperature of 16°C (60°F). Sow thinly in pots and only just cover the seeds. Use any good growing medium. Prick off seedlings and harden off in the usual way. Plant out 15cm (6in) apart.

Take care
Remove flowers regularly to keep foliage neat. 138▸

Ranunculus gramineus

- **Sow in early spring**
- **Ordinary soil**
- **Sun or partial shade**

One of a great number of species of the buttercup family *R. gramineus* is an extremely valuable plant to have in the garden. Buttercup flowers are produced in sprays on 30cm (12in) stems. The leaves are grey-green and grass-like. Appearing from late spring to midsummer, the yellow blooms are 2cm (0.8in) in diameter, shiny in texture and very free flowering. Mainly used in drifts in slightly moist areas, these plants will also give a good account of themselves in most borders, especially in conjunction with annual grasses or the blue linums.

Raise plants each year from seed by sowing in a frame or under cloches. Sow directly into the ground during early spring in shallow drills. Thin out the seedlings and remove the frame top or cloche in mid-spring. Grow on until autumn, then plant in final flowering positions.

Take care
Keep young plants cool through the summer months. 139▸

Reseda odorata

(Mignonette)

- **Sow in early spring or autumn**
- **Most soils except very acid ones**
- **Sunny location**

Having a very distinctive sweet scent, mignonette has long been a favourite. Flowers are carried on branching upright stems 75cm (30in) in height. Individual flowers are made up of very small petals in the centre of which is a mass of orange tufted stamens; clusters of these blooms are formed into a loose head. Leaves are a light green and spathe shaped, smooth and terminating just below the blooms. Planted towards the back of a border mignonette will look and smell fine.

Sow seeds where they are to flower, in early spring or autumn. Take out drills and lightly cover the seed. To assist germination and better-shaped plants, firm the soil well after sowing, either with the back of the rake or by treading lightly with your feet. Thin out subsequent seedlings to 15-23cm (6-9in) apart. Flowers will appear from early summer onwards.

Take care

Do not overwater mature plants. 139▸

Ricinus communis

(Castor oil plant)

- **Sow in early spring**
- **Ordinary well-cultivated soil**
- **Sunny location**

Treated as a half-hardy annual for normal garden work, this species originates from Africa.

Grown for the beautiful large palmate leaves up to 30cm (12in) across, castor oil plants are best used at the back of an informa border to give height and character. Depending on the cultivar the leaves will be green, purple or bronze. Petal-less flowers are produced in summer, followed by large spiky round seedpods; these can be poisonous if the internal seeds are eaten.

Sow seeds in early spring in a heated greenhouse at a temperature of 21°C (70°F). Sow in individual pots of a good growing medium. Move on into larger pots (10cm/4in), and reduce the temperature to 10°C (50°F). Harden off the plants in a cold frame at least two weeks before planting out in early summer.

Take care

Staking will be necessary. 140▸

Rudbeckia hirta 'Marmalade'

(Black-eyed Susan; Cone flower)

- **Sow in spring**
- **Any soil**
- **Sunny position**

The common names of this species allude to the centre of the flower, which has a very dark brown to purple colour and is cone-shaped. The outer petals are lovely shades of yellow, golds and brown, and the cultivar 'Marmalade' is a rich yellow with a central cone of purple-black – very striking. It flowers from early summer, and blooms will be carried in great profusion until late autumn on stems 45cm (18in) long. Individual flowers will be up to 10cm (4in) across.

To obtain flowering plants each year, sow seeds in boxes of any good growing medium in spring. Heat will not be required and they can be raised in either a cold greenhouse or a frame. Prick out the young seedlings into boxes and place these in a cold frame to protect them from frosts. Harden off in late spring and plant out into flowering positions in very early summer, 23cm (9in) apart.

Take care

Watch out for slug damage. 140▶

Salpiglossis sinuata 'Grandiflora'

- **Sow in very early spring**
- **Ordinary but well-cultivated soil**
- **Open and sunny position**

Although usually grown as a pot plant this species is a worthwhile subject to use outdoors in the summer months as a bedding plant.

'Grandiflora' and its hybrids will provide a wealth of colour in shades of crimson, scarlet, gold, rose, blue and yellow. Each flower has a velvet texture and the throat of the tubular flowers is often deeply veined with a contrasting colour. Size of individual blooms will vary between named cultivars of the species but they are on average about 5cm (2in) long and the same in diameter. Up to 60cm (24in) in height, the stems are slender and carry wavy-edged narrow leaves of a dark green.

Sow seed under glass in very early spring to produce plants for growing outdoors in summer. Use a peat-based growing medium for raising the seed, and keep in a temperature of 18°C (65°F). Prick out seedlings into boxes, harden off and plant out in early summer, 23cm (9in) apart.

Take care

Keep well watered at all times. 141▶

Above: **Phlox drummondii 'Carnival'**
This sweetly scented dwarf mixture includes many lovely colours with contrasting eyes. 133▸

Below: **Portulaca grandiflora**
In dry sunny situations these fleshy leaved plants will abound with bright flowers during the summer. Water established plants sparingly. 133▸

Above: **Pyrethrum ptarmicaeflorum 'Silver Feathers'**
The elegant silver-grey foliage of this plant makes it ideal for edging. Raise new plants from seed each year. 134▸

Left: **Ranunculus gramineus**
For masses of yellow flowers in late spring plant this dwarf buttercup in generous drifts in the border. Will tolerate partial shade. 134▸

Right: **Reseda odorata**
An established favourite, this plant deserves to be widely grown for its sweet scent alone. Ideal for the back of the border. 135▸

Above: **Ricinus communis**
These stately plants add height and interest to the border. Plant in early summer and provide support. 135▸

Below: **Rudbeckia hirta 'Marmalade'**
These long-lasting golden flowers are borne on tall stems. 136▸

Above: **Salpiglossis sinuata 'Grandiflora'**
Velvety textured, multicoloured flowers are borne on stems up to 60cm (24in) in height. A fine summer bedding plant that can be cut. 136▸

Left: **Salvia horminum**
The striking blue or purple bracts surround the true flowers, which are insignificant. Grow these attractive plants in well-drained soil in a sunny location for best results. 153▸

Right: **Salvia sclarea**
This is a useful plant for a large border, both for its bold foliage and for its elegant sprays of true flowers and showy bracts. Grow this biennial in sun on light soil. 154▸

Below: **Salvia splendens 'Flarepath'**
The bright scarlet spikes of true flowers and bracts make a vivid contrast against the dark green foliage of these well-loved plants. Superbly showy for formal beds, containers and window boxes. 155▸

Left: **Sanvitalia procumbens**
These miniature flowers are borne on branching stems that reach only 15cm (6in) high. Ideal as an edging and ground cover plant, it will thrive in an open sunny position. 155▸

Right: **Schizanthus pinnatus 'Angel Wings'**
Delicate butterfly flowers float above the fine feathery foliage. This free-flowering cultivar grows 30cm (12in) high and does not need staking. Suitable for containers. 156▸

Below: **Silybum marianum**
Grow these striking plants at the back of the border, where their bold green leaves flecked with white will add height and interest. Thistle flowers in late summer. 156▸

Left: **Thunbergia alata**
This vigorous annual climber will grow well outdoors in a sunny and sheltered spot. The pretty flowers are freely produced throughout the summer. Provide support. 159▸

Right: **Tropaeolum peregrinum**
Also a climber, this colourful plant will quickly spread over a fence or trellis, producing masses of lovely fringed flowers in summer. Feeding will give leaves, not flowers. 160▸

Below: **Tagetes erecta 'Orange Jubilee' F1**
This fine marigold holds its large flowerheads well above the dense foliage. The lovely blooms are double and will last well if cut. 157▸

Above: **Ursinia anethoides 'Sunshine'**
Bright golden yellow flowers that need sunshine to open fully. 161▸

Below: **Venidium fastuosum**
Stunning blooms up to 10cm (4in) across are borne on tall stems. Excellent as cut flowers indoors. 161▸

Above:
Verbascum bombyciferum
Bold architectural plants. Flowering stems reach a height of about 120cm (48in) and bear masses of yellow blooms. Give them room. 162▶

Above: **Verbena 'Florist Mixed'**
A bright mixture with a wide range of colours, many showing contrasting eyes. Grow this dwarf verbena on the rock garden, border edges, and in containers and window boxes. 163▶

Above: **Viola x wittrockiana Swiss Giant type**
This is one of the many varieties of garden pansy available. The colourful flowers are produced over a long period in the summer. 164▸

Below: **Viola cornuta**
This miniature viola is quite hardy and will flower continuously in the summer. In a moist fertile soil it will be equally happy in sun or in partial shade. Ideal for rock gardens. 163▸

Above: **Viscaria elegans 'Love'**
Sow these pretty annuals where they are to flower for a colourful, early summer display in the border. 164▸

Below: **Zinnia elegans 'Hobgoblin Mixed'**
A bright mixture of medium-sized, weather-resistant double flowers. 166▸

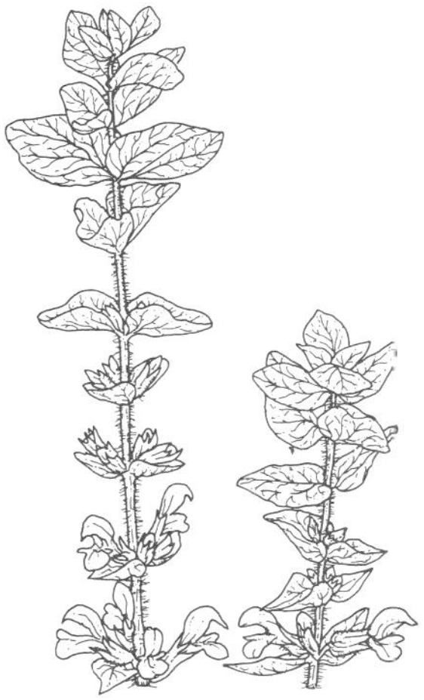

Salvia coccinea

- **Sow in early spring**
- **Ordinary soil**
- **Sunny position**

Often confused with *S. splendens* because of their close resemblance, *S. coccinea* has slightly longer flowers and is more slender in habit. Growing to 60cm (24in) it is more suited to the mixed or herbaceous border than for formal planting in beds. Deep scarlet tubular flowers show colour later than those of its more popular cousin, usually about midsummer onwards. Leaves are cordate or ovate, hairy and a lightish green. The species is variable and a number of sub-species are available, such as 'bicolor', 'lactea' and 'nana', all excellent for specific purposes.

S. coccinea should be grown from seed each year during early spring. Sow seeds in a peat-based growing medium under glass, in a temperature of 18°C (65°F). Prick off the seedlings singly into individual peat pots; in this way stronger plants will be obtained. Grow on in a reduced temperature. Harden off and plant out in early summer at 30cm (12in) intervals.

Take care
Check for slug or snail damage.

Salvia horminum

(Clary)

- **Sow in early spring or autumn**
- **Ordinary well-drained soil**
- **Sunny position**

This salvia from S Europe will provide a completely different range of colour from the *S. splendens* scarlet cultivars. Dark blue or purple bracts are produced around the insignificant true flowers. Mixtures are available, but the cultivar 'Blue Beard' is recommended for its very deep purple bracts on erect branching square stems, 45cm (18in) high. These also carry the ovate mid-green leaves. Grow towards the front of a border, or as a formal bedding plant with a few silver spot plants.

These hardy annuals may be sown direct outdoors in spring or autumn. If earlier colour is required plants can be raised under glass by sowing in seed mixture in spring at a temperature of 18°C (65°F). Prick off into individual pots or seed trays. Grow on cooler and harden off to plant out at 23cm (9in) apart in early summer. Too high temperatures will produce soft elongated growth.

Take care
Thin seedlings sown outdoors before they become crowded. 142▸

Salvia patens

- **Sow in early spring**
- **Ordinary soil**
- **Sunny spot**

Another species of the useful sage family, *S. patens* originates from Mexico. When plants are in flower the vivid blue colour is probably the best of its shade in the summer months. Individual blooms will be 5cm (2in) long, tubular in shape, consisting of lower and upper joined lips. Up to 45cm (18in) in height, the plants have sage-like leaves that are ovate and pointed, of a lovely green; the stiff stems are square. Although these plants are half-hardy perennials, they are usually treated as annuals for most purposes.

Sow seeds in very early spring in a warm greenhouse, keeping a constant temperature of 18°C (65°F). Use any good growing medium for seed raising and pricking out. The latter should be done into individual small pots. Grow on until hardening off in early summer. Plant out into final positions, 30cm (12in) apart.

Take care
Pinch out tips of young plants for bushy growth.

Salvia sclarea

(Clary)

- **Sow in spring**
- **Light and fertile soil**
- **Full sun**

This handsome biennial was grown in the past for use as a culinary herb but is now surpassed by the various species of sage. The oil, however, is still extracted commercially for use in the manufacture of perfumes. Reaching a height of 75cm (30in), the stems carry large, very hairy triangular leaves of mid-green. Flowers are tubular in shape, about 2.5cm (1in) long, and white-blue in colour. Below the true flowers, bracts of purple or yellow will accentuate the whole blooms, which show colour from midsummer onward. These are good border plants, which will enhance an otherwise flat area; use them towards the back of the border.

This species is biennial in habit. The seeds are sown in spring where they are to flower. Take out drills 38cm (15in) apart; thin out seedlings to 30cm (12in) apart when they are large enough to handle.

Take care
Use leaves for culinary purposes from midsummer onwards. 143▸

Salvia splendens 'Flarepath'

(Scarlet sage)

- **Sow in early spring**
- **Ordinary well-drained soil**
- **Sunny position**

Of all summer annuals the scarlet flowers (actually, bracts) of *S. splendens* must be the most vivid. Planted in formal beds or borders with contrasting silver- or grey-leaved plants they provide a stunning spectacle. Of the many cultivars available 'Flarepath' is well recommended and enjoys great popularity. The flowers are produced on 30cm (12in) stems above the rich green ovate leaves; they usually start to appear in early summer.

This tender plant requires a greenhouse for propagation. Sow seed in early spring in a peat-based growing compost. Keep the temperature about 18°C (65°F). Prick out seedlings into individual small pots and grow on in a slightly lower temperature. Harden off and plant out in summer about 23cm (9in) apart after late frosts are over.

Take care

Provide ample moisture when the plants are established. 143▸

Sanvitalia procumbens

(Creeping zinnia)

- **Sow in spring**
- **Ordinary soil**
- **Sunny site**

Very aptly named, the zinnia-like flowers of this hardy annual are quite striking. Bright yellow single flowers have jet black cone centres. They are 2.5cm (1in) across, produced on semi-prostrate branching stems only 15cm (6in) high from early summer onwards. Leaves are ovate, pointed and a useful green.

For successful results, fork peat or other humus into the top layer of soil before sowing the seed. To have plants flowering through the summer months, sow seeds outdoors in spring or earlier under glass; the latter will produce stronger, earlier-flowering specimens. Take out shallow drills where the plants are to flower, and lightly cover the seed with soil. Thin out the spring-sown seedlings as soon as they are large enough to handle; those sown in heat should be hardened off for later planting. In either case, thin out to 7.5cm (3in) apart.

Take care

Keep well watered if in hanging baskets. 144▸

Schizanthus pinnatus 'Angel wings'

(Butterfly flower)

- **Sow in spring**
- **Ordinary well-drained soil**
- **Sunny position**

The very tall cultivars of this species are now being replaced by more manageable dwarfer forms for garden work. Use them as border plants or even in formal bedding. 'Angel Wings' is a cultivar well worth trying for all purposes. Only 30cm (12in) tall the plants are very free-flowering, compact and almost conical in shape, and will not require staking. Flowers are orchid-shaped and come in a wide variety of colours; the spotted petals and open throats of the blooms are most attractive. Stems and leaves are a light green, the latter being deeply cut and fern-like.

As this is a half-hardy annual, sow seeds under glass in spring at a temperature of 16°C (60°F). Use a peat-based growing medium for sowing and for the subsequent pricking-off of seedlings. Harden off and plant out into flowering positions in early summer, 23cm (9in) apart.

Take care

Avoid watering overhead in very hot weather. 145▸

Silybum marianum

(Our Lady's milk thistle)

- **Sow in spring or autumn**
- **Any soil**
- **Sunny and open site**

Beautiful thistle flowers of a violet colour are produced in late summer by this lovely plant from the Mediterranean. More often than not, though, it is grown for its remarkable foliage; the attractive dark green leaves are mottled or flecked with white. Ovate in shape, they carry spines in and around the lobes. Stems carrying the flowers can be up to 1.5m (5ft) in height and arise from rosettes of the beautiful glossy leaves. Use this as an architectural plant at the back of a mixed, annual or herbaceous border.

Stronger plants will be obtained if seed is sown in autumn rather than in the spring. In either case take out drills where the plants are to be effective. Sow the seed and lightly cover over. Thin out the young seedlings as early as possible, to 60cm (24in) apart. Despite their height these plants should not require staking, and it should be avoided, or the effect can be spoiled.

Take care

Give plants enough space. 146▸

Tagetes erecta 'Orange Jubilee' F1

(African marigold)

- **Sow in spring**
- **Any soil**
- **Open and sunny site**

Nearly all marigolds are very reliable, and the cultivar 'Orange Jubilee' is no exception. One of a strain of Jubilee types growing to 60cm (24in) tall, they are often referred to as 'hedge forms' because of the dense foliage. 'Orange Jubilee' is an F1 Hybrid and although seeds are relatively expensive they are worth the extra cost because of the reliable uniformity of flower. Carnation-shaped double blooms are produced on the almost erect stems of very sturdy plants; light orange in colour, individual flowers can be 10cm (4in) in diameter. Foliage, kept below the flowers, is light green and deeply cut. All parts of the plant are very pungent. This cultivar can be used for nearly all purposes. The plants will look well formally planted with other complementary subjects.

Raise young plants as other *Tagetes* described here. Plant out 'Orange Jubilee' at 30cm (12in) apart.

Take care

Dead-head to prolong flowering. 146◆

Tagetes patula 'Yellow Jacket'

(French marigold)

- **Sow in spring**
- **Ordinary, even poor soil**
- **Open and sunny site**

Few annuals provide such good value as the marigolds. They tolerate most conditions except shade, and even on poor soils they do remarkably well. Continual dead-heading of plants will give a longer flowering season. Recent introductions – and there have been many–can make it difficult to choose, but 'Yellow Jacket' is strongly recommended for its dwarfness. Only 15cm (6in) in height, it has large double carnation-like flowers of bright yellow, which shine in warm sunny conditions; they are also slightly crested. These lovely flowers are formed on very compact plants carrying dark deeply cut leaves.

Sow under glass in spring. Use any good growing medium to raise the seed. Keep in a temperature of 18°C (65°F). Prick off the young seedlings in the usual way. Harden off and plant out in early summer, 15cm (6in) apart, after the risk of frost.

Take care

Spray against aphid attacks.

Tagetes patula 'Florence'

- **Sow in spring**
- **Ordinary soil**
- **Open and sunny site**

For many years, crosses have been made between the French and African marigolds, resulting in 'hybrida' strains. 'Florence' is a cultivar of this type and is well recommended for garden use. Single, orange-gold flowers 6cm (2.4in) across are produced on 50cm (20in) branching erect stems; these also carry lovely light green finely cut foliage. The bushy compact plants will provide early and continuous flowers from early summer onwards. For a good display near the house, plant them in containers in late spring; otherwise use them in beds or borders with suitable annuals of a contrasting colour, planting out in early summer. Make sure the site is open and sunny. Enrich the soil with humus before planting out.

Sow seed under glass in the usual way, during spring. Keep in a temperature of 18°C (65°F). Harden off and plant out in summer, at 25cm (10in) intervals.

Take care
Dead-head to prolong flowering.

Tagetes patula 'Silvia'

(Dwarf French marigold)

- **Sow in spring**
- **Most ordinary soil**
- **Sunny position**

Rather a misnomer, the French marigold originates from Mexico. The number of cultivars to choose from increases each year; the recent introduction of 'Silvia' is a dwarf form of the species, growing only 20cm (8in) high. The large yellow blooms are remarkably resistant to unfavourable weather conditions. These compact plants are ideal subjects for edging around formal beds and borders. They are also very useful for the front of window boxes and other containers on a patio or yard. In such conditions water well.

As half-hardy annuals, tagetes need to be raised under glass. Sow seed in spring, in pots or boxes of any good growing medium. Keep in a temperature of 18°C (65°F). Germination is usually very quick, and pricking out should be done as soon as the young seedlings are manageable. Harden off and plant out in early summer, at 23cm (9in).

Take care
Keep established plants on the dry side unless in containers.

Tagetes signata pumila 'Starfire'

(T. tenuifolia)

- **Sow in spring**
- **Ordinary well-cultivated soil**
- **Open sunny location**

These marigolds are noted for their continuous flowering. The dwarf 23cm (9in) plants thrive in sunny positions. This new mixture includes colours from lemon to yellow, orange-brown and mahogany, with many different markings. The finely divided light green leaves are pleasantly scented.

Seeds may be sown in seed mixture under glass from early spring in a temperature of 16-18°C (60-65°F) and lightly covered until germination, which should take about one week. Prick off into trays and grow on in a lower temperature until ready for hardening off; plant out in early summer after danger of frost is past. Space plants about 20cm (8in) apart.

Take care

Overwatering and overfeeding result in too much foliage.

Thunbergia alata

(Clock vine; Black-eyed Susan)

- **Sow in spring**
- **Ordinary, well-drained soil**
- **Sunny and sheltered position**

Surely one of the finest annual climbers, the clock vine comes from S Africa. It freely produces 5cm (2in) wide tubular flowers of orange-yellow, the centre of the tube being dark purple-brown. Blooms are formed from the axils of the ovate light green leaves, which are carried on twining stems up to 3m (10ft) long. This is an ideal climbing plant for the cool greenhouse. If given a sheltered sunny site it will do equally well in the garden: grow it against a south-facing wall, or on tall peasticks in an annual or mixed border. If space and position allow, let this species twine amongst a blue clematis – a lovely combination.

Sow seeds in spring under glass in a temperature of 16-18°C (60-65°F): use any good growing medium. Prick off the seedlings singly into individual small pots and place a split cane in each to give support. Plant out after hardening off in summer.

Take care

Keep young plants well spaced under glass to prevent tangling. 146▶

Tropaeolum majus 'Whirlybird'

(Nasturtium)
- **Sow in spring**
- **Poor soil**
- **Sunny position**

Many of the old cultivars have been superseded by modern forms, a number of which are less vigorous and rambling; 'Whirlybird' mixture is one of these. The short trumpet-shaped flowers lack the usual spur associated with these flowers, and the semi-double blooms face upwards above the foliage. Reaching an ultimate height of 23cm (9in), this cultivar has smooth light green circular leaves. This lovely foil enhances the cherry-rose, gold, mahogany, orange, scarlet or tangerine flowers.

To flower on the border, plant seeds in spring, two seeds per station, 2.5cm (1in) deep. Space seeds at 15cm (6in) intervals. To grow as young plants for planting out in early summer, sow seeds in pots, either one or two seeds per pot. Use a growing medium without nutrients. Keep in a temperature of 13°C (55°F). Plant into flowering positions after hardening off, in early summer.

Take care
Spray against blackfly.

Tropaeolum peregrinum (T. canariense)

(Canary creeper)
- **Sow in spring**
- **Average soil**
- **Sun or partial shade**

This choice climber, related to the nasturtium, is well worth a place in the garden if you have a suitable site. Strictly short-lived perennials they are treated as annuals for cultivation purposes. The elegantly fringed yellow flowers, 2.5cm (1in) across, have graceful green spurs, and are produced freely from thin twining stems that can reach a height of 4m (13ft) in a single season. Peltate leaves of five lobes, and green-blue in colour, are carried on the full length of the stems. This species is useful over trellis work or on wires.

Sow seeds in early spring to produce flowering plants in the summer. Use any good growing medium, plant two seeds per pot, and keep in a temperature of 13°C (55°F). Place a split cane in each pot to provide support; plant out in early summer, after hardening off.

Take care
Avoid overwatering and do not feed: otherwise plants will make leaves but very few flowers. 147▸

Ursinia anethoides 'Sunshine'

- **Sow in spring**
- **Ordinary or dry soil**
- **Sunny location**

Blooms are daisy-like and come in shades of golden-yellow or orange; often they are banded towards the base of each flower in a striking black or maroon, the central base being in similar colours. Individual blooms will be up to 5cm (2in) across. Stems are 30cm (12in) in height, with finely cut leaves of a light green.

It is very important to plant ursinias in full sunshine, because they tend to close their flowers in dull weather and at night. Make bold plantings of this attractive annual on borders or in formal beds. Useful as a pot plant, they will be quite happy planted into various containers for the yard or patio, as long as the site is sunny.

Sow seeds under glass in spring, and keep a constant temperature of 16°C (60°F). Use any good growing medium that is free draining. Prick off the seedlings into boxes. Harden off in late spring and plant out into flowering positions in early summer, 23cm (9in) apart.

Take care

Add sand to heavy soils. 148▸

Venidium fastuosum

(Monarch of the veldt)

- **Sow in spring**
- **Light, well-drained soil**
- **Sunny position**

As its common name implies, this species originates from S Africa. Up to 60cm (24in) in height, the stems carry terminal blooms of a rich orange, 10cm (4in) in diameter. The petals are banded towards the bottom of each flower in shades of purple-brown. The central cone or disc is black. This striking contrast has no real equal among the summer-flowering annuals. The stems and deeply lobed leaves are often a silver-white texture, giving a woolly effect; this highlights the flowers even more. These plants are excellent for borders when planted in bold drifts, or they can be used for containers. The cut flowers last well.

Sow seeds in spring under glass, in a temperature of 16°C (60°F). Use any good growing medium, and prick out and harden off in the usual way: Plant out in early summer, 30cm (12in) apart. Alternatively, sow seeds where they are to flower, in mid-spring.

Take care

Support with bushy peasticks. 148▸

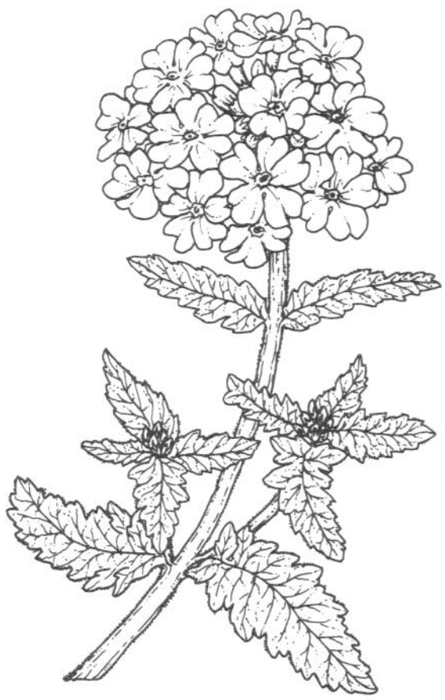

Verbascum bombyciferum

(Mullein)

- **Sow in late spring**
- **Ordinary well-drained soil**
- **Full sun**

Borders often lack plants of good height, colour and architectural effect for the back, but this species of mullein will meet most of those requirements even when not in full flower. Up to 1.3m (4ft) in height, the stems arise from a rosette of large ovate pointed leaves, which have a fine felty texture made up of masses of white-silver hairs. Stems are very erect, and bear a profusion of sulphur-yellow flowers. These are saucer-shaped, up to 5cm (2in) across, with pronounced stamens.

As this is a biennial, seeds will need to be sown in late spring to ensure good flowering plants in the following year. Sow in boxes or pots of any good growing medium, and place in a cold frame. Once germinated, plant out into nursery rows, 20cm (8in) apart. Keep watered and weeded through the summer. Plant out in early autumn, 45-60cm (18-24in) apart.

Take care

Stakes plants in windy sites. 149▸

Verbena × hybrida 'Dwarf Compact Blaze'

(Vervain)

- **Sow in early spring**
- **Ordinary but fertile soil**
- **Sunny location**

Only 18cm (7in) high, this dwarf cultivar is a very useful addition to the general group of verbenas. Plants can provide colour in a small garden without taking up too much precious space; try them beneath half or full standard fuchsias. The vivid scarlet flowers are produced on stems carrying dark green leaves. Plants are free-flowering from early summer until well into the autumn. The compact plants are better raised each year from seed, rather than by the old method of taking cuttings at the end of each flowering season.

Sow seeds in early spring under glass, in a temperature of 18-21°C (65-70°F). Use any good growing medium that is free draining. Germination may be slow so do not be tempted to overwater. Prick off the seedlings into boxes, and harden off in the usual way. Plant out in early summer, 23cm (9in) apart.

Take care

Water freely in very dry conditions, especially on light soils.

Verbena × hybrida 'Florist Mixed'

(Vervain)

- **Sow in early spring**
- **Any fertile soil**
- **Sunny position**

Another dwarf form of verbena, 'Florist Mixed' provides a diverse colour range. The stems, 23cm (9in) in height, tend to spread and make a mat. The rainbow shades of the flowers are produced above the foliage, which is dark green, and this gives a jewel-like effect. This cultivar is very useful as a front plant for window boxes, the edge of containers, or flower beds and borders. Small pockets on the rock garden make ideal sites.

Sow seeds in pots or boxes in early spring under glass. Keep at a temperature of 16°C (60°F). Use any good growing medium. Prick off the young seedlings as soon as they are ready, into boxes or trays. Harden off and plant out into flowering positions in early summer. Those for containers and window boxes can be planted out slightly earlier as long as they are in sheltered positions. Spacing should be 23cm (9in) apart.

Take care

Water freely in very dry weather. 150▸

Viola cornuta

- **Sow in early spring**
- **Fertile and moist but well-drained soil**
- **Sun or partial shade**

This comes from the Pyrenees and is therefore quite hardy for most garden purposes. The species is usually represented by the lovely lavender- or violet-coloured flowers, although there is the white form 'Alba'. Blooms are angular, and about 2.5cm (1in) across, carried on semi-prostrate soft stems not much longer than 30cm (12in). Leaves are oval to ovate, and green. Use them as an early or midsummer annual for the edge of a border or bed and for the odd pocket in the rock garden. They will tolerate dappled shade as long as the soil is moist.

Sow seeds during early spring under glass, in a temperature of 16°C (60°F). Use a soil-based growing medium. Prick off seedlings into boxes or trays, harden off in the usual way and plant out in late spring, 23cm (9in) apart. Alternatively, broadcast the seeds where they are to flower and thin out later.

Take care

Keep plants moist. 151▸

Viola wittrockiana

(Pansy)

- **Sow in early spring and summer**
- **Well-cultivated soil**
- **Sun or partial shade**

Pansies are hardy, and will flower in sun or partial shade. Many large-flowered F1 and F2 hybrids have recently been introduced. There are several strains able to flower during winter and early spring.

For summer and autumn flowering, seed may be sown in gentle heat under glass in late winter or early spring, or under cold glass in spring. The seedlings should be pricked out and grown cool ready for planting out when large enough. Summer and autumn sowings can be made in a sheltered position in the open or in cold frames for the following year. Pansies appreciate good fertilized soils enriched with well-rotted compost or manure. Prompt removal of dead flowers will promote continual flowering. Keep watered in dry weather and watch for aphids, which check growth.

Take care

Plant on a fresh site each year to avoid soil diseases. 151▸

Viscaria elegans 'Love'

(Silene coeli-rosa)

- **Sow in autumn or spring**
- **Ordinary soil**
- **Sun or partial shade**

The cultivar 'Love' has lovely rose-carmine flowers that start to flower in early summer. Salver-shaped and 2.5cm (1in) across, the blooms of this hardy annual are carried on very slender stems 25cm (10in) high. Leaves are grey-green and tend to be oblong in shape. Overall, plants have a light appearance. This species of the campion family will tolerate some shade, which makes it useful for the difficult position where colour is required in such a situation. Being medium in height, it is suitable towards the front of an annual or mixed border.

These plants are easily raised from seed. Sow them where they are to flower. Take out shallow drills during autumn or spring, and lightly cover the seed. Thin out seedlings to 15cm (6in) apart when they are large enough to handle. Autumn-sown plants will be stronger and flower slightly earlier.

Take care

Avoid watering overhead in hot sunny weather. 152▸

Zea japonica 'Harlequin Mixed'

(Ornamental maize)

- **Sow in mid- or late spring**
- **Fertile and well-cultivated soil**
- **Sunny position**

This is a form of maize prized in the large annual or mixed border. The 'Harlequin' mixture has a variable pleasing colour range: the large strap-like leaves are striped through the basic green with cream, white, pale pink or rose. Up to 2m (6.5ft) the plants will provide extra height where needed; they give greater impact if planted in groups of three or five, preferably at the back of a border in full sunshine.

Sow seed under glass in spring to produce plants for planting out in early summer. Sow individual seeds into single peat pots of any good growing medium. Keep at a temperature of 16°C (60°F). Harden off carefully and plant out when all risk of frost has passed; space them 45cm (18in) apart. Alternatively, in late spring sow seeds where they are to produce foliage; sow two seeds per station, 45cm (18in) apart, and take out the weaker of the two when germination is complete.

Take care

Water well in the summer

Zinnia elegans 'Chippendale Daisy'

- **Sow in spring**
- **Ordinary well-drained soil**
- **Sunny location**

Zinnias are invaluable for bedding purposes. 'Chippendale Daisy' is a very vivid cultivar: the single flowers have intense dark red centres surrounded by bright yellow petal tips – very striking. Blooms measure up to 5cm (2in) in diameter. Stems carrying these blooms have ovate pointed light green leaves. In height, plants will be no more than 60cm (24in). 'Chippendale Daisy' is ideally suited for most purposes, as long as you can provide a sunny site. On borders, plant towards the centre, near light-coloured flowers of a similar height.

Sow under glass in spring at a temperature of 16°C (60°F). Use any good growing medium. When pricking off, use individual peat pots for each single seedling; this will avoid any major disturbance of the roots or stems at planting-out time. Harden off carefully in the usual way at the end of spring and plant out in early summer, 30cm (12in) apart.

Take care

Do not plant out too early.

Zinnia elegans 'Hobgoblin Mixed'

- **Sow in spring**
- **Ordinary, well-drained soil**
- **Sunny position**

The 'Hobgoblin' mixture has a particularly good range of colour, in shades of red, pink, yellow and gold.

Stem length is about 25cm (10in); they are branched and make good bushy compact plants. Leaves are ovate, pointed and light green. Both stems and leaves are covered with stiff hairs. These plants are ideal for borders and beds in a sunny situation although the 'pumila'-type flowerheads are very weather-resistant, and the rain easily runs off the individual blooms.

As a tender half-hardy annual, this plant will need to be raised from seed under glass in spring. Sow seeds in any good growing medium that is free-draining. Keep at a temperature of 16°C (60°F). Prick out seedlings into individual peat pots; this will avoid handling the stems at a later date, which can be damaging. Grow on in the usual way and harden off at the end of spring. Plant out carefully in early summer, 23cm (9in) apart.

Take care

Avoid overwatering at any stage. 152▸

Zinnia elegans 'Ruffles Hybrids'

- **Sow in spring**
- **Ordinary, well-drained soil**
- **Sunny position**

Another zinnia of great potential, the 'Ruffles Hybrid' gives extra height for the annual border or large formal bed. The stems, 60-75cm (24-30in) tall, carry quite weather-resistant flowers of yellow, cherry, pink, scarlet, orange and white. The stiff ruff-like blooms have water-repellent properties. Long branching stems provide useful cut flowers for the house, but plant good-sized drifts in the middle of a large border, or formal beds for a continuous show of colour throughout the summer.

Sow seeds of this tender half-hardy annual during spring. Keep the greenhouse temperature at a constant 16°C (60°F) while seeds are germinating. Use a peat-based growing medium for sowing and pricking off. Pot the seedlings singly into small pots; in this way, less harm will be caused to them at planting-out time. Harden off in the usual way and plant out carefully in summer, 30cm (12in) apart.

Take care

Do not plant out too early.

Part Two

PERENNIALS

Filipendula purpurea

Author

Noël J. Prockter is an experienced garden writer. Trained at Kew, he became manager of a leading plant nursery in southern England and then an Assistant Editor of 'Amateur Gardening' magazine. He has contributed to many radio gardening programmes and has authored several books and articles on a wide range of gardening subjects. He is at present Chairman of the Hardy Plant Society of Great Britain.

Tropaeolum speciosum

Index of Scientific Names

The plants are arranged in alphabetical order of Latin name.
Page numbers in **bold** refer to text entries; those in *italics* refer to photographs.

Acanthus mollis	**184**	*180*
Achillea filipendulina	**184**	*181*
Achillea millefolium 'Cerise Queen'	**186**	*181*
Aconitum napellus	**186**	
Actaea alba	**187**	
Agapanthus	**187**	*183*
Alchemilla mollis	**188**	*182*
Alstromoeria ligtu	**189**	
Anaphalis triplinervis	**189**	
Anaphalis yedoensis	**189**	*184*
Anchusa azurea	**190**	*201*
Anemone x hybrida	**190**	*202*
Anthemis tinctoria	**191**	*202*
Aquilegia hybrids	**191**	*203*
Ballota pseudodictamnus	**198**	*209*
Baptisia australis	**198**	
Bergenia cordifolia	**199**	*209*
Brunnera macrophylla	**199**	*210*
Buphthalmum salicifolium	**200**	
Campanula lactiflora	**200**	*210*
Campanula persicifolia	**217**	
Catananche caerulea	**217**	
Centaurea macrocephala	**218**	*211*
Centranthus ruber	**218**	
Cephalaria gigantea	**219**	
Ceratostigma willmottianum	**219**	
Chelone obliqua	**220**	*211*
Chrysanthemum maximum	**220**	*212*
Cimicifuga racemosa	**221**	

Armeria plantaginea 'Bee's Ruby'	**192**	
Artemisia lactiflora	**192**	
Arum italicum 'Pictum'	**193**	
Aruncus sylvester	**193**	*204*
Asphodeline lutea	**194**	
Aster amellus	**194**	*204-5*
Aster x frikartii 'Mönch'	**195**	*206*
Aster novae-angliae	**195**	
Aster novi-belgii	**196**	*206*
Astilbe x arendsii	**197**	*207*
Astrantia major	**197**	*208*
Clematis heracleifolia	**221**	
Clematis recta	**222**	
Coreopsis grandiflora	**222**	*213*
Coreopsis verticillata	**223**	*214*
Cortaderia selloana	**223**	*215*
Corydalis lutea	**224**	*214*
Crambe cordifolia	**224**	
Crocosmia pottsii	**225**	
Delphinium Belladonna varieties	**226**	
Dianthus	**226**	
Dicentra spectabilis	**227**	*216*

Dictamnus albus	**227**	*216*	Hemerocallis	**258**	*242-3*
Dierama pendulum	**228**		Hesperis matronalis	**259**	
Digitalis grandiflora	**228**		Heuchera sanguinea 'Red Spangles'	**259**	*244*
Doronicum 'Miss Mason'	**229**	*233*	Hosta fortunei 'Albopicta'	**260**	*244*
Eccremocarpus scaber	**229**		Iberis sempervirens	**260**	*246*
Echinacea purpurea	**230**	*234*	Incarvillea mairei	**261**	*247*
Echinops ritro 'Taplow Blue'	**230**	*235*	Inula helenium	**261**	*246*
Erigeron 'Quakeress'	**231**		Iris florentina	**262**	*248*
Eryngium bourgatii	**231**	*235*	Iris unguicularis	**262**	
Eupatorium purpureum 'Atropurpureum'	**232**	*236*	Kniphofia	**263**	*265-6*
Euphorbia characias	**232**		Lathyrus latifolius	**263**	
Euphorbia griffithii 'Fireglow'	**249**	*236-7*	Lavateria olbia rosea	**264**	*266*
Festuca glauca	**249**	*237*	Liatris spicata 'Kobold'	**264**	*267*
Filipendula purpurea	**250**	*239*	Libertia formosa	**281**	
Francoa sonchifolia	**250**		Ligularia 'Gregynog Gold'	**281**	
Gaillardia aristata	**251**		Linaria purpurea	**282**	
Galega officinalis	**251**	*238*	Liriope muscari	**282**	*269*
Gentiana asclepiadea	**252**	*240*	Lobelia cardinalis	**283**	*268*
Geranium endressii	**252**	*238*	Lunaria rediviva	**283**	*269*
Geranium pratense 'Johnson's Blue'	**253**		Lupinus polyphyllus	**284**	*270-1*
Geranium macrorrhizum	**253**		Lychnis coronaria 'Abbotswood Rose'	**284**	*270*
Geum chiloense	**254**		Lysimachia punctata	**285**	*271*
Gillenia trifoliata	**254**		Lythrum salicaria 'Firecandle'	**285**	*272*
Gypsophila paniculata	**255**	*241*	Macleaya cordata	**286**	
Helenium 'Wyndley'	**255**	*240-1*	Malva moschata	**286**	*273*
Helianthus decapetalus	**256**	*242*	Melianthus major	**287**	*274*
Helichrysum angustifolium	**256**		Mertensia virginica	**287**	
Heliopsis scabra	**257**		Monarda didyma 'Cambridge Scarlet'	**288**	*275*
Helleborus corsicus	**257**	*243*	Morina longifolia	**288**	
Helleborus orientalis	**258**				

Index of Common Names

Aaron's rod 322
Algerian iris 262
Alkanet 190
Asphodel 194

Baby's breath 255
Baneberry 187
Bear's breeches 185
Bee balm 288
Bergamot 288
Black-eyed Susan 317
Black-leaved lily turf 291
Black snake-root 221
Blanket flower 176
Bleeding heart 227
Blue indigo 198
Blue penstemon 293
Bouncing bet 318
Bridal wreath 250
Bugbane 221
Burning bush 197

Cape figwort 296
Cardinal flower 283
Catmint 289
Chalk plant 255
Columbine 191
Cone flower 230
Coral bells 259
Corsican hellebore 257
Cotton thistle 290
Cranesbill 253
Crosswort 295
Cupid's dart 217
Curry plant 256

Dame's violet 259
Day lily 258
Dropwort 170
Drumstick primrose 315
Dusty meadow rue 323
Dusty miller 284
Dutchman's breeches 227

Elecampane 93
Everlasting flower 189

Fair maids of France 316
Fairy's wand 228
False goat's beard 197
False indigo 198
False Solomon's Seal 322
Fern-leaf yarrow 185
Fleabane 231
Flowering seakale 224
Foetid crucinella 143
Fortune's saxifrage 318

Garden pinks 226
German catchfly 326
Giant scabious 219
Globe flower 324
Glory flower 229
Goat's beard 193
Goat's rue 251
Golden groundsel 281
Golden Marguerite 191
Golden rod 322
Great Cape honeyflower 287
Greek mallow 303

Hardy arum lily 326
Hardy plumbago 219
Helmet flower 186
Herbaceous virgin's bower 222
Himalayan cinquefoil 314
Himalayan whorlflower 288
Hound's tongue 225

Ice plant 320
Indian physic 254
Italian arum 193
Italian bugloss 190
Italian starwort 194

Jacob's ladder 313
Jerusalem sage 294
Joe Pye Weed 232

King's spear 194

Lady's mantle 196
Lamb's ear 323
Lamb's tongue 323
Large-rooted cranesbill 253
Lenten rose 258

Myrrhis odorata	**289**	*275*
Nepeta faassenii	**289**	*276*
Oenothera missouriensis	**290**	*276*
Onopordon acanthium	**290**	*277*
Ophiopogon planiscapus nigrescens	**291**	
Osmunda regalis	**291**	*279*
Paeonia officinalis 'Rubra Plena'	**292**	*278*
Papaver orientale	**292**	*279*
Penstemon glaber	**293**	
Perovskia atriplicifolia	**293**	
Phlomis russeliana	**294**	*280*
Phlox paniculata	**294-5**	*297*
Phuopsis stylosa	**295**	*298*
Phygelius capensis	**296**	
Physostegia virginiana	**296**	*299*
Polemonium foliosissimum	**313**	*300*
Polygonatum x hybridum	**313**	*300*
Polygonum amplexicaule 'Atrosanguineum'	**314**	*301*
Potentilla atrosanguinea	**314**	*301*
Primula denticulata	**315**	
Pulmonaria officinalis	**315**	
Pyrethrum roseum	**316**	
Ranunculus aconitifolius 'Flore Pleno'	**316**	*302*
Rudbeckia fulgida	**317**	*302*
Salvia superba	**317**	*303*
Saponaria officinalis	**318**	*304*
Saxifraga fortunei	**318**	
Saxifraga x urbium	**319**	
Schizostylis coccinea	**319**	*137*
Schrophularia aquatica 'Variegata'	**320**	
Sedum 'Autumn Joy'	**320**	*305*
Sedum spectabile 'Carmen'	**320**	*305*
Sidalcea malvaeflora	**321**	*306*
Sisyrinchium striatum	**321**	*306*
Smilacina racemosa	**322**	
Solidago 'Goldenmosa'	**322**	*307*
Stachys olympica 'Silver Carpet	**323**	*309*
Thalictrum speciosissimum	**323**	*308*
Tradescantia virginiana 'Isis'	**324**	*309*
Trollius x cultorum	**324**	*310*
Tropaeolum speciosum	**325**	*310-111*
Veronica spicata	**325**	*311*
Viscaria vulgaris 'Splendens Plena'	**326**	
Zantesdeschia aethiopica 'Crowborough'	**326**	*312*

Leopard's bane 229
Ligtu hybrids 188
London pride 319
Long-branched sage 317
Loosestrife 285
Lungwort 315
Lupin 284

Masterwort 197
Michaelmas daisy 196
Milfoil 186
Milky bellflower 200
Monkshood 186
Mountain fleece-flower 314
Musk mallow 286

New England aster 295

Obedient plant 296
Old double crimson 292
Orange sunflower 257
Oris root 262
Oriental poppy 292
Ox-eye chamomile 191
Ozark sundrops 290

Pampas grass 223
Peach-leaved bellflower 217
Pearly everlasting 189
Perennial candytuft 260
Perennial honesty 283
Perennial larkspur 226
Perennial pea 263
Phlox 294, 295
Pig squeak 199
Plaintain lily 260
Plume poppy 336
Prairie mallow 321
Purple loosestrife 279
Purple toadflax 282
Pyrethrum 316

Red hot poker 263
Red valerian 236
Rose campion 284
Royal fern 296
Russian sage 293

Satin flower 321
Scarlet avens 254
Scotch flame flower 325
Scotch thistle 290
Sea holly 231
Sea pink 192
Shasta daisy 220
Sheep's fescue 249
Siberian bugloss 199

Soapwort 318
Soldiers and sailors 315
Solomon's seal 313
Sneezeweed 255
Spiderwort 324
Spiked speedwell 325
Spike gayfeather 364
Spire lily 252
Spurge 249
Steel globe thistle 230
Sub-shrubby spurge 232
Summer hyacinth 252
Sunflower 256
Sweet Cicely 289
Sweet rocket 259

Thrift 192
Tickseed 223
Torch lily 263
Tree mallow 264
Trumpet flower 261
Tube clematis 221
Turf lily 282
Turtlehead 220

Variegated figwort 319
Virginian cowslip 287

White mugwort 192
Willow-leaf ox-eye 260
Windflower 190
Wolf's bane 186

Yarrow 186
Yellow-flowered chamomile 191
Yellow foxglove 228
Yellow fumitory 224
Yellow hardhead 218
Yellow hardweed 218

Introduction

What is a perennial plant? Correctly, all plants except annuals and biennials are perennial, as they last from season to season. Annuals and biennials have a limited life. However, the term perennial is usually used to refer to herbaceous perennials. These are plants that live from one season to another, but die down to soil-level during winter. Fresh shoots arise from the base of the plant in spring, and during the same year they produce foliage and flowers.

Some perennials, however, do not lose all of their leaves in autumn. These include London Pride (*Saxifraga* x *urbium*), Bergenia, Liriope and Geum. These plants have an advantage in creating interest throughout winter, and can look very attractive when the leaves are covered with frost.

Because some perennials are best grown as biennials, a few such plants are included in this section. These include the Scotch Thistle (*Onopordum acanthium*), which seeds itself and grows up to 2.1m (7ft) high. Also included is the hardy, shrubby Russian Sage (*Perovskia atriplicifolia*), so often grown with herbaceous perennials. This is because it produces its best foliage when cut down to about 30cm (1ft) above the soil in spring.

Most herbaceous plants have a mass of fibrous roots that form a mat around them. Others have bulbous, tuberous or rhizomatous roots. These are all underground food storage organs that both absorb food and water from the soil, and act as a reservoir of energy that perpetuates the plant from season to season. Such plants include the False Solomon's Seal (*Smilacina racemosa*) the Algerian Iris (*Iris unguicularis*), and Aunt Liza (*Curtonus paniculatus*).

Because perennial borders are usually formed of a mixture of plants, many bulbous plants from Part Three of this book can be interplanted with true herbaceous perennials.

Left: *A beautiful example of a 'classic' herbaceous perennial border. Alive with colour for many months of the year, such a border is a constant delight. Plants of different height, colour and texture have been skilfully blended here to produce a stunning effect. Edging plants along the path give way to subjects of medium height in the centre and these are backed up by tall perennials and shrubs.*

Right: **Lysimachia punctata**
A vigorous perennial that thrives in sunshine or partial shade. 285▶

first spit or two of top soil (a spit is one spade's depth), then fork over the bottom spit of sub-soil and cover with the next one or two top spits. When digging, remove all pernicious weeds such as bindweed, ground elder, docks and dandelions (which my wife calls malignant weeds). Once these irritants are removed, the bed or border has been properly dug with humus incorporated, and the soil has settled, the ground is ready for planting. Always plant firmly and use a hand-fork to make the hole, rather than a trowel. Humus can be well-rotted garden compost, well-rotted farmyard manure or leafmould. Initial preparation is paramount, for once the plants are in the ground there is little one can do; though a gardener I knew mulched all around his plants each year with farmyard manure. Today many gardeners use pulverized bark as a mulch to prevent the soil from drying out during summer, and this also acts as a good weed preventative.

Many plants require ample moisture during hot dry weather. Spray them with clear water in the evening after sunset. Where water has to be applied to the roots of plants, apply a mulch of rotted garden compost or farmyard manure to prevent evaporation.

Stakes and supports

Not all perennials require staking or support; many are sturdy enough to remain upright. But for those that do require some form of support, staking should be carried out at the start of the season, before growth has become too advanced. Peasticks are excellent if inserted in and around the plants or clumps so that the new growth can grow through them; when the plants come into flower the supports are well camouflaged.

Today there are special plant supports for herbaceous border plants; neither sticks nor string is required, just a stout wire stake that supports a galvanized wire ring 20-25cm (8-10in) wide, and the plants grow through them so that the supports become almost invisible. Other types are a triangle with three supports, or a ring with cross pieces and three supports.

Beds and borders

The traditional herbaceous border was planted rather like a shop window, with short, medium and tall plants ranged from front to back. Usually at the back of the border there was a wall, fence or hedge, often a yew hedge. Some gardeners now plant perennials in island beds cut out of a lawn, and this is an ideal method for a small garden because it gets rid of rigid straight lines. Island beds can be round, oval or rectangular. By this method the gardener can get right around the bed.

Choice of plants

Most gardeners have their favourite plants that they wish to grow. Remember that a bed or border can look rather dull during late autumn and winter, and this can be partly avoided by growing a few clumps of plants that retain their foliage throughout the year, such as *Liriope, Saxifraga × urbium* (London pride), *Iberis sempervirens* (Candytuft), *Bergenia, Helleborus, Dianthus, Heuchera, Phlomis russeliana, Sisyrinchium striatum* and *Iris foetidissima.*

To add interest a few shrubs can be included with the herbaceous plants, such as helianthemums, *Ruta graveolens* 'Jackman's Blue', *Rosmarinus* 'Jessop's Upright', *Senecio* 'Sunshine', *Hypericum*

Above: **Rudbeckia fulgida 'Goldsturm'**
Lovely daisy-like blooms on stems up to 60cm (24in) in height. 317▸

Left: *The perfect match of a superb lawn and richly planted borders.*

Above:
Cortaderia selloana 'Pumila'
A lovely compact pampas grass. 223▸

Right:
Anemone 'Honorine Jobert'
Superb for late summer flowers. 190▸

elatum 'Elstead variety', *Lavandula* 'Hidcote Blue', *Hebe pinguifolia* 'Pagei', *Euonymus* 'Emerald 'n Gold', *Berberis thunbergii* 'Aurea'.

When planning a border or island bed, remember that many plants look more effective when planted in groups of three, four or five to the square metre or yard. In a small garden, however, some plants are best grown alone, eg *Aruncus sylvester, Stipa pennata* (a handsome grass), *Cortaderia selloana* 'Pumila' (a dwarf pampas grass).

Propagation

A vast number of perennials can be increased from seed and in many cases the seedling plants will be like their parents. In other instances they will vary in colour: for example, *Lupinus polyphyllus* (the Russell lupin) produces a wide range of colours from one packet of seed. Therefore with many plants it will be necessary to divide them to retain a desirable colour, in either autumn or spring.

Division can be performed in several ways: pull a plant apart with the hands; cut through it with a stout sharp knife; use two hand-forks, placing them back to back, then grip the handles together and ease the plant apart gradually.

Plants such as anchusas and poppies can be increased by taking root cuttings in the autumn or winter months. To do this cut the roots into approximately 3-5cm (1.2-2in) lengths, making a horizontal cut at the top and a slanting cut at the base to avoid inserting the cuttings upside down. Where cuttings are up to 5cm (2in) long, a box will need to be 8cm (3.2in) deep. Fill the box with a mixture of 1 part medium loam, 2 parts granulated peat and 3 parts coarse silver sand (all parts by volume); no fertilizers are required with this mixture. I have used

this mixture many times but if peat has not been available I have used well-rotted oak or beech leaf-mould. Today many growers use a soil-less mixture, which is fine; when the cuttings are rooted they can be potted or lined out in a nursery row.

When using peat, make sure it is properly moistened before mixing it with loam and sand; unless it is, water will not be soaked up afterwards. When using pots, boxes or pans, always make certain that they are clean before use, and well crocked, ie place broken pieces of pot and dry leaves in the bottom of the container to ensure good drainage. When using soil-less mixtures, crocks are not necessary, and the mixture must not be made too firm.

Pests and diseases

Perhaps the worst pest – apart from a cat scratching around newly cultivated soil – is the slug, which adores luscious new shoots. Today there are plenty of slug-killers on the market. Snails also do damage, especially to new young shoots. Another very common pest is the greenfly or aphid. To control these, spray or dust with pyrethrum or malathion. The best way to avoid phlox eelworm – a small pest that cannot be seen by the naked eye – is to increase phlox from root cuttings taken from clean stock. Phlox roots are rather like bootlaces. Cut them into 8cm (3.2in) lengths, lay them on the cuttings mixture, and cover. Another pest that often causes havoc is the Solomon's seal sawfly, which disfigures foliage by chewing it to pieces. Control by hand picking, or by spraying with malathion. Ants, too, can be a nuisance; pyrethrum will help to control them, but there are also various specific ant-killers on the market.

Above: **Achillea filipendulina 'Coronation Gold'**
The pale yellow flowerheads are borne on stout stems up to 90cm (3ft) high. Plant in a sheltered spot or provide adequate support. 185▸

Left: **Acanthus mollis**
Both the flowers and foliage of this dramatic looking plant are handsome. A single specimen would suit a small garden because its roots can be invasive. 185▸

Right: **Achillea millefolium 'Cerise Queen'**
A lovely plant for the front of the border. The flat flowerheads are carried on stems 60cm (24in) tall and may need support. 186▸

Above: **Aconitum wilsonii**
Up to 180cm (6ft) in height, this stately plant produces striking blue flowers in late summer. Grow in deep fertile soil for best results; keep moist if planted in full sun. 186▶

Left: **Alchemilla mollis**
This adaptable plant is prized by flower arrangers for its grey-green silky foliage. In the garden it is useful as ground cover. 188▶

Right: **Agapanthus 'Headbourne Hybrids'**
These beautiful plants are hardy, except in the coldest and wettest areas. Their handsome flowers, in varying shades of blue, are borne on stout stems up to 90cm (3ft) high. 187▶

Above: **Anaphalis yedoensis**
The papery white 'everlasting' flowers are carried on stems 60cm (24in) tall above broad green leaves that are white felted beneath. Soak the stems before drying in winter. 189▶

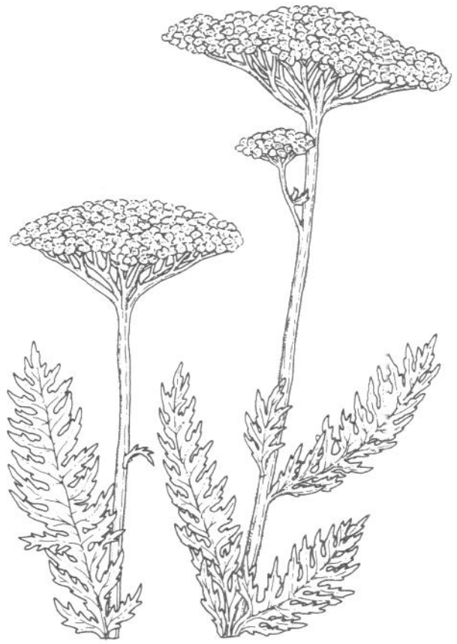

Acanthus mollis

(Bear's breeches)

- **Sunny position**
- **Well-drained soil**
- **Late summer flowering**

This attractive architectural plant has green glossy foliage; the mauve-pink foxglove-like flowers are rather sparingly produced on stems 120cm (4ft) or higher. As plants can spread as much as 90cm (3ft), in small gardens it is advisable not to grow more than one plant; its roots can be invasive. Any good fertile soil suits acanthus, provided it is well drained. Plant in spring, and during the first winter, especially in cold districts, give a mulch of leaf-mould or well-rotted garden compost.

A. spinosus is similar in many respects, except that it has nasty spines at the end of each dark green, deeply divided leaf. Each leaf is about 60-90cm (2-3ft) long. The flowers of *A. spinosus* are borne more freely; when dried they have a pleasant scent. The dried flowers are used for winter decorations.

Propagate by seed sown in spring in a cold frame; or by root cuttings in late autumn or winter; or by division in spring.

Take care

Protect from frost and drying winds in their first winter. 180▸

Achillea filipendulina

(Fern-leaf yarrow)

- **Sunny position**
- **Tolerates dry soils**
- **Summer flowering**

The large yellow plate-like flowers of *A. filipendulina* are best seen in the variety 'Gold Plate'; this most spectacular plant has flat bright-yellow heads at the top of stout erect stems 150cm (5ft) tall. Each flowerhead can be as much as 13cm (5in) across, and the plant can spread as much as 45cm (18in).

A more recent introduction is called 'Coronation Gold'; this has pale yellow flat heads, and the 90cm (3ft) stems rise out of grey-green feathery foliage.

Propagate by seeds or division in spring, or by cuttings in early summer. Plant in spring, in good retentive soil. A few peasticks will be needed to protect the heavy heads in wet weather, particularly in windswept gardens.

The tall varieties should be cut down to ground level during the autumn. The flowerheads can be dried for winter decoration indoors.

Take care

Plant this species in a sheltered spot, if possible. 181▸

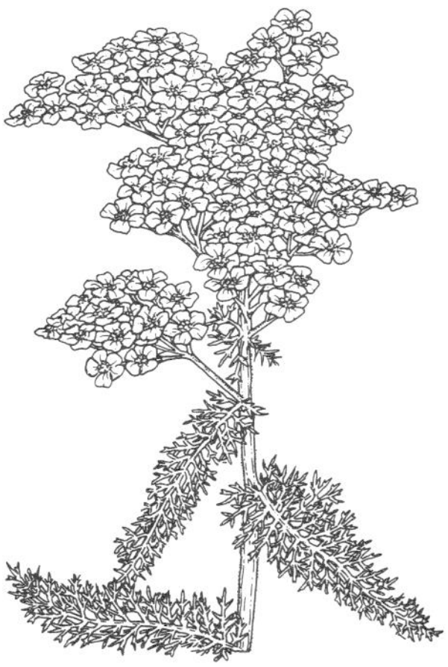

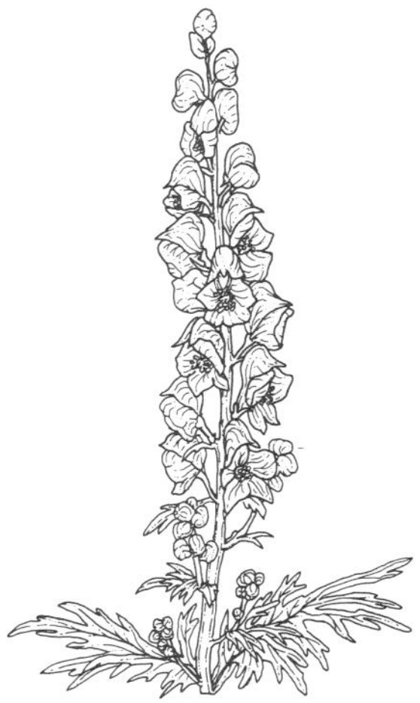

Achillea millefolium 'Cerise Queen'

(Yarrow; Milfoil)

- **Sunny position**
- **Well-drained soil**
- **Summer flowering**

Although the common yarrow *A. millefolium* can become a headache to the lawn purist, the variety 'Cerise Queen' is quite attractive. It has wide flattish heads of rose-cerise flowers, each floret with a paler centre, on stout 60cm (24in) stems in summer. The dark green feathery foliage makes a mat-like plant. It is ideal for the front of the border, but beware – it can become invasive.

Propagate either by sowing seed in spring in a cold house or frame, or by taking cuttings in early summer, again in a cold house or frame, or by division in autumn. A few stout peasticks inserted around the plants will prevent them being blown over in windy gardens.

The varieties of *Achillea* will grace any border with summer colour. For best results plant them in well-drained soil in a sunny position.

Take care

Plant this species in a sheltered spot, if possible. 181▸

Aconitum napellus

(Monkshood; Wolf's bane; Helmet flower)

- **Full sun; tolerates partial shade**
- **Fertile, retentive soil**
- **Summer and late summer flowering**

Possibly this plant is sometimes known as wolf's bane because its roots are poisonous, but this need not stop us having these stately delphinium-like flowering plants in our gardens. The blue helmet-shaped flowers are held at the top of stout 90-120cm (3-4ft) stems, and clothed with dark green finger-like foliage. To-day there are many varieties to choose from, and among the finest are 'Blue Sceptre', with blue and white bicolour flowers, 60cm (24in) stems, and a pretty neat dwarf plant; 'Bressingham Spire', a taller grower, with 90cm (3ft) stems; and the common monkshood, *A. napellus*, with indigo-blue flowers in late summer. *A. wilsonii* is also worth trying, with flowering stems up to 180cm (6ft) in late summer.

Propagate by seeds in spring or by division in spring or autumn. Plant out in late autumn.

Take care

A spring mulch of compost, and thinning out of surplus stems, will both improve flowering. 182▸

Actaea alba

(Baneberry)

- **Partial shade**
- **Moist, fertile soil**
- **Late summer and early autumn flowering**

The common name, baneberry, is due to the poisonous berries. *A. alba*, from eastern North America, has white flowers, and fresh green foliage similar to that of astilbe. The fluffy white flowers, on rather thin wiry stems up to 90cm (3ft) tall, later change to pea-sized white berries. The red baneberry, *A. rubra*, from North America has bright scarlet berries above green fern-like foliage on 45cm (18in) stems in early autumn. *A. spicata* is similar to *A. rubra* except that it has shining black berries. This is a useful plant to grow among shrubs. Be careful during the winter not to disturb the roots, as the stems and foliage die right down.

Propagate by fresh seeds in spring, but avoid using old seed; or divide the roots in spring. Choose a cool, partially shaded spot in retentive fertile soil.

Take care

Keep moist.

Agapanthus

- **Sunny position**
- **Moist, fertile soil**
- **Summer flowering**

The blue African lily, *Agapanthus umbellatus*, belongs to the family Liliaceae, but is not, in fact, a lily; it is hardy out of doors only in gardens that are usually frost-free. Today, however, there are some very fine garden forms that are hardy. During the 1950s and 1960s the 'Headbourne Hybrids' were developed from *A. campanulatus*; they are in varying shades of blue.

All agapanthus plants have lily-like flowers that are arranged in an umbel, ie like an upturned umbrella. The flowers are borne on stoutish stems, 60-90cm (2-3ft) high. They are deciduous, and the dark green strap-like foliage dies down in the winter, so it is wise to mark the spot where they grow so that when the border is dug over, the plants are not damaged. Choose moist rather than dry soil, but avoid very wet ground.

Propagate by division in spring, as the new growth appears.

Take care

Avoid deep planting. 183▶

Alchemilla mollis

(Lady's mantle)

- **Not fussy where it grows**
- **Avoid very wet ground**
- **Early summer flowering**

Since the Second World War and the great rise of interest in flower arranging, *A. mollis* has become very popular for this purpose. The rounded silky-haired pale grey-green leaves and tiny sulphur-yellow frothy sprays of flowers last a long while, beautifying either the flower border or the flower arranger's vase. This precious plant is also a superb ground cover plant. Its seeds can be invasive, however; to prevent it spreading, remove the flowerheads before the seeds ripen, and this will save many self-sown seedlings appearing where they are not wanted. It grows to about 45cm (18in) in height. *A. mollis* has the useful ability of being able to grow happily beneath trees or in full shade.

Propagate by division in spring or autumn. Plant this species in any good fertile soil, in sun or shade. Insert twiggy sticks for support in windswept locations.

Take care

Put this plant where it can spread. 182▶

Alstroemeria aurantiaca

(Peruvian lily)

- **Sun or partial shade**
- **Deep, well-drained sandy soil**
- **Summer flowering**

This is the easiest of the alstroemerias and hardier than most species. Lax leafy stems carry umbels of a dozen or more orange lily-like flowers, each up to 4cm (1.6in) long; the stems are 90cm (3ft) high. They have fleshy finger-like roots, which can be invasive once established; for this reason, put them in a bed or border where they can romp away on their own. The flowers are loved by floral arrangers because they are long lasting.

When planting, lay out the roots in the ground 15-20cm (6-8in) deep. Plant between early autumn and early spring. If the soil is heavy, especially clay soils, work in a mixture of moistened peat and sand at the base of each planting hole. Do not be surprised if there is poor or no growth the first year after planting, but once established there will be no stopping this alstroemeria. Propagate by division or by seed.

Take care

The soil should contain humus.

Anaphalis triplinervis

(Everlasting flower)

- **Sun or partial shade**
- **Well-drained soil**
- **Late summer flowering**

This is a beautiful plant, with white flowers in tightly bunched heads, 7.5-10cm (3-4in) across. These are borne during mid to late summer among silvery-grey leaves. Their undersides are smothered with white, woolly hairs.

It grows about 30cm (1ft) high, and spreads 30-38cm (12-15in). Its size enables it to be planted quite near the front of the border, but if you want a slightly smaller form try 'Summer Snow' which has heads of white flowers and silvery-grey leaves.

Anaphalis margaritacea is another Everlasting flower, growing slightly higher at 30-45cm (1-1½ft) high. The grey-green leaves provide a superb foil for the pearly-white flowers that adorn the plant during mid to late summer.

Propagate by dividing clumps in autumn or spring. Alternatively, take 7.5cm (3in) long basal cuttings in late spring.

Take care

Avoid planting them under trees, as water drips will damage the foliage.

Anaphalis yedoensis

(Pearly everlasting)

- **Sun or partial shade**
- **Well-drained soil**
- **Late summer or autumn flowering**

This plant has broad green leaves that are white felted beneath, and flat papery white flowerheads with enchanting yellow centres. These develop from late summer through to early autumn, reaching up to 10cm (4in) across each flowerhead. Although its foliage dies back in the winter, silvery-white shoots soon appear as spring approaches. It will reach a height of 60cm (24in). When pearly everlasting flowers are gathered for drying, for use in winter flower arrangements, give the stems a good drink before hanging them up to dry off. *A. yedoensis* is best when grown in full sun, although it can tolerate the shade of a wall (but not of trees).

Propagate by division in autumn, or by seeds sown out of doors in spring. Plant them in any good retentive soil.

Take care

These plants will soon droop if they get too dry at the root, so keep them moist. 184▶

Anchusa azurea

(Alkanet; Italian bugloss)
- **Sunny position**
- **Well-drained soil**
- **Early summer flowering**

The anchusas are tall coarse-growing branching herbaceous perennials that have rough hairy stems and foliage with charming large forget-me-not blue flowers. *A. azurea* is still sometimes also known as *A. italica*. There are several excellent varieties: 'Morning Glory' is bright blue, and reaches 150-180cm (5-6ft); 'Opal' is an old favourite, soft blue, 150cm (5ft); 'Royal Blue', rich royal blue, 90cm (3ft); and the late spring to early summer flowering 'Loddon Royalist', gentian blue, 90cm (3ft). Anchusas will grow in any good soil. Choose young plants when setting them out in a border.

Propagation is easy. Cut roots into lengths of about 4cm (1.6in), making a clean cut at the top of each and a slanting one at the base – this will prevent them being inserted upside down. Place pots of these roots in an unheated frame. Plant out in early mid-spring.

Take care

Stake early to prevent damage. 201▸

Anemone × hybrida

(Windflower)
- **Sun or partial shade**
- **Good ordinary soil**
- **Early autumn flowering**

Of all the many windflowers, the best-known are the many hybrids of the Japanese anemones *A. × hybrida* (also known as *A. japonica*). These vary in height from 45 to 120cm (18-48in), and their individual flowers vary in size from 4 to 6cm (1.6-2.4in) across, each with five or more petals. Each flower has a central boss of yellow stamens. The stems are clothed with vine-like leaves. Their roots are like stiff black leather bootlaces. Choose from the following selection: 'Bressingham Glow', a semi-double rosy red, 45cm (18in) tall; 'Luise Uhink', white, 90cm (3ft); 'September Charm', single soft pink, 45cm (18in); 'White Queen', 90-120cm (3-4ft); and 'Honorine Jobert', white, 120cm (4ft).

Propagate by cutting the roots into 4-5cm (1.6-2in) lengths and inserting them in a deep box filled with peat and sand mixture.

Take care

Good drainage is needed, and preferably a sunny position. 202▸

Anthemis tinctoria

(Yellow-flowered chamomile; Ox-eye chamomile; Golden Marguerite)

- **Full sun**
- **Well-drained soil**
- **Summer flowering**

This species is a free-flowering herbaceous perennial. The daisy flowers are held on single-flowered stems above a base of parsley-like foliage.

There are several named varieties, varying in height from 60 to 90cm (2-3ft). The pale primrose-yellow 'E.C. Buxton' is 60-75cm (24-30in) tall; 'Loddon' has deep buttercup-yellow flowers, 75-90cm (30-36in) high; of similar height is the bright golden-yellow 'Grallagh Gold', which has flowers almost 6.5cm (2.6in) across; and the 60-90cm (2-3ft) 'Wargrave' has lemon-yellow flowers.

Propagate this species by division in spring. To encourage good strong basal growth before winter, cut the plants down as soon as they have finished flowering.

Take care

Cut plants down immediately after they have flowered. 202▸

Aquilegia hybrids

(Columbine)

- **Sun or partial shade**
- **Any well-drained fertile soil**
- **Early summer flowering**

The many hybrid strains of aquilegia are elegant plants. The 'long-spurred hybrids' have rather glaucous foliage. The flowers range in colour from pure white, through yellow to pink, soft rose, red, crimson, purple, and blue. Good effects can be had by growing these 90cm (3ft) tall plants in partial shade in the dappled light given by deciduous trees. Provided they are grown in well-drained fertile soil that does not dry out, they will give a good account of themselves.

The common columbine *Aquilegia vulgaris* and its double form are short-spurred and these, too, come in a variety of colours. They reach 60cm (24in) in height.

Propagate by seeds sown in a cool greenhouse or frame in spring, or out of doors in early summer. Division of named varieties can take place in early spring.

Take care

In full sun the flowers drop quickly; dappled sunlight gives a longer season of bloom. 203▸

Armeria plantaginea 'Bee's Ruby'

(Thrift; Sea pink)

- **Sunny position**
- **Well-drained soil**
- **Early summer flowering**

This large-flowered thrift is very free-flowering. The bright rose-pink globular flowerheads are held on stout erect smooth 35-45cm (14-18in) stalks, above dense cushion-like hummocks. The round flowerheads have papery petals. The long broad leaves, 8mm (0.3in) wide, frequently have curled edges. This popular hardy herbaceous perennial is superb as an edging. It is both a good garden plant and an excellent cut flower, as it is very long lasting.

Armerias like plenty of sun and a well-drained soil, and they are especially useful on lime or chalk soils. They are an ideal plant to grow if your garden is near the sea. Propagate them by pulling off cuttings in late summer or early autumn. You could try division but it is not easy; this also is best done in autumn.

Take care
Do not let these become waterlogged in winter.

Artemisia lactiflora

(White mugwort)

- **Sun or partial shade**
- **Moist fertile soil**
- **Late summer flowering**

This tall sturdy ornamental herbaceous perennial makes a fine clump and even in winter it has a tuft of green parsley-like foliage. Arranged at the top of its stout 150-180cm (5-6ft) stems, clothed in deeply cut chrysanthemum-like foliage, are plumes of branching sprays of milky-white scented flowers in late summer. It is good as a cut flower.

This species resents poor dry soil; it needs a good fertile soil and moisture, or the leaves and flowers will look dry and untidy. It will thrive in a sunny position given moisture at the roots and will also tolerate partial shade.

When a clump becomes worn out, lift it and replant the healthy pieces on the outside of the clump in well-prepared ground. Propagate by division in spring.

Take care
These plants must not lack moisture, if they are to give of their best.

Arum italicum 'Pictum'

(Italian arum)

- **Sun or partial shade**
- **Retentive fertile soil**
- **Spring flowering**

A. italicum has been known since 1683, but even after 300 years it is still not seen as often as it should be. However, in recent years, *A. italicum* 'Pictum' has been sought after by flower arrangers for indoor decoration. Only recently in the winter sunshine I saw an impressive clump of this particular variety, looking charming with its prettily spotted marbled foliage of grey and cream. During early summer the foliage dies down entirely, reappearing in the autumn. Greenish white spathes appear before the leaves come in spring, followed in autumn by orange-red poisonous berries. 'Pictum' is shy at flowering, not nearly as free as lords and ladies, *A. maculatum*; but its foliage is so beautiful that it is worth a place in any garden.

It enjoys moisture, and will thrive in sunshine or partial shade. Propagate this species by taking offsets of the tubers in autumn.

Take care

Plant the tubers 10cm (4in) deep.

Aruncus sylvester

(A. dioicus)

(Goat's beard)

- **Sunshine or shade**
- **Deep rich fertile soil**
- **Summer flowering**

Goat's beard has had its botanical name changed several times, but nurserymen still use the name *A. sylvester*. It is a tall and rather handsome plant, with broad fern-like foliage on stiff wiry stems 120-150cm (4-5ft) tall; above are impressive plumes of creamy white stars throughout the summer.

Plants make bold hummocks, which need a great deal of strength to lift out of the ground once they are well established, and even more strength when division is necessary. They do better in a deep rich fertile soil with some shade.

The male and female flowers are on different plants; the male flowers are more feathery than the female ones, and they are not so troublesome by germinating self-sown seedlings. Even so, the female seedheads come into their own for drying. Propagate by spring-sown seed or divide clumps in late autumn.

Take care

Male plants are more free-flowering than female plants. 204▸

Asphodeline lutea

(Asphodel; King's spear)
- **Sunny position**
- **Deep sandy loam**
- **Late spring flowering**

For many years this species has also been known as *Asphodelus luteus*. It even has a third common name, Jacob's rod, which perhaps refers to its flower spikes. It is a stately looking hardy perennial. At its base there is a tuft of glabrous, dark green grassy furrowed leaves with glaucous or paler green lines. Its 90cm (3ft) erect flower spikes also carry leaves. The bright yellow fragrant silky starry-looking flowers, 1cm (0.4in) across, are arranged in buff-coloured clusters, and they will last for many weeks.

These fleshy-rooted plants are best in deep sandy loam, though I have seen plants flourishing in heavier soils. Propagate them by dividing the roots in spring or in early autumn. Take great care not to cut or damage the fleshy thong-like roots themselves.

Take care

Leave the flower spikes once they are over, as the seedheads are also decorative for the flower arranger.

Aster amellus

(Italian starwort)
- **Sunny position**
- **Retentive well-drained soil**
- **Late summer and early autumn flowering**

A. amellus has large solitary flowers with golden-yellow centres, with several clusters to each strong branching stem. The grey-green foliage is rough when handled, also the stems. These plants form a woody rootstock.

Four varieties to choose from are: 'King George', with soft blue-violet 8cm (3.2in) flowers with golden-yellow centres, introduced seventy years ago; the 60cm (24in) tall 'Nocturne', with lavender-lilac flowers; the large-flowered pink 'Sonia', 60cm (24in); and the compact dwarf 45cm (18in) 'Violet Queen'.

They object to winter wetness and are happiest in a good well-drained retentive soil. They are best planted in spring. Propagate by basal cuttings in spring, or by division where possible.

Take care

Do not let them have wet rootstocks in winter. 204-205▸

Aster × frikartii 'Mönch'

- **Sunny position**
- **Good well-drained soil**
- **Summer to autumn flowering**

Aster × frikartii 'Mönch' is a hybrid between *A. amellus* × *A. thomsonii*. Its flowering period is considerably longer than *A. amellus* varieties. 'Mönch' has stout branching stems up to 90cm (3ft) bearing an abundance of clear lavender-blue flowers with yellow rayed centres, lasting until the frosts begin in autumn. Every collection of hardy herbaceous perennials should possess a plant or two.

Grow this hybrid aster in good well-drained soil in an open sunny position. Make sure that there is sufficient moisture in the soil to sustain the autumn flowers but avoid excessive wetness during the winter months.

Propagate this variety by basal cuttings in spring, or by division where possible. It is best planted in spring.

Take care

This plant must not have a wet rootstock in winter. 206▸

Aster novae-angliae

(New England aster)

- **Sunny position**
- **Good fertile soil**
- **Late summer, early autumn flowering**

The New England aster does not seed itself about nor run its roots underground, but makes a tough vigorous compact rootstock. The leaves are rough to the touch, and a light shade of green. Beautiful clusters of flowers, each measuring up to 5cm (2in) across, are produced during the late summer and early autumn. Several lovely varieties are available, all excellent as cut flowers.

The warm pink flowers of 120cm (4ft) tall 'Harrington's Pink' were introduced 40 years ago; the semi-double phlox-purple 'Lye End Beauty' is 135cm (4.5ft) tall. Two lovely varieties are both 105cm (3.5ft) tall, 'Alma Potschke' with branching heads of salmon-tinged bright rose flowers, and the startling ruby-red 'September Ruby'.

Propagate these plants by dividing their tough rootstocks in autumn, by placing two strong forks back to back.

Take care

Do not let these vigorous plants exhaust the nutrients in the soil.

Aster novi-belgii

(Michaelmas daisy)

- **Sunny location**
- **Ordinary fertile soil**
- **Early autumn flowering**

The true Michaelmas daisy needs to be grown in well-enriched soil, or plants will soon exhaust the ground. Some varieties are very invasive.

Here are seven varieties to choose from: the stately purple 'Orlando' is 150cm (5ft) tall; the pure white semi-double 'Blandie' is 105-120cm (3.5-4ft) tall; the fine dark blue 'Mistress Quickly' reaches 120cm (4ft); the fully double 'Coombe Rosemary' has violet-purple flowers 3-5cm (1.25-2in) across; and 'Winston S. Churchill' has rich ruby-crimson flowers 75cm (30in) tall. A fine double is the light blue 'Marie Ballard', 90cm (36in) tall; the semi-double rich red 'Freda Ballard' has 90cm (36in) stiff straight stems. There is a good selection of dwarf hybrid *novi-belgii* Michaelmas daisies, which are free-flowering and long-lasting in bloom. 'Audrey' has large pale blue flowers, 30-40cm (12-16in) tall; of similar height is 'Blue Bouquet', a bright blue; 'Lady in Blue' has semi-double rich blue flowers, very free blooming, makes perfect little hummocks and is only 25cm (10in) high. Of the pink and red shades there is 'Little Pink Beauty', a superb semi-double 40cm (16in) tall, or the double pink 'Chatterbox', 45cm (18in); 'Dandy' is 30cm (12in), with purple-red flowers, and 'Little Red Boy', of similar height, is a deep rosy red. Finally, the late-flowering 30cm (12in) 'Snowsprite' makes perfect little hummocks.

Propagate all these by division in spring. To keep them thriving, divide and replant every three years; when doing so choose the strongest and healthiest young pieces on the outside of the clump, and resist replanting any woody pieces.

Take care

If mildew attacks, spray with flowers of sulphur. 206▸

√89 √89

Astilbe × arendsii

(False goat's beard)

- **Sunshine or partial shade**
- **Moist fertile soil**
- **Summer flowering**

Astilbes are one of our most decorative hardy herbaceous perennials. The arendsii hybrids vary from white, through pale pink, deep pink, coral and red, to magenta. Not only are they good garden plants but they also force well under glass in an unheated greenhouse. The foliage varies from light to dark green, with some of purplish and reddish purple shades. The fluffy panicles of flowers are held on erect stems 60-90cm (2-3ft) tall, but the dwarf varieties are only 45cm (18in).

They will grow in full sun or partial shade and thrive in most soils. They have a long flowering period and their rigid erect stems do not require staking. There are too many varieties to mention, but all are worth a place in any garden.

Propagate by division in spring. Alternatively, roots may be divided in autumn and potted for forcing or spring planting.

Take care

Do not cut old flower stems back before spring. 207▸

Astrantia major

(Masterwort)

- **Sunshine or partial shade**
- **Retentive fertile soil**
- **Summer flowering**

The masterwort *A. major* is a fascinating perennial. Each flowerhead has outer bracts that are stiff, papery and pointed, and in the centre of each individual flower are many tiny florets. The whole umbel presents a number of star-like flowers. The foliage is palmate. The colour of the flowers is a pure rose-pink, with a pinkish collar of the petal-like bracts. The flowers are held on wiry stems 60cm (2ft) high. Other varieties have greenish white or pale green collars of bracts. One variety, 'Sunningdale Variegated', has leaves prettily splashed with yellow and cream, but as the season advances they lose their variegation unless old flower stems are cut back.

To be successful, astrantias must be in a soil that does not dry out in summer; a thinly dappled or partial shade is an advantage.

Propagate by seed sown as soon as it has been gathered, or by division in spring.

Take care

Do not let these plants become too dry in summer. 208▸

Ballota pseudodictamnus

- **Sunny location**
- **Well-drained ordinary soil**
- **Summer flowering (insignificant)**

This white woolly hardy perennial has a bush-like habit; it is a good ground cover and looks well throughout the year. The small mauve flowers are almost invisible, so it is the white woolly foliage that is the attraction. Established plants have a woody base, and new shoots are smothered with pale apple-green egg-shaped pointed deeply indented leaves. The many-flowered whorls of pale green bracts are widely displayed at each pair of leaves; the lower leaves remain apple-green but those nearer the top of each 45-60cm (18-24in) stem become more and more woolly. Dried ballota is much used by flower arrangers.

In late spring plants need pruning; leaves that have suffered winter damage can be cut back. Propagate by taking heel cuttings in early summer.

Take care

Give dried material a good drink before storing. 209▸

Baptisia australis

(False indigo; Blue indigo)

- **Sunny location**
- **Good deep fertile soil**
- **Early summer flowering**

This handsome leguminous plant is from North America, although the specific name is *australis*. Its vetch-like trifoliate leaves, on stout 75-90cm (30-36in) stems, carry 23cm (9in) branching spikes of rich blue pea-shaped lupin-like flowers in early summer. In very good fertile soil plants can reach 120cm (4ft).

For some reason, this plant is not widely grown; this may be because it takes a while before it is properly established. It is a useful hardy herbaceous perennial and can be grown from seed, but it will take two years before the plants become established. Although plants can be divided they are best left alone unless they really need transplanting. Propagate by division in autumn or early spring. Or seeds can be sown in pans or boxes and placed in a cold greenhouse in the spring.

Take care

Provide good well-enriched soil.

Bergenia cordifolia

(Pig squeak)

- **Sunshine or shade**
- **Not fussy about soil**
- **Spring flowering**

Bergenia has gone through a series of generic names: at one time it was *Megasea*, and then *Saxifraga*.

In recent years bergenias have come into their own, partly due to the interest in flower arranging. The large leathery green or dark green foliage often takes on attractive hues of red, crimson and brown-red. Their flowers, displayed on stout stems 30cm (12in) high, rise above the mass of green leathery foliage. A large clump in my garden is *B. cordifolia* 'Purpurea', which has large rounded leaves that turn to purplish hues in winter; in spring it displays bright magenta-coloured flowers.

To write about bergenias and not mention the pretty white-flowered *B. stracheyi* 'Silver Light' or 'Silberlicht' would be a bad omission. The pure white flowers take on a pinkish tint as they age, but they are still lovely.

Propagate bergenias by division, immediately after flowering or in autumn.

Take care

Do not let them dry out. 209▸

Brunnera macrophylla

(Siberian bugloss)

- **Sunshine or a little shade**
- **Damp soil**
- **Spring flowering**

B. macrophylla, when I first knew this plant, was called *Anchusa myosotidiflora*, the species name indicating that the flowers were like forget-me-nots.

It is one of the first of the border plants to produce blue flowers in spring. The basal leaves are rough, heart-shaped and large, on stalks about 38-45cm (15-18in) long, which carry sprays of small blue flowers. In the garden, young plants from self-sown seed can easily be removed and replanted to form a new clump, or given away.

There is also an attractive variegated form, *B. macrophylla* 'Variegata', which has prettily marked creamy white leaves. The variety needs a sheltered spot, and the soil must not dry out.

Propagate by root cuttings, which are like thick black leather bootlaces, or by division in early autumn.

Take care

To prevent self-sown seedlings, remove flowerheads as soon as they have faded. 210▸

Buphthalmum salicifolium

(Willow-leaf ox-eye)

- **Sun or partial shade**
- **Good fertile soil**
- **Early summer to early autumn flowering**

This hardy herbaceous perennial has narrow willow-like sharp-pointed leaves, slightly hairy, which clothe the stiff slender stems. The stems are crowned by masses of solitary 4cm (1.6in) wide bright golden-yellow daisy-like flowers; the narrow pointed petals are like golden stars.

It is a plant that will grow almost anywhere, and it blooms from early summer through to early autumn. If not staked, the plants will create neat tumbling bushes, 45-60cm (18-24in) high; they are better left to grow naturally. This is an ideal plant to grow near the front of the border.

Propagate *B. salicifolium* by division of the roots during spring or in the autumn. Cuttings can be taken, ideally in the summer for the best plants. Seeds sown in spring also produce good plants.

Take care

Allow them to grow informally; they do not look so attractive if staked.

Campanula lactiflora

(Milky bellflower)

- **Full sun**
- **Deep fertile soil**
- **Early to late summer flowering**

This is a superb perennial which will reach a height of 120-150cm (4-5ft), and in partial shade may reach 180cm (6ft), though it is better in full sun. Its stout stems require staking in windy gardens. The rootstock, although vigorous, fortunately does not rampage in the soil. The rigid stems carry loose or dense panicles of white or pale blue to deep lilac flowers. The stems are clothed with small light green leaves. The flesh-pink 'Loddon Anna' is a lovely form of *C. lactiflora*, reaching 120-150cm (4-5ft). The baby of this species, 'Pouffe', only 25cm (10in) high, is an ideal dwarf plant, with light green foliage forming mounds that are smothered for weeks with lavender-blue flowers during the early and midsummer months.

Propagate by division or by cuttings in spring

Take care

These campanulas need moisture during the growing season. 210▸

Above: **Anchusa azurea**
Lovely blue flowers adorn this plant in midsummer. Several varieties are available, differing in height from 90 to 180cm (3-6ft). Grow in full sun, and stake plants early on. 190▸

Above:
Anemone 'Honorine Jobert'
This lovely white form was a 'sport' from a red-flowered variety in the garden of M. Jobert, in 1858. 190▸

Left: **Anthemis tinctoria 'Wargrave'**
A fine variety with lemon yellow flowers on 90cm (3ft) stems. 191▸

Above right:
Aquilegia 'McKana Hybrids'
These large-flowered hybrids have a fine selection of beautiful colours. 191▸

Right:
Aquilegia 'Long-spurred Hybrids'
Elegant wiry stemmed plants that will grow best in dappled shade. 191▸

Above:
Aster amellus 'King George'
This large-flowered aster has held its popularity since it was bred in 1914. The soft blue-violet blooms are borne on 60cm (2ft) stems. 194▸

Left: **Aruncus sylvester**
This handsome and tenacious hardy herbaceous perennial has magnificent plumes of creamy white flowers in the summer. Grow it in some shade in deep fertile soil. 193▸

Right: **Aster amellus 'Nocturne'**
This recommended variety has a compact bushy habit and semi-double lilac-lavender flowers in summer. Grow it in free-draining soil and avoid winter wetness. 194▸

Above: **Aster × frikartii 'Mönch'**
A splendid hybrid that blooms earlier and for a longer period than the Aster amellus *varieties. Its 75cm (30in) stems carry lavender-blue flowers well into the autumn.* 195▸

Below: **Aster novi-belgii 'Orlando'**
Panicles of pink-purple 5cm (2in) flowers are freely borne on stems up to 150cm (5ft) in height during the autumn. These plants need a fertile soil and a sunny location. 196▸

Above: **Astilbe × arendsii**
These hardy herbaceous perennials are ideal in a garden where the soil does not dry out. Astilbes flower over a long period and do not need to be staked. Good for sun or shade. 197▸

Above: **Astrantia major**
For those who favour 'everlasting flowers' the paper-like florets of the astrantias are very attractive. Dappled shade and a moist soil suit these summer-flowering plants. 197▶

Above: **Ballota pseudodictamnus**
This compact plant is grown for its white woolly foliage rather than for the insignificant purple blooms. Excellent for drying for indoor decoration during the winter. 198▸

Below: **Bergenia cordifolia**
Clusters of attractive pink-purple flowers are produced in spring on robust stems. Towards autumn the fleshy leaves take on a bronze colour that gives added interest. 199▸

Left: **Brunnera macrophylla**
Tiny blue flowers appear above the large hairy leaves of this plant during the spring months. 199▸

Below left:
Campanula lactiflora 'Pouffe'
This charming miniature campanula has little green hummocks covered in lavender-blue flowers. 200▸

Right: **Centaurea macrocephala**
Striking golden flowerheads borne on erect stems up to 120cm (4ft) in height make this plant a handsome addition to the summer garden. 218▸

Below: **Chelone obliqua**
A perennial with unusually shaped flowers that resemble a turtle's head. Do not grow near weaker plants; it will spread quickly. 220▸

Left: **Chrysanthemum maximum**
Every garden should contain a clump of these dependable perennials. They tolerate all soils and are available with single or double blooms. Excellent as cut flowers. 220▸

Right **Coreopsis grandiflora 'Sunray'**
This bright perennial creates a wealth of colour from mid to late summer. The mid-green leaves create a superb background. 222▸

Below: **Cimicifuga japonica**
At 90cm (3ft) tall, this is the smallest of the cimicifugas. The elegant racemes of snow white blooms appear in midsummer. Grow in moist fertile soil for best results. 221▸

Above: **Coreopsis verticillata**
The starry yellow flowers borne from midsummer to autumn on stiff stems are ideal for flower arranging. Be sure to keep the plant well watered during hot dry weather. 223▸

Right: **Cortaderia selloana 'Sunningdale Silver'**
This splendid variety of pampas grass produces creamy white plumes about 210cm (7ft) high during the autumn. Keep moist in hot dry weather. 223▸

Below: **Corydalis lutea**
This adaptable perennial keeps on flowering throughout the summer. Plants will seed freely, but self-sown seedlings can be cleared easily. 224▸

Above: **Dicentra spectabilis**
Planted in a position sheltered from wind and frost, this charming plant will bloom in early summer. 227◆

Below: **Dictamnus albus**
Spikes of fragrant white flowers appear in early summer above the finely divided foliage. 227◆

Campanula persicifolia

(Peach-leaved bellflower)

- **Sun or partial shade**
- **Good fertile soil**
- **Summer flowering**

The peach-leaved bellflower is a perennial with an evergreen basal rosette of pleasing dark green foliage. It reaches a height of about 60cm (24in), but named varieties will be about 90cm (36in) tall. The slender stems carry numerous open cup-shaped bell-like flowers.

Varieties include: the large double white 'Fleur de Neige', with cup-shaped flowers, 7cm (2.75in) wide, on stiff stems 75-90cm (30-36in) tall; the semi-double 'Pride of Exmouth', with rich lavender-blue flowers on 60cm (24in) slender stems; and the new variety 'Hampstead White', with single cup-and-saucer flowers on 70cm (28in) stems.

Propagate by division in spring, or take basal cuttings in early autumn. As this campanula is surface rooting, its life expectancy is not as long as some perennials; lift, divide and replant it in spring every third year. Rust can disfigure the foliage; pick off affected leaves and spray plant.

Take care

Replant stock every third year.

Catananche caerulae

(Cupid's dart)

- **Full sun**
- **Well-drained light soil**
- **Summer flowering**

This attractive cornflower-like perennial forms clumps of hairy grass-like leaves, from which emerge 60cm (24in) spikes each carrying silvery papery bracts and lavender-blue everlasting flowers. The best form, *C. caerulea* 'Major', has larger and richer blue flowers. There is also a white variety, 'Ferry's White'.

To extend the season of flowering, grow two or more clumps, and cut one down when it comes into flower; this will then bloom later. The flowers can be cut and dried, like everlastings, and used for indoor decoration. All catananches are best in full sun and in well-drained soil. If plants are cut back in early autumn, this enables them to pull through the winter.

Propagate by root cuttings in autumn, or by division in spring or by seeds sown out of doors in spring.

Take care

These plants should have good drainage.

Centaurea macrocephala

(Yellow hardhead; Yellow hardweed)

- **Full sun**
- **Light, sandy soil**
- **Summer flowering**

This member of the knapweed family is a very handsome perennial, the strong erect stems of which are 90-120cm (3-4ft) tall; at the top of each stem appears a round golden flowerhead, as large as a tennis ball. Each flower is surrounded by rough brown papery bracts forming a collar that protects the inner florets. If situated in the middle of a border this plant makes an outstanding individual display. The flowerheads dry well, and are useful for winter decorations for the flower arranger.

It would be wrong not to mention *C. dealbata* 'John Coutts'; this perennial cornflower is free-flowering and, from my experience, can be left in one position for many years. The cornflower blooms are large and clear pink, on 90cm (3ft) stems.

Propagate when necessary by division in spring or autumn.

Take care

These plants need full sun, and will do well in a limy soil. 211▸

Centranthus ruber

(Red valerian)

- **Full sun**
- **Ordinary garden soil**
- **Summer flowering**

Although this perennial may be classed as a wilding, it is worth garden space, especially if you have a lime or chalk soil, as this is something it revels in. Plants can often be seen growing on old walls or mortar rubble dumps. The closely packed heads of red or deep pink flowers are carried on 60-90cm (2-3ft) glaucous stems and foliage. The red flowers are certainly more colourful than the pink ones, and it is as well to remember this when buying. There is also a white form available, *Centranthus ruber* 'Albus'.

Propagate by seeds sown out of doors during late spring or the seeds can be sown as soon as they are ripe where the plants will eventually flower. Alternatively, plants can be divided in late autumn or spring.

This plant has also been known as *Kentranthus ruber*.

Take care

Choose a well-coloured form when buying.

Cephalaria gigantea

(Giant scabious)

- **Sunny location**
- **Any good ordinary soil**
- **Early summer flowering**

What fun botanists have in changing names. For years I have known this giant scabious-like plant as *C. tartarica*, which indicates that it comes from Central Asia. Nevertheless, *C. gigantea* is a good name for this spectacular hardy herbaceous perennial, as it grows up to 180cm (6ft); it needs to be planted near the back of a border, or, if you have island beds, then place these plants in the centre. It has large, deeply toothed leaves, soft green above and paler beneath. The large heads of light yellow flowers grow on 60cm (2ft) branching stalks. The flowers last for several weeks during the early summer.

Propagate this plant by dividing the stout roots in spring or by sowing seeds out of doors in spring and transplanting the seedlings in late spring.

Take care

Do not put this tall handsome cephalaria in front of shorter plants.

Ceratostigma willmottianum

(Hardy plumbago)

- **Full sun**
- **Fertile well-drained soil**
- **Late summer and autumn flowering**

This plant is generally found in nurserymen's shrub catalogues, but its treatment is almost identical with that of fuchsias; it has to be cut back in late winter or very early spring to encourage strong new growth for the coming season. It makes a wiry, bushy plant up to 90cm (3ft) tall; its small rough leaves are green, set on brown twiggy stems that are topped by branching shoots bearing clear cobalt-blue flowers.

Two plants that I was told were *C. willmottianum* were in fact *C. plumbaginoides*. The stems are 30cm (12in) high, and in late autumn dark blue bristly flowers are borne at the end of each stem. This is an ideal plant for the front of a border.

Propagate *C. willmottianum* by softwood cuttings in early summer, inserted in a heated propagator. Take half-ripe cuttings from *C. plumbaginoides* in midsummer, or divide in spring.

Take care

Grow these in well-drained soil.

Chelone obliqua

(Turtlehead)

- **Sun; tolerates light shade**
- **Fertile well-drained soil**
- **Autumn flowering**

This rather strange-looking perennial derives its popular name from the unusual shape of the flowers. It is a close relation of the penstemons and is sometimes confused with them. Its dark green leaves are broad to oblong in shape, 5-20cm (2-8in) long, and arranged in pairs, the last two being just below the erect crowded truss of rosy-purple flowers. The square stems are 60-90cm (2-3ft) tall. Provided it is given a sunny position in the border, this plant will produce blooms for several weeks in autumn: the flowers are very weather resistant, which is useful in wet seasons. Its roots have a spreading habit, and plants soon form a mat.

Propagate by seed sown in spring under glass in a temperature of 13-18°C (55-65°F), or in late spring without heat in a cold frame; or by division of roots in spring, or in late autumn as soon as the flowers fade.

Take care

Chelones may crowd out less tough growing plants. 211▸

Chrysanthemum maximum

(Shasta daisy)

- **Sunny location**
- **Any good fertile soil**
- **Summer flowering**

The Shasta daisy, a native of the Pyrenees, is a must for any perennial border. The height varies from 60 to 90cm (2-3ft). The flowers are single or double, with plain or fringed petals. On account of the large flat heads, rain and wind can soon knock plants over; short peasticks should be inserted in the ground before the plants are too advanced.

One of the best-known varieties is 'Esther Read', 45cm (18in) tall, with pure white, fully double flowers; 'Wirral Pride' is a 90cm (36in) beauty with large anemone-centred blooms; another variety is the fully double white-flowered 'Wirral Supreme', 80cm (32in) high. If you prefer a large, fully double frilly-flowered variety, plant 'Droitwich Beauty', 80-90cm (32-36in) tall; a creamy-yellow variety is 'Mary Stoker', 80cm (32in) high.

Propagate by softwood cuttings in summer, or by division in autumn or spring.

Take care

Be sure to provide support. 212▸

Cimicifuga racemosa

(Black snake-root; Bugbane)

- **Sun or partial shade**
- **Rich fertile moist soil**
- **Summer flowering**

This plant is commonly known as bugbane because of the rather unpleasant smell that is given off by the leaves of some species. Such a name is misleading, however, as no perennial can be more beautiful when its tall branching stems are displaying the feathery sprays of creamy-white flowers during late summer. The stems are 150-180cm (5-6ft) tall. The fluffy flowers droop gracefully above shining green divided foliage. Another fine cimicifuga is *C. japonica,* with snow white blooms on stems up to 90cm (3ft) tall.

Cimicifugas will grow in dry soils but are far finer where their roots are growing in rich deep well-cultivated soil, preferably moist. Propagate them by seed sown as soon as it has been gathered, or by division in spring or autumn.

Take care

This plant needs full sun, and must not become dry or starved. 212-213▶

Clematis heracleifolia

(Tube clematis)

- **Sunny location**
- **Ordinary fertile soil**
- **Late summer flowering**

This species is popularly called the tube clematis because of its tube-shaped flowers. It is not a climbing plant, but a hardy herbaceous perennial, bearing clusters of sweetly scented flowers resembling the individual florets of a hyacinth. Clusters of small purple-blue flowers are borne on leafy stems about 60-90cm (2-3ft) in height. Later, frothy seedheads provide an added bonus. The form called *C.h. davidiana* has large leaves that are slightly coarse in texture; it bears clusters of deliciously scented rich blue hyacinth-like flowers on 90-120cm (3-4ft) stems.

Propagate by division during the dormant season. Both *Clematis heracleifolia* and *C.h. davidiana* need to have all their top growth cut back and the previous season's dead shoots removed during the winter.

Take care

Remove all dead shoots and cut the plants back in spring.

Clematis recta

(Herbaceous virgin's bower)

- **Full sun**
- **Ordinary fertile soil**
- **Summer flowering**

This outstanding hardy perennial clematis has pinnate glistening dark green leaves. During the summer an abundance of billowing sweetly-scented white flowers is carried on branching sprays at the top of straggling stems. Each flower forms a star and can be as much as 2.5cm (1in) across. Plants reach a height of 120-150cm (4-5ft), and sometimes higher. Place a few peasticks around the plant, allowing the stems to clamber through them; in autumn, when flowering has finished, the mound will be covered with clouds of silvery seedheads.

This fine clematis will thrive in full sun in ordinary garden soil, and also do well in an alkaline soil. A spring mulch of peat or rotted manure will be beneficial.

Propagate this species by division during the dormant season.

Take care

Prune the plant down to ground level during the winter.

Coreopsis grandiflora

- **Full sun**
- **Fertile soil**
- **Flowers ideal for cutting**

This robust plant from North America has beautiful, deeply toothed, narrow leaves. They are light to mid-green, and provide a perfect background for the bright yellow flowers, up to 6cm (2½in) wide. These are borne on long stems from early to mid-summer. The normal species grows 30-45cm (1-1½ft) high, but there are several attractive forms that are slightly taller. 'Sunray', at 60cm (2ft) high, is long-flowering and easy to grow. 'Sunburst' grows 75cm (2½ft) high and displays rich yellow, double flowers. 'Badengold' is even taller, at 90cm (3ft), and bears large, golden-yellow flowers. 'Mayfield Giant' is an old favourite, at nearly 75cm (2½ft) high and with golden flowers. 'Goldfink', sometimes called 'Goldfinch', is a dwarf form, growing 20-25cm (8-10in) high and bearing deep golden-yellow flowers.

Propagate by division in autumn or spring. Ensure that each new plant has several healthy shoots.

Take care

Remember to stake the tall varieties, from an early stage.

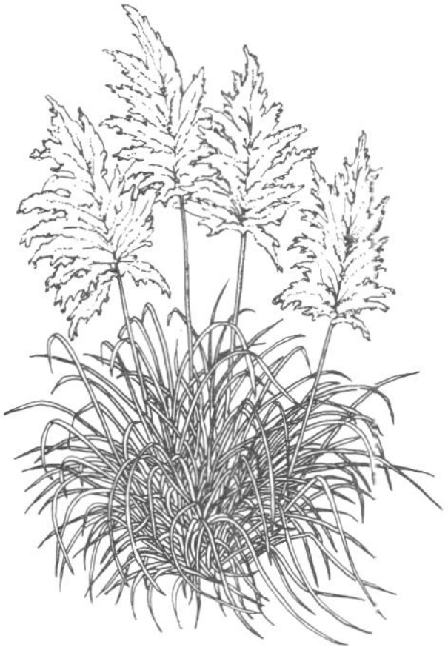

Coreopsis verticillata

(Tickseed)

- **Full sun**
- **Fertile soil**
- **Summer and autumn flowering**

This plant from the eastern United States is one of the best perennials for the front of the border. It makes a dense bushy plant; the deep green foliage is finely divided, on stiff needle-like stems that support bright yellow starry flowers as much as 4cm (1.6in) across, and the blooms have a very long season. The flowers are fine for cutting, and mix particularly well with the light lavender-blue flowers of *Aster* × *frikartii* hybrids.Coreopsis must not be left in the same place too long without being lifted and divided, or the plants will become starved. This species does not require support

Today there is also an improved and larger-flowered variety called *C. verticillata* 'Grandiflora', which has warmer yellow flowers than the species.

Propagate this plant by division in spring.

Take care

Do not let this plant dry out in warm weather; water in the evening. 214▶

Cortaderia selloana

(Pampas grass)

- **Full sun**
- **Light retentive fertile soil**
- **Late summer and early autumn flowering**

Pampas grass has masses of gracefully arching leaves that forms a good base for the erect stems to carry their silky silvery white plumes. For indoor decoration gather plumes as soon as they are fully developed.

Varieties include: 'Monstrosa', creamy-white plumes, 275cm (9ft) stems; compact 'Pumila', with short foliage, creamy white plumes, erect 150cm (5ft) stems; 'Sunningdale Silver', creamy white open plumes, 210cm (7ft) stems; 'Rendatleri', silver-pink plumes, 180-240cm (6-8ft) stems.

They are not fussy over soil but are happiest in light soils enriched with humus or well rotted farmyard manure or good garden compost. Plant in either autumn or spring. Winter care entails allowing the grass to die down. Never cut it with shears; wear stout leather gloves to pull the leaves out of established clumps.

Propagate by seed under glass in spring, or by division in spring.

Take care

Give ample moisture during very hot weather. 178▶ 215▶

Corydalis lutea

(Yellow fumitory)

- **Sunny location**
- **Any well-drained soil**
- **Late spring to late summer flowering**

The yellow fumitory may be only a wilding, but its small bright yellow trumpet-like flowers, which rise among a hummock of soft divided pretty fern-like foliage, in all about 30cm (12in) tall, are well worth growing. This charming little plant will make a gay display from late spring and throughout the summer, well into the autumn. It will readily naturalize once it is established.

Although it can often be seen flourishing in old walls, it also looks well when growing in odd places where perhaps other plants could not or would not exist.

Propagate by sowing seed out of doors in spring, where they are to flower; but plants may also be divided in spring. Self-sown seedlings will appear profusely; keep them in check by uprooting any unwanted ones regularly.

Take care

Keep plants in check. 214▸

Crambe cordifolia

(Flowering seakale)

- **Full sun**
- **Good rich soil**
- **Early summer flowering**

To many people the common name of seakale will conjure up that most delectable blanched vegetable, but *Crambe cordifolia* is a dramatic perennial; some authorities say it is for only the larger garden, but there is nothing to stop the small garden having an isolated plant. This magnificent species has large deep unequally lobed and toothed heart-shaped leaves, 30-90cm (24-36in) long. From a mound of foliage arise 150-180cm (5-6ft) flower spikes on which massive branching sprays of hundreds of small white flowers appear. The width of one plant can be as much as its height.

Propagate by root cuttings taken off after flowering has ceased, or by seed sown out of doors in spring, but it will be three years before seedling plants will flower. As a perennial it is not long lasting; therefore restock with a new plant.

Take care

Spray it with malathion if the cabbage white fly attacks.

Crocosmia pottsii

- **Sun or partial shade**
- **Well-drained, fertile soil**
- **Mid to late summer flowering**
- **Light sandy fertile well-drained soil**
- **Summer flowering**

This species is hardier than other crocosmias, and has become very popular. The 4cm (1½in) long, trumpet-shaped flowers appear from mid to late summer on 90cm (3ft) long stems. Their colours range from yellow to dark red.

Many varieties have been developed, and include 'Bressingham Blaze', with intense, orange and flame-red flowers. 'Vulcan' is equally well known, with bright orange-red flowers. 'Jackanapes' is especially attractive, combining yellow and deep orange. They are borne on wiry stems.

These plants grow best in the shelter of a south-facing wall. Alternatively, set them among shrubs or herbaceous perennials, where they will gain some protection.

Propagate by lifting and dividing clumps every three or four years. This is best done in spring.

Take care

This plant requires well-drained soil if the corms are to survive during winter.

Cynoglossum nervosum

(Hound's tongue)

- **Sunny or lightly shaded**
- **Rich, well-drained soil**
- **Mid-summer flowering**

This easily grown and amenable border plant gains its common name from the shape of its large, narrow, mid-green leaves that are hairy and rough. The plant grows 45-60cm (1½-2ft) high, with a bushy and dense stance. During mid-summer it creates a mass of intense blue flowers that resemble those of Forget-me-nots. It is the strong blue colour that first catches the eye.

Set the plants in position during either autumn or spring. The latter is the best time in cold areas. If the soil is rich, the stems grow rapidly in early summer, and soon need staking with twiggy sticks. In autumn, cut down the plants to soil level. However, in cold areas do not cut down the plants until spring.

Propagate by sowing seeds in a cold frame in spring, pricking out the seedlings into a nursery bed as soon as they are large enough to handle. Alternatively, divide congested plants in autumn or spring.

Take care

Support the young growth before it starts to flop over.

Delphinium Belladonna varieties

(Perennial larkspur)

- **Full sun**
- **Deep rich well-drained retentive soil**
- **Summer and autumn flowering**

Belladonna delphiniums are bushy, and their deeply cut foliage produces stems that display branched spikes of pretty blue flowers. The majority of belladonnas do not require staking, except in very windswept gardens. As a group they are also stronger and easier to cultivate than their taller sisters. The Belladonna delphiniums available today are the result of selection and hybridization that has been performed throughout the 20th century.

The gentian-blue 'Wendy' is 120cm (4ft) tall. Three varieties just over 90cm (3ft) tall are 'Pink Sensation' (cerise-pink), 'Moerheim' (white) and the semi-double 'Naples' (brilliant blue).

Propagate these delphiniums by division or by cuttings rooted in a cold frame, in spring.

Take care

Avoid cold wet soils, and plant in spring.

Dianthus

(Garden pinks)

- **Full sun**
- **Well-drained rich soil**
- **Early summer flowering**

Varieties of garden pinks include: 'Mrs Simkins', with scented double white flowers 20cm (8in) high; the sweetly scented semi-double pale pink 'Inchmery', 30cm (12in); the double 'White Ladies', 45cm (18in); and the double salmon-pink 30cm (12in) 'Doris'.

The main requirement of garden pinks is a well-drained open soil with plenty of humus, rotted farmyard manure, rotted garden compost and an ample supply of lime or old mortar rubble; however, they will flourish in an acid soil. To encourage new growth cut them back when the plants have finished flowering. The new growth will enable them to withstand the winter, and provide propagating material. Plant garden pinks in early autumn so that they become established before winter. Propagate them by cuttings taken from non-flowering basal shoots, or by layering in midsummer.

Take care

Suport taller varieties with twigs.

Dicentra spectabilis

(Bleeding heart; Dutchman's breeches)

- **Partial shade or full sun**
- **Rich well-cultivated fertile soil**
- **Late spring and early summer flowering**

This charming plant has a fragile look; the glaucous finely divided foliage has attractive arching sprays off the stoutish stems, about 60cm (2ft) high, sometimes taller, from which dangle crimson and white lockets. When open, the flowers are rosy pink with white tips. It makes a good cut flower, and roots potted in autumn can be forced into flower in an unheated greenhouse.

These delicate-looking plants can be damaged by late spring frosts, and it is advisable to plant them where the sun does not reach the plants before the frost has gone. Plant *D. spectabilis* where it can be protected by a wall or evergreen shrubs. A mulch of leaf-mould or well-rotted garden compost should be given each spring.

Propagate in spring by cutting the roots with a sharp knife, or by root cuttings taken in spring and rooted in an unheated frame.

Take care

Protect against wind and frost. 216▶

Dictamnus albus

(Burning bush)

- **Full sun**
- **Well-drained deep fertile soil**
- **Early summer flowering**

The burning bush so called because on hot dry days, when the seedpods are ripening, it is possible by holding a lighted match at the base of the flower stalk to ignite the volatile oil given off by the plant without doing any damage to the dictamnus itself. Other common names that have been used for this plant are dittany and fraxinella, and in America it is called gas plant.

The smooth divided light green leaves are on erect stems that are lemon scented. The erect stems bear white flowers that have very long stamens. The plant usually seen in our gardens is *D. albus purpureus,* which has soft mauve-purple flowers, veined with red. Both are 90cm (3ft) tall. As the plants are deep rooted they can remain in one place for a number of years.

Propagate by root cuttings in late autumn or winter, or by division in spring.

Take care

Give water in very dry weather. 216▶

Dierama pendulum

(Fairy's wand)

- **Full sun**
- **Light sandy soil**
- **Mid-summer flowering**
- **Late summer flowering**

This Wand Flower is much smaller than its related species, *Dierama pulcherrimum*. When in flower it reaches 75cm (2½ft) high. The pendulous, pink-purple flowers appear during mid-summer, amid the thin, graceful and arching stems and leaves.

There is a white-flowered form called 'Album'.

Well-drained soil enriched with leaf-mould or compost is essential, as is a sunny and sheltered position. Plant the corms 10-15cm (4-6in) deep in autumn or spring. In all but the coldest places they can be left in the soil throughout winter. Cut the plant down to soil-level in autumn or spring. The latter is the best time in cold regions.

Propagate by lifting and dividing plants in autumn or spring. Small offsets can be kept in a nursery bed for a year or so, until large enough to be planted into the garden.

Take care

Avoid draughty and windswept positions.

Digitalis grandiflora

(D. ambigua)

(Yellow foxglove)

- **Sun or partial shade**
- **Ordinary soil**
- **Summer flowering**

Most gardeners are familiar with the biennial common foxglove, *D. purpurea,* but the yellow foxglove, *D. grandiflora,* is a perennial evergreen. It has normal 5cm (2in) foxglove flowers in a pale creamy yellow, prettily blotched with brown spots. The individual flowers are smaller than those of the common foxglove, but it has a larger quantity of flower spikes. The whole plant is hairy. The oblong leaves, notched at the edges, clasp the 60cm (24in) stems.

Foxgloves grow in ordinary garden soil, but the ground needs humus to prevent the plants drying out during hot weather. To guard against root rot ensure that the soil does not remain excessively wet during the winter months. Propagate by sowing seed out of doors in spring, or by division in spring.

Take care

When raising from seed, cull poor forms when seedlings bloom.

Doronicum 'Miss Mason'

(Leopard's bane)

- **Full sun or partial shade**
- **Any good fertile soil**
- **Spring flowering**

The leopard's bane is one of the first perennials to brighten the garden as spring approaches; the large yellow star-shaped flowers are a good follow-on after the early daffodils are over.

'Miss Mason' is probably a hybrid of *D. austriacum* or *D. caucasicum*. Its bright yellow daisy-like flowers are in bloom for several weeks. The smooth heart-shaped leaves have scalloped edges, and are bright green; the flowers are carried at the top of wiry stems 45cm (18in) high. This variety makes an excellent cut flower. When flowering is over, the leaves of 'Miss Mason' do not die down as this hybrid is evergreen. To have a good display, plant them in groups of five or six.

Propagate by division in early autumn or spring. Plants should be divided every third or fourth year.

Take care

Remove faded blooms so that plants produce a further crop of flowers in the autumn. 233▶

Eccremocarpus scaber

(Glory flower)

- **Full sun**
- **Any fertile soil**
- **Summer flowering**

This semi-woody perennial evergreen climber needs to be treated as an annual in cold and wet areas or where hard frosts are usual. The stems are 3.7-4.6m (12-15ft) long and at the end of each fern-like leaf is a tendril used to attach the plant to its support. The 2.5cm (1in) tubular orange-yellow and orange-scarlet flowers are carried on graceful 15-25cm (6-10in) racemes bearing 10-20 flowers.

Eccremocarpus will thrive in almost any type of soil except chalk. Grow it against a sheltered and sunny wall. Prune each spring by cutting out all dead or frosted growth, and shortening a few main shoots to produce new growth.

Propagate by seed sown under glass in a temperature of 13°C (55°F) in spring or by cuttings of ripened shoots in autumn in heat under glass.

Take care

Do not plant before late spring.

Echinacea purpurea

(Cone flower)

- **Sunny location**
- **Well-drained soil**
- **Summer flowering**

For many years this strongly-growing perennial was known as *Rudbeckia purpurea*. It is a stately plant with dark green foliage, rough to the touch, on stiff stout stems.

The rich reddish-purple flowers have a central boss of orange-brown which makes them quite outstanding. Over the years there have been many varieties raised. The variety I remember when first working in a nursery was called 'The King', 120cm (4ft) tall, and it is still available. An earlier flowering variety is the broad-petalled erect carmine-purple flowered 'Robert Bloom', which is 90cm (3ft) tall. If you want a variety of colours, the Bressingham Hybrids, also 90cm (3ft) tall, are well worth planting.

The echinaceas are best planted in spring. Add leaf-mould or well-rotted compost to the soil at the time of planting. Propagate by seed sown in spring, by root cuttings in autumn, or by division in spring.

Take care

Choose a sunny spot. 234▶

Echinops ritro 'Taplow blue'

(Steel globe thistle)

- **Full sun**
- **Not fussy over soil**
- **Late summer flowering**

Globe thistles have round drumstick heads in varying tones of blue. They are coarse growing; attached to the stout rough wiry stems is deeply cut greyish spiny foliage, woolly beneath. Bees are especially attracted to the globular flowers. The flowerheads can be dried for winter decoration. The variety 'Taplow Blue' is 150cm (5ft) tall, with dark blue globular flowers that have a metallic steely lustre. A variety with a slightly richer blue is 'Veitch's Blue'. There is also the white species *E. nivalis (E. niveus)*. These hardy herbaceous perennials can be grown successfully in the poorest of soils, whether sand or chalk, but should be well drained.

Propagate by root cuttings in late autumn or winter, or by division in autumn or spring.

Take care

Provide a good depth of soil, as the thong-like roots of this plant are very penetrating. 235▶

Erigeron 'Quakeress'

(Fleabane)

- **Sunny location**
- **Not fussy over soil**
- **Summer flowering**

With a pretty name like 'Quakeress', it is unfortunate that this erigeron has the common name 'fleabane'. All the erigerons have a long flowering period, and their daisy-like flowers are in varying shades of blue, pink, mauve or violet. 'Quakeress' has pale blue flowers, and is 60cm (24in) high. Of similar height is 'Charity', a light pink, or 'Darkest of All', a deep violet blue. Where shorter varieties are needed, plant the semi-double light blue 'Prosperity', only 45cm (18in) high, or the very dwarf pink-flowered 'Dimity'.

Erigerons are real sun-lovers, and if they have well-drained soil they will not present any problems. Plant in spring, in batches of five or six plants to each square metre/square yard.

Propagate by seeds sown out of doors in spring, or by division in spring or autumn.

Take care

Avoid waterlogged soil.

Eryngium bourgatii

(Sea holly)

- **Sunny location**
- **Fertile well-drained soil**
- **Summer and late summer flowering**

As their name implies, the sea hollies have spiny holly-like foliage which is especially attractive, and thistle-like flowerheads in varying shades of blue. They are hardy, and flourish by the sea coast. *E. bourgatii* is a native of the Pyrenees having grey-green foliage and blue-green thistle-like flowers, borne on wiry branching stems. A beautiful evergreen sea holly from Morocco is *E. variifolium.* The spiny toothed rounded leaves are small compared with many eryngiums, and each leaf has distinctive white veins. The flowers, which are not striking, are borne in late summer and carried on erect stems. The British sea holly, *E. maritimum,* has glaucous leaves and charming blue flowers.

Propagate eryngiums by taking root cuttings in late winter or by sowing seed during early spring.

Take care

Do not allow these plants to become waterlogged. 235▸

Eupatorium purpureum 'Atropurpureum'

(Joe Pye weed)

- **Sunny location**
- **Any good fertile soil**
- **Early autumn flowering**

This plant has always attracted my attention by its tall handsome upright purplish stems, bedecked with large fluffy branching heads of flowers in varying shades of pale purple, mauve-pink, cinnamon-pink, purplish rose, and purple-lilac. My reason for giving such a list of colours is that much depends on the individual admirer of this 150-180cm (5-6ft) dominating perennial. The variety 'Atropurpureum' has foliage that is purplish, and its fluffy flowers are rosy lilac.

In a large border it needs to be planted well behind shorter-growing plants, or they will be hidden. This North American needs good rich soil if it is to give of its best; a mulch in spring with well-rotted farmyard manure or good garden compost will be welcome. This is an ideal perennial to grow in a wild or semi-wild garden. Propagation is by division in autumn.

Take care

Make sure plants are not starved. 236▸

Euphorbia characias

(Sub-shrubby spurge)

- **Sun or shade**
- **Fertile soil, moderately drained**
- **Early spring flowering**

This evergreen is a sub-species of *E. wulfenii*. Here is a plant which appears in lists of hardy herbaceous perennials although, as I have said, it is an evergreen and therefore its shoots do not die down in winter, as is usually the case with hardy herbaceous perennials. *E. w. characias* has narrow flower spikes that are green with dark brown centres; *E. wulfenii* has broader flower spikes, also green, but with yellowish centres. Their erect stems are about 120cm (4ft) tall, with grey-green glaucous foliage, each stem turning over rather like a shepherd's crook. The following spring each stem is topped by a flowerhead, after which the stems die down to the base and eventually have to be removed.

Propagate by seed or softwood cuttings in spring.

Take care

The white sap from shoots can irritate some skins.

Above: **Doronicum 'Miss Mason'**
The yellow daisy-like flowers of this lovely hybrid are a welcome sight in spring. Carried on wiry stems up to 45cm (18in) tall, these blooms are excellent for cutting. 229◆

Left: **Echinacea purpurea**
This hardy perennial is a stately plant, its richly coloured flowers appearing in midsummer. It is a strongly growing subject that will thrive in sunshine and warmth. 230▸

Right: **Echinops ritro**
The globe thistles are coarse, prickly foliaged plants which in late summer are festooned with blue globular flowers about 5cm (2in) across. Easy to grow in full sun. 230▸

Below: **Eryngium bourgatii**
On a fertile well-drained soil this striking plant will produce its lovely thistle-like flowers on stems up to 45cm (18in) tall in summer. Decorative grey-green foliage. 231▸

Above: **Euphorbia griffithii 'Fireglow'**
This plant produces red-tipped shoots from the base that gradually develop into attractive green foliage which, in early summer, is enhanced by striking orange-red bracts. 249▶

Left: **Eupatorium purpureum 'Atropurpureum'**
The purplish foliage of this pretty variety is an added bonus to the autumnal rose-lilac flowers. 232▶

Right: **Festuca glauca**
This densely tufted perennial grass is a useful plant for the front of the border. It will thrive in sun. 249▶

Above: **Galega officinalis**
Galegas have a sprawling habit and are best planted near the back of the border. Small pea-shaped blooms are borne on branching stems. 251▸

Right: **Filipendula purpurea**
A splendid plant for a cool moist spot. The handsome foliage is crowned with lovely carmine-rose flowers on stems 60-120cm (2-4ft) high. 250▸

Below: **Geranium endresii 'A.T. Johnson'**
A superb geranium for planting at the side of a gravel path or at the front of a border. 252▸

Left: **Gentiana asclepiadea**
This is a most attractive gentian with glossy green willow-like leaves and rich blue flowers in the early autumn. Partial shade and moist conditions suit this plant best. Leave undisturbed to naturalize. 252▸

Right: **Gypsophila paniculata**
A magnificent display of feathery white flowers covers this plant in midsummer. It is deep-rooted and needs well-prepared soil and full sunshine to become established. 255▸

Below:
Helenium autumnale 'Wyndley'
The heleniums enrich the garden with bright daisy-like flowers in shades of yellow and orange. This lovely variety has large coppery-yellow blooms on erect stems. 255▸

Left: **Helianthus decapetalus**
The perennial sunflowers produce large daisy-like flowers on stout stems up to 150cm (5ft) in height. They are vigorous plants. 256▶

Right: **Helleborus corsicus**
Clusters of fascinating pale green cup-shaped flowers are produced by this plant from winter until early spring. The three-lobed leaves make a handsome display on their own. 257▶

Below:
Hemerocallis 'Pink Damask'
The beautiful pink lily-like blooms of this recommended variety are carried on stems up to 75cm (30in) in height. Allow these superb plants to grow undisturbed in good soil. 258▶

Above: **Heuchera sanguinea 'Red Spangles'**
This is one of the best varieties to grow; its blood-red bell-shaped flowers are borne on slender stems up to 50cm (20in) in height. 259▸

Right: **Hosta rectifolia 'Tall Boy'**
A lovely hybrid for the border. 260▸

Below: **Hosta fortunei 'Albopicta Aurea'**
Grown for its stunning foliage. 260▸

Above: **Iberis sempervirens**
This half-shrubby perennial is an ideal edging plant. Its dark evergreen foliage forms hummocks that are covered with white flowers in spring and early summer. 260▸

Left: **Inula helenium**
A hardy herbaceous perennial with many deep yellow daisy-like blooms carried single on wiry stems above a dense display of narrow leaves. It thrives in a moist spot. 261▸

Right: **Incarvillea mairei**
Beautiful pink-purple flowers with yellow throats adorn this plant in early summer. It grows to 30cm (12in) in height and so is ideal for the front of a sunny border. 261▸

Above: **Iris florentina**

This intermediate bearded iris creates a dominant splash of colour in early summer. The roots have been extensively used in perfumery. 262▶

Euphorbia griffithii 'Fireglow'

(Spurge)

- **Sun or partial shade**
- **Good fertile soil**
- **Early summer flowering**

E. griffithii has bright yellow flowers 45cm (18in) high; it was introduced from the Himalayas, and was first exhibited in 1954. The flowerheads of 'Fireglow' are a rich burnt orange shade (frequently described as brick red), and carried on erect stems. My own plant has not flowered so far and I am anxiously looking forward to it blooming, when its 75cm (30in) stems will carry their handsome coloured 'flowers', which are in fact bracts.

'Fireglow' does best in an open sunny spot or partial shade. It has slow-spreading shoots, which appear around the base. The dull red asparagus-like shoots soon develop into dark green foliage, reddish beneath.

Propagate this plant by division in spring or autumn.

Take care

Its roots may become invasive, but if you admire it you will probably not mind. 236▸ 237▸

Festuca glauca

(Sheep's fescue)

- **Sunny location**
- **Well-drained soil**
- **Midsummer flowering**

This useful and accommodating grass is a form of sheep's fescue, *Festuca ovina. F. glauca* is a densely tufted perennial, with little plumes like miniature pampas grass. The neat clumps have flower spikes 23-25cm (9-10in) tall. It is an ideal plant for the front of a border or as an edging. The foliage is steely blue-grey or a glaucous grey. As it is a slow grower it does not require replanting for several years. Other fescues are *F. amethystina,* which has stems of powder blue 23cm (9in) tall, and *F. punctoria,* which is a steely blue and only 15cm (6in) high.

All these fescues like full sun and are at their best on dry soils. Propagate them by sowing seeds in spring or by division in early autumn or spring.

Take care

Plant in early autumn or spring, and always in light well-drained soil. 237▸

Filipendula purpurea

(Dropwort)

- **Sun or partial shade**
- **Cool moist conditions**
- **Summer flowering**

This Japanese hardy herbaceous perennial is one of half a dozen dropworts. It can still be found in some nursery catalogues and garden centres under its old name, *Spiraea palmatum*. This is a most handsome plant, and if it has moist soil or is growing near the side of a pond, it will not fail to attract attention. It has large lobed leaves and above the elegant leafy crimson stems are large flat heads bearing many tiny carmine-rose flowers, each stem reaching a height of 60-120cm (2-4ft). The pinkish *F. rubra* has large flowerheads up to 28cm (11in) across. In damp soil it will form huge clumps, in either sun or shade.

To obtain the best results, grow this plant in partial shade and in rich fertile moist soil. Propagate by seeds sown in pans or boxes under glass in autumn, or by division in autumn.

Take care

Make sure that this plant does not lack moisture. 239▸

Francoa sonchifolia

(Bridal wreath)

- **Sun or partial shade**
- **Any well-drained soil**
- **Summer flowering**

The best-known bridal wreath is *F. racemosa*, which needs to be grown indoors. The so-called half-hardy *F. sonchifolia* is much hardier. It is a graceful plant, and the long erect wand-like stems rise 45-60cm (18-24in) above the deeply lobed dark green foliage. At the top of these wands are carried numerous heads of white and deep pink flowers with red spots at the base of each petal. The flowers are long lasting, and even when over they look quite attractive at first, but as winter draws near they are best cut down.

Grow *F. sonchifolia* in any well-drained soil in a sunny position or one providing partial shade. The lovely flowers are produced in midsummer.

Propagate by seed sown in spring under glass, or by division in spring.

Take care

Choose a sheltered spot and plant in spring for best results.

Gaillardia aristata

(Blanket flower)

- **Sunny location**
- **Light well-drained soil**
- **Summer flowering**

The gaillardias are among the most colourful perennials, and the hybrids are chiefly derived from *G. aristata*, better known in the nursery trade as *G. grandiflora*. These vivid flowers can be had in shades of yellow, bronze, orange, flame, brown and maroon-red. Their large daisy-like saucer-shaped flowers are ideal for cutting. The height varies from 60-90cm (2-3ft). All parts of the plant are sticky, and its soft leaves have an aromatic scent.

As they are short-lived, gaillardias should be grown in well-drained soil, and they will flourish in calcareous soils, ie chalk or lime. Fortunately, they grow with the minimum of attention; the long flowering season lasts from mid to late summer.

Propagate by seeds sown under glass in late winter or out of doors in early summer, or by root cuttings in autumn or softwood cuttings in midsummer.

Take care

As gaillardias are rather floppy, support them with a few peasticks.

Galega officinalis

(Goat's rue)

- **Full sun**
- **Any good soil, or even poor soils**
- **Summer flowering**

This is a perennial that needs to be at the back of the border, as it has a rather sprawling habit, so plant it behind perennials that can shield it when the flowers have faded and the plant is looking a little the worse for wear. What a joy goat's rue is, as it will thrive in any sunny corner and in any good soil. The small pea-shaped flowers of *G. officinalis* are mauve, and they are borne on branching stems up to 150cm (5ft) tall. As a contrast to *G. officinalis* there is an attractive white variety called 'Candida'.

Plant galegas in autumn or early spring and allow sufficient room for them to develop. They will thrive in a sunny location and are generally free of pests and diseases.

Propagate by division in autumn or spring.

Take care

Insert a few peasticks in the ground early in the year, so that the plants can grow through to hide them. 238▶

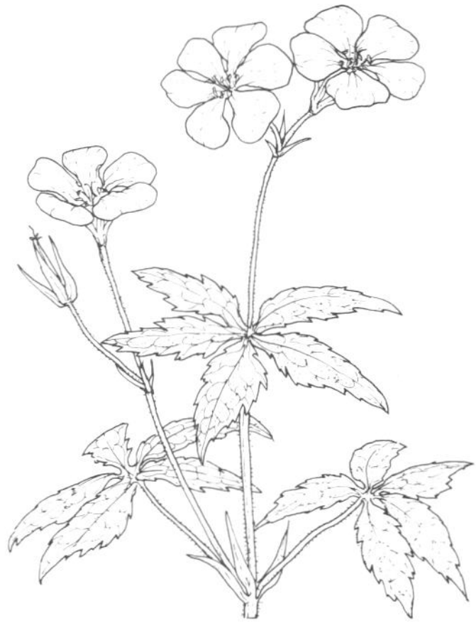

Gentiana asclepiadea

(Willow gentian)

- **Shade or partial shade**
- **Rich moist soil**
- **Early autumn flowering**

This European charmer has graceful stems and willow-like foliage. The arching stems, 45-60cm (18-24in) long, carry glossy leaves, and pairs of azure-blue to almost bluish purple tubular flowers, singly in the axils of the leaves, in the early autumn.

To get the best from this plant it needs dappled sunlight in woodland, but if a really moist soil is available, even a chalk soil, the willow gentian can be grown. It does need a rich moist soil containing a good proportion of humus, such as rotted leaf-mould. Once established, plants will seed themselves and become naturalized.

Propagate by seed, sown as soon as it is ripe: the seedlings will take at least two years before they flower. Alternatively, propagate by division in spring.

Take care

Plant firmly, and in spring. 240▸

Geranium endressii

'A.T. Johnson'

- **Sunny position**
- **Fertile well-drained soil**
- **Early to mid-summer flowering**

This is a superb plant for covering the soil with a mass of glossy, mid-green, deeply-lobed leaves and 2.5cm (1in) wide, silver-pink flowers. It has the ability to create mounds of colour at the sides of paths or at the fronts of borders through most of the summer. It grows 30cm (1ft) high, with a 38-45cm (15-18in) spread.

There are several other superb varieties, such as 'Wargrave Pink', which grows to about 30cm (1ft), with clear pink flowers. 'Rose Clair' is slightly higher, at 45cm (1½ft), bearing salmon-pink flowers with beautiful purple veining.

Set the plants in position in autumn or spring – the latter in cold areas. They need little attention and are remarkably resilient.

Propagate by lifting and dividing congested clumps in autumn or spring. The best parts to reuse are those from around the edges of the old clump.

Take care

Ensure that the plant has well-drained soil.

Geranium pratense 'Johnson's Blue'

(Cranesbill)

- **Sunny location**
- **Fertile well-drained soil**
- **Early summer flowering**

This geranium is a most captivating plant. Above the elegantly divided foliage that covers the ground, the wiry 30-35cm (12-14in) stems carry lavender-blue cup-shaped flowers with darker veins. The flowers are produced profusely from early summer onwards; each measures up to 5cm (2in) across. A second flush of these lovely blooms can be encouraged by cutting down old flowering stems. A border of this plant in front of a hedge of white floribunda roses looks really stunning.

Provided this and other geraniums have good ordinary soil and good drainage, very little else is needed. Plant in autumn or spring, five plants to the square metre/square yard. Protect young plants from the ravages of slugs. Propagate by division of roots in autumn or spring.

Take care

Give geraniums good drainage.

Geranium macrorrhizum

(Large-rooted cranesbill)

- **Sun or partial shade**
- **Well-drained soil**
- **Late spring flowering**

This woody rooted cranesbill is a perfect ground cover. The palmate five-lobed leaves, over 5cm (2in) across, are light green or dull purplish-crimson, clammy to the touch and aromatic; in mild winters they are semi-evergreen. When growing in well-drained poorish soil, the leaves become very decorative in autumn. The leaves are a light purplish crimson underneath. The flowers are white stained with pink, and appear freely in early summer. The flower stalks are 30cm (12in) high, with several blooms on each stalk. It is from the aromatic foliage of this geranium that the oil of geranium in commerce is extracted.

Propagate by seed sown in early spring under glass, or by division in autumn or spring.

Take care

Clear the ground of any pernicious weeds, for once geraniums are established, it is difficult to weed them effectively.

Geum chiloense

(Scarlet avens)

- **Sun or partial shade**
- **Good fertile soil**
- **Early summer flowering**

This is probably the parent of the double red 60cm (24in) variety 'Mrs Bradshaw' and the double yellow 'Lady Stratheden' of similar height. These two geums have wild-rose-like flowers on fairly stiff wiry stems, and dull green strawberry-like foliage. The quite separate hybrid 'Borisii' is not so tall, having 30cm (12in) stems, and above clumps of rich green roundish hairy foliage are single rich orange-red flowers. *G. rivale* 'Leonard's Variety' is also only 30cm (12in) high, and bears on hairy red stems its drooping sprays of deep red calyces surrounded by pinkish brown petals.

These hardy perennials will grow in almost any soil, provided it is not too dry. Propagate them by division, but cut away any pieces that are woody.

Take care

Divide geums every two or three years, and replant only the youngest pieces.

Gillenia trifoliata

(Indian physic)

- **Sun or partial shade**
- **Moist fertile soil**
- **Summer flowering**

Among hardy herbaceous perennials this one must rate quite high, for it is an elegant plant. The 60cm (24in) or more slender reddish stems carry bunches of small white strap-like flowers forming an open star; the flowers are not unlike those of a spiraea or astilbe. The white flowers are backed with wine-red calyces, and the latter remain on the flower stalks long after the white petals have dropped. The flower sprays are suitable for cutting and can be easily arranged. It is quite hardy and easily grown; it prefers a moist peaty soil and partial shade, but will tolerate sun.

Propagate by division in either early autumn or early spring. Seed can be used, but it is a very slow process.

Take care

Plant in spring, as they need enrichment in the soil; well-rotted garden compost is satisfactory.

Gypsophila paniculata

(Chalk plant; Baby's breath)

- **Sunny location**
- **Well-drained, preferably limy soil**
- **Summer flowering**

The flowerheads of *G. paniculata* are a mass of small feathery flowers, white or pink. The glaucous leaves are also small. The branching flowerheads are used by flower arrangers to add a light cloud effect to arrangements of other flowers. *G. paniculata* 'Bristol Fairy' is the best double form, 90cm (3ft) tall.

As gypsophilas are deep-rooted, the ground must be well prepared before planting; it should be bastard trenched, ie double dug. To do this, take out the first spit or spade's depth of soil, break up the bottom spit with a fork and fill up with the next top spit. Also enrich the ground with well-rotted farmyard manure or well-rotted garden compost. Provided they have full sun and well-drained soil, gypsophilas should be no trouble.

Propagate 'Bristol Fairy' by taking softwood cuttings in late spring to very early summer.

Take care

Insert a few peasticks for support. 241▶

Helenium autumnale 'Wyndley'

(Sneezeweed)

- **Full sun**
- **Prefers heavy soil**
- **Late summer flowering**

The North American helenium is one of those perennials with daisy-like flowers, chiefly in late summer and autumn. The variety 'Wyndley' has large coppery yellow, flecked flowers, 60cm (24in) tall and fairly rigid. Like all helenium flowers, they have a prominent central disc. The 50cm (20in) 'Crimson Beauty' has brownish-red flowers.

Although these plants will grow in almost any type of soil, they prefer a fairly stiff loam. The fact that their stems are fairly rigid can make plants flop over in heavy rain so push in a few peasticks around the plant at an early stage; then the stems will grow through and cover the sticks. Their pleasing branching stems make heleniums useful as cut flowers, and they last well in water.

Propagate heleniums by softwood cuttings in early summer, or by division in autumn or spring.

Take care

Keep moist during hot dry spells in summer. 240-241▶

Helianthus decapetalus

(Sunflower)

- **Full sun**
- **Well-drained stiff loam**
- **Late summer flowering**

H. decapetalus, from North America, is probably the species from which we have gained several good hybrid sunflowers. All have coarse, rough foliage. The double-flowered 'Loddon Gold' bears rich yellow blossoms on 150cm (5ft) stout stems. The semi-double 'Triomphe de Gand' has large golden-yellow flowers with ball-shaped centres, 120-150cm (4-5ft) high. Another rich yellow variety, 'Morning Sun', has anemone-centred flowers, and this erect and sturdy grower is 120cm (4ft) tall. The graceful, lemon-yellow single-flowered *H. orgyalis* 'Lemon Queen', reaches 150cm (5ft) high.

Grow these plants in a well-drained loamy soil and ensure that they receive plenty of sunshine.

Propagate perennial sunflowers by division in autumn or spring. Divide and replant every three or four years.

Take care

Do not let perennial sunflowers starve; they are greedy feeders. 242▶

Helichrysum angustifolium

(Curry plant)

- **Full sun**
- **Poor well-drained soil**
- **Mid-summer flowering**

This is a hardy evergreen perennial or sub-shrub, but it usually appears in authoritative works on border perennials. The common name curry plant is most descriptive; on a hot day, if it is brushed against, a wonderful aroma of curry fills the air. In spring the foliage is bright silver. This tarnishes as the summer advances, but even in winter it is still a delightful plant, reaching a height of 35cm (14in) and a width of 45-60cm (18-24in).

In midsummer it bears flat terminal crowded heads of small yellow flowers. To prevent it flowering use the shears on the plant as soon as the flower shoots push their way through the silver foliage. This will encourage a fresh batch of young foliage. Propagate in summer by taking half-ripe cuttings with a heel.

Take care

Avoid cold wet soil.

Heliopsis scabra

(Orange sunflower)

- **Full sun**
- **Good fertile soil**
- **Late summer flowering**

Despite its common name, this hardy herbaceous perennial is not a sunflower. It is a stiff upright plant and normally no staking is required. It has strong woody branching stems, and the spear-shaped foliage is dark green; stems and foliage are very rough. Several single or double, yellow or orange flowers, 7.5-10cm (3-4in) across, are carried on each stem. They are very resistant to drought, but will grow in moist or rich soil and become very lush. They flower from midsummer to early autumn.

The perfectly shaped 'Light of Loddon' has anemone centred bright yellow flowers 105-120cm (42-48in) high; it is free flowering and if cut in the evening blooms will last well in water.

Propagate by division, or by basal cuttings in spring.

Take care

Cut down flowering stems to ground level in late autumn.

Helleborus corsicus

(Corsican hellebore)

- **Partial shade or some sun**
- **Well-drained fertile retentive soil**
- **Winter and spring flowering**

This native of the Balearic Islands, Corsica and Sardinia is an outstanding and lovely hellebore, which has been known as *H. argutifolius* and *H. lividus corsicus*. Here is a perennial worth waiting for after it is first planted. It is a bushy plant, 60cm (24in) tall, with tripartite leathery glaucous leaves with spined tipped edges. Above its handsome foliage are clusters of pale green cup-like drooping flowers, with centres of pale green stamens; the flowers last for many months, from winter well into spring, but unfortunately, they do not make successful cut flowers.

Propagate by seeds sown in spring or autumn, or by division of the roots in spring.

Take care

Remove old stems as they die, cutting each stem back almost to ground level. 243▶

Helleborus orientalis

(Lenten rose)

- **Partial or full shade**
- **Not fussy over soil, provided it is not bog**
- **Winter and spring flowering**

This native of Greece and Asia Minor has produced a large number of good garden varieties in many colours, including pure white, cream, green, pink, rose, purple, plum-colour or almost black, and prettily spotted maroon or crimson. They are 45cm (18in) tall, and have large open cup-like flowers. The foliage is evergreen, and once established they act as very useful ground cover.

The variety 'Kochii' is a little shorter than *H. orientalis* and blooms a little earlier, having large coarsely toothed foliage; in bud it is yellowish green, later opening its nodding primrose-yellow flowers.

Provided the soil is fertile and the plants are growing in partial or full shade, they should give pleasure for many years. Propagate by seeds sown in spring or autumn, or by division of the roots in spring.

Take care

These hellebores do not make good cut flowers.

Hemerocallis

(Day lily)

- **Sun or partial shade**
- **Any soil but avoid dry ones**
- **Summer flowering**

The day lilies are hardy, the large clumps producing an abundance of bright green arching foliage and a display of scented lily-like flowers over a long period. The flowers of early day lilies lasted for only one day, but modern varieties last two or sometimes three days. The lily-like flowers are carried at the top of stout 90cm (36in) stems.

Three modern varieties are: 'Pink Damask', with pretty pink flowers, 75cm (30in); 'Nashville', large, creamy yellow with streaked orange-red throat markings, 90cm (36in); and the glowing bright red 'Stafford', 75cm (30in).

Propagate day lilies by division in spring. Plants can be left undisturbed for many years; lifting and divide them only when clumps become overcrowded.

Take care

In very hot dry weather, give plants a thorough soaking. 242-243▶

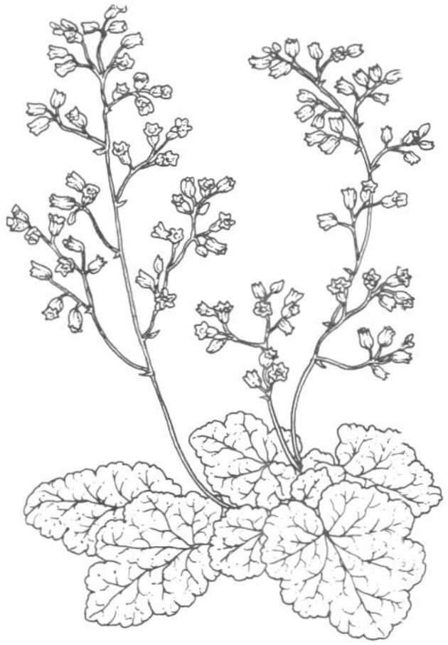

Hesperis matronalis

(Sweet rocket; Dame's violet)

- **Sun or partial shade**
- **Well-drained moist soil**
- **Summer flowering**

The single hesperis is not a long-lived perennial, and it is therefore necessary to raise fresh stock. Single seed is available in shades of lilac, purple and white. As a cut flower choose the double white. The singles are easier to grow than the doubles. Plants are 105-120cm (42-48in) in height. The cross-shaped blooms develop on spikes up to 45cm (18in) long in midsummer and are sweetly fragrant during the evening. Once they have finished flowering it is best to cut the flower spikes down.

To be successful, hesperis needs good drainage and a moist sandy loam. Propagate the singles as biennials, sowing seed out of doors in spring; the double varieties can be divided in spring, or cuttings of basal growth taken in midsummer or early autumn. However, singles will seed themselves about, once established.

Take care

Seek doubles, but at least try the singles.

Heuchera sanguinea 'Red Spangles'

(Coral bells)

- **Sun or partial shade**
- **Well-drained fertile soil**
- **Early summer flowering**

Heucheras have evergreen heart-shaped leaves and their pretty tiny bell-shaped flowers hang down from slender wiry stems. The foliage comes in various shades of green, sometimes with zonal markings marbled like pelargoniums. 'Red Spangles' has crimson-scarlet flowers and is 50cm (20in) tall.

Heucheras make bold clumps as much as 30cm (12in) wide, but deteriorate if not divided and transplanted every few years; throw out woody pieces, keeping only the young vigorous ones. Work in well-rotted garden compost or well-rotted manure before planting. Heucheras prefer a light, well-drained fertile soil, but dislike cold clay, wet or very acid soils. Given good feeding, flowers will be produced from spring to early autumn. Propagate by division in late summer or early autumn.

Take care

Keep moist during hot dry days in the summer. 244▶

Hosta fortunei 'Albopicta'

(Plaintain lily)

- **Dense or partial shade**
- **Rich fertile soil**
- **Summer flowering**

The hosta, previously called *Funkia*, has become popular since the second World War, because the large and beautiful foliage is used for flower arrangements. 'Albopicta' has large scrolled leaves exquisitely marbled in shades of golden yellow and edged with pale green. As summer advances the golden yellow becomes primrose coloured and the pale green turns darker. Above this magnificent foliage are 45-60cm (18-24in) stems carrying bell-like flowers. A recent introduction is *H. rectifolia* 'Tall Boy' with green leaves and violet-mauve flowers.

Provided hostas are not allowed to become dry during summer, and are well laced with rotted farmyard manure or well-rotted garden compost, the gardener will be rewarded handsomely for his labours. Propagate these plants by division in spring.

Take care

Do not let hostas become dry 245▸

Iberis sempervirens

(Perennial candytuft)

- **Full sun**
- **Any soil**
- **Spring and early summer flowering**

This is half-shrubby, but a superb plant to grow either as an edging to a path or as a bold clump. Even when it is not in flower, its bright to darkish evergreen foliage looks attractive. In spring and early summer the mounds of evergreen foliage are covered with dense wreaths of snowy white flowers; the hummocks of green are about 30cm (12in) high.

Provided they grow in good soil, plants will flourish for a number of years. After flowering has finished, cut off the old flowerheads; this encourages new growth and keeps the tufts neat and tidy. Propagate by taking half-ripe cuttings during early summer, inserting them in a cold frame or under a large glass jar.

Take care

The ground where iberis is to be planted should be free of perennial weeds, as it is difficult to eradicate such weeds once the plants are established. 246▸

Incarvillea mairei

(Trumpet flower)

- **Full sun**
- **Light fertile soil**
- **Early summer flowering**

This handsome perennial, sometimes known as *Incarvillea grandiflora brevipes*, is 30cm (12in) tall, with deeply pinnate foliage. The flowers, held well above the foliage, are a rich pinkish purple, with a yellow throat.

The fleshy root needs to be planted 7.5cm (3in) deep. Incarvilleas need a light sandy well-drained soil in full sun. As this species is only 30cm (12in) high, it needs to be planted near the front of the border. In gardens where frost could cause damage, put a covering of bracken or a pane of glass over these plants during the winter.

Propagate by sowing seed as soon as possible after ripening. Although division can be done in spring, the crowns may be too tough to split easily and so seed is perhaps a wiser way to increase them.

Take care

As slugs are attracted by incarvilleas, put down slug pellets. 247▸

Inula helenium

(Elecampane)

- **Sunny location**
- **Moist soil**
- **Summer flowering**

The inulas are showy sun-loving hardy herbaceous perennials with brightly coloured daisy-like flowers. Although they can be grown in the herbaceous border they are really more at home in a moist situation, beside the margin of a pond or stream.

I. helenium reaches a height of 90-120cm (3-4ft), it has bright yellow flowers similar to small sunflowers, and large leaves. A real beauty (when it can be obtained) is *I. royleana*, with yellow rayed flowers, 10-12cm (4-4.75in) wide, on 60cm (24in) stems; this species must have moisture. Two other varieties are *I. ensifolia* 'Compacta', with golden rayed flowers on stems 25cm (10in) high and *I. ensifolia* 'Golden Beauty', which is 60cm (24in) high, and has golden flowers that last for weeks.

Propagate inulas by seed sown in spring, or by division in autumn or spring.

Take care

Do not let the soil dry out. 246▸

Iris florentina

(Oris root)

- **Sunny position**
- **Well-drained soil**
- **Early summer flowering**
- **Early summer flowering**

This intermediate bearded iris is often classified as *Iris germinica florentina,* a form of the London Flag or Purple Flag. However, whatever the name botanists now call it, few people would not say it is a beautiful iris. It grows 45-75cm (1½-2½ft) high, with upright, sword-like leaves. During early summer it develops 7.5-15cm (3-5in) wide, white flowers.

The roots have the odour of violets and have been used in the perfumery trade. This is probably the reason that they are said to have been chewed by those with offensive breath!

Plant the roots shallowly in late summer, and keep the soil moist until they are established. If they are subsequently lifted by frost, cover them with light, friable soil. Do not press down the roots as they may break. Propagate by dividing congested clumps in late summer.

Take care

When planting, trim the leaves by half to prevent roots being rocked by strong winds.

Iris unguicularis

(Algerian iris)

- **Full sun**
- **Well-drained soil**
- **Winter flowering**

This winter-flowering iris, known for many years as *I. stylosa,* is more correctly *I. unguicularis.* The lilac-lavender flowers are prettily veined, on 30cm (12in) stems, and the abundant glossy foliage is 60cm (24in) long.

This plant needs a poor dry soil. Choose a sunny well-drained site and plant in autumn – not in spring, as often advised – because the roots need plenty of moisture, which they can get from autumn and winter rains. In autumn cut back the foliage on established plants to about 15-20cm (6-8in) from ground level. Pull out dead leaves, using leather gloves, as the leaves can cut. Give a spring dressing of the following, all by weight: 4 parts superphosphate of lime; 2 parts sulphate of ammonia; and 1 part sulphate of potash. Apply this at 85gm (3oz) per square metre/yard. In early summer apply 57gm (2oz) of magnesium sulphate per square metre/yard. Propagate by division in autumn.

Take care

Choose a hot sunny site.

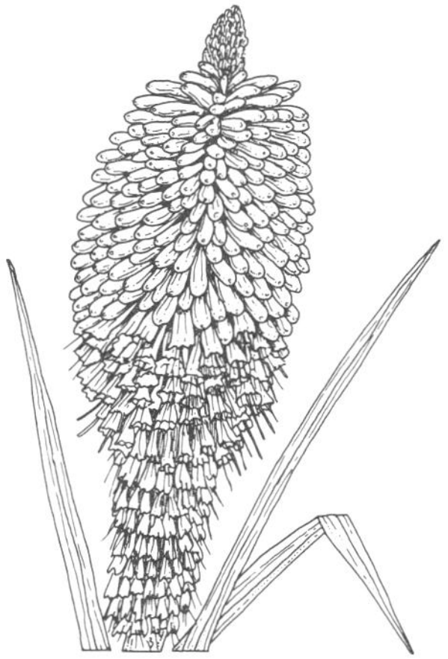

Kniphofia

((Red hot poker; Torch lily)

- **Full sun**
- **Rich retentive well-drained soil**
- **Early summer to autumn flowering**

Kniphofias will come through most winters. To ensure their safety, tie the foliage into a kind of wigwam in winter, to keep the crowns dry. The flowers are carried on stout stems; one beauty is 'Little Maid' about 60cm (24in) tall, with attractive creamy flower spikes. *K. galpinii* 'Bressingham Seedlings' produce graceful spikes in orange shades, 45-90cm (18-36in) tall, through summer to autumn. *Kniphofia praecox* has brilliant scarlet flowers on 180-210cm (6-7ft) stems.

Kniphofias require a fairly rich soil with ample humus such as rotted manure or garden compost. After clumps have been divided, do not allow them to dry out before or after planting. A mulch of rotted manure or garden compost should be given annually in spring; otherwise they can remain untouched for several years. Plant them three or four to the square metre/yard. Propagate by division in spring.

Take care

Protect crowns during winter.

Lathyrus latifolius

(Perennial pea)

- **Sunny location**
- **Good fertile soil**
- **Summer to early autumn flowering**

Large sheets of bloom of the perennial pea can often be seen along railway embankments. It is excellent for planting beside a wire fence, on trellis or supported by a few peasticks. The flowers are rosy pink to reddish purple; there is also a good white form, 'White Pearl , and 'Rose queen' has pink flowers with a white eye. Sprays of flowers arranged in pairs are carried on the end of stiff stems. Perennial peas bloom throughout the summer until early autumn; the flowers are useful for cutting for indoor decoration. Plants are 150-165cm (5-5.5ft) in height.

These plants enjoy a well-enriched soil. Propagate them by seed sown in spring, or by division of the roots in spring. Be sure to protect seedlings and young plants from slugs, which can cause serious damage to stems and leaves.

Take care

Insert peasticks early in the season.

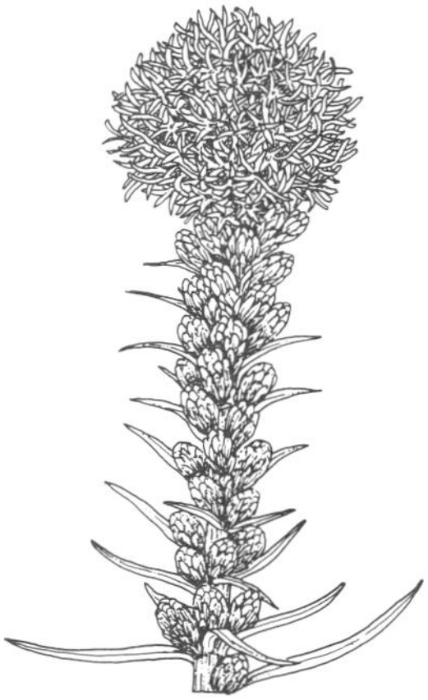

Lavatera olbia 'Rosea'

(Tree mallow)

- **Full sun**
- **Well-drained fertile soil**
- **Summer and autumn flowering**

The tree mallow is a woody plant and correctly classed as a sub-shrub, but it is usually grown in hardy flower borders. It grows especially well in coastal areas where frost is not a problem. Plants reach a height of 150cm (5ft) and as much in width, so they should be placed in a border where they will not overshadow other plants. The large hollyhock-like flowers of a deep old-rose pink are profusely borne on branching woody stems. The vine-like foliage is a dull green.

This species needs a rich well-drained soil. Always have young stock plants. Once frosts are past, cut back all young growth annually to near the base. Propagate by seeds sown in spring under glass, or by half-ripe cuttings in summer.

Take care

Keep plants in good shape by annual pruning. 266▸

Liatris spicata 'Kobold'

(Spike gayfeather)

- **Full sun**
- **Ordinary well-drained soil**
- **Summer flowering**

The flowers of liatris open at the top first, whereas most plants that have spike-like flowers open from the base, and those at the top open last. The small strap-like leaves form a rosette near the ground; the flower stems also have small leaves. The flowerheads are closely packed and look not unlike a paint brush. The variety 'Kobold' has brilliant pinky mauve flowers, 60cm (24in) tall. Also recommended is *L. pycnostachya*, the Kansas feather, with pinky purple crowded flowerheads, 15-20cm (6-8in) long, on rather floppy 120cm (4ft) stems. It makes a fine display in late summer and early autumn. Liatris are useful as cut flowers and ideal for drying for winter flower arrangements.

The species is better in poor soil, and prefers firm ground. Propagate by seed sown in pans in early spring, or by division in late spring.

Take care

Do not grow liatris in rich soil. 267▸

Above: **Kniphofia 'Little Maid'**
This is a particularly attractive variety to grow; its creamy white blooms are 60cm (24in) tall and excellent for cutting. Grow these plants in a well-drained soil. 263◆

Left: **Kniphofia praecox**
This is a tall variety – up to 210cm (7ft) tall – with magnificent spikes of tubular crimson flowers that make a fine display in late summer and early autumn. 263▶

Right: **Liatris spicata 'Kobold'**
The frothy flowers of the liatris have the unusual habit of opening from the top downwards. This lovely variety has pink-purple flower spikes that can be cut for indoors. 264▶

Below: **Lavatera olbia 'Rosea'**
This is a shrubby perennial that grows up to 150cm (5ft) tall with attractive pink flowers in summer and early autumn. Pruning in spring will keep the plant in good shape. 264▶

Left: **Lobelia 'Cherry Ripe'**
This is one of the best of the many hybrids of Lobelia cardinalis *and* L. fulgens. *Its bright cerise-scarlet flowers appear in late summer on stems up to 120cm (4ft) tall.* 283▸

Right: **Liriope muscari**
A hardy evergreen perennial with arching grass-like foliage that forms a neat hummock in the border. In late summer and autumn erect stems of lilac-mauve blooms appear. 282▸

Below: **Lunaria rediviva**
The perennial form of the popular plant 'honesty' bears pretty lilac to lavender flowers in spring and flat papery seedpods that can be used for indoor decoration. 283▸

Above: **Lupinus polyphyllus 'Russell Hybrids'**
The Russel lupins provide a good mixture of colours for the garden on stems up to 120cm (4ft) tall. Grow these on acid or neutral soil. 284▶

Left: **Lychnis coronaria 'Abbotswood Rose'**
Branching sprays of rose-crimson flowers adorn this plant during the summer. The silvery foliage is an excellent foil to the blooms. 284▶

Right: **Lysimachia punctata**
In moist situations this vigorous perennial will provide a long display of bright yellow flowers during the summer. It grows 90cm (3ft) tall and will tolerate semi-shade 285▶

Above: **Macleaya microcarpa**
An imposing perennial that should be given ample room to spread. The branching plumes of buff or flesh tinted flowers reach a height of about 240cm (8ft) in late summer. 286▸

Left: **Lythrum salicaria 'Firecandle'**
Handsome spikes of deep rosy red flowers adorn this dependable plant in late summer. It will thrive in moist retentive garden soils. 285▸

Right: **Malva moschata 'Alba'**
This pure white form of the musk mallow is a lovely perennial with flowering stems 75cm (30in) tall. It is short lived but self-sown seedlings are always plentiful. 286▸

Above: **Monarda didyma 'Cambridge Scarlet'**
Both the foliage and flowers of this summer-blooming perennial are fragrant. Grow it in sun or partial shade and be sure to keep it moist. 288▸

Left: **Melianthus major**
An evergreen sub-shrub grown for its large, deeply serrated leaves. It is best suited to mild areas and must have protection against frost to survive. Ideal for poor soils. 287▸

Below: **Myrrhis odorata**
This delightful herb has aromatic fern-like foliage and creamy white flowers in early summer. As autumn approaches the leaves turn red. A useful, dependable plant. 289▸

Left: **Nepeta × faassenii**
Excellent for edging and beneath roses, this charming plant has aromatic foliage irresistible to cats and lovely sprays of lavender-blue flowers for many weeks during the summer. Grow in full sun. 289▸

Right: **Onopordon acanthium**
Although strictly a biennial, this impressive thistle is usually grown in the herbaceous border. Stems can be 210cm (7ft) tall, with grey foliage and attractive purple flowers. 290▸

Below: **Oenothera missouriensis**
A superb ground cover plant with dark green narrow leaves that hug the ground and red-spotted bright yellow flowers borne on red stems 23cm (9in) high. It must have a freely draining soil to succeed. 290▸

Above: **Paeonia officinalis 'Rubra Plena'**
This old favourite among peonies has large heads of double crimson blooms on stems up to 60cm (24in) tall. Best left undisturbed. 292◆

Above: **Osmunda regalis**
A noble fern that thrives in partial shade and moist conditions. Lovely yellow and russet autumn hues. 291▸

Below: **Papaver orientale**
Unsurpassed for their large colourful blooms, the Oriental poppies thrive in a well-drained sunny location. 292▸

Above: **Phlomis russeliana**
Whorls of rich yellow hooded flowers are borne on stately spikes up to 90cm (3ft) above the heart-shaped basal leaves. The seedheads are ideal for indoor decoration. 294▸

Libertia formosa

- **Full sun**
- **Well-drained fertile soil**
- **Summer flowering**

This evergreen perennial from Chile is not hardy in the coldest areas, but in a sunny sheltered situation it will come through most winters. It has attractive dark green sword-shaped foliage forming dense tufts from which arise 75cm (30in) stems. During summer it bears sprays of ivory-white saucer-shaped flowers, enhanced by a boss of yellow stamens. In autumn orange-brown seedheads are produced. *L. grandiflora* and *L. ixioides* also have foliage that turns an attractive orange-brown in winter.

Libertias must have well-drained soil; add moistened peat, leaf-mould and sharp sand when preparing the ground for planting in spring. Propagate by seeds sown as soon as ripe, in late summer to early autumn, or by dividing the fibrous roots in spring.

Take care
Provide good drainage, and ample moisture in summer.

Ligularia 'Gregynog Gold'

(Golden groundsel)

- **Full sun or partial shade**
- **Moist conditions**
- **Late summer to early autumn flowering**

This handsome perennial is a hybrid between *L. dentata* and *L. vietchianus.* Above its large handsome heart-shaped leaves, up to 30cm (12in) across, arise stout stems 60-90cm (24-36in) high, on top of which are erect spike-like flower sprays up to 7.5cm (3in) across. The magnificent blooms are a beautiful orange-gold with bronzy maroon discs and prettily freckled with yellow. The flowers look partiuclarly attractive when seen in autumn sunshine. This fine hybrid, known for almost 50 years, deserves to be more popular.

This ligularia does best when growing in moist soil, in a boggy situation beside a pool or stream. Propagate it by division in spring.

Take care
Keep plants moist.

Linaria purpurea

(Purple toadflax)

- **Full sun or partial shade**
- **Well-drained soil**
- **All summer flowering**

This S European perennial may become a weed, but when properly understood it will be appreciated for its long season of flowering. Its small antirrhinum-like flowers are carried on thin wiry stems, and it has greyish narrow leaves. The blooms are a lovely purple-blue with a beard of white. An excellent garden variety is 'Canon Went', with bright pink flowers that have an orange spot on the lip of each flower. Both *L. purpurea* and the variety 'Canon Went' grow 60-90cm (24-36in) tall. No staking is necessary. Plants will thrive in a well-drained soil and will tolerate sun or semi-shade.

Linaria seeds itself freely, yet it is easy enough to cull unwanted plants. Propagate by sowing seeds in late spring out of doors, or by division in spring.

Take care

Keep this species within bounds.

Liriope muscari

(Turf lily)

- **Sunny location**
- **Fertile soil with moderate drainage**
- **Late summer or autumn flowering**

As its name suggests, *L. muscari* is not unlike an outsize grape hyacinth. Its foliage arches over, forming a neat hummock from which the 23-30cm (9-12in) stems arise, bearing lilac-mauve flowers crowded together and looking rather like a bottle brush. I have seen liriope used most effectively as an edging to a border of shrubs; it is always useful to have a few of these evergreen plants in a border during winter.

Having grown liriope in a clay soil with a pH 6.5 reading, which is an almost neutral soil, I am now growing it in a light acid soil with a pH of 5 to 5.5, and the plant in the light acid soil looks very much happier. In my experience, this tuberous-rooted plant does better in full sun than in shade or partial shade. Propagate it by division in spring.

Take care

Give these plants a sunny spot in which to grow. 269▸

Lobelia cardinalis

(Cardinal flower)

- **Sunny location**
- **Rich fertile moist soil**
- **Late summer flowering**

The cardinal flower is one of the most handsome herbaceous perennials. Above a rosette of green leaves, which also cover the stem, are brilliant scarlet blooms. The stems are 90cm (3ft) high.

Planting is best done in spring; initial preparation is essential, and plenty of moistened peat, leaf-mould or well-rotted garden compost should be incorporated. This species likes rich moist soil. If the ground is not forked over or cleaned for the winter, plants will come through unscathed in areas that are more or less frost-free; if doubtful, lift them in autumn and store in a dry frost-proof shed, covering the roots with peat or leaf-mould. Propagate by division in spring when the plants can be taken out of store.

Take care

Never let the roots suffer from drought during the growing season, and ensure that they have adequate moisture. 268▶

Lunaria rediviva

(Perennial honesty)

- **Partial shade**
- **Good light soil**
- **Spring flowering**

The biennial honesty, *L. annua* is well-known and loved by flower arrangers because of its white papery seedpods, which can be used in winter flower arrangements. Seeds sown in spring will flower the following spring (ie 12 months later).

L. rediviva has four-petalled lavender to lilac fragrant flowers, which are borne on 60-90cm (2-3ft) stems above a rosette of foliage at the base. This pretty perennial honesty blooms in spring. It is to be hoped that one day it will become more popular; but it has been around since 1596. It has white papery seedpods but they are a different shape, lanceolate and tapering gradually at each end, and 8cm (3.2in) long. The leaves are larger and less serrated than those of the biennial honesty.

L. rediviva does best in half shade in good light soil. Plant it in spring, about 30cm (12in) apart. Propagate by division in spring.

Take care

Buy the perennial honesty. 269▶

Lupinus polyphyllus

(Lupin)

- **Sun or light shade**
- **Light sandy loam**
- **Early summer flowering**

Lupins enjoy sun and well-drained soil; avoid lime, and heavy wet clay soils. Before planting, see that the ground is well cultivated, with an ample supply of well-rotted farmyard manure or garden compost. On well-drained soils, plant in autumn; otherwise, wait until spring.

With established plants restrict the number of flower spikes to between five and seven, when stems are about 30cm (12in) high. Give a light spraying of plain water in the evening during dry springs. As a rule staking is not necessary. Named varieties can be obtained, but the Russell hybrids have a good mixture of colours, and vary in height from 90 to 120cm (3-4ft). In very windy gardens sow the dwarf 'Lulu' lupin; this is only 60cm (24in) tall.

Propagate by basal cuttings in early spring, when 7.5-10cm (3-4in) long; insert in a cold frame.

Take care

Remove faded flowerheads to prevent them forming seeds, which will take strength from the plant. 270▶

Lychnis coronaria 'Abbotswood Rose'

(Rose campion; Dusty miller)

- **Full sun**
- **Fertile well-drained soil**
- **Summer flowering**

This species is popularly known as dusty miller because of its soft furry foliage; its leaves are coated with fine silver hairs, which almost cover the entire plant. The leaves are borne in pairs from a basal clump up the 60cm (2ft) stems on which the branching sprays of dianthus-like brilliant rose-crimson flowers of 'Abbotswood Rose' are carried (some call the flowers rose pink). It is a lovely plant, and a clump of five plants to a square metre/square yard will add charm and colour to any perennial border.

There is also a variety 'Alba', which has white flowers; apart from the colour, it is similar to the variety 'Abbotswood Rose'.

Propagate by division in autumn, but if the soil is cold and wet, leave it until spring.

Take care

These plants need a fertile soil. 270▶

Lysimachia punctata

(Loosestrife)

- **Sun or semi-shade**
- **Ordinary garden soil, preferably damp**
- **Summer flowering**

This loosestrife is quite unconnected with the purple loosestrife, *Lythrum salicaria*, but one must admit that both plants have tall and dominating flower spikes. *Lysimachia punctata* has straight stems bearing whorls of bright yellow five-petalled flowers; each stem is about 90cm (3ft) high, and it blooms for at least two months during the summer.

Plants can be invasive so it should not be grown near other perennials that could become swamped. It grows in full sun or partial shade, but although it will grow in dryish soil, it is happier where it has damp or moist soil conditions. Grouped in clumps of four plants it can give brightness to an otherwise dull corner in a garden.

Propagate by division in spring or autumn. Cuttings of young shoots can be taken in spring and inserted in sandy soil under glass. Seeds can be sown in pots or boxes in spring in a cold frame.

Take care

Do not allow these plants to crowd out weaker perennials. 271▸

Lythrum salicaria 'Firecandle'

(Purple loosestrife)

- **Sunny location**
- **Fertile moist soil**
- **Late summer flowering**

The purple loosestrife is one of the most handsome perennials during summer, when it is found growing wild on river banks, ditches and marshes. This indicates the type of soil and situation in which to grow garden varieties. But although they prefer to grow in damp boggy soil, they succeed quite happily in any moist border. The showy spikes of flowers are borne on 120cm (4ft) wiry stems. They are hardy, long lived and long flowering. The variety 'Firecandle' has deep rosy red flowers borne in the leaf axils on spikes 90cm (3ft) tall. A dwarfer one is the clear pink 'Robert', only 75cm (30in) tall. Plant bold clumps of five in the middle of the border.

Another lythrum is *L. virgatum* 'The Rocket', which is 90cm (3ft) high with erect spikes of rose-red flowers borne in the leaf axils.

Propagate by root cuttings in spring; as the rootstock is very woody division is difficult.

Take care

The ground should be moist. 272▸

Macleaya cordata

(Plume poppy)

- **Sun or light shade**
- **Rich fertile soil**
- **Late summer flowering**

This impressive and dramatic-looking hardy herbaceous perennial may grow to 210cm (7ft) tall. The rough fig-like palm-shaped sculptured glaucous foliage, silver beneath, forms a dominating clump from which stiff tall stems arise displaying the small panicles of yellow plume-like fluffy flowers without petals. It is a plant for an isolated bed or at the back of a large border, for if too near the front it will obscure any plants behind it. For a slightly earlier display of flesh-tinted buff flowers grow the similar *M. microcarpa*.

The plume poppy has wandering roots but this should not put anyone off; if you can find a suitable part of the border or garden, it is well worth growing. Plant in spring. Propagate by half-ripe cuttings in early summer, by suckers or root cuttings in autumn, or by division in spring.

Take care

Choose the ideal position for this dramatic plant. 273▸

Malva moschata

(Musk mallow)

- **Sunny location**
- **Fertile and moderately well-drained soil**
- **Summer flowering**

This European perennial is not long lived and in very hot weather plants have been exhausted through heat. The musk mallow has mid-green finely cut buttercup-like foliage; when bruised, this gives off a pleasant musk-like odour, which is more pronounced in spring. The soft pink hollyhock-like flowers are carried in terminal and axillary clusters on stems about 60-75cm (24-30in) high. The pure white *M. m. alba* is equally charming.

Provided the soil is moderately well drained, malvas are easily cultivated. It pays to gather seed, so that young stock is always available to replace exhausted plants. Propagate by sowing seed in spring in sandy soil; bury them 12mm (0.5in) deep, and place in a cold frame. Keep moist during very hot dry weather.

Take care

Stake if plants are in a position where they may be windswept. 273▸

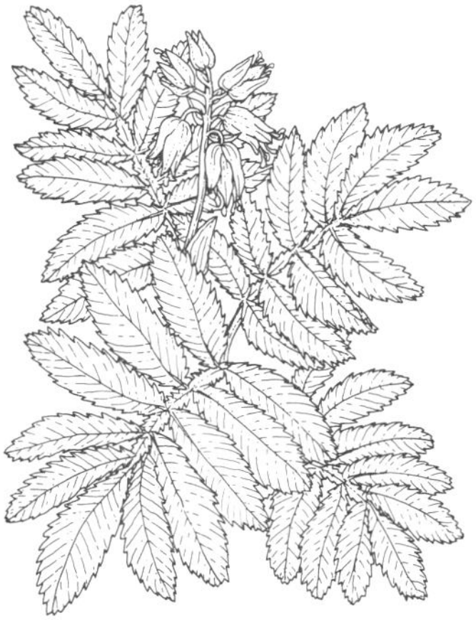

Melianthus major

(Great Cape honeyflower)
- **Sunny location**
- **Poor soil**
- **Late summer flowering**

Even though this is not a hardy herbaceous perennial but a semi-woody evergreen sub-shrub, its distinct handsome alternate pinnate leaves make it a worthwhile border plant for gardeners near the sea or in mild localities. The large glaucous-green leaves, deeply serrated, have an unpleasant smell when bruised. Where the leaves join the main or side stems are glaucous-green stipules not unlike an individual globe artichoke scale. The 'flowers' are in fact reddish-brown bracts. Plants can grow as high as 210cm (7ft). This species is certainly one of the most handsome foliage plants in my garden.

Propagate by softwood cuttings taken in spring and rooted in a mist propagator, or sow seed under glass in late summer.

Take care

Protect plants against frosts during winter and early spring. 274▶

Mertensia virginica

(Virginian cowslip)
- **Partial shade**
- **Well-drained fertile soil**
- **Spring flowering**

This spring-flowering perennial is a hardy plant that thrives in good ordinary well-drained fertile soil in a partially shady position. The tubular flowers of cool purplish-blue cascade in bunches among soft blue-grey leaves, from the top of 45cm (18in) stiff stems.

During midsummer little can be seen of this mertensia, as the stems and foliage die down; for this reason it is ideal for a woodland site where it can rest until it comes into leaf and flower the following spring. The spot where it has flowered should be marked. The tuberous roots are only just under the surface, so care should be taken not to damage them or plants will die.

Propagate them by seed sown as soon as ripe, or by division of the tuberous black roots in early autumn.

Take care

Give this species partial shade, and do not disturb it unnecessarily.

Monarda didyma 'Cambridge Scarlet'

(Bergamot; Bee balm)

- **Full sun or partial shade**
- **Moist fertile soil**
- **Summer flowering**

This fragrant perennial has nettle-like foliage. It has erect square stems, and at each joint there are pairs of pointed leaves. At its base the leaves form a dense clump. Above the several whorls of leaves, at the top of each stem, there is a crowded head of hooked scarlet flowers, also in the axil of the pairs of opposite leaves; the flowers have a pleasant fragrance.

The mat-like roots are not as a rule invasive though in well-cultivated soil they can widen, but plants are easily divided in spring, and this should be done about every third year. Today, apart from the old favourite 'Cambridge Scarlet', there are several other good varieties: 'Croftway Pink' has clear pink flowers; 'Prairie Night' is a rich violet-purple; 'Snow Maiden' is white. All are 90cm (36in) tall, except the bright ruby 'Adam', a showy variety, which is 100cm (39in).

Propagate all varieties by division in spring.

Take care

Do not let the soil dry out. 275▸

Morina longifolia

(Himalayan whorlflower)

- **Full sun**
- **Well-drained sandy loam**
- **Summer flowering**

This handsome Nepalese evergreen perennial is not seen as often as it should be. It has large slightly spiny thistle-like foliage, and leaves at the base of the stems are fragrant. The hooded tubular flowers are pink, red, yellow or white, and carried on long spikes arranged in whorls around the stout 75-90cm (30-36in) stems. Flowering starts at midsummer and goes on into early autumn.

This species needs good fertile soil, well drained but retentive, as the plant must have a certain amount of moisture. It will not tolerate cold wet soil in winter, however. Shelter should be given against spring frosts.

Propagate by sowing seed out of doors, in a well-prepared bed of rich porous soil. Apart from thinning, do not disturb the plants. The dried stems can be used by flower arrangers for winter decoration.

Take care

Protect against frost in spring.

Myrrhis odorata

(Sweet Cicely)

- **Sun or partial shade**
- **Any good soil**
- **Early summer flowering**

This old-fashioned herb is delightful in a flower border. The 75cm (30in) bush has mid-green fern-like foliage, similar in flavour to sweet liquorice. In autumn it turns a charming burnished red, which gives another interest in a flower border. The heads of small creamy white flowers brighten other plants around it; the flowers are followed by large narrow seedheads, first green, then black. This is indeed a pretty and useful hardy perennial.

The leaves of this plant have been used in salads and the seeds were at one time used to scent and polish furniture and oak floors. The plant is also attractive to bees.

As self-sown seedlings appear regularly, this species is not easily lost among other plants. The best planting time is autumn. Propagate by seed sown in early autumn or spring, or by division of the carrot-like roots in autumn or spring.

Take care

Remove unwanted self-sown seedlings. 275▸

Nepeta × faassenii

(Catmint)

- **Sunny location**
- **Well-drained soil**
- **Early and late summer flowering**

Cats love nestling in a clump of catmint. To prevent them sitting on your plants, insert a few prickly twigs; any cat will then soon realize that it is no place for a nap. This plant was for many years called *N. mussinii*. The soft lavender-blue flowers have a long season of bloom from early summer to late summer, and often into early autumn. The flower sprays are on thin wiry grey small-leaved stems, 45cm (18in) tall. Nepeta makes a good edging and is especially useful in a bed of roses.

It is not a particularly long-lived plant, especially on cold clay soils; it needs a light, well-drained soil. On heavy soil, work in sand or gritty material around the plants. Cut the plants back after the first flush of flowers; this encourages more flowers, and provides material to use as cuttings. Plant in spring, where an individual clump is required, putting four plants to a square metre/square yard. Propagate by softwood cuttings in early to mid-summer.

Take care

Avoid winter wetness. 276▸

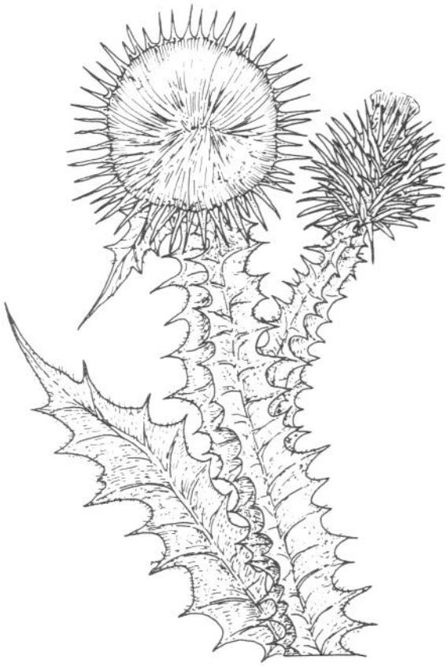

Oenothera missouriensis

(Ozark sundrops)

- **Sunny location**
- **Well-drained soil**
- **Summer and autumn flowering**

This lovely perennial ground-hugging plant, which belongs to the evening primrose family, is a native of the southern United States of America, hence its rather unusual common name, Ozark sundrops. The dark green narrow leaves lie prostrate on the ground, and above them are produced canary-yellow flowers about 7.5cm (3in) across, on 23cm (9in) reddish stems, in succession for many weeks during the summer. The flowers, which open in the evening and last for several days, are followed by equally large seedpods. Often the buds are spotted with red.

This is a superb plant for the front of a border, but to succeed it must have a well-drained soil. It is ideal for the rock garden but allow it sufficient space, because it can spread up to 60cm (24in). Propagate this species by seed in spring.

Take care

Choose a well-drained soil. 276▶

Onopordon acanthium

(Scotch thistle; Cotton thistle)

- **Sunny location**
- **Ordinary soil**
- **Summer flowering**

As the Scotch thistle is a hardy biennial, and usually found growing in a hardy flower border, it is right to include this handsome tall grey-leaved and grey-stemmed architectural plant. Both leaves and stems are covered with woolly cobweb-like hairs, and on top of its 150-210cm (5-7ft) high stems are carried purplish mauve to pale lilac thistle-like flowers.

These plants seed themselves freely, and once a plant is established the owner will never be without a plant or two in the border. Nevertheless, it is easy to eradicate any unwanted seedlings, or to give them away to friends. Position these plants at the back of the border and allow at least 90cm (3ft) for them to spread. Propagate by seeds sown out of doors in well-drained soil in spring.

Take care

Stake plants, if necessary, in windswept borders. 277▶

Ophiopogon planiscapus nigrescens

(Black-leaved lily turf)
- **Sun or partial shade**
- **Sandy well-drained soil**
- **Summer flowering**

This black-stemmed and black-leaved plant is probably of Japanese origin. The ophiopogons are related to the liriopes. It is grown for its foliage; and as it creeps slowly, it is a useful ground cover plant. The pale purple to white flowers appear in summer, and are followed by black berries. The flower stems are 15cm (6in) tall. Ophiopogon needs to be planted in front of light-leaved plants, so that the dark foliage will be more outstanding.

Not having grown this plant, I cannot write from experience, but it is said that it will grow in dry sand or (according to some authorities) in clay soils; nevertheless, my advice is to keep to well-drained soils. To be successful with ophiopogon it should be planted where it can have the benefit of shelter from a fence, wall or hedge.

Propagate this species by division in spring.

Take care
Position at the front of a border.

Osmunda regalis

(Royal fern)
- **Partial shade**
- **Moist peaty soil**
- **Early spring flowering**

This deciduous hardy perennial needs a moist peaty soil, and is best grown in half shady places, though it can be grown in full sunshine if its roots are constantly in moist soil and the plant is sheltered from cold winds. The sterile delicate pale green fronds are 120-150cm (4-5ft) long, whereas the fertile portion may be as much as 150-180cm (5-6ft). As the elegant fronds emerge from their solid clumps in spring, they look like shepherds' crooks, and in autumn they take on bright yellow and russet hues. Flower arrangers gather them, because they press and dry well.

This fern can be propagated by sowing the spores during summer, but for the amateur, propagation by division in spring is more satisfactory; the mass of black roots needs to be sliced through with a sharp spade.

Take care
The royal fern must always have its roots in moist soil. 279▸

Paeonia officinalis 'Rubra Plena'

(Old double crimson)

- **Full sun or partial shade**
- **Rich well-drained soil**
- **Late spring flowering**

'Rubra Plena' is a beautiful old peony, introduced in the sixteenth century. The large heads of double blooms are held above deeply cut foliage on stems 45-60cm (18-24in) high. Apart from 'Rubra Plena' there is the white 'Alba Plena' and the larger flowered light pink 'Rosea Superba Plena'. All three of these peonies are well worthwhile.

Peonies will grow in full sun or partial shade. Choose a site where the plants will not catch the early morning sun, as frosts can injure flower buds. When preparing the site incorporate well-rotted farmyard manure, garden compost or leaf-mould. An application of liquid manure as the buds start to swell will be beneficial. A feed of bonemeal and a mulch of humus should be worked into the soil every autumn.

Propagate them by division in early autumn, or in early spring before new growth starts.

Take care

See that plants have enough moisture in dry weather. 278▶

Papaver orientale

(Oriental poppy)

- **Full sun**
- **Well-drained soil**
- **Early summer flowering**

The Oriental poppies have the largest and most flamboyant flowers of all hardy herbaceous perennials. They vary in height from 30 to 100cm (12-39in). The first colour break came in 1906 with the salmon-pink 'Mrs Perry', 90cm (36in) tall. To name only a few other varieties: 'Fireball', with double orange-scarlet flowers, 30cm (12in) tall; 'Marcus Perry', orange-scarlet, 75cm (30in); 'Perry's White', 90cm (36in); 'Curlilocks', ruffled vermilion petals, 75cm (30in); 'Black and White', white flowers with a black centre zone, 100cm (39in); and a recently introduced seedling, 'Cedric's Pink', with large greyish pink curled petals with a purple-black blotch at the base.

These poppies will thrive in full sunshine in a well-drained soil. Propagate by root cuttings in autumn or winter.

Take care

Do not let these poppies swamp less vigorous plants. 279▶

Penstemon glaber

(Blue penstemon)

- **Sunny location**
- **Well-drained fertile soil**
- **Summer flowering**

Having grown it recently for several years I can thoroughly recommend the blue penstemon. It has dark green glabrous strap-like leaves, 5-8cm (2-3.2in) long. Plants form thick clumps and send up flower spikes 45-60cm (18-24in) high, bearing bright blue to purple, broad-mouthed tubular flowers.

No staking is needed. Cut off the first flush of flowers and a second crop will soon take its place. One can justly call this a trouble-free hardy perennial. Even in winter the dark green foliage makes a pleasant mound in the border.

Would-be planters of this outstanding plant may need to search for it and visit several garden centres, but do persevere; it is well worth the trouble!

Propagate by taking half-ripe cuttings just below a node in late summer and inserting them in a cold frame or propagator.

Take care

Remove the first flush of flowers.

Perovskia atriplicifolia

(Russian sage)

- **Sunny location**
- **Well-drained soil**
- **Late summer flowering**

This is a sub-shrubby deciduous hardy perennial, though more often than not it is grown in herbaceous borders rather than among shrubs. The whole plant has a sage-like odour, especially when it is brushed against. It has coarsely toothed grey-green foliage, and a profusion of soft lavender-blue flowers during late summer. A variety worth growing is 'Blue Spire', with deeply cut leaves and larger lavender-blue flowers.

This species needs to be grown in full sun, in well-drained loamy soil. An annual pruning should be given just as buds start to break in spring; cut all shoots hard back to the base, leaving perhaps two buds to develop on each. The plant will then send up new shoots 90-150cm (3-5ft) high. Propagate by cuttings of half-ripe shoots in midsummer, inserted in sandy cuttings mixture in a propagating frame.

Take care

Give this plant plenty of room.

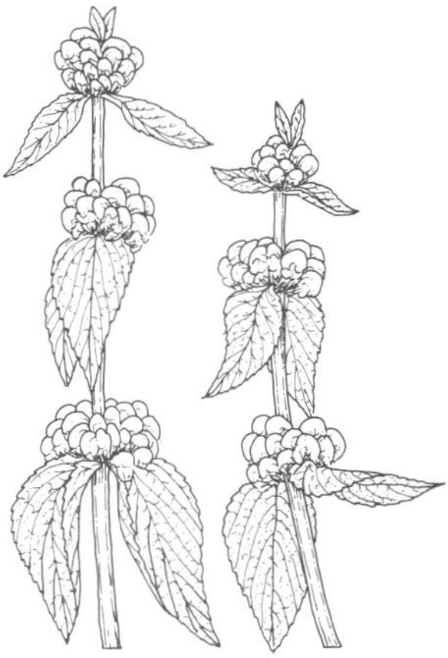

'Vintage Wine'

Phlomis russeliana

(Jerusalem sage)

- **Sunny location**
- **Well-drained ordinary soil**
- **Summer flowering**

The Jerusalem sage is also found under other specific names: one is *P. samia,* which is frequently used by nurserymen, and another is *P. viscosa*. But, for our purposes, *P. russeliana* is its name. This handsome weed-smothering plant, or ground coverer, has large rough puckered heart-shaped felty sage-like grey-green leaves. Among the foliage stout flower spikes, 75-90cm (30-36in) high, carry whorls of soft rich yellow hooded flowers in early to mid-summer. The attractive seedheads can be used successfully in flower arrangements, whether green or dried. Phlomis will grow in ordinary garden soil in an open, sunny location.

Propagation of this plant is by seed, cuttings or division, in spring or autumn.

Take care

Plant phlomis against a suitable background, such as a red-leaved Japanese maple. 280▸

Phlox paniculata

(Phlox)

- **Sun or light shade**
- **Light fertile soil**
- **Summer to late summer flowering**

Although many amateurs favour common or popular names, as far as I know phlox are simply phlox. The species *P. paniculata* is the ancestor from which all the colourful named varieties have sprung. Their brilliant and quiet colours and wonderful musky fragrance can never be forgotten. The times of day to enjoy phlox to perfection are daybreak or sunset.

Many older varieties are no longer easily available, but there is still a good selection of varieties and colours. The purple-red 'Vintage Wine' has huge trusses, on 75cm (30in) stems; 'Windsor' is clear carmine with a magenta eye, 110cm (44in) tall; the strong 'Border Gem' is cyclamen-purple with a peony-purple eye, 90cm (36in) tall; 'Mother of Pearl' has pretty pink trusses and is 75cm (30in) tall; the dark-foliaged blue 'Hampton Court' is of similar height; and for a variegated variety there is 'Harlequin' bearing rich purple flowers, 90cm (36in) tall. 'Prince of Orange' is a stunning orange-salmon colour, also 90cm (36in) high; the pure white Fujuyana

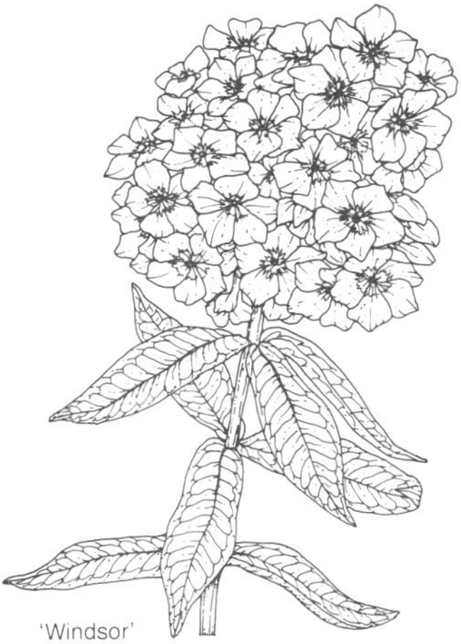

'Windsor'

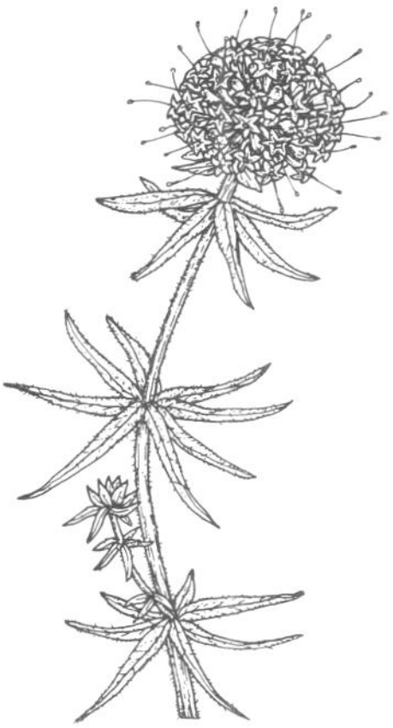

from the USA has magnificent cylindrical trusses and is 75cm (30in) tall; two 90cm (36in) beauties are the pale lilac 'Prospero' and the deep crimson 'Red Indian'. For a pure white choose 'White Admiral', 75cm (30in) high; and for a real dwarf the 45cm (18in) 'Pinafore Pink', a charming variety with large trusses of bright pink.

Phlox are best in a light soil with a good supply of humus, well-rotted farmyard manure or well-rotted garden compost, and – in very dry weather – sufficient moisture for their needs. What they do not like is chalk or clay soils. Gritty or gravelly soils are satisfactory, provided there is enough humus and the soil is never allowed to dry out.

Only one pest attacks phlox, that is the eelworm. To avoid it, propagate plants from root cuttings, in autumn or winter.

Take care

Do not let phlox dry out in very hot dry summers 297▸

Phuopsis stylosa

(Crosswort; Foetid crucinella)

- **Full sun**
- **Sandy or chalky soils**
- **Summer flowering**

This little mat-forming gem from Persia and the Caucasus was for many years known as *Crucinella stylosa,* but now its genus is *Phuopsis.* It gets its common name foetid crucinella because of its fox-like musky odour, though personally I have never found it objectionable. The 25-30cm (10-12in) stems are clothed in small slender foliage; on these stems are borne pretty little tubular flowers that form a crosswise design, hence its other common name, crosswort. The bright rosy-pink flower clusters make an attractive display throughout the summer. It is a first-rate plant for the front of the border or as an edging plant to a path. There are other coloured forms with scarlet and purple flowers.

Propagate crosswort by sowing seeds in the open ground in spring, or by division of the roots in early autumn.

Take care

This plant likes plenty of sun. 298▸

Phygelius capensis

(Cape figwort)

- **Sunny location**
- **Well-drained fertile soil**
- **Summer and autumn flowering**

In its native habitat this South African beauty is a shrub, but it is equally happy growing as a hardy perennial. The flowers are not unlike those of a fuchsia. The opposite leaves are attached to stiff stalks which carry the candelabra-like tubular flowers, which are crimson-scarlet with yellow throats. The flowers hang down like trumpets, enhanced by the protruding stamens.

Where plants are growing in maritime districts or are trained to a sunny sheltered wall, they can be grown as shrubby perennials. Plants trained against a wall can reach 180cm (6ft) or more. In more exposed gardens, plants may become badly damaged by frost; when this happens cut them back to encourage new growth and healthy shoots in spring.

Propagate this species by half-ripe cuttings in summer or by seed sown in gentle heat in spring.

Take care

Protect plants in unsheltered areas or frost pockets.

Physostegia virginiana

(Obedient plant)

- **Sun or partial shade**
- **Any good fertile soil**
- **Late summer flowering**

This hardy herbaceous perennial is well named the obedient plant, because its flowers have hinged stalks and can be moved from side to side and remain as altered on their square stems. The long narrow dark green glossy leaves are toothed and grow in four columns; the dull rose-pink flowers terminate the square tapering spikes, 45-105cm (18-42in) tall. They bloom from summer to autumn, until the frosts spoil their beauty. Physostegia has vigorous stoloniferous rootstocks that spread underground.

There are several good varieties: 'Rose Bouquet' has pinkish mauve trumpet flowers; 'Summer Snow', pure white, is about 75cm (30in) high; and 'Vivid' bears rose-crimson flowers on stalks 30-45cm (12-18in) tall.

Propagate by division in spring, or by root cuttings in winter.

Take care

Give this plant sufficient moisture during dry summer weather. 299▸

Above: **Phlox paniculata 'Vintage Wine'**
This purple-red variety has fairly compact flower trusses that are freely produced on stems 75cm (30in) tall. Beautifully fragrant. 294▸

Above: **Physostegia virginiana 'Rose Bouquet'**
Spires of tubular pink-mauve flowers up to 60cm (24in) long are carried above the large, coarsely toothed leaves during late summer. 296▸

Right:
Physostegia virginiana 'Alba'
One of the attractive white varieties of this hardy perennial. Grow these plants in fertile soil and water well during hot dry weather. 296▸

Left: **Phuopsis stylosa**
A mat-forming plant ideal for the front of the border or for edging a path. It thrives in bright sun, producing its delightful rosy pink flowers throughout the summer. 295▸

Left: **Polemonium foliosissimum**
Rich lavender-blue flowers on stems 75cm (30in) high grace this hardy perennial during the summer. Grow in deep fertile soil. 313▶

Below left:
Polygonatum × hybridum
This adaptable hardy perennial bears arching stems of sweetly scented bell-shaped flowers in spring. 313▶

Right: **Polygonum amplexicaule 'Atrosanguineum'**
Crimson flower spikes are freely produced by this vigorous perennial from summer into the autumn. 314▶

Below: **Potentilla atrosanguinea 'Gibson's Scarlet'**
Stunning single red flowers are produced on 30cm (12in) stems above strawberry-like foliage. 314▶

Above: **Rudbeckia fulgida 'Goldsturm'**
These bright flowers are superb for cutting from late summer. 317▸

Below: **Ranunculus aconitifolius 'Flore Pleno'**
Attractive double button-like blooms on stems up to 60cm (24in) tall. 316▸

Above: **Salvia superba**
This is a hardy and adaptable plant that will thrive in any soil. It produces abundant spikes of lovely violet-purple flowers over a long period from early summer. 317▸

Above:
Sedum spectabile 'Autumn Joy'
Easy to grow and spectacular in bloom, the ice plants are to be recommended. This variety has rose flowers changing to salmon pink. 320▸

Left: **Saponaria officinalis**
This is the original single-flowered form, with fragrant rose-pink blooms carried on erect stems up to 90cm (3ft) in height. Double-flowered forms are also available. 318▸

Right: **Sedum spectabile 'Carmen'**
This beautiful border plant is well able to brighten the garden in late summer and autumn. The flowers slowly assume richer colours. 320▸

Above: **Sidalcea malvaeflora**
Lovely flowers in varying shades of pink are borne on stems up to 135cm (4.5ft) tall depending on variety. Cut down after flowering to encourage lateral shoots to develop. 321▸

Left: **Sisyrinchium striatum 'Variegatum'**
Slender stems with yellowish-white flowers grow to a height of about 90cm (3ft) in summer; the foliage remains through the winter. 321▸

Right: **Solidago 'Goldenmosa'**
This superb variety grows to about 75cm (30in) in height with lovely frothy yellow flowers in late summer. It will grow vigorously in any good soil, in sun or partial shade. 322▸

Above:
Thalictrum speciosissimum
This plant is much prized by flower arrangers, particularly for its long-lasting glaucous foliage. Yellow flowers are borne in summer. 323▶

Above: **Stachys olympica 'Silver Carpet'**
An excellent ground cover plant that does not produce flowers. 323▸

Below:
Tradescantia virginiana 'Isis'
The striking purple-blue flowers are long-lasting in summer. 324▸

Left: **Trollius × cultorum 'Fire Globe'**
This is a plant that will thrive in a moist situation, next to a pond for example. It flowers in the spring at a height of 75cm (30in). 324▶

Right: **Veronica spicata**
Plant these at the front of a sunny border and they will provide a colourful display in summer. This is the original species; the varieties offer other colours. 325▶

Below: **Tropaeolum speciosum**
Bright scarlet flowers appear on the twining stems of this attractive plant throughout the summer months. An excellent subject for growing over an evergreen shrub. 325▶

Above: **Zantedeschia aethiopica 'Crowborough'**
This fairly hardy arum lily will grow in an open border or in moist ground next to a pond or stream. White spathes appear in summer. 325▸

Polemonium foliosissimum

(Jacob's ladder)

- **Sunny location**
- **Deep rich fertile soil**
- **Early to late summer flowering**

The polemonium has been known since Roman times, and its generic name is after King Polemon of Pontus. Most gardeners know *P. caeruleum*, which seeds so freely. *P. foliosissimum* (a mouthful of a name) is the longest-lived of these pretty hardy perennials. It has pinnate foliage bearing clusters of pretty five-petalled lavender-blue flowers, enriched by orange-yellow stamens, and massed together on upright 75cm (30in) stems from early to late summer. There is also an earlier flowering variety called 'Sapphire', which has light blue flowers on 45cm (18in) stems and is equally long lived.

Grow polemoniums in a rich fertile soil for a fine display of flowers. Propagate these plants by division in early autumn or spring.

Take care

Buy plants of the long-lived *P. foliosissimum*, as it hardly ever produces seed. 300▸

Polygonatum × hybridum

(Solomon's seal)

- **Sun or shade**
- **Fertile retentive soil**
- **Late spring flowering**

This is a most graceful hardy herbaceous perennial, with fat rhizomatous roots that need to be grown in groups. The 90cm (36in) stems, which have a pretty arching habit, are clothed with stalkless alternate broad ribbed lance-like fresh green foliage. On the opposite side to each leaf, pretty little greenish white fragrant bells hang down from horizontal arching stems. Gather stems when the flowers are in bud and take them indoors; when they open they will fill a room with their scent.

The rhizomes should be just below soil level. Solomon's seal is happiest in a retentive soil well endowed with leaf-mould or well-rotted garden compost. Propagate it by division in autumn or spring.

Foliage can be skeletonized by the Solomon's seal sawfly. At the first sign of a holed leaf, spray or dust at once with malathion.

Take care

Keep moist when growing in full sun during very dry weather. 300▸

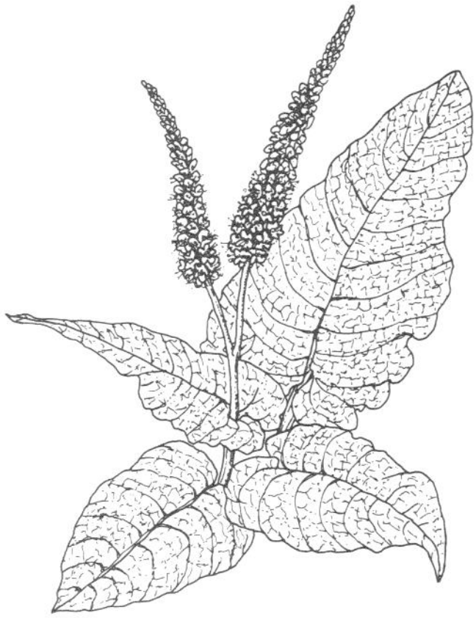

Polygonum amplexicaule 'Atrosanguineum'

(Mountain fleece-flower)

- **Sun or partial shade**
- **Good moist soil**
- **Summer to autumn flowering**

A polygonum that is a must for any flower border. This attractive hardy herbaceous perennial has a woody rootstock, from which arise erect 105-120cm (42-48in) flower stems clothed in heart-shaped foliage, with an abundance of tiny rosy crimson flowerings forming spikes up to 15cm (6in) long at the end of each shoot during summer and into autumn. Plants form a large leafy clump, increasing in size every year. Grow at least four plants together, as one on its own does not make much of a show. Provide rich moist soil for best results and grow in sun or semi-shade.

Propagate this polygonum by seed sown in a cool house or frame in spring, or by division of roots in spring, which is the more satisfactory method.

Take care

Keep moist; if they become dry at the roots, flowering will be poor. 301▶

Potentilla atrosanguinea

(Himalayan cinquefoil)

- **Full sun**
- **Fertile well-drained soil**
- **Early and late summer flowering**

The best-known variety of *P. atrosanguinea* is 'Gibson's Scarlet', which has brilliant single red flowers on 30cm (12in) stems from mid- to late summer. Larger-flowered varieties include the double orange-flame 'William Rollison', also the double mahogany-coloured 'Monsieur Rouillard'; and the grey-foliaged 'Gloire de Nancy', which has semi-double orange-crimson flowers almost 5cm (2in) across, on 45cm (18in) branching stems; all bloom from early to late summer.

The potentillas, with strawberry-like foliage, are best in full sun, but can tolerate partial shade. They enjoy good well-drained soil, but if the soil is too rich it results in extra lush foliage at the expense of the flowers. Avoid growing potentillas in moist or stagnant ground in winter.

Propagate by division in spring or autumn.

Take care

These potentillas sprawl, so give ample space; plant in groups. 301▶

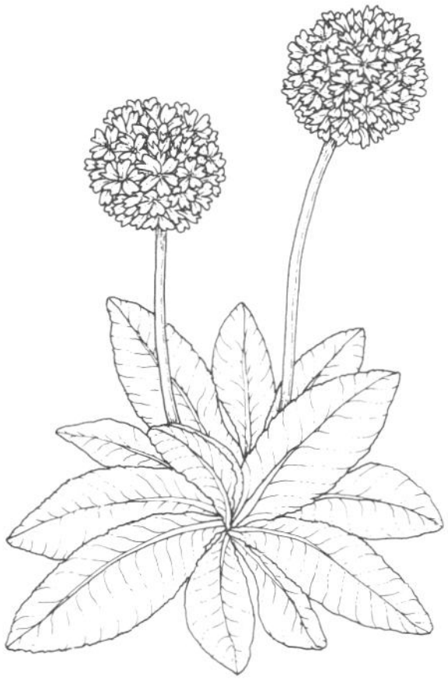

Primula denticulata

(Drumstick primrose)

- **Partial shade**
- **Cool rich retentive soil**
- **Spring flowering**

In spring this Himalayan primula produces dense globular heads of fragrant flowers of pale lavender, mauve, lilac, lilac-purple, rich carmine or deepest purple, on stout olive-green stalks about 30cm (12in) high. There is also an attractive white form, *P. denticulata alba*. The erect stalks are lightly covered with a powdered meal, as is the pale green foliage, which forms large tufts at the base of each plant.

Although this perennial is perfectly hardy, early sharp frosts can sometimes slightly damage the foliage; if a sheltered place can be found, damage is less likely to happen. The drumstick primroses, when grown in a sunny border, need moisture throughout the summer, or a deep moist rich soil. Propagate them from seeds sown as soon as ripe in summer in a shady spot. To keep forms true to colour, increase by root cuttings in winter.

Take care

Choose a semi-shady position.

Pulmonaria officinalis

(Lungwort; Soldiers and sailors)

- **Full or partial shade**
- **Any good fertile soil**
- **Spring flowering**

This early flowering perennial is so called because its spotted leaves are said to resemble (and were once thought to cure) diseased lungs. The flowers of *P. officinalis*, carried on 25cm (10in) stems, are bright pink when first open, turning later to a purplish-blue; the large leaves are spotted with white. *P. saccharata* has longer and narrower leaves, almost grey and moderately spotted, and its pink and blue tubular flowers are carried on 30cm (12in) stems. *P. officinalis* and *P. saccharata* are more or less evergreen, but one that almost dies down in late autumn and winter is *P. angustifolia* 'Munstead Blue' or 'Munstead Variety'; the 15cm (6in) stems emerge with clusters of pretty pinkish purple buds in late winter, and the blue tubular flowers appear in early spring.

Divide plants in autumn or spring.

Take care

Do not plant pulmonarias too near to trees when in full shade; the tree roots can rob the soil of moisture.

Pyrethrum roseum
(Chrysanthemum coccineum)
(Pyrethrum)
- **Sunny location**
- **Good fertile soil**
- **Early summer flowering**

Many fine varieties of pyrethrums have been introduced and named, both single and double forms. 'Eileen May Robinson' a large single pale rose-pink variety, has erect stout stems that are 80cm (32in) tall, with flowers 7.5cm (3in) across. Pyrethrum 'Brenda' is also single, with Tyrian purple flowers 9.5cm (3.75in) across on erect 90cm (3ft) stems. For a double, choose the large-flowered pink 'Progression', 90cm (3ft) tall, or the pure white double 'Aphrodite', of perfect shape, 60-70cm (24-28in) high. All these varieties are excellent as cut flowers.

Propagate pyrethrums by division in early autumn or early spring, doing this every second year. They will thrive in a fertile well-drained soil in an open, sunny position.

Take care
Support with twiggy peasticks, from early in the season.

Ranunculus aconitifolius 'Flore Pleno'
(Fair maids of France)
- **Sun or partial shade**
- **Well-drained soil**
- **Late spring flowering**

The common name conjures up in one's mind that here is a plant which must be delicately lovely and it is. The double-flowered 'Flore Pleno' has dark green deeply cut buttercup-like foliage, and on 60cm (24in) stems it bears delightful sprays of perfect pure white buttons, those elegant 'fair maids of France'. These flowers are about 1.25cm (0.5in) across and appear during the early summer months. It is a fine plant where it will flourish.

Provided this ranunculus has good fertile soil and is not allowed to become dry, the little beauty should be no bother. In a sheltered position it will grow equally well in sunshine or partial shade. Propagate it by division, either in spring or immediately after flowering.

Take care
Do not let the soil dry out during hot dry weather. 302▸

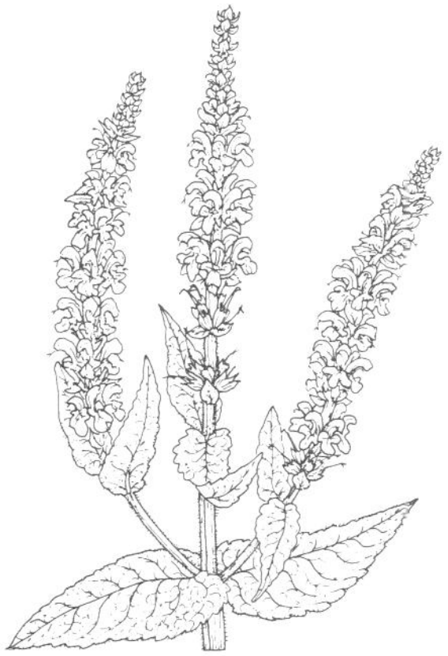

Rudbeckia fulgida

(Black-eyed Susan)

- **Full sun**
- **Moist fertile soil**
- **Late summer and autumn flowering**

This species has also been known as *R. speciosa* and *R. newmanii*; but whatever one calls it, it is one of the most useful border and cut flowers in late summer and autumn. Erect 60cm (24in) stems rise from leafy clumps, displaying several large golden-yellow daisy-like flowers with short blackish-purple central discs or cones, hence the name black-eyed Susan. The narrow leaves are rather rough to handle. Other garden forms of *R. fulgida* are the free-flowering *deamii*, 90cm (36in) tall, and 'Goldsturm', which above its bushy growth has stems 60cm (24in) tall carrying chrome-yellow flowers with dark brown cones. Rudbeckias make good cut flowers and blend very well with *Aster amellus* 'King George'.

Propagate by dividing the plants, in autumn or spring.

Take care

Do not let these dry out during the summer. 302▶

Salvia superba

(Long-branched sage)

- **Sun or partial shade**
- **Any good fertile soil**
- **Early summer to late autumn flowering**

For many years this plant was known as *S. virgata nemerosa*. Each erect 90cm (36in) stem carries branching spikes of violet-purple flowers, with reddish-brown bracts (ie modified leaves). Today there are also dwarf varieties, such as 'Lubeca', with masses of spikes of violet-blue flowers, 75cm (30in) high; and 'East Friesland', violet-purple, and only 45cm (18in) tall. These salvias look well when planted on their own.

Salvias are both fully hardy and perennial, and will grow in any good fertile soil or on chalk, but they dislike dry soils, and should not be allowed to dry out. Some form of support should be given, such as peasticks pushed in around the plants to allow them to grow through. Propagate salvias by division in spring or autumn.

Take care

Support the tall varieties. 303▶

√89

Saponaria officinalis

(Bouncing bet; Soapwort)

- **Sunny location**
- **Well-drained soil**
- **Summer to early autumn flowering**

This plant is called soapwort because a lather can be made from the foliage and used for cleaning old curtains. This wilding can be seen in hedgerows in summer and early autumn. It is a handsome perennial, but its roots can spread beneath the ground. It has panicles of large fragrant rose-pink flowers, 2.5-3cm (1-1.2in) across, carried on terminal loose heads on erect 60-90cm (24-36in) stems. The three-veined leaves are 5-13cm (2-5in) long and 5cm (2in) wide. Double forms are 'Roseo Plena', which is pink, and the white 'Albo Plena'.

All do well in good well-drained soil, but lime or chalk soils should be avoided. Propagate by half-ripe cuttings in summer, or by division in spring.

Take care

These plants can spread and become untidy, but do not exclude them from your garden on this account. 304▸

Saxifraga fortunei

(Fortune's saxifrage)

- **Shady location**
- **Rich fertile soil**
- **Autumn flowering**

Even though it is 120 years since this saxifrage was introduced from China by Robert Fortune, it is still not freely planted. It flowers in autumn, and into early winter in some years. Above the glossy fleshy bright green foliage, which is reddish beneath, are the delicate sprays of pure white, unevenly rayed star-shaped flowers carried on fleshy branching 30-45cm (12-18in) stems. It makes a useful cut flower in autumn.

This species needs a cool shady situation in rich soil, preferably one offering some degree of shelter. *Saxifraga fortunei* 'Wada's Form' has purplish leaves which are crimson beneath.

Propagate by division of the plant, either in spring or immediately after flowering has finished.

Take care

Plant in a cool shaded spot such as the edge of a woodland border.

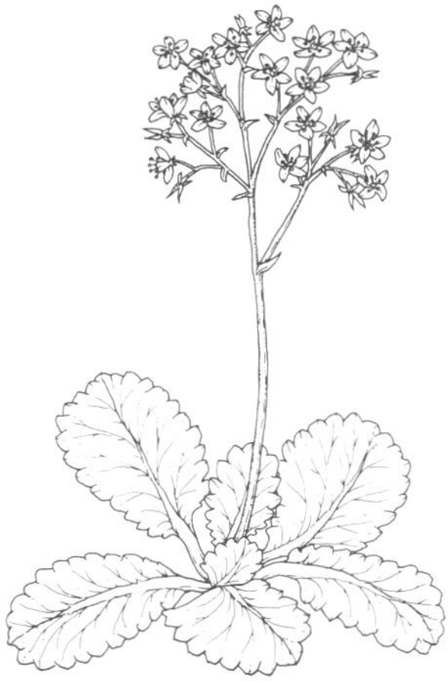

Saxifraga × urbium

(London pride)

- **Full sun or partial shade**
- **Any ordinary soil**
- **Late spring to early summer flowering**

London Pride is one of those charming plants that should be grown in every garden. It is named not after the City of London, but after George London, a partner in an 18th century nursery firm. No doubt if *S. × urbium* (once known as *S. × umbrosa*) was difficult to grow it would be more appreciated. This evergreen perennial has rosettes of oblong slightly fleshy leaves with slender 30cm (12in) needle-like stems that carry sprays of star-shaped flowers, pinkish white and freely dotted with delicate red spots. There are also variegated forms such as *S. × urbium* 'Variegata' and *S. × u.* 'Variegata Aurea' with pretty yellow spots.

The variegated forms must be grown in full sunshine or they will lose their markings. They will need moisture in summer, and an annual mulch of humus. Propagate by division in autumn or spring.

Take care

Plant in partial shade if possible, except variegated forms.

Scrophularia aquatica 'Variegata'

(Variegated figwort)

- **Partial shade**
- **Moist soil**
- **Spring to autumn**

An evergreen hardy perennial grown for its variegated foliage; the leaves are prettily striped, with creamy markings. Its insignificant flowers are best removed, to encourage better-marked and stronger foliage and also to prevent self-sown seedlings popping up where not wanted. The rigid upright 60cm (24in) stems are clothed with opposite leaves from spring to autumn.

It is happiest growing in semi-shade, as in full sun the foliage may become dry and lose some of its lovely markings. The old stems can be cut back in early winter when they look untidy. Propagate by dividing and replanting during the spring. Alternatively, take almost ripe cuttings in the autumn and insert them in sandy soil in a cold frame.

Take care

Provide ample moisture during summer months.

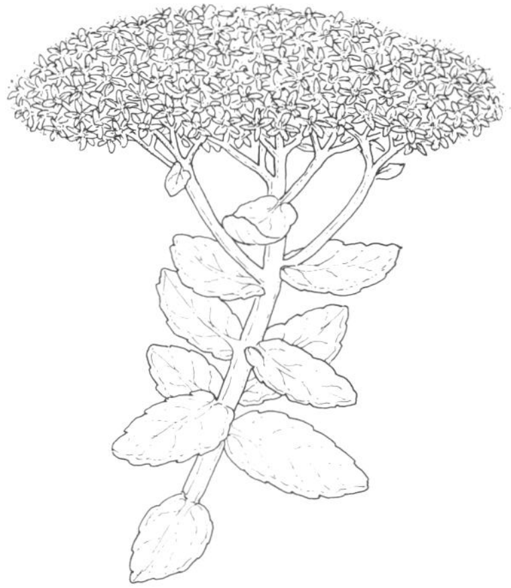

Sedum 'Autumn Joy'

(Ice plant)

- **Full sun**
- **Well-drained soil**
- **Late summer/autumn flowering**

The name 'Ice plant' probably originated because this species has glaucous, glistening foliage. The leaves grow opposite or in threes, and clasp stout, erect, stems 30-60cm which are (1-2ft) high. Above these stems are borne large, slightly-domed, 10-20cm (4-8in) wide, flower heads. The flowers are pink when they first open, slowly changing to deep orange-red and later to orange-brown.

It can be grown with the minimum of attention, needing only well-drained soil and full sun.

Leave the plants undisturbed during winter, as the flower heads look attractive when covered with frost. In spring, remove dead stems. Propagate by lifting and dividing congested plants in autumn or spring. Alternatively, take stem cuttings in mid-summer, inserting them in sandy compost and placing in a cold frame.

Take care

Give this sedum plenty of room – about five plants to a square metre

Sedum spectabile 'Carmen'

(Ice plant)

- **Full sun**
- **Well-drained soil**
- **Late summer/autumn flowering**

Of all the late summer and autumn-flowering border plants it is often the varieties of *Sedum spectabile* that create the greatest impact. 'Carmen', with bright carmine flower heads, is one of the most attractive. Others include 'Brilliant', deep rose; and 'Meteor', deep carmine-red. Some catalogues also include 'Autumn Joy' under this species, but it is now considered to be a cross between *Sedum spectabile* and *Sedum telephium*, another good border plant.

'Carmen', and its related varieties, grows 30-38cm (12-15in) high, with a spread of 45cm (1½ft).

Well-drained soil and full sun are essential. Set the plants in the border during autumn or spring. The latter is the best in extremely cold areas. After flowering, leave the plants as they are until spring, then remove dead stems.

Propagate by division in autumn or spring.

Take care

Although relatively drought resistant, it does appreciate damp soil.

Sidalcea malvaeflora

(Greek mallow; Prairie mallow)

- **Full sun**
- **Good ordinary soil**
- **Summer flowering**

These mallow-flowered beauties are most graceful perennials. The funnel-shaped flowers in varying shades of pink are carried in terminal branching spikes on stout stems 120-135cm (4-4.5ft) high. The leaves are divided like a hand. Varieties to choose from include: 'Croftway Red', a deep rich red, 90cm (3ft) tall; 'Rose Queen', deep rosy pink, 120cm (4ft); 'William Smith', salmon-pink, 105cm (42in); and 'Sussex Beauty', a clear satiny rose-pink, 90cm (3ft).

They may be attacked by hollyhock rust, but there is no need to worry. Propagate them by division, in autumn or spring. Support the taller varieties with canes and cut down plants after flowering to encourage the development of lateral shoots to flower the following season.

Take care

If hollyhock rust attacks, spray the plants with zineb. 306▸

Sisyrinchium striatum

(Satin flower)

- **Sunny location**
- **Well-drained soil**
- **Summer flowering**

This Chilean species is liked by some, but bitterly disliked by others. It is evergreen, and it gives grey-green sword-like foliage throughout the year. In winter its 45-60cm (18-24in) iris-like foliage makes a handsome fan in the borders, and in summer the 75-90cm (30-36in) rigid slender stems are closely packed with many pale yellowish-white flowers; the reverse of the petals is striped with purple. The flowers are carried on about half the total length of the stems. Grow it in a sunny place in well-drained soil with added leaf-mould or peat.

After a year or so plants suddenly die, but it seeds itself freely. It is a good idea to cut down the faded flower stems and any dead leaves during the autumn. Propagate it by division in autumn.

Take care

Transplant self-sown seedlings to form a tidy clump. 306▸

Smilacina racemosa

(False Solomon's seal)
- **Shade**
- **Moist rich soil**
- **Spring flowering**

Smilacina enjoys similar conditions to lily of the valley. Its slender pointed fresh green spear-like leaves are downy beneath, and stick out right and left alternately from the stem. The little trusses of creamy-white scented frothy flowers are also arranged alternately, and are distributed on the underside of the arching 75cm (30in) stems. In autumn the flowers are followed by red berries.

Provided it is given shade and moisture, and no lime, this species will not be any bother. It must not be allowed to dry out during summer; therefore if at all possible choose a site where it will have shade and moisture at its roots. Propagate by division of the rhizomatous roots in autumn. Do not divide in the first year after planting; the roots spread slowly underground and should not be disturbed until the plant is fully established.

Take care

Do not let the roots dry out.

Solidago 'Goldenmosa'

(Aaron's rod; Golden rod)
- **Sun or partial shade**
- **Good ordinary soil**
- **Late summer flowering**

Golden rod, at one time, meant some small yellow one-sided sprays at the top of tall stout hairy stems. Today, there is a much larger selection. The variety 'Goldenmosa' has pretty frothy flowers, miniature heads of the original golden rod, similar to mimosa; the rough hairy flower spikes are 75cm (30in) tall. Two smaller varieties are the 45cm (18in) 'Cloth of Gold', with deep yellow flowers, and 'Golden Thumb', with clear yellow flowers on 30cm (12in) stems, which produces neat little bushes ideal for the front of the border.

These vigorous plants will thrive in any good soil well supplied with nutrients. A sunny location or one in partial shade will suit them equally well. Propagate them all by division in spring.

Take care

Apply humus to taller varieties. 307▸

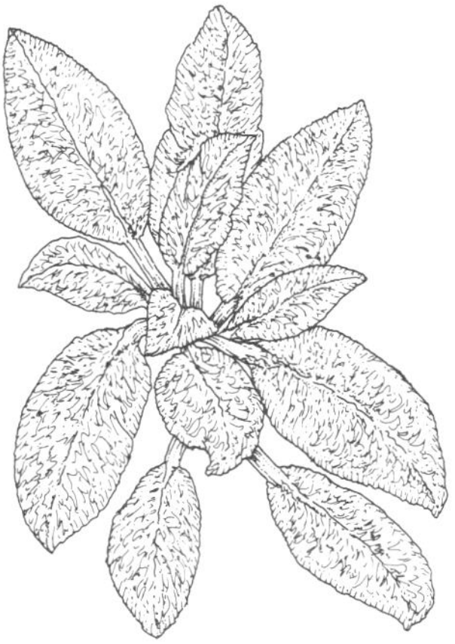

Stachys olympica 'Silver Carpet'

(Lamb's ear; Lamb's tongue)

- **Full sun**
- **Well-drained soil**
- **Non-flowering**

S. olympica (once *S. lanata*) flowers very freely, but 'Silver Carpet' is a non-flowering variety. It makes excellent ground cover and does not have the disadvantage of producing flower stems, which look untidy once the plant has finished flowering. If you have *S. olympica*, cut off the flowerheads as soon as they are over. Both *S. olympica* and 'Silver Carpet' are evergreen.

A quite different stachys is *S. macrantha* (syn. *S. grandiflora*), or big betony. This has heart-shaped hairy white foliage which is a soft green and very wrinkled. The rosy-violet flowers are held on erect stems 30cm (12in) high. Varieties of this include 'Robusta', 60cm (24in) high, with large violet-mauve flowers, and the rosy pink 'Rosea Superba'. They flower during summer.

Propagate stachys by division, in spring or autumn.

Take care

Do not let these encroach on other perennials. 309▸

Thalictrum speciosissimum

(Dusty meadow rue)

- **Sun or light shade**
- **Any good fertile soil**
- **Summer flowering**

Some meadow rues are much sought after by flower arrangers for their foliage. *T. speciosissimum* (also known as *T. flavum glaucum*) has lovely glaucous leaves pinnately cut and divided. The foliage lasts longer than the frothy pale yellow flowers carried on huge panicles at the top of stout 150cm (5ft) stems. This is a back of the border perennial, or on its own if grown for cutting.

T. delavayi (generally known as *T. dipterocarpum*) is another lovely meadow rue, with branching panicles of rosy mauve flowers with bright yellow stamens. It needs rich well-cultivated soil, and staking if planted in a windy site. The form 'Hewitt's Double' has rich mauve flowers.

Propagate by division in spring, and 'Hewitt's Double' by offsets also in spring.

Take care

Obtain the correct plant when buying these thalictrums. 308▸

Tradescantia virginiana 'Isis'

(Spiderwort)

- **Sun or partial shade**
- **Any good fertile soil**
- **Summer and autumn flowering**

The spiderworts are probably better known as house plants, but the hardy herbaceous perennials are much larger. *T. virginiana* has a number of varieties from which to choose. These perennials have smooth almost glossy curving strap-shaped leaves, ending in a cradle-like effect, where a continuous display of three-petalled flowers emerges throughout summer and autumn.

The variety 'Isis' has deep blue flowers and is 45cm (18in) high. The pure white 'Osprey', has three-petalled crested flowers, and another pure white of similar height is 'Innocence'. Two 50cm (20in) varieties are the carmine-purple 'Purewell Giant' and the rich velvety 'Purple Dome'.

Plant them in clumps, not singly; on their own they are not effective, but clumps make a splash of colour. Propagate them by division in spring or autumn.

Take care

Plant near the front of a border. 309▸

Trollius × cultorum

(Globe flower)

- **Sun or dappled shade**
- **Moist soil**
- **Spring flowering**

Globe flowers thrive best in moist soil, and they need plenty of humus such as leaf-mould, well-rotted farmyard manure or good garden compost, especially in drier ground.

The following varieties are worth considering 'Fire Globe' is 75cm (30in) tall, with deeply cut large dark green foliage and rich orange-yellow globular flowers; of similar height, 'Goldquelle' is a vigorous plant with pale buttercup-yellow globular flowers; 'Canary Bird' is not quite 60cm (24in) high, with coarsely divided dark green foliage and large cup-shaped bright golden-yellow flowers. If your soil does not dry out, plant 45cm (18in) 'Earliest of All', with medium-size foliage, and bright golden-yellow, cup-shaped flowers in early spring.

Propagate all varieties by division in spring.

Take care

Keep moist in summer. 310▸

Tropaeolum speciosum

(Scotch flame flower)

- **Shade and sun**
- **Retentive moist soil**
- **Summer and autumn flowering**

This beautiful perennial can be bitterly disappointing, because its fleshy roots are difficult to establish. Once settled it is a joy. Pretty six-lobed leaves are carried on twining stems that are best seen rambling over evergreen shrubs or hedges. From midsummer through to the autumn the plant is covered with superb scarlet flowers about 4cm (1.6in) across and with attractive spurs. The plant is best suited to cool moist country gardens; it is not ideal for towns and cities.

The warm ochre-yellow flowers of *T. polyphyllum* are equally lovely, but it prefers its fleshy roots in well-drained hot sunny positions.

Propagate by seed sown in spring in a cold frame, or by division in spring.

Take care

Be patient. 310-311▸

Veronica spicata

(Spiked speedwell)

- **Full sun**
- **Good ordinary soil**
- **Summer flowering**

Provided these cultivated speedwells have reasonably good soil and are grown in a sunny position near the front of the border, the result will be very pleasing. The rich rose pink spikes of 'Barcarolle' form above a deep green mat on 30-45cm (12-18in) stems. The light pink 'Minuet' is of a similar height but has grey-green foliage. Two recent varieties are 'Blue Fox', with bright lavender-blue flowers on 30-40cm (12-16in) spikes, and the long-flowering deep-coloured 'Red Fox' with 35cm (14in) erect stems.

A late summer flowering Australian species is *V. perfoliata*, the Digger's speedwell. It has grey glaucous leaves, and the 60cm (24in) stems carry sprays of Spode-blue flowers.

Propagate all these speedwells by division in autumn or spring.

Take care

Plant near the front of the border. 311▸

Viscaria vulgaris 'Splendens Plena'

(German catchfly)

- **Sunny location**
- **Fertile moderately drained soil**
- **Early summer flowering**

For many years this species was called *Lychnis viscaria*, but now it is *Viscaria vulgaris*. The branching 45cm (18in) stems of 'Splendens Plena' bear sprays of double cerise flowers in early summer. At the base of each plant is a tuft of narrow dark green grass-like foliage. All parts of the German catchfly are sticky, which gives the plant its common name. The white variety, 'Alba', has lighter green foliage; its single white flowers are shaded cool green, and carried on 23cm (9in) stalks. The single *V. vulgaris* has carmine-pink flowers on 25cm (10in) stalks.

All three are excellent as border edging. When planted as a clump, five or six plants are needed for each square metre/yard. Propagate them by seed sown out of doors in spring, or by division of plants in autumn or spring.

Take care
Divide and replant every third or fourth year.

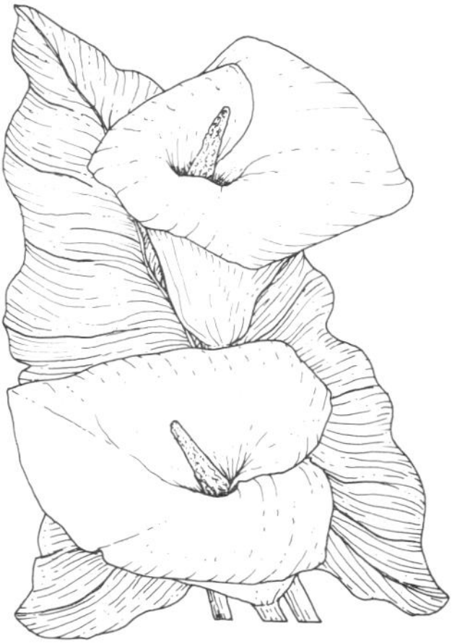

Zantedeschia aethiopica 'Crowborough'

(Hardy arum lily)

- **Sunny location**
- **Dry or wet soil**
- **Summer flowering**

This is a hardy arum lily, but during its first few years after planting some form of protection should be given. This hardy variety is about 90cm (3ft) high and has white fleshy spathes with spear-shaped foliage. The bright yellow 'true' flowers are borne on a fleshy spadix enclosed by the large white spathe, which is a modified bract.

In future years, once the plants are established, give a good thick mulch of leaf-mould or bracken. When planting, place the roots about 10cm (4in) below soil level; as plants mature it will be found that the roots will penetrate more deeply. 'Crowborough' will put up with dry as well as moist conditions, and will flourish in heavy soil.

Propagate in late spring, by removing young offsets at the base of the plants.

Take care
Protect newly planted stock. 312▸

Part Three

BULBS

Nerine bowdenii

Author

David Papworth is a freelance writer and illustrator on horticultural subjects. He is also involved in preparing garden designs for show houses, exhibitions and private homes. For a period of over 12 years David was Gardening Editor of Ideal Home magazine. He has written two other books: 'Patios and Water Gardens (1973) and 'Patios and Windowbox Gardening' (1983).

Colchicum speciosum

Index of Scientific Names

The plants are arranged in alphabetical order of Latin name.
Page numbers in **bold** refer to text entries; those in *italics* refer to photographs.

Achimenes heterophylla **345**
Acidanthera bicolor murielae **345**
Agapanthus campanulatus **346** *340*
Allium giganteum **346**
Allium moly **347**
Allium sativum **347**
Allium schoenoprasum **348**
Alstroemeria aurantiaca **348** *341*
Amaryllis belladonna **349** *341*
Anemone blanda **349** *343*
Anemone coronaria **350** *342*
Anemone nemorosa **350** *343*
Arisaema speciosum **351**
Arisarum proboscoideum **351**
Colchicum autumnale **358** *365*
Colchicum speciosum **359** *366*
Convallaria majalis **359**
Crinum x powellii **360** *367*
Crocosmia x crocosmiiflora **360** *368*
Crocosmia masonorum **377** *369*
Crocus aureus 'Dutch Yellow' **377** *368*
Crocus chrysanthus 'Blue Bird' **378** *370*
Crocus tomasinianus **378** *370*
Crocus vernus 'Striped Beauty' **379** *371*
Curtonus paniculatus **379**

Arum italicum **352**
Begonia x tuberhybrida **352-3** *344, 361*
Begonia boweri **354**
Begonia masoniana **354**
Begonia rex **355**
Brodiaea laxa **355**
Calochortus venustus **356** *362*
Camassia leichtlinii **356**
Canna x hybrida **357** *363*
Cardiocrinum giganteum **357** *364*
Chionodoxa luciliae gigantea **358** *364*
Cyclamen hederifolium **380** *372*
Cyclamen persicum **380**
Dahlia (Single-flowered) **381**
Dahlia (Anemone-flowered) **381** *372-3*
Dahlia (Collarette) **382** *374*
Dahlia (Paeony-flowered) **382** *375*
Dahlia (Decorative) **383** *375-6*
Dahlia (Ball) **383** *393*
Dahlia (Pompon) **384**
Dahlia (Cactus) **384** *394*
Dahlia (Semi-cactus) **385** *395-6*
Dahlia (Bedding) **385** *397*

Dierama pulcherrimum	**386**	
Endymion hispanicus	**386**	*397*
Endymion non-scriptus	**387**	
Eranthis hyemalis	**387**	*398*
Eremurus robustus	**388**	
Erythronium dens-canis	**388**	*398*
Erythronium tuolumnense	**389**	*399*
Eucomis bicolor	**389**	
Freesia x hybrida	**390**	*400*
Fritillaria imperialis	**390**	*401*
Fritillaria meleagris	**391**	
Galanthus nivalis	**391**	*402*
Galtonia candicans	**392**	*402*
Gladiolus byzantinus	**392**	*403*
Gladiolus (Large-flowered)	**409**	*405*
Gladiolus (Primulinus hybrids)	**409**	*404*
Gladiolus (Miniature hybrids)	**410**	*404*
Gladiolus (Butterfly hybrids)	**410**	
Gloriosa rothschildiana	**411**	
Haemanthus natalensis coccineus	**411**	
Hedychium gardnerianum	**412**	
Hyacinthus orientalis (Dutch)	**412**	*406*
Hyacinthus orientalis (Garden)	**413**	*406*
Hymenocallis x festalis	**413**	*407*
Ipheion uniflorum	**414**	*407*
Iris (Pogoniris/Arillate)	**414**	
Iris (Pogoniris/Eupogon)	**415**	*408*
Iris (Apogon/Californicae)	**415**	*425*
Iris (Apogon/Hexagona)	**416**	
Iris (Apogon/Laevigatae)	**416**	*427*
Iris (Apogon/Sibirica)	**417**	
Iris (Apogon/Spuria)	**417**	
Iris (Crested section)	**418**	*426*
Iris (Juno subsection)	**418**	*426*
Iris (Reticulata)	**419**	*429*
Iris (Xiphium)	**419**	
Ixia viridiflora hybrids	**420**	
Ixiolirion pallasii	**420**	
Lachenalia aloides	**421**	*428*
Leucojum aestivum 'Gravetye Giant'	**421**	*428*
Liatris spicata	**422**	
Lilium Asiatic cvs	**422**	*430*
Lilium Martagon hybrids	**423**	
Lilium candidum cvs	**423**	
Lilium American cvs	**424**	*431*
Lilium longiflorum cvs	**424**	
Lilium Trumpet and Aurelian cvs	**441**	*432*
Lilium Oriental cvs	**441**	*431*
Lilium regale	**442**	*432*
Lilium tigrinum	**442**	*433*
Muscari armeniacum	**443**	*434*

Index of Common Names

African corn lily 420
Arum lily 486
Autumn crocus 358, 359

Bearded irises 414, 415
Beardless irises 416-417
Blood lily 411
Blue windflower 349
Bulbous irises 418, 419
Bunch-flowered narcissus 444

Cape cowslips 421
Chilean crocus 476
Chincherinchee 341
Chives 348
Crested irises 418
Crown imperial 390
Cuban lily 356

Dog's tooth violet 388
Dutch hyacinth 412

English bluebell 387
Eyelash begonia 354

Foxtail lily 388

Garden hyacinth 413
Garlic 347
Giant lily 357
Ginger-wort 412
Glory lily 411
Glory of the snow 358
Gloxinia 474
Grape hyacinth 443
Guernsey lily 450

Harlequin flower 474

Narcissus cyclamineus **443** *434*
Narcissus pseudonarcissus **444** *435*
Narcissus tazetta **444**
Narcissus (Division 1) **445** *436*
Narcissus (Division 2) **445** *436-7*
Narcissus (Division 3) **446**
Narcissus (Division 4) **446** *438*
Narcissus (Division 5) **447**
Narcissus (Division 6) **447** *439*
Narcissus (Division 7) **448**
Narcissus (Division 8) **448** *438*
Narcissus (Division 9) **449** *440*
Narcissus (Division 10) **449**
Nerine bowdenii **450** *457*
Nomocharis saluenensis **450**
Notholirion thomsonianum **451**
Ornithogalum thyrsoides **451** *458*
Ornithogalum umbellatum **452**
Oxalis adenophylla **452**
Pancratium maritimum **453**
Polianthes tuberosa 'The Pearl' **453**
Puschkinia scilloides **454** *458*
Ranunculus asiaticus **454** *459*
Rechsteineria cardinalis **455**
Rhodohypoxis baurii **455**
Schizostylis coccinea **456** *460*
Scilla peruviana **456**
Scilla sibirica 'Atrocoerulea' **473** *461*
Scilla tubergeniana **473** *461*
Sinningia speciosa **474** *462*
Sparaxis tricolor **474**
Sprekelia formosissima **475** *463*
Sternbergia lutea **475** *463*
Tecophilaea cyanocrocus **476** *464*
Tigridia pavonia **476** *465*
Trillium grandiflorum **477**
Trillium sessile **477**
Tritonia crocata **478** *465*
Tulip (Division 1) **478** *466*
Tulip (Division 2) **479**
Tulip (Division 3) **479** *467*
Tulip (Division 4) **480** *466*
Tulip (Division 5) **480** *468*
Tulip (Division 6) **481** *468*
Tulip (Division 7) **481** *469*
Tulip (Division 8) **482** *469*
Tulip (Division 9) **482**
Tulip (Division 10) **483** *470*
Tulip (Division 11) **483** *470-1*
Tulip (Division 12) **484** *471*
Tulip (Division 13) **484** *472*
Tulip (Division 14) **485**
Tulipa tarda **485** *472*
Tulipa turkestanica **486**
Zantedeschia aethiopica **486**

Iron Cross begonia 354
Ixia lily 420

Kaffir lily 456

Lent lily 444
Lily of the valley 359

Mariposa lily 356
Montbretia 360
Mouse plant 351

Pineapple flower 389

Quamash 356

Regal lily 339

Sea lily 453
Snake's head fritillary 391
Snowdrop 391
Snowflake 421
Star of Bethlehem 452
Striped quill 454
Summer hyacinth 392
Sweet-scented gladiolus 345

Tiger flower 476
Tiger lily 442

Wandflower 386
Water-lily tulip 484
Wild daffodil 444
Winter aconite 387
Wood anemone 350

Introduction

What exactly are bulbs, corms, rhizomes and tubers; what have they in common; and why are they different?

All these root forms are food storage systems built up in one season when the weather allows nutrients to be readily available, and then used during the following season when the plants need to grow rapidly and flower at a time when drought, frozen soil or other poor growing conditions occur.

A *bulb* is a collection of old leaf bases around an embryo bud and new leaves that will emerge the next season. A *corm* is the thickened end of a stem that will shoot up and produce leaves along its length. A *rhizome* is a horizontal stem – sometimes above ground and at other times below the surface – which will sprout tufts of leaves; sometimes it runs under the ground and emerges some distance from the parent plant. A *tuber* is a swollen root that stores goodness for the coming year.

Most of these plants produce underground offshoots that can be removed and grown on separately to become mature plants. Bulbs often produce small bulbs around the root area, called *bulblets,* which can be separated and replanted in protected nursery beds. Corms produce a new corm either above or next to the old one, and often smaller ones are also produced, which can be treated like bulblets to reach maturity. Rhizomes and tubers are usually divided by cutting but each piece must have an eye or small shoot to grow; if there is a root system as well, each section must have some rooting growth in order to survive.

Buying bulbs

There are many places for buying bulbs – garden centres, nurseries, supermarkets and mail order specialists – and it is quite a simple matter to find what you are looking for; but do be wary of cheap offers, for in this field you get only what you pay for. It is better to buy one good bulb than a dozen poor ones.

Left: **Tulip 'Bing Crosby'**
A Triumph tulip grown from a bulb that produces a plain red bloom, but colour breaking can occur. 480▸

Below: *Four types of food reservoir: (A) Bulb (leaf storage); (B) Corm (stem supply); (C) Rhizome (swollen stem) and (D) Tuber (enlarged root).*

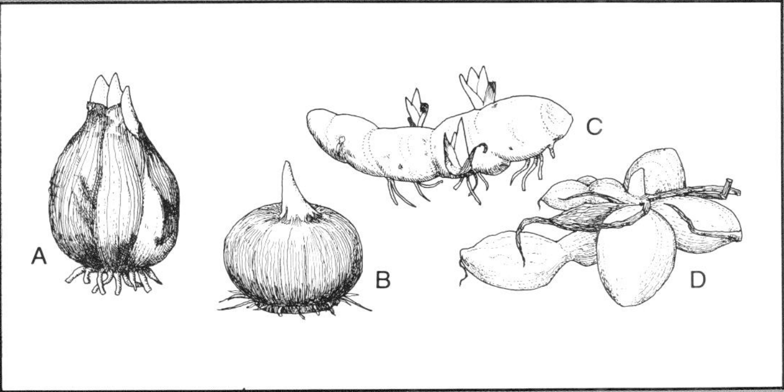

Bulbs come in different sizes and forms. In the narcissus family there are 'mother' bulbs, which will produce a number of shoots and flowers, and can then be divided up to give several individual bulbs. 'Double nose' bulbs should give two shoots and flowers. Offsets are unlikely to be mature enough to flower in the first year. Some suppliers give quantity discounts, and these should be treated as genuine bargains and not confused with cheap offers. Bruised or damaged bulbs, or ones that show signs of insect attack or mould, should be avoided where possible. Spare bulbs from friends or neighbours may carry disease and pests; if you use them, give the bulbs and the surrounding soil a dose of pesticide and fungicide.

Storing bulbs
At the end of the growing season it is sometimes necessary to lift and store bulbs. They should be sorted, named and treated with a fungicide. Some will need to be covered with moist peat, but others will require a dry covering. Keep them in a cool place that is frost-free, not too dry (or the bulbs will shrivel) and protected against marauding pests such as mice. Inspect your store of bulbs during the winter and remove any that are beginning to rot or show disease. Tubers that are drying out and look shrivelled can be soaked in water overnight, then dried on the surface and replaced in store. By taking care during the winter months you should have healthy bulbs to plant when the season is right.

Health
To keep disease and pest attack to a minimum it is best to prevent trouble before it starts, by treating the plant and the surrounding soil with an appropriate preparation. This can be a chemical, but for

Above: **Crocus 'Firefly'**
Crocuses grow from a corm, the thickened end of the stem that will release food when nutrition is short.

Above: **Iris innominata**
An American beardless iris grown from a rhizome, a swollen underground stem. 415▶

those who have deep feelings against chemicals there are natural products that will help to fend off any attack. Whether they are man-made or natural, treat every such product with respect, and keep to the manufacturer's instructions. A solution may look weak, but resist the temptation to make it stronger; it is when we fail to use the right dose that trouble starts. As a general rule, a good healthy plant will keep disease at bay and shrug off a few pests; it is the weak plants that attract trouble.

Planting

Before planting takes place, a little preparation is important. First, plan where the bulbs are to be placed, how many, and in what shape or order. Once this is decided, then the area of soil can be prepared and dug over, all weed roots removed and drainage supplied if necessary: often a good dose of bulky manure, sharp sand or leaf-mould is sufficient to open the texture of the soil and improve the drainage. Peat can be added where there is a need for more moisture; this, together with manure and leaf-mould, can be either dug well in or left as a thick layer, or mulch, on the surface, but do take care that manure is not in direct contact with the bulb and that the manure used is old and well rotted. Where the soil is boggy a series of land drains should be laid to drain the soil; if this is impossible, it is better to use the land to good advantage, and make a bog garden planted with moisture-loving specimens.

Feeding

It is important to provide food each season, so that every plant will have built up strength to produce leaves and flowers during the next growth period. In most cases, feeding takes place either when the leaves are mature and can absorb nourishment even if the flowers have finished blooming, or – in the case of the colchicum – before the flowers appear. A surface dressing of a general fertilizer will be washed into the soil by the rain and taken up by the roots. A mulch of compost will follow the same path with the added advantage of supplying humus to improve the soil. A good dose of liquid manure will feed the plant through its leaves as well as through its roots. All these types of feed will do wonders to the plant, fattening up the roots and storage growths for the next year, when the size and blooms will be much improved. Watering is important, too; make sure that the bulb is kept moist during the feeding period. If drought occurs, check that the soil has not dried out, and if it has, give a copious draught so that the soil is thoroughly soaked down to the bulb roots. A mere sprinkle of water will just dampen the surface and encourage the roots to grow towards the moisture, which will quickly dry out.

Propagation

In general the increase of plants occurs naturally through seed, by increase of roots, or by *layering* (stems touch the soil and develop a new root system, and gradually become independent). In most cases bulbs produce small bulblets around the parent bulb, which grow into full-sized ones in a year or two; these should replace other bulbs that are lost through age, disease, drought, pests or poor conditions. Plants grown from seed will in some cases take six years or more to reach the flowering stage, and for most of us this is far too long to wait – even waiting for bulblets to produce blooms is sometimes more than we can bear, so we have to resort to buying bulbs to give us instant gardens. Even if we purchase bulbs, however, we can still keep a small bed of bulblets or even a pot in a sheltered part of the garden. To keep the young plants from being choked with weeds, grow them in a sterilized potting mixture. This will give them a balanced soil to grow in, a good start in life, and a better chance to reach maturity. Where seed is recommended for increasing stock, a seed-growing mixture should be used and the instructions given in the text of this book should be followed.

Indoor forcing

To provide blooms out of season or even a few weeks earlier the bulb growers have devised a system of cultivation using cold and warm storage, so that spring flowers are available during the winter months. Plant them in containers of peat and charcoal, provide them with moisture, and keep them in the dark to sprout. When the shoot has emerged from the bulb and grown to the desired length bring the plants out into the light and warmth, where they will bloom. After flowering they can be planted out in the garden, but some bulbs take a long time to recover their natural cycle. Many bulbs suitable for growing indoors are sold complete with pot and soil.

Selection

The bulbs featured in this section have been selected to give a broad range of different types, and most are readily available commercially. They include hardy, half-hardy and tender forms. Hardy plants will survive in the colder regions of the temperate zone, and can withstand prolonged frost and moderately hot weather. Half-hardy ones are from warmer regions of the temperate area, stand up to the occasional frost, and thrive in heat. Tender types are best kept to areas where there is little frost or where protection can be given. In the case of dormant bulbs a thick layer of straw, compost, bracken or peat will insulate them. In colder areas it is best to treat the tender plants as pot specimens to be kept in the greenhouse or indoors. The choice of plants in this book gives a variety of flower, leaf and size; you should be able to find plants that you can fit into existing schemes without having to alter the planting to see the new varieties. There are small subjects suitable for the alpine garden as well as for the border, larger ones for the back of the herbaceous border, and middle-sized ones that can stand on their own or be mixed with other plants. Whichever sort you choose you can have flowers the whole year round provided you pick the right varieties.

Names given are, in most cases, the Latin ones that are known in all countries; the common names vary from district to district. The most common names are given after the Latin name to help identification. The planting depths indicate the distance between the top of the bulb and the soil surface.

Below: **Dahlia 'Scaur Princess'**
A decorative dahlia that is a fine example of a tuberous plant; the swollen root system feeds the plant when it cannot draw nutrition from the soil. Protect from frost.

Above:
Agapanthus campanulatus
This plant forms a delightful focal point in the garden, with its sword-like leaves and delicate blooms. Ideal for border or containers. 346▶

Above: **Alstroemeria aurantiaca**
The rich colour and exotic markings of this plant contrast with the blue-grey leaves in summer. Place it in a sheltered site in full sun. 348▶

Below: **Amaryllis belladonna**
An exotic plant that is ideal in a sheltered border or among shrubs, where the large blooms make a fine spectacle in late summer. 349▶

Above:
Anemone blanda 'Blue Pearl'
This fine low-growing plant brightens up the border and rock garden in late winter and early spring with its finely shaped blooms. It forms a clump and will grow happily in either sun or shade and in a well-drained soil. 349▶

Left: **Anemone coronaria**
The cultivated anemone that every florist stocks; available in a variety of colours with dark centres. They are very popular as garden plants and will grow well in the border as well as in the rock garden. 350▶

Right: **Anemone nemorosa**
This plant enjoys the light shade provided by thin woodland and forms a low-growing mass. Where the soil is moist it will increase and produce a prolific display of white flowers in early spring. 350▶

Above: **Begonia × tuberhybrida**
A fine example of the picotee begonia, which is noted for its delicate edging along the petals in a contrasting colour. They are ideal for bedding plants, and in containers and hanging baskets, where they provide a touch of vivid colour. Avoid too much sun. 352▶ 353▶

Left: **Begonia × tuberhybrida**
The rich colour of the large blooms stands out against the dark green leaves and, provided it is kept out of too much sun and is given a moist soil and high humidity, it will reward the owner with a succession of blooms from early summer to late autumn. A pot or bedding plant. 352-353▶

Achimenes heterophylla

- **Light position, but avoid strong sunshine**
- **Soil on the dry side**
- **Plant tubers 2.5cm (1in) deep**

This tender tuberous bushy plant has mid-green, toothed and hairy leaves, borne in threes, that drop in the autumn. In a greenhouse, it will grow to 30cm (12in). The long-lasting flowers start trumpet shaped, opening out to flat pansy-like blooms in shades of bright orange and crimson, almost 4cm (1.6in) across.

Using a peat-based mixture place the tubers 2.5cm (1in) deep in a flowerpot, six to a 12.5cm (5in) pot, and gently moisten the mixture. Once tubers have sprouted, feed them with liquid fertilizer every two weeks, keeping the plant at 16°C 60°F). Support the plant with canes or string. Keep the foliage out of strong sun, misting the leaves with water in hot weather. In autumn allow the plant to dry out, and then place in a frost-free position until spring. These plants are generally pest- and disease-free.

Take care

Avoid direct fierce sunlight and overwatering.

Acidanthera bicolor murielae

(Sweet-scented gladiolus)

- **Sunny sheltered position**
- **Any garden soil that is not waterlogged**
- **Plant 10cm (4in) deep**

This half-hardy plant will not stand frost reaching the corm. It should be either grown as a greenhouse subject or used for bedding unless in a very sheltered frost-free area. It will grow to 90cm (36in), with sword-shaped leaves. In late summer the scented star-shaped flowers appear, up to eight per stem, white with deep purple centres, about 5cm (2in) across.

Plant the corms in any garden soil with reasonable drainage, at a depth of 10cm (4in) in spring, about 20cm (8in) apart, in a sunny position. Lift the plants before the first hard frost and dry them off in the greenhouse. Separate young corms from the parent corm and keep them all in a warm dry place until spring. For greenhouse use put up to six in a 15cm (6in) pot in winter for midsummer blooms. Use pesticides to stop slugs and thrips.

Take care

Keep corms frost-free, and grow in a well-drained soil.

Agapanthus campanulatus

- **Sunny position**
- **Well-drained soil**
- **Plant crowns 5cm (2in) deep**

This fleshy-rooted plant grows in clumps of sword-like foliage that die back in winter to emerge again the following spring. Plants grow up to 75cm (30in) tall and should be 45cm (18in) apart. The late summer flowers are in ball-like groups on the end of tall stems almost 1m (39in) long, and vary in colour from white to amethyst.

They thrive in a warm sunny position with well-drained soil, but most withstand winter frosts. When the flowers die back, cut the stems to ground level, and cover the crowns with bracken, compost, straw or ashes if sited in a frost pocket. The roots can be lifted, divided and replanted in late spring; growing fresh stock from seed takes up to three years from sowing to flowering. Seeds should be sown in spring in seed mixture at 13-16°C (55-60°F); transplant them to boxes and on to flowerpots as they mature. Overwinter in a frost-free place and plant out in late spring.

Take care

Do not plant in waterlogged soil. 340▸

Allium giganteum

- **Sunny site**
- **Well-drained soil**
- **Plant with 15cm (6in) of soil above bulb**

This bulbous plant is grown mainly for its decorative flowerhead, which stands well above other herbaceous plants. The leaves are grey-blue and strap-like, making a clump up to 45cm (18in) in height, with flowerheads 10cm (4in) across. The flowers in midsummer are deep lilac. As soon as the flowers die, cut the heads off but leave the stalks to feed the bulb for the following year; dead leaves and stems should be removed in autumn.

Grow them in a sunny place in well-drained soil, and leave untouched for a few years; then lift, split and replant in spring or autumn with more space around the bulbs. Seeds can be sown in autumn, winter or spring; leave them for 12 months, then replant in nursery rows out of doors, keeping the soil moist.

Watch for slugs and white rot. Infected bulbs should be destroyed, and the soil dusted with calomel dust. Do not grow alliums there for 10 years.

Take care

Stake plants on windy sites.

Allium moly

- **Sunny site**
- **Well-drained soil**
- **Plant with 7.5cm (3in) of soil over the bulb**

This allium is suitable for the rock garden, as it grows only 30cm (12in) tall. It has strap-like grey leaves, and bright yellow star-like flowers that form clusters 5cm (2in) wide on the end of the flower stems in midsummer. The plants spread 15cm (6in) across and should be planted this distance apart.

Plant the bulbs in autumn in well-drained soil with some moisture; they prefer a sunny site. Leave them for a few years, until the flowers become crowded; then lift the clump in spring or autumn, split and replant with more space. This can be grown as a pot plant provided it is kept cool until the flower buds start to open and then it can be brought indoors. Sow seeds in winter or spring, and after 12 months replant in a nursery bed for another two years.

Protect from slugs, and watch for white rot. If white fungus appears at the base of the bulbs, destroy the plants and do not grow alliums in this soil for 10 years.

Take care

Avoid waterlogged soil.

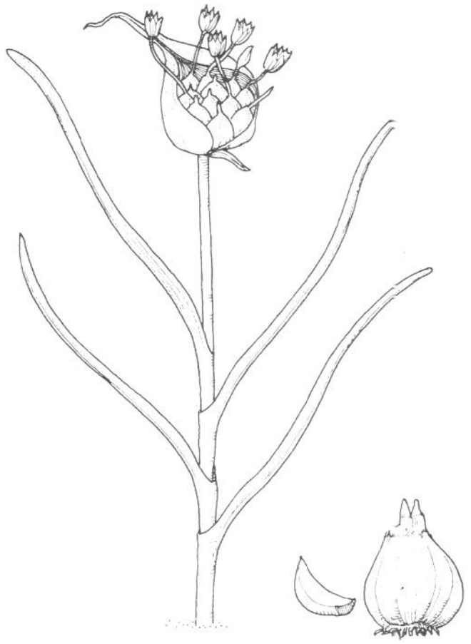

Allium sativum

(Garlic)

- **Sunny position**
- **Moist light soil fed with manure**
- **Plant 15cm (6in) deep; cloves 7.5cm (3in) deep**

Garlic is a member of the onion family and grows to 60cm (24in) tall, with narrow grey-green leaves. The bulb itself is made up of several segments known as cloves, which are held together with a thin dryish skin. The plant has heads of tiny white blooms flushed with red at midsummer; remove these to keep the bulbs well-formed.

Garlic thrives in a light soil that has manure in it to keep the bulbs moist and fed. They are ready for harvesting in late summer. Plant bulbs in winter at a depth of 15cm (6in), but if cloves are used instead of bulbs, keep 7.5cm (3in) of soil over them. When the leaves turn yellow in summer, the bulbs can be lifted and laid out in the sun to dry; then they can be stored for the winter in a cool but frost-free place. Pick out the best bulbs for planting next season. Garlic is generally pest-free, but if it is attacked by fungus disease, destroy the plant to stop it spreading.

Take care

Keep the soil moist during the growing season.

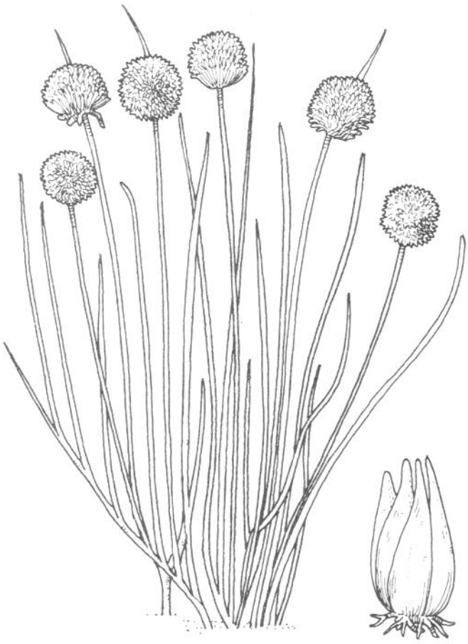

Allium schoenoprasum

(Chives)

- **Full sun or partial shade**
- **Good soil**
- **Plant 1.25cm (0.5in) deep**

This hardy perennial herb, used in the kitchen for flavouring, produces a clump of hollow grass-like leaves. In midsummer the spherical flowers appear, rose-pink in colour and 2.5-4cm (1-1.6in) across.

Chives should be grown in a good soil in full sun or partial shade. In dry periods, water the plant to keep it moist. To keep a supply of leaves, all flowers should be removed. The plants die back in winter and resprout the following spring. Use cloches to cover the plants in winter, to get early leaves to pick in spring. Spread compost or manure over the area in spring. Plants can be divided in autumn and replanted to give more space. At this time, lift one or two clumps and put them into pots; kept on the kitchen windowsill they will provide fresh leaves through the winter. Chives are normally pest- and disease-free.

Take care

Pinch out flowerheads to give a continuous supply of leaves.

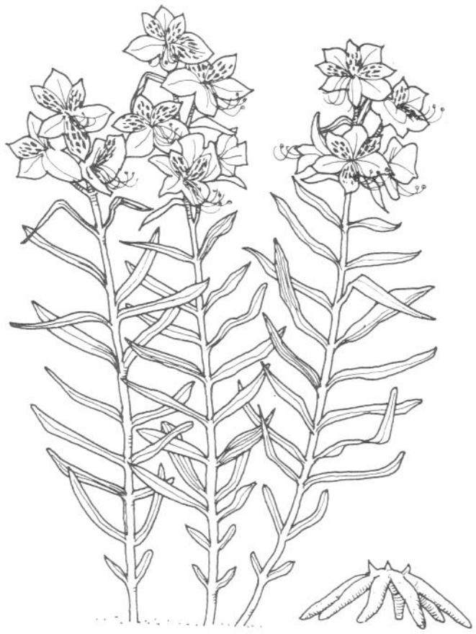

Alstroemeria aurantiaca

- **Sunny, sheltered site**
- **Well-drained fertile soil**
- **Plant tubers 10-15cm (4-6in) deep**

This tuberous-rooted plant has twisted blue-grey leaves, and grows to a height of 90cm (36in). Borne on leafy stems, the flowers are trumpet-shaped in orange-reds, the upper two petals having red veins.

Plant the tubers in spring. Cover with a mulch of compost or well-rotted manure in spring. As they grow, support to prevent them being blown over. Dead-head plants to encourage more blooms. In autumn cut stems down to the ground. In spring the plants can be divided, but take care not to disturb the roots unduly. Sometimes the plant will not produce any stems, leaves or flowers during the first season, but once established it can be left for years. Sow seed in spring in a cold frame, and plant out a year later.

Watch for slugs and caterpillars, and use a suitable insecticide if necessary. When the plant shows yellow mottling and distorted growth, destroy it – this is a virus disease.

Take care

Avoid damaging the roots. 341▶

Amaryllis belladonna

- **Sunny sheltered position**
- **Well-drained soil**
- **Plant 15-20cm (6-8in) deep**

This bulbous plant has strap-like leaves, lasting from late winter through to midsummer. After the leaves die down, flower stems appear and grow to a height of 75cm (30in). The trumpet-shaped fragrant pink or white flowers vary from three to 12 on a stem.

Plant the bulbs in summer in a warm sheltered situation in well-drained soil. Bulbs can be divided in summer and should be replanted immediately. Dead-head the flowers as they fade, and remove leaves and stems as they die.

Hippeastrum bulbs, often sold as Amaryllis, are tender indoor subjects. Plant one bulb in a 15-20cm (6-8in) pot of well-draining mixture, leaving a third of the bulb exposed. Water a little until the flower stem appears and then water and feed liberally. Bulbs bloom about three months after planting. Prepared bulbs planted in late autumn flower during midwinter.

Take care

Keep moist when transplanting. 341▶

Anemone blanda

(Blue windflower)

- **Sun or light shade**
- **Well-drained soil**
- **Plant 5cm (2in) deep**

This spring-flowering plant grows to 15cm (6in) tall; the daisy-like flowers, in white, pink, red-tipped, lavender or pale blue, and 3.5cm (1.4in) across, appear during spring. They make an ideal rockery plant and can be grown in clumps under trees.

They tolerate either alkaline or acid soils provided they are well-drained. Corms should be planted 10cm (4in) apart in autumn. Lift the corms after leaves die down in early autumn; divide, and remove offsets for replanting. Sow seeds in late summer, and germinate in a cold frame; transplant seedlings, and grow on for two years before moving to final positions.

If plant and soil are treated with a general insecticide you should have little trouble. Stunted yellow leaves and meagre flowers indicate a virus attack; destroy plants before the virus can spread.

Take care

Soak corms for 48 hours before planting. 342-343▶

Anemone coronaria

- **Sunny or lightly shaded position**
- **Well-drained soil**
- **Plant corms 5cm (2in) deep**

This E Mediterranean plant flowers in spring, and the blooms vary from white to blue or red. From this plant have developed the De Caen and the new robust St. Piran, both with single flowers, and the St. Brigid anemone with double or semi-double blooms. These grow to a height of 30cm (12in) and flowers are up to 7.5cm (3in) across.

Corms should be planted in early autumn, 15cm (6in) apart; by planting in other months a succession of blooms can be had throughout the year. Corms deteriorate, and should be replaced every couple of years. Anemones can be grown from seed, sown in late summer and kept in a cold frame. Transplant the seedlings, leave for a year, and then move to their flowering position. Treat these plants with a general pesticide to stop insect attack. If the plant looks sick and the leaves turn yellow, destroy it before the virus spreads.

Take care

Replace corms every other year. 342▸

Anemone nemorosa

(Wood anemone)

- **Light shade**
- **Well-drained soil with leaf-mould**
- **Plant 5cm (2in) deep**

This anemone has white flowers with a touch of pink or blue on the outside of the petals. The low-growing plant reaches 10cm (4in) high, although some varieties grow to twice this size. The flowers are single, about 2.5cm (1in) across, but there are some double varieties.

These plants are easily grown from corms, provided they are planted in autumn in a shady place with moist soil, and they will bloom in spring. They may be attacked by a number of insects, such as flea beetles, caterpillars, cut worms, aphids or slugs. These should be treated with a suitable insecticide when damage is seen. Virus and rust disease can affect the plants, leaving yellow spores on the leaves and stems and yellowing of leaves with twisted flowers; if either of these symptoms is seen, destroy the plant.

Take care

Do not plant in a hot dry position. 343▸

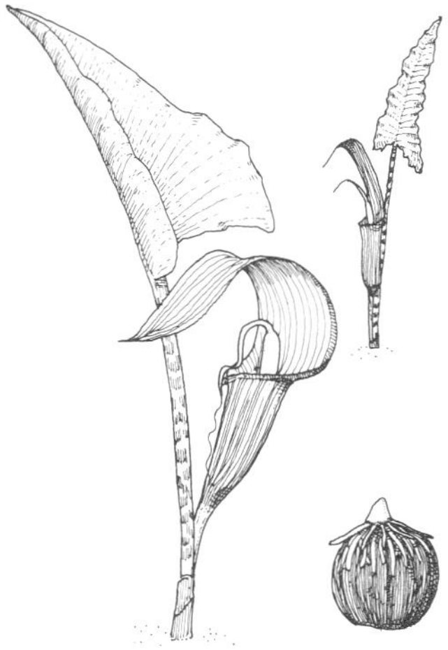

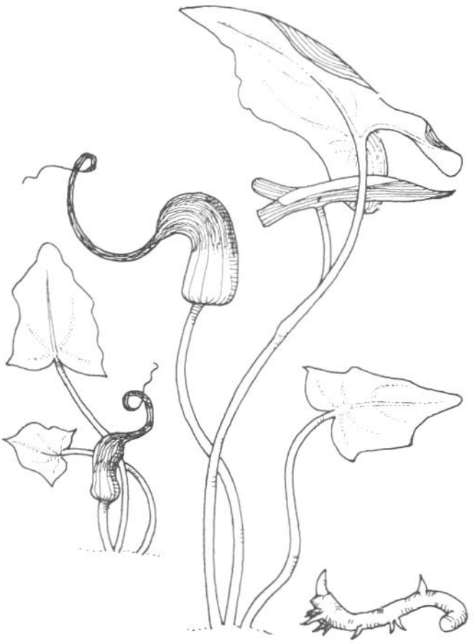

Arisaema speciosum

- **Shady woodland**
- **Moist soil with leaf-mould**
- **Plant 15cm (6in) deep**

Originating from the E Himalayan forests, this tuberous plant has mid-green leaves edged with red, and unusual flowers. The true flowers are very small, and form around the base of a central pencil-like stem that tapers to a length of 50cm (20in); this is surrounded by a petal-like spathe 15cm (6in) long and 10cm (4in) wide, striped in purple and white. The plant grows to a height of 45cm (18in) excluding the flower stem. The flowers appear in late spring.

The tubers should be planted in summer in a moist, shady place where there is plenty of leaf-mould in the soil. Cover the area with a layer of bracken to protect the plants during winter. When necessary, lift the plant in late summer, divide and replant with more space. Generally arisaemas are pest-free, but treat with a fungicide to prevent the roots from rotting.

Take care

Watch for root rot in heavy wet soils.

Arisarum proboscideum

(Mouse plant)

- **Shady area**
- **Moist fibrous soil**
- **Plant 15cm (6in) deep**

This plant thrives in woodland areas where it is partially shaded. It will grow to 12.5cm (5in) tall, but it spreads to form a dense mat of arrow-shaped leaves under which the mouse-like flowers are borne in late spring, lasting until late summer. The flowers are the size and shape of a mouse, joined to the stem at the 'head' end, and the colour is a mouse brown.

These plants are hardy and easy to grow in a moist soil containing plenty of humus; too much sun would dry up the plant. Tubers should be planted in autumn, 15cm (6in) deep. When they are established, they can be lifted and divided, and the offsets removed, in spring. They should be replanted before the root system dries out; this will enable the plant to settle before new growth appears. The arisarum is generally both pest- and disease-free.

Take care

Plant where there is both moisture and shade.

Arum italicum

- **Partial shade**
- **Well-drained soil with leaf-mould**
- **Plant 7.5cm (3in) deep**

This hardy perennial grows to a height of 30cm (12in) from a rhizome. Large heavily marbled leaves in white and dark green appear in autumn. In spring there are unusual creamy-green flowers, followed in autumn by bright red berries that are 1.25cm (0.5in) across, grouped on compact spikes 15cm (6in) long.

Plant in summer in a dry soil that has plenty of humus added in the form of leaf-mould; the rhizome should be planted 7.5cm (3in) deep in semi-shade. In severe winters a mulch of compost, leaf-mould or bracken spread over the plants will protect them against hard frost. To increase stock the seeds can be sown when they are ripe in autumn; or the plant can be lifted in the summer, divided and offsets removed, and replanted. Normally the plant is free from pests but the root is susceptible to rot from excess moisture; treat soil with fungicide.

Take care

Keep the soil well-drained.

Begonia × tuberhybrida

- **Slight shade**
- **Humid atmosphere, moist soil**
- **Plant flush with the soil**

The parents of this tuberous-rooted group come from China, Japan and Socotra, an island in the Indian Ocean. The plants form a very popular series of hybrids or crosses with large rose-like flowers and mid-green ear-shaped leaves. The plants grow to 60cm (24in) tall, with a spread of 45cm (18in). Both male and female flowers are borne on the same plant: the females are single blooms, but the males are more noticeable, being double in form and 7.5-15cm (3-6in) across. They flower from summer to late autumn, and are very popular as both bedding and pot plants. The range of colours is wide, with brilliant hues of yellow, orange, reds, pink and white; some have bands of red edging to the petals, and are known as picotee begonias.

The tubers are started in damp peat when a temperature of 16°C (60°F) can be kept, the tubers being placed just level with the surface and with the flat or slightly hollow surface uppermost. As the leaves start shooting, the tuber should be lifted

Begonia × tuberhybrida
The drawing shows one of the very attractive picotee begonias, with blooms edged in a darker colour.

Begonia × tuberhybrida
The pendulous hybrid shown in the drawing has relatively small flowers borne profusely on slender stems.

and put into a pot with moist growing medium. As the roots fill the pot, move to a larger container and support the stems with a cane. Once established the pots should be given an occasional liquid feed. At the end of spring the danger of frost should have passed and they can be planted out in the open.

To retain deep colours, keep the plant out of direct sunshine and prevent over-heating by spraying it with water. Larger flowers can be produced by removing the single female blooms and allowing only one shoot to each tuber; remove the other shoots and use them as cuttings. Push these into a sharp soil and keep moist until rooted. Sow seeds in winter at the same temperature as when tubers are started and you should get flowers the same year; tubers will be formed and they can be kept for the following year. At the end of the growing season, when the leaves start to turn yellow or the first frost occurs, the plants can be lifted and kept in a frost-free place until they have died back. The tubers can be separated from the dead leaves and stem, and stored in peat where there is protection from frost through the winter until the following year, when they can be started off again on their next cycle.

Pendent varieties are ideal for hanging baskets, containers and windowboxes where they can spill over the edge. The winter-flowering Lorraine begonias are grown in spring from cuttings and should be kept at 10°C (50°F) for the flowers to continue throughout the winter. These plants should be kept just moist. When growing from seed, mix the seeds with some fine sand, spread the mixture over the surface of the seed-growing medium, press down and put no additional soil on top; this will even the distribution of the seeds. Begonias can also be propagated by dividing the tubers, or by leaf cuttings. Keep pests to a minimum with a general pesticide; diseases are generally due to over-wet conditions encouraging moulds, so use a fungicide too. 344▶ 361▶

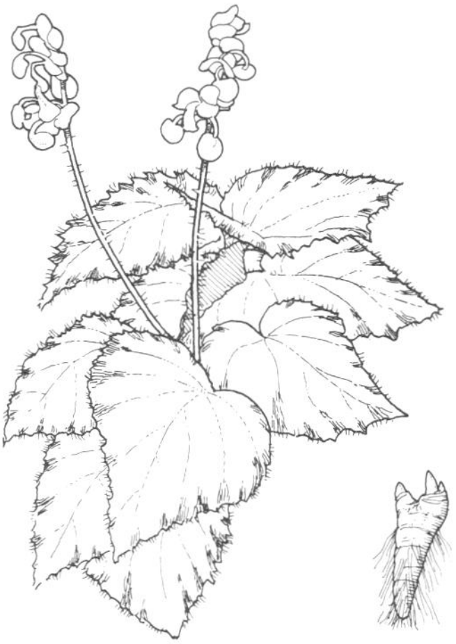

Begonia boweri

(Eyelash begonia)

- **Moist and shady**
- **Frost-free place in winter**
- **Plant on the surface**

This very small evergreen begonia grows from a rhizome. It is cultivated for its small decorative hairy leaves, which are emerald-green with a margin of dark brown blotches. The white or pale rose flowers are only 1.25cm (0.5in) across and appear in spring in small groups. They can be increased by dividing the rhizome in spring, making sure each section has a healthy growing point. Treat as pot plants, or use for windowboxes and outside containers.

Seeds should be sown in early spring at 16°C (60°F). As the seeds are very fine, mix them with some sand before sowing; do not cover the seeds with soil. Once plants are large enough to handle, transplant into pots or boxes. They can be put out into the open in late spring for flowering.

Avoid pests by treating soil and plant with a general pesticide. Disease attack is usually mould or fungus, encouraged by the warm moist conditions, so use a fungicide.

Take care
Make sure plants are shaded.

Begonia masoniana

(Iron Cross begonia)

- **Light shade**
- **Light soil with peat**
- **Plant flush with the surface**

This attractive evergreen begonia is grown for its foliage. The ear-shaped leaves are tightly crinkled, hairy and bright green, with a cross pattern of dark purplish bars. It grows to a height of 23cm (9in) and a spread of 30cm (12in), and it rarely flowers.

It grows from a rhizome and can be increased in spring by dividing the rhizome into pieces, making sure that each has a growing point. This begonia is usually grown as a pot plant, but do not place it in a room with a gas fire, as the fumes can kill it. It prefers a warm moist soil, and some shade from direct sunlight. When it becomes pot-bound, move it to a larger pot at any time from spring to autumn. During winter the plant should be kept just moist – not too much, or rot will occur.

A general pesticide will keep insects away, and a fungicide will deter the fungus and mould infections attracted to the warm moist conditions.

Take care
Keep moist in summer, but almost dry in winter.

Begonia rex

- **Light shade**
- **Light moist soil**
- **Plant just flush with the surface**

These begonias can be used as pot specimens or as bedding plants. They grow to 30cm (12in) high, and spread to 45cm (18in). The leaf colour can vary, with silver markings on dark green to a spectrum of yellows, reds, creams and purples in bands and patterns. Occasionally pale rose flowers, 1.25cm (0.5in) across, appear during summer.

This begonia prefers a light shade: direct sun can bleach the colour, and dry out the plant in summer. In winter it needs a frost-free situation with a little water to keep the plant moist – too much, and the plant can be affected by rot and mildew. Propagate by leaf cuttings, or even sections of leaves about 5cm (2in) square can be placed on moist peat at a temperature of 21°C (70°F) and will develop roots from the underside. *B. rex* can also be grown from seeds, sown in early spring at 16°C (60°F) and transplanted when the first true leaf appears.

Take care
Syringe the plants with water if summer heat makes them wilt.

Brodiaea laxa

- **Sunny position**
- **Well-drained soil**
- **Plant 7.5cm (3in) deep**

These plants have long narrow leaves, and trumpet flowers on leafless stems. They grow up to 60cm (24in) tall, with flowers of blue, mauve or white, almost 4cm (1.6in) across, from spring to midsummer.

Brodiaeas prefer a heavy soil in a warm place, and show well when treated as a drift, the corms 15cm (6in) apart, or planted in clumps. Plant corms in late summer in well-drained soil or in pots. Soak well with water after planting, and keep just moist until the first leaf appears; they should be kept well watered until flowering has finished, then let them dry. The plants should be lifted every few years; divide the corms and replant with more space around them. They can be grown from seed but take up to five years to mature. They are generally both pest- and disease-free.

Take care
Do not overwater after flowering.

Calochortus venustus

(Mariposa lily)

- **Full sun**
- **Dry, well-drained sandy soil**
- **Plant 7.5cm (3in) deep**

These bulbous plants thrive in light woodland and open grassland; in light sandy soil they grow to over 45cm (18in) tall. The calochortus forms a spindly plant with insignificant foliage of long slender leaves that appear in early spring; the summer flowers vary from white to yellow, orange, rose, dark red or purple, with very decorative markings, and reach 5cm (2in) across.

Plant in autumn in a sunny situation, with a dry sandy soil that has some leaf-mould in it. The bulbs should be planted 7.5cm (3in) deep and kept away from excessive moisture, so ensure that the soil is well drained. When foliage dies down keep the plant dry until growth starts again; then keep it just moist until it flowers. It will grow well in a pot in the greenhouse. To keep the plant free from attack, treat with both a pesticide and a fungicide.

Take care

Keep this plant on the dry side. 362▸

Camassia leichtlinii

(Quamash)

- **Sun or light shade**
- **Moist soil**
- **Plant 15cm (6in) deep**

This plant grows to a height of 90cm (36in) and has pointed sword-like leaves. The flowers, on stems that grow above the leaves, are star-shaped in blue or white, about 4cm (1.6in) across, and appear in summer.

This species should be planted in a heavy moist soil with plenty of leaf-mould or peat to prevent drying out by spring winds and summer droughts. The bulbs should be planted in autumn, 15cm (6in) apart. They can be left for a few years; then in autumn lift the bulbs, split up and replant to give them more space. To prevent strength being taken from the bulbs, dead flowerheads should be removed. To increase your stock, bulblets can be removed from around the older bulbs in early autumn and replanted immediately; they should reach flowering size in three years. Seeds can be sown, but may take up to five years to flower.

Take care

Do not let the bulbs dry out in spring and early summer.

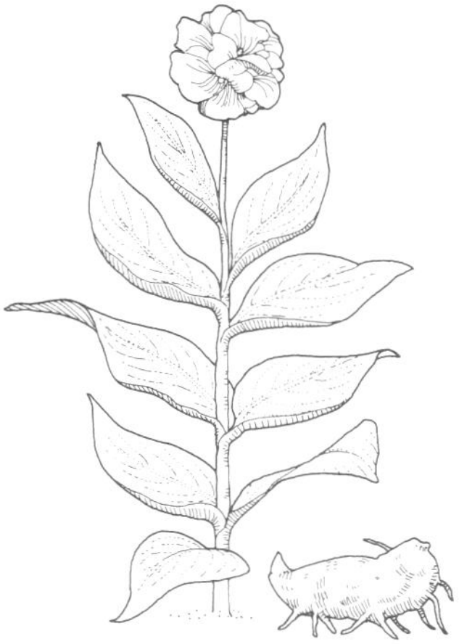

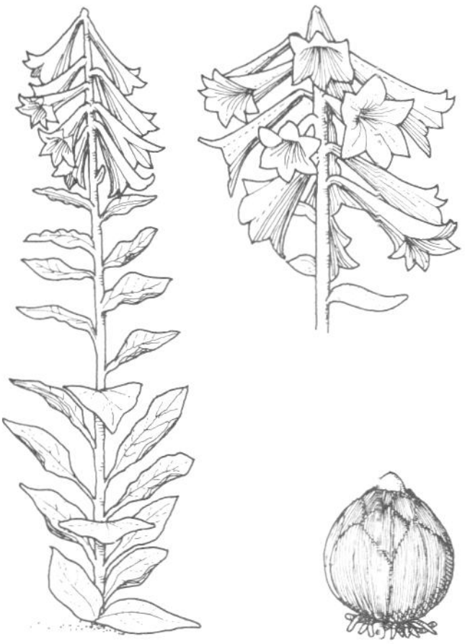

Canna × hybrida

- **Sunny and sheltered position**
- **Rich peaty soil**
- **Just cover the rhizome**

These tropical plants have broad leaves and bright flowers. The plants grow to a height of 120cm (4ft) and should be kept at least 30cm (12in) apart. Cannas fall into two groups, those with green leaves and those with brown to purple ones; the leaves can be up to 60cm (24in) long and 30cm (12in) wide. The flowers are about 7.5cm (3in) long, in brilliant orange or yellow.

Plant the rhizomes in pots in early spring, and keep them at 16°C (60°F). If more than one shoot appears the rhizome can be divided; make sure that each section has a shoot, a piece of rhizome and some roots. In late spring they can be planted outside in a sheltered sunny place. Bring plants indoors before autumn frosts, and keep in a cool but not cold place during the winter. Treat soil and plants with a general pesticide to deter slugs, leather-jackets and cutworms. Cannas are usually disease-free.

Take care

Keep frost-free in winter. 362-363▸

Cardiocrinum giganteum

(Giant lily)

- **Sheltered, in light shade**
- **Well-drained but rich soil**
- **Plant just below the surface**

This hardy bulbous perennial has dark green heart-shaped leaves that grow in a spiral from ground level to just below the first flower. The plants can reach 3m (10ft) high, and should be planted 90cm (3ft) apart. The flowers are borne on a long stem in summer; they consist of a series of trumpets, often over 15cm (6in) long, in cream or palest green streaked with red-brown or purple.

The bulbs die after flowering but usually leave offset bulbs, which mature and flower in three to five years. Sets of bulbs can be bought to give continuous flowering, and as the last bulb dies the first's offsets are ready to flower. Adult bulbs should be planted in autumn, with the neck just below the surface. Water freely in dry spells; a layer of garden compost or manure spread over the bulbs is beneficial. Seeds can be sown, but take up to seven years to flower. Normally these plants are disease- and pest-free.

Take care

Keep moist in dry spells. 364▸

Chionodoxa luciliae gigantea

(Glory of the snow)

- **Open sunny site**
- **Ordinary soil**
- **Plant 5-7.5cm (2-3in) deep**

This early-flowering bulb grows to 20cm (8in) tall. The strap-like leaves have blunt tips, and the six-petalled violet-blue flowers with white centres are 4cm (1.6in) across. They are ideal for growing in rock gardens, at the front of beds and in grass; they come into flower in late winter and last until spring.

Plant bulbs 5-7.5cm (2-3in) deep and 7.5-10cm (3-4in) apart in the autumn; for a good effect plant in groups. Lift the plants after several years, divide the bulbs and replant to give more space; the best time is when foliage is dying back. Seeds can be sown in late spring, left for a year and then transplanted into flowering position. Slugs are the worst pest; put down slug bait in the area. Black sooty areas around the flowers are caused by smut; lift and destroy the infected plants, and spray other chionodoxas with Bordeaux mixture.

Take care

Watch for slugs and smut attack. 364▸

Colchicum autumnale

(Autumn crocus)

- **Sun or partial shade**
- **Well-drained soil**
- **Plant 10cm (4in) deep**

This corm produces large mid- to dark green leaves in spring and early summer; these then die back, and from the bare earth spring the stemless flowers in autumn. The leaves grow up to 25cm (10in) long. The flowers are 15cm (6in) long, and from each corm can come several blooms of lilac, rose or white; one variety has double pink flowers.

The corms should be planted in late summer if purchased corms, or from lifted plants when the leaves die down in midsummer. Position them 20cm (8in) apart in clumps, where they can get some sun. Grown from seed, they may take seven years to reach flowering; offsets take only a couple of years to mature. Do not plant too close to smaller plants that may be smothered by the leaves in spring. The area round the corms should be treated to prevent slug attack. Colchicums are normally disease-free.

Take care

Do not let the large leaves smother smaller adjacent plants. 365▸

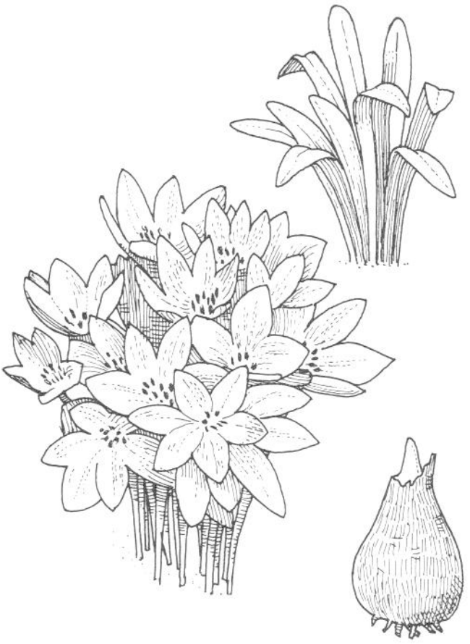

Colchicum speciosum

(Autumn crocus)

- **Sun or partial shade**
- **Well-drained soil**
- **Plant 10-15cm (4-6in) deep**

This plant flowers in autumn; the flowers are white, rose, purple, violet or crimson, some with coloured veining. Leaves show in spring and last till early summer, 30cm (12in) long and 10cm (4in) wide, four to each bulb.

It is easily cultivated in ordinary well-drained soil, and increases well in grass. Plant a little deeper than *C. autumnale*, in early autumn. Make sure that the leaves do not choke smaller neighbours in spring. Colchicums can be grown from seed, but take up to seven years to reach flowering. Offsets from existing corms will take only two or three years to flower. Lift corms when the leaves have died down in summer, remove the offsets and replant. Keep slugs off with slug bait; the plants are usually disease-free.

Take care

Watch for slug attack on leaves and shoots. 366-367▶

Convallaria majalis

(Lily of the valley)

- **Cool shade**
- **Ordinary soil with leaf-mould**
- **Plant just below the surface**

This plant grows from a creeping horizontal rhizome, and given the right conditions it will spread rapidly. It is spring-flowering, with delicate tiny white or pink scented bells, up to eight bells on a stem. The leaves are in pairs, mid-green and elliptical.

Lilies of the valley grow best in cool moist shade; the soil ought to contain garden compost or leaf-mould to retain moisture. Plant rhizomes in autumn just below the surface, with the pointed end uppermost. Plants can be lifted during late autumn and winter, and divided for replanting. Sow seeds in late summer; they will take up to three years to mature. Grow them first in trays, then move to a nursery bed for two years before transplanting to their final position. Treat the soil with a pesticide to prevent caterpillars, and do not plant this species in wet or boggy areas, as this can cause grey mould.

Take care

Keep the roots moist, but not wet.

Crinum × powellii

- **Warm sheltered site**
- **Rich well-drained soil**
- **Plant up to 30cm (12in) deep**

Crinums are tender, and unless you possess a sheltered border, they are best grown as pot plants. They have mid-green sword-like leaves, and form clumps up to 45cm (18in) tall. The trumpet-like flowers are borne in late summer, 15cm (6in) long, in white or pink or striped with both.

The bulbs should be planted in a warm border in late spring; cover them with ashes, bracken or garden compost to protect from late frosts. If you prefer to grow one as a pot plant, place the bulb in a large pot of rich soil and keep in the greenhouse or indoors until late spring; then it can be moved outside until mid-autumn, when it should be brought indoors again for the winter. Crinums grown from seed can take five years to flower; it is quicker to propagate with offsets from the bulbs, which are removed in spring, potted up and kept moist, and will reach flowering size in three years. They are generally pest- and disease-free.

Take care

Watch for late frosts. 367▸

Crocosmia × crocosmiiflora

(Montbretia)

- **Sunny position**
- **Light sandy soil**
- **Plant 7.5cm (3in) deep**

This well-known plant has sword-like leaves and small but profuse flowers borne on 90cm (36in) stems; the trumpet-shaped blooms, up to 10cm (4in) long, in yellow, orange or deep red, appear throughout the summer.

The plants are hardy and quite invasive. Corms should be planted 7.5cm (3in) deep in a well-drained soil that will retain moisture in the summer, preferably in full sun. The leaves should be cut off in spring before the new growth begins to sprout. Every few years, lift, divide and replant the bulbs with more space around them, just after flowering or in spring. Seeds sown in autumn in pots, and kept in a cold frame, germinate in the spring, and should flower in one or two years. This plant is generally free from pests and diseases.

Take care

Keep this invasive plant under control. 368▸

Above: **Begonia × tuberhybrida**
An exotic double picotee that will grow happily out of doors or under glass as long as the soil is moist and the air is humid. Keep out of direct sun by giving light shade. 352-353▶

Left: **Calochortus venustus**
A simple flower with beautiful markings that tops the delicate tracery of the plant in the summer. Grows well in a dry sandy soil in full sun, or can be grown as a pot plant. 356▸

Right:
Canna × hybrida 'King Humbert'
Justifiably popular for their large leaves, some with a brown to purple colour, and bright blooms that are not unlike those of a gladiolus. 357▸

Below: **Canna × hybrida 'Assault'**
When grouped together in a bed these plants form a fine display, standing over 1m (39in) in height. The flowerheads shine throughout the summer months. 357▸

Above: **Cardiocrinum giganteum**
A really spectacular plant that towers above people and is topped with large trumpets in midsummer. It needs a rich, well-drained soil and a lightly shaded location offering plenty of space. 357▸

Left:
Chionodoxa luciliae gigantea
These delicate looking plants bloom during early spring and will look fine in the rock garden, borders and in grass. Thrives in ordinary soil. 358▸

Right: **Colchicum autumnale**
An unusual plant that has prolific leaves in spring and summer. In the autumn these die back and the crocus-like blooms spring from the bare earth, giving a delightful display when other plants are fading. 358▸

Above: **Colchicum speciosum**
A corm that blooms after the leaves have died back, producing flowers during the autumn. It enjoys either sun or some shade and brings needed colour to the garden. 359▸

Left:
Colchicum speciosum 'Album'
A white variety that is useful in giving a bright patch in the autumn garden. A low-growing plant that thrives in ordinary soil in either semi-shade or in direct sun. 359▸

Right: **Crinum × powellii**
Invaluable in a sheltered border, where the plant will thrive in a good, well-drained soil. Produces the fine trumpet like blooms in late summer. Can also be grown as a pot plant. 360▸

Above: **Crocosmia × crocosmiiflora 'Emily McKenzie'**
Commonly known as montbretia, this is one of the many large-flowered varieties available. 360▸

Left:
Crocus aureus 'Dutch Yellow'
Fine for rock and sink gardens as well as for borders and growing in grass. Provides spring colour. 377▸

Right: **Crocosmia masonorum**
This plant gives a continuous display of blooms throughout the summer, provided it has plenty of sun and the soil is not too moist. 377▸

Above: **Crocus tomasinianus**
One of the first crocuses to flower, it produces blooms in late winter. The plant needs some protection to give it a good start but will then thrive in most areas of the garden. 378▸

Left:
Crocus chrysanthus 'Blue Bird'
This crocus shows a blue bud that opens out to reveal the creamy-white inside with a deep orange centre. It will thrive in full sun in any well-drained soil. 378▸

Right:
Crocus vernus 'Striped Beauty'
A large-flowering crocus with very delicate veining on the petals. The plant will increase naturally if the soil is free-draining and sunny. 379▸

Left: **Cyclamen hederifolium**
Shade-loving plants that enjoy a woodland situation, where they will spread naturally. They flower from midsummer until late autumn, providing well needed colour at ground level under the trees. 380▸

Right: **Dahlia 'Claire de Lune' (Anemone-flowered)**
Often growing to over 1m (39in) in height, these dahlias will flower all summer until the late autumn frosts. Ideal for the back of the border. 381▸

Below: **Dahlia 'Scarlet Comet' (Anemone-flowered)**
These are grown for their brilliant colours and spectacular blooms with an inner ring of petals that surround the centre like a halo. Highly suited to the border where colour is needed. 381▸

Above: **Dahlia 'Geerling's Elite' (Collarette)**
Brilliantly coloured blooms to grace any border, each with a small collar of petals around the centre. These are very free-flowering plants. 382▸

Above: **Dahlia 'Bishop of Llandaff' (Paeony-flowered)**
These blooms have rings of flat petals surrounding the central core of stamens. Fine border plants. 382▸

Below: **Dahlia 'Yma Sumac' (Decorative)**
These dahlias are recognised by the double blooms with the petals often twisted. Wide choice of sizes. 383▸

Above: **Dahlia 'Vicky Jackson' (Decorative)**
A beautiful bloom that would grace any garden. Decorative dahlias are available in delicate shades and are free-flowering from midsummer until the frosts of late autumn. The blooms can vary from 10cm (4in) to 25cm (10in) across. 383▸

Left: **Dahlia 'Schwieter's Kokarde' (Decorative)**
Decorative dahlias can reach up to 150cm (5ft) tall, with flowers in proportion to suit most borders and beds. The taller varieties should be staked against wind damage. 383▸

Crocosmia masonorum

- **Sunny place**
- **Well-drained sandy soil**
- **Plant 7.5cm (3in) deep**

This South African plant has sword-like leaves with pronounced centre spines, and grows to 75cm (30in) tall. The flowers are bright orange, 2.5cm (1in) long, and the plant will give a succession of blooms from midsummer.

These plants can be invasive; confine them by planting in a bottomless container sunk into the ground. The corms should be planted in spring, 7.5cm (3in) deep and 15cm (6in) apart, in a sunny position. The plants need a well-drained soil, but keep it moist during summer droughts. The flowers are often used for cutting; if they are left on the plants, remove them as soon as they die. Cut off dead leaves before the new ones appear in spring. Corms should be lifted every few years; divide after flowering and before new growth appears. They are normally pest- and disease-free.

Take care

Stop plants spreading too far. 369▸

Crocus aureus 'Dutch Yellow'

- **Sunny position**
- **Well-drained soil**
- **Plant 7.5cm (3in) deep – more in a light soil**

The yellow flowering crocus has fine grass-like leaves, and produces its bright blooms in early spring, growing to 10cm (4in) long. It prefers well-drained soil and a sunny situation, and is recommended for rock gardens. It also thrives in short grass, provided no mowing occurs before the leaves turn yellow in late spring.

Corms should be planted in autumn to flower the following spring, in groups or drifts; plant them 7.5cm (3in) apart. Crocuses multiply by cormlets produced around the parent corm, or by seeding. Cormlets can be removed in early summer and grown on to flower in two years' time; seed takes up to four years to flower, and should be sown in summer and transplanted into nursery beds when large enough to handle. A general pesticide will keep most trouble at bay. Also use a fungicide.

Take care

Bird attack can be averted by black cotton stretched over the plants. 370▸

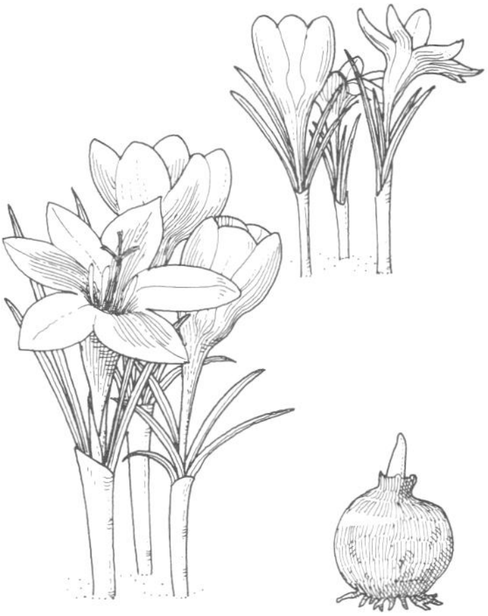

Crocus chrysanthus 'Blue Bird'

- **Sheltered sunny position**
- **Well-drained soil**
- **Plant 7.5cm (3in) deep**

This spring-flowering crocus has a bloom with a mauve-blue exterior edged with white, a creamy white inside and a deep orange centre, and it flowers profusely. The short narrow leaves of pale green have a paler stripe along the spine.

These crocuses are ideal for the border or rockery, and do well in pots in a cold greenhouse. Corms can be planted in any free-draining soil. If the soil is very light, they can be planted 15cm (6in) deep, but otherwise 7.5cm (3in) is recommended. If crocuses are grown in grass, delay mowing until the leaves turn yellow and die back; if you cut sooner, the corms will produce very poor blooms next season. Treat the soil with a general pesticide and fungicide. Mice and birds can be deterred by the use of mouse bait and black cotton stretched over the plants; but a cat is as good a deterrent as any.

Take care

Keep the corms from becoming waterlogged. 370▶

Crocus tomasinianus

- **Sunny site sheltered against cold winds**
- **Ordinary well-drained soil**
- **Plant 7.5cm (3in) deep**

This winter-flowering crocus has smaller flowers than the spring crocus, up to 7.5cm (3in) long. The delicate blue-lavender flowers bud in winter and open in very early spring. They naturalize well in grass and sunny borders, given a sheltered position, and do well also in groups under deciduous trees or on rockeries. The varieties available are mostly deep purples such as 'Bar's Purple' and 'Whitewell Purple', but a white variety called 'Albus' is for sale from some specialists.

Corms should be planted 7.5cm (3in) deep, but if the soil is very light and summer cultivation is likely to disturb the roots, they can be planted as deep as 15cm (6in). Do not remove flowers as they die, and leave foliage until it can be pulled off. Increase stock by growing the cormlets, which should flower in two years. Treat soil with a pesticide and fungicide.

Take care

Leave flowers and leaves on the plant until leaves turn yellow. 371▶

Crocus vernus 'Striped Beauty'

- **Sheltered but sunny place**
- **Well-drained soil**
- **Plant 7.5cm (3in) deep**

C. vernus is the parent of the large Dutch crocuses, which over several centuries have resulted in blooms of great variety, up to 12.5cm (5in) long. 'Striped Beauty' has a large flower of silver white with dark purple-blue stripes and a violet-purple base to the petals.

Corms should be planted 7.5cm (3in) deep, or more if the soil is light and sandy, and not less than 10cm (4in) apart. Over the years the corms will multiply naturally to form dense mats of flowers, which are spectacular in grass under deciduous trees. The grass-like leaves should pull off easily when they turn yellow after flowering. At this time the corms can be lifted and divided; remove the cormlets and keep in a nursery area, where they will mature in two years. Treat the soil with a general pesticide and fungicide.

Take care

Do not dead-head or cut leaves until the leaves die back. 371▸

Curtonus paniculatus

- **Sheltered border**
- **Well-drained soil with plenty of humus**
- **Plant 15cm (6in) deep**

This plant is sometimes classified as *Antholyza* or *Tritonia*; it is closely related to crocosmias, freesias ixias and sparaxis. It is hardy, and in the herbaceous border it will grow to 120cm (4ft); in ideal conditions it may reach 150cm (5ft). The sword-like leaves are up to 75cm (30in) long. In late summer the plant produces a succession of blooms on tall branching stems; at each division it bears an orange-red trumpet-shaped flower, 5cm (2in) long.

Corms should be planted 15cm (6in) deep in autumn, in a well-drained soil containing fibrous material. The position should be warm and protected against frost until it is established, when it will be hardy. When flowers die back in autumn, the stems should be cut. At this time the plants can be lifted and divided, but keep them moist until growth starts. This species is generally pest- and disease-free.

Take care

Protect from frost until established.

Cyclamen hederifolium

- **Shade**
- **Soil with added leaf-mould**
- **Plant just under the surface**

This Mediterranean plant is hardy and will grow in poor soil, but it thrives if covered with a 2.5cm (1in) layer of leaf-mould in late spring, after the leaves have died down. The plant grows to only 10cm (4in), often much less. The silvery leaves have dark green markings on the upper surface, and underneath they are red.

Plant the corms 10-15cm (4-6in) apart in a light soil that has plenty of leaf-mould in it; they will thrive in woodland if left undisturbed. Grow cyclamen from seed: sow in pots or trays in late summer and leave the container outside on its side to prevent it becoming waterlogged. Germination will occur the following spring, and seedlings can be potted on, planting out when they are large enough to handle easily, in either late spring or late summer. Treat with a general pesticide; disease is mainly due to wet conditions, so treat the area also with a fungicide.

Take care

Ensure that the soil is well-drained and not waterlogged. 372▸

Cyclamen persicum

- **Sheltered and shady situation**
- **Well-drained soil with plenty of humus**
- **Plant 5cm (2in) deep**

This cyclamen group is much larger than *C. hederifolium*. The original variety is parent to a wide range of plants, forming two main groups: first, the less hardy garden cyclamen, with flowers up to 6.5cm (2.6in) long, in colours ranging from white through pinks and reds to purple, and some with decorative leaf markings; and second, the tender, florists' pot plants with even larger blooms, some of which are scented.

The outdoor varieties grow well in sheltered areas out of direct sun. If you are growing the pot varieties use a soil mixture that has plenty of leaf-mould or peat. Keep the pots cool, moist and shaded from hot sun, keep at 13-16°C (55-60°F) and place in full light. If the air is dried by central heating, keep cyclamen moist. The plants will bloom through the winter, and can be rested during summer. Use a general pesticide and fungicide.

Take care

Avoid watering the centre of the cyclamen.

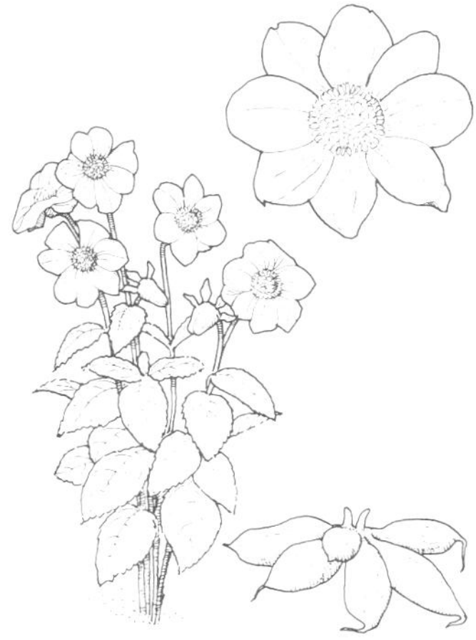

Dahlia (Single-flowered)

- **Open sunny site**
- **Rich well-drained soil**
- **Plant 10cm (4in) deep**

These half-hardy tuberous plants are popular as border specimens. They come into flower in summer and continue until the first frost. The single-flowered varieties have blooms up to 10cm (4in) across, in red, lilac or pink, and consist of a single row of petals around a central disc of stamens. The plants grow up to 75cm (30in) tall.

Plant the tubers outdoors in mid-spring, but if they are already sprouting keep them in a frost-free place until late spring, when they can be planted out. A rich, well-drained soil is needed, with fertilizer or manure added before planting. Place in an open and sunny situation and give the growing plant some support. Remove dead flowers and pinch out leading shoots to encourage larger blooms. Tubers should be lifted and stored each autumn. Spray with a general pesticide and fungicide. If the leaves turn yellow and wilt, destroy the plant to stop the virus.

Take care

Protect young shoots from cold winds and late frosts.

Dahlia (Anemone-flowered)

- **Open sunny site**
- **Rich well-drained soil**
- **Plant 10cm (4in) deep**

This variety will grow to 105cm (42in), with blooms some 10cm (4in) in diameter. The flowers are double, with the outer petals flat and the inner ones tubular and much shorter often in contrasting colours. Blooms appear in summer and continue through to the autumn frosts, giving a brilliant show of red, purple, yellow or white.

Tubers can be started in the warmth but must not be planted out until the danger of frosts has passed. Unsprouted tubers can be planted in late spring; the shoots will not pierce the surface until the frosts have gone. The soil should have plenty of organic material added to it, to feed the roots and to retain moisture during dry periods. Remove dead flowers. Lift the plant in autumn and store the tubers in a frost-free place during winter. Spray with a pesticide and fungicide. If leaves turn yellow and wilt, destroy the plant to prevent spread of virus.

Take care

Keep tubers moist in droughts. 372-373▸

Dahlia (Collarette)

- **Sunny sheltered place**
- **Rich and moist but well-drained soil**
- **Plant 10cm (4in) deep**

This half-hardy plant will grow to 120cm (4ft) tall, with a spread of 75cm (30in). The leaves are bright green and make a good foil for the blooms, which are up to 10cm (4in) across in white, yellow, orange, red or pink. The flowers have an outer ring of flat petals with an inner collar of smaller petals around the central disc of stamens. Blooms appear from late summer to the frosts in autumn, when the plant should be lifted and the tuber stored.

The following spring they can be started off in the greenhouse, and the sprouting plant put out in late spring; or the unsprouted tuber can be put out in mid-spring. The soil should be rich in organic material, compost, bonemeal or manure. Plant in full sun; shelter plants from wind or support the dahlia with a stake. Spray with a general pesticide and fungicide. Destroy plants if the leaves wilt and turn yellow.

Take care

Protect against frost both when growing and in store.

Dahlia (Paeony-flowered)

- **Open sunny site**
- **Rich well-drained soil**
- **Plant 10cm (4in) deep**

This dahlia is descended from Mexican species, and grows to 90cm (36in) tall, with a spread of 60cm (24in). The flowers, 10cm (4in) across, consist of an outer ring of flat petals and one or more inner rings of flat petals around a central core of stamens, in orange, red or purple. Plant the tubers 10cm (4in) deep in well-drained soil with plenty of organic material mixed in to supply nutrients and retain moisture. This border plant should be grown with other dahlias for best effect. The flowers start in late summer and continue until the late autumn frosts.

The tuber should then be lifted and stored free from frost until the following year, when it can be planted out in spring. Alternatively, keep the tuber in a greenhouse to encourage early sprouting, but then it should not be planted out until late spring. Spray with a pesticide and fungicide. If the leaves turn yellow and the plant wilts, destroy it.

Take care

Do not damage the growing points on the tuber. 375▸

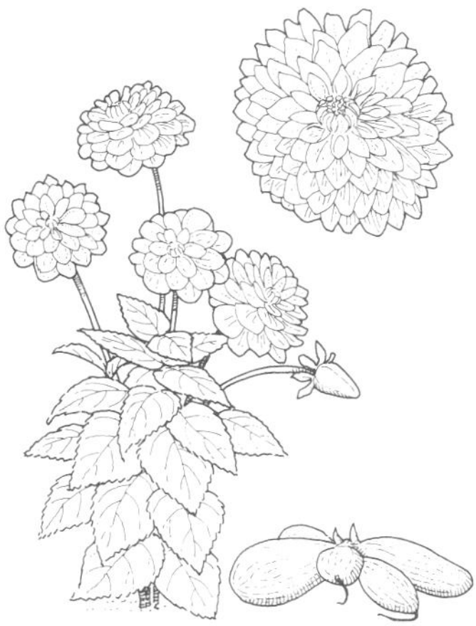

Dahlia (Decorative)

- **Open sunny position**
- **Rich well-drained soil**
- **Plant 10cm (4in) deep**

This group of dahlias is distinguished by the truly double blooms of flat petals, often twisted and normally with blunt points. The group divides into five sections: giant, large, medium, small and miniature. The giants grow to 150cm (5ft), with blooms up to 25cm (10in) across; the miniatures have a height of 90cm (3ft), with flowers 10cm (4in) in diameter. The colours include white, yellow, orange, red, pink, purple and lavender, with some multicolours.

They all flower from late summer until the autumn frosts. Then the plants should be lifted and the tubers stored in a frost-free place until spring. Support plants with stakes, particularly the taller varieties, which are more prone to wind damage. Remove all but one bud from each stem to encourage larger blooms. Remove dead flowers to ensure further flowering. Treat the plants with a pesticide and fungicide.

Take care

Inspect tubers in winter, and destroy diseased or damaged ones. 375▸ 376▸

Dahlia (Ball)

- **Open sunny place**
- **Rich well-drained soil**
- **Plant 10cm (4in) deep**

This group is noted for the ball-shaped blooms. They are fully double; the petals appear to be tubular and open out at the blunt end, and they are arranged in a spiral. The group is split into two sections the standard ball has blooms over 10cm (4in) in diameter; and the miniature ball has blooms under 10cm (4in). Both will grow to 120cm (4ft) tall, and spread 75cm (30in). The colours include white, yellow, orange, red, mauve and purple.

Plant tubers in a well-drained soil rich in organic material, in an area that is open to the sun but sheltered from the wind; mature plants should be staked to prevent wind damage. Sprouted tubers should not be planted in the open until danger of frost has passed, unsprouted ones can be planted out in spring. Spray plants with a pesticide and fungicide. Wilting plants with yellow leaves must be destroyed at once.

Take care

Stake plants to keep wind damage to a minimum. 393▸

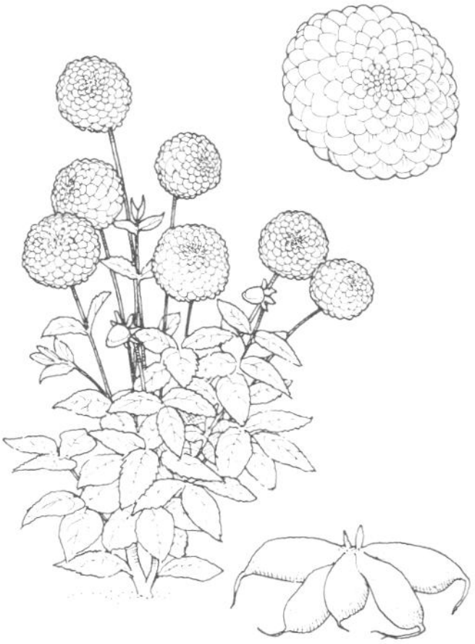

Dahlia (Pompon)

- **Open sunny site**
- **Well-drained rich soil**
- **Plant 10cm (4in) deep**

These plants are similar to the ball dahlias but their blooms are only 5cm (2in) in diameter, the shape is more ball-like, and the petals are tubular for their whole length. They flower in late summer and continue to the first frosts; colours include lilac, red, purple and white. They grow to 120cm (4ft) tall, and 75cm (30in) across.

Plant in a section of the garden that is open but sheltered from the wind. The tubers, if unsprouted, can be planted in mid-spring, but sprouted tubers should be kept in the greenhouse until late spring. Give the plants some support and pinch out the leading shoots one month after planting. When the plants are cut down by frosts, lift and store the tubers in a frost-free place until the following spring. Plants should be treated with a pesticide and fungicide; wilting dahlias with yellow leaves should be destroyed.

Take care
Keep soil moist in droughts.

Dahlia (Cactus)

- **Open sunny site**
- **Rich well-drained soil**
- **Plant 10cm (4in) deep**

This group of dahlias can be divided into five sections: miniature, small, medium, large and giant. They are exotic, with the petals rolled back or quilled for over half their length; the largest flowers reach 25cm (10in) in diameter, but the smallest are only 10cm (4in). The colours include white, yellow, orange, red and purple, with some delicate shades of pink and lilac. The larger plants grow to 150cm (5ft) tall and almost 120cm (4ft) across; the smaller ones are 90cm (36in) tall and 75cm (30in) across.

Tubers should preferably be planted in open sun, but will stand some shade. Plant them outdoors in mid-spring or start them off in a greenhouse and plant out in late spring. Spray with a pesticide and fungicide; wilting plants with yellow leaves should be destroyed.

Take care
Winter storage of tubers must be frost-free. 394▶

Dahlia (Semi-cactus)

- **Open but sheltered site**
- **Well-drained rich soil**
- **Plant 10cm (4in) deep**

Very closely related to the cactus dahlia, the semi-cactus has broader petals that are not tubular or quilled for half their length. Sizes are the same, ranging from 10-25cm (4-10in). The plants have the same bright green leaves and range of flower colour, but the spikiness is less distinct and some have fluted ends to the petals.

Plant in a good well-drained soil rich in humus, and in sunshine, though if necessary they can stand partial shade. The tubers should be planted 10cm (4in) deep in spring, provided they have not started sprouting; otherwise keep them in a frost-free place until late spring, when frosts are over. Provide some support to prevent wind damage. After flowering, remove the dead heads to encourage further flowers. When frost has cut down the dahlias, lift and store the tubers. Spray with a pesticide and fungicide.

Take care

Keep tubers from standing in waterlogged soil. 395▸ 396▸

Dahlia (Bedding)

- **Open sunny site**
- **Well-drained rich soil**
- **Plant 5-10cm (2-4in) deep**

These small dahlias are normally grown from seed and treated like annuals. They grow 30-50cm (12-20in) tall with a similar spread. The leaves are bright green; flowers can be single, semi-double or double, in colours from white through yellows and reds to lilac, and 5-7.5cm (2-3in) in diameter. They start to bloom in midsummer and continue until the autumn frosts.

After the first year, when they are grown from seed, tubers are formed and can be lifted and kept in a frost-free place during winter. If tubers shrivel, soak them in water overnight and then dry them before putting them back into storage. They can be planted the following year in spring unless they have started to sprout, in which case keep them in moist peat until late spring, when they can be planted outside. Seed can be sown in late winter at a temperature of 16°C (60°F), transplanted when large enough to handle, and planted out in late spring in the flowering position. Spray with a pesticide and fungicide.

Take care

Cover plants if frost is forecast. 397▸

Dierama pulcherrimum

(Wandflower)

- **Sunny sheltered site**
- **Ordinary well-drained soil**
- **Plant 10-15cm (4-6in) deep**

This cormous plant is hardy except in the coldest areas. It grows to 180cm (6ft) tall, with grass-like leaves reaching 90cm (36in) in length. The trumpet-shaped hanging flowers, on arching stems, are often 2.5cm (1in) long, and the spread of the plant will reach 60cm (24in). The flowers, in red, violet, purple or white, appear in late summer and last until autumn.

Plant the corms in well-drained soil; there should be at least 10cm (4in) of soil over the corm, and preferably 15cm (6in). Plant in either spring or autumn, and leave undisturbed. If plants become overcrowded they can be lifted in autumn, divided and replanted. In cold areas, lift the corms in autumn and store until spring. Offsets can be removed from the corms in autumn, and will reach flowering in 18 months. Seed can be sown and takes up to three years to flower. Normally plants are pest- and disease-free.

Take care

Leave plants undisturbed.

Endymion hispanicus

- **Open or lightly shade position**
- **Moist but not boggy soil**
- **Plant 10-15cm (4-6in) deep**

This plant was included in the genus *Scilla* but now has its own genus. It grows to a height of 30cm (12in), with broad strap-like leaves, and bell-shaped white, blue or pink flowers from spring to midsummer. It thrives on neglect and is ideal for growing in the open.

Bulbs should be planted 10-15cm (4-6in) deep, in a moist soil with plenty of organic matter. The bulbs have no outer skin, and should be out of the soil as little as possible. Do not store bulbs, as they shrivel when dry or go mouldy if too wet.

Propagate by lifting the bulbs and removing offsets, which can then be replanted with more space around them. Seed sown on leaf-mould may take six years to flower. Yellow spots that turn to dark brown blotches indicate rust; remove and destroy infected leaves, and spray with zineb.

Take care

Avoid waterlogged soil. 397▸

Endymion non-scriptus

(English bluebell)

- **Open sun or light shade**
- **Moist but not waterlogged soil**
- **Plant 10-15cm (4-6in) deep**

This bulbous plant, widespread throughout Western Europe, gives spectacular shows of blue in light woodland and open ground. In Scotland, it is called the wild hyacinth. The strap-like leaves are a glossy mid-green; the purple-blue, white or pink bell-shaped flowers appear in spring. The plant grows to 30cm (12in), and has a spread of 10cm (4in), although the mature leaves will spread further as they become less erect.

The bulbs should be planted 10-15cm (4-6in) deep. They have no outer skin, so the less time they spend out of soil the better. Choose a moist soil with plenty of leaf-mould in it. Plants are increased by lifting and dividing the bulbs after the foliage has died down in autumn. Seed can take up to six years to flower. Endymions are normally pest- and disease-free.

Take care

Replant bulbs quickly, and handle as little as possible.

Eranthis hyemalis

(Winter aconite)

- **Sun or partial shade**
- **Well-drained heavy soil**
- **Plant 2.5cm (1in) deep**

This European tuberous-rooted plant grows to a height of 10cm (4in) with a spread of 7.5cm (3in). The leaves are pale green and deeply cut, and the bright yellow flowers appear in late winter; in mild winters it may start blooming in midwinter. The flowers are about 2.5cm (1in) across and look like buttercups but with a collar of pale green leaves just below the flower.

Plant tubers in a well-drained soil that is moist throughout the year – a heavy loam is ideal. Grow them in either sun or light shade. To propagate, lift the eranthis when the leaves die down, break or cut the tubers into sections, and replant these immediately, at least 7.5cm (3in) apart. Seed can be sown in spring and kept in a cold frame; transplant in two years, and flowering will start after another year. Watch for bird attack. If sooty eruptions occur on the plant, destroy it to stop the spread of smut disease.

Take care

Keep soil moist in spring. 398-399▸

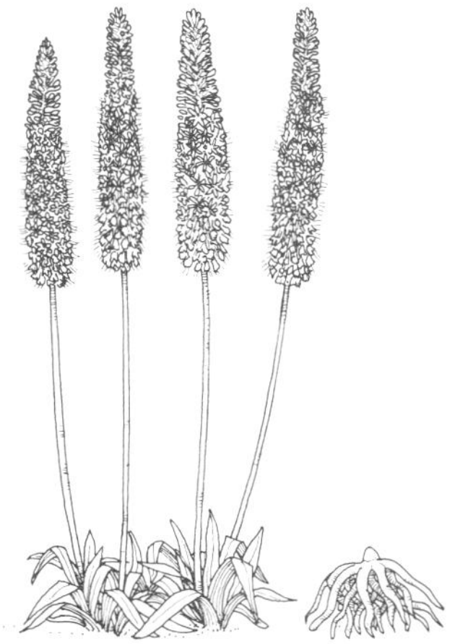

Eremurus robustus

(Foxtail lily)

- **Sunny sheltered border**
- **Well-drained soil**
- **Plant 1.25cm (0.5in) deep**

This dramatic plant reaches 3m (10ft) high, with bright sword-like leaves 120cm (4ft) in length. The flowers, which have the appearance of bushy foxtails, are 120cm (4ft) spikes of star-like blooms, peach-buff to pink in colour. They appear in summer.

The plants should be kept in a sheltered border, with an aspect to catch midday to evening sun, and the soil should be well-drained with plenty of fibre. The crown of the tuber should have only 1.25cm (0.5in) of soil over it, although some growers recommend planting as deep as 15cm (6in) in light soils. Leave undisturbed until tubers become crowded, then lift, divide and replant in autumn. The flower stems should be cut down when blooming stops, unless seed is needed. Spread well-rotted manure or compost over the area in autumn. Seeds are slow to germinate and take several years to reach flowering size.

Take care

Not suitable for windy sites.

Erythronium dens-canis

(Dog's tooth violet)

- **Semi-shade**
- **Moist well-drained soil**
- **Plant 7.5cm (3in) deep**

This cormous plant grows only 15cm (6in) tall. The spotted leaves vary from plant to plant, and some are particularly attractive. The 5cm (2in) flowers appear in spring and the petals are folded back like a cyclamen; they are available in white, pink, red and violet, each flower having a pair of leaves up to 10cm (4in) long.

Corms should be planted in autumn, preferably in groups of at least a dozen for show, in a moist but well-drained soil; choose a partially shaded site. Here they can be left for many years undisturbed. Increasing stock by growing from seed can take over five years to reach flowering size. It is quicker to remove offsets in late summer, when the leaves have died down, and to grow them separately in a nursery bed for a year or so; they should take two years to start flowering, and then they can be planted out in autumn. Generally pest- and disease-free.

Take care

Keep these plants moist. 398▸

Erythronium tuolumnense

- **Shady situation**
- **Moist but not waterlogged soil**
- **Plant 10cm (4in) deep**

This plant grows to 30cm (12in), with a spread of 15cm (6in). It has bright green leaves that are broad and pointed. The spring flowers have six pointed yellow petals and are rather like small lilies.

The corms should be planted 10cm (4in) deep, in a moist but not boggy soil that has plenty of leaf-mould to keep it well-drained, and with some shade. They should be planted in late summer and can be left undisturbed until they become overcrowded; then lift, divide and replant when the leaves die down in summer. Seed takes over five years to reach flowering; it is quicker to increase stock from offsets, which reach flowering in three years. Make sure the soil does not dry out when plants are young, as they need constantly moist soil to thrive. A good layer of well-rotted manure or compost spread over the plants in autumn keeps the organic level high.

Take care

Keep the soil moist (but not wet) until plants are established. 399▸

Eucomis bicolor

(Pineapple flower)

- **Open position or light shade**
- **Rich well-drained soil**
- **Plant 2.5cm (1in) deep**

This plant reaches 70cm (28in) tall, with a spread of 45cm (18in). It has long broad strap-like leaves with pronounced centre spines, and cream flowers in summer borne on fleshy stems crowned with rosettes of petal-like leaves.

It thrives in a rich well-drained soil with plenty of leaf-mould in it. This plant is hardy and needs only a mulch of well-rotted manure each autumn to protect it from hard frosts in winter. Bulbs can be lifted in very early spring, and the offsets separated and replanted; the parent bulbs then have more space to grow, and offsets reach flowering size in two or three years provided they are kept moist all summer and shaded from the sun.

If this species is grown as a pot plant, it should be kept moist in summer but the pot should be rested on its side during winter to allow the soil to dry out. Grown from seed it takes several years to flower.

Take care

Protect from hard frosts.

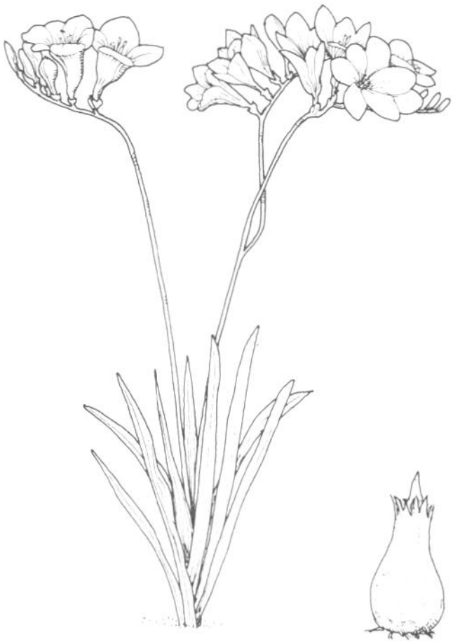

Freesia × hybrida

- **Sheltered sunny situation**
- **Light sandy soil**
- **Plant 5cm (2in) deep**

These plants grow to 45cm (18in) tall, with a spread of 15cm (6in). The leaves are narrow and sword-like, and the flower stems have spikes of scented trumpet-shaped 5cm (2in) blooms in summer. Although most are suitable for the greenhouse only, some are available for growing out of doors, being planted in spring to flower in the summer of the first season only. A wide variety of exquisite colours is available, from white through yellow to pink, red, magenta and violet.

Freesias need a light sandy soil and a position that is sunny and sheltered from cold winds. Plant the corms in spring unless you have a frost-free area, where they can be planted in late summer to flower the following spring. After flowering the corms can be lifted and treated as greenhouse bulbs where they can provide flowers in early spring, but they need a minimum temperature of 5°C (41°F). Offsets removed in late summer flower the following year.

Take care

Protect from frost. 400▶

Fritillaria imperialis

(Crown imperial)

- **Full or partial shade**
- **Well-drained soil**
- **Plant 20cm (8in) deep**

This plant grows up to 90cm (36in) tall, with a centre stem on which is carried a series of narrow pointed glossy leaves to half the total height; the top half of this stem carries a circle of large beautiful drooping flowers about 5cm (2in) long, which is topped with a green crown of leaves. The range of bloom colour is yellow, orange and red.

The bulb should be planted in autumn in a rich well-drained soil in shade, preferably where it can be left undisturbed. Handle bulbs carefully and do not let them dry out. Plant the bulb on its side to stop water getting into the hollow crown and rotting the bulb. In heavy soil a handful of coarse sand around the bulb will speed drainage. Cut the stems down when they die off in summer. Seed will not produce flowering bulbs for six years. It is quicker to use offsets taken from the parent bulb in late summer; plant them out in a nursery bed for two years, then transplant them to the flowering position.

Take care

Do not bruise or dry the bulb. 401▶

Fritillaria meleagris

(Snake's head fritillary)

- **Full or semi-shade**
- **Well-drained fertile soil**
- **Plant 15cm (6in) deep**

These fritillarias have delicate blooms with a fine chequerboard pattern. They grow to 45cm (18in) tall with fine grass-like leaves mid- to blue-green in colour. The blooms are just under 5cm (2in) in length and hang down like bells, appearing in spring. The flowers are purple, brown, violet-red and white; the white varieties do not have the chequerboard pattern, but some have fine green veining instead.

They should be planted in the autumn, 15cm (6in) deep on their side, in rich fertile soil that is well-drained, and in full or partial shade. Leave undisturbed for at least four years; then they can be lifted, and the bulblets removed and replanted in a nursery bed for two years, then transplanted to their final flowering positions. When young, they should be kept moist but not wet; if the soil is too wet, mix in plenty of sharp sand to aid drainage. Fritillarias are generally pest- and disease-free.

Take care

Avoid waterlogged sites.

Galanthus nivalis

(Snowdrop)

- **Partial shade**
- **Rich well-drained soil**
- **Plant 10-15cm (4-6in) deep**

Snowdrop leaves are flat, sword-shaped and often blue-green in colour. The flowers are either single or double, in white with green markings on the inner petals, and can be as long as 2.5cm (1in). Snowdrops' time of flowering depends on the severity or mildness of the winter weather, but normally starts around midwinter. One variety flowers in late autumn, before the leaves appear. They can grow up to 20cm (8in) tall in rich soil and in partial shade.

The bulbs should be planted 10cm (4in) deep in heavy soil, or 15cm (6in) deep in light soil, in autumn; the soil should be moist but well-drained. Move bulbs after they have finished flowering, while the soil is moist. Seed may take five years to bloom, so it is better to split clusters of bulbs and spread them out. Take care when lifting not to damage the roots or to let them dry out. Use a soil insecticide and fungicide.

Take care

Leave bulbs undisturbed for several years for improved flowering. 402-403▸

Galtonia candicans

(Summer hyacinth)

- **Full sun**
- **Moist well-drained soil**
- **Plant 15cm (6in) deep**

This plant grows up to 120cm (4ft), with narrow sword-like pointed leaves 75cm (30in) long. The dozen or so scented flowers appear in late summer on a single stem; they are bell-shaped, almost 5cm (2in) long, and white in colour with green markings at the tip and base of the petals.

The large round bulbs should be grouped and planted in spring in a rich well-drained soil. They are hardy in the more temperate areas but where there are hard frosts it is better to treat galtonias as pot plants. As pot plants they should be started in autumn in order to flower late the following spring, but keep them at a temperature of not less than 4°C (39°F) for success. Seed takes up to five years to flower; but offsets taken in autumn will flower in two years. Treat the soil with slug bait around the plants, and spray with fungicide to keep grey mould to a minimum, especially with newly planted bulbs.

Take care

Protect from severe frost by covering with bracken or a thick mulch. 402▸

Gladiolus byzantinus

- **Full sun**
- **Ordinary rich garden soil**
- **Plant 10cm (4in) deep**

This hardy plant, up to 60cm (24in) tall, has a flower spike about 40cm (16in) long. A succession of wine-red blooms, 5-7.5cm (2-3in) across, appear along the spike in midsummer. The leaves are sword-shaped with pointed tips.

Plant in full sun in ordinary garden soil fed with manure, in either autumn or spring. Plant a little deeper in light soil, to give more anchorage. In heavy soil a base of sharp sand under the corm will help drainage and prevent rot. Keep the young plants weeded, and after 10 weeks of growth start watering well. In the autumn the leaves will die back; remove them when they virtually fall off. After a few years lift them and remove the cormlets to increase the stock; these take up to three years to flower. Treat the plant with a pesticide and fungicide to prevent trouble. If a plant looks sick and turns yellow, destroy it to stop the virus spreading.

Take care

Avoid waterlogged soil. 403▸

Above: **Dahlia 'Kay Helen' (Ball)**
A very neat and compact bloom that will look equally splendid in either the garden border or as a cut flower indoors. Dahlias will thrive in a rich soil and a sunny position. 383◆

Above: **Dahlia 'Match' (Cactus)**
A lovely example of a multicoloured bloom, with its spiky double flowers and the petals rolled or quilled. 384▶

Below: **Dahlia 'Salmon Keene' (Cactus)**
One of the more regular shaped blooms of this group. 384▶

Above: **Dahlia 'Earl Marc' (Semi-cactus)**
Not as quilled or tubular as the cactus, this bloom has flatter petals. Semi-cactus flowers can reach 25cm (10in) across. 385▸

Left: **Dahlia 'Primrose Bryn' (Semi-cactus)**

These sun-loving plants thrive in an open border with rich garden soil. The blooms continue throughout the summer until late autumn. 385▸

Right: **Dahlia 'Gypsy Dance' (Bedding)**

Ideal for the front of borders and in bedding arrangements. The small brightly coloured flowers come in single and double forms. 385▸

Below: **Endymion hispanicus**

Often referred to as the Spanish bluebell, this plant enjoys a moist soil and thrives on neglect. It will grow in either the open or in the light shade of woodland. 386▸

Left: **Erythronium dens-canis**
A low-growing plant that has beautifully marked leaves and delicate blooms that appear in the spring and often continue until summer. Provide some shade. 388▸

Right: **Erythronium tuolumnense**
This plant loves a moist soil and shade, where it will flower in spring with yellow lily-like blooms. It likes to be left alone and undisturbed; a woodland site is ideal. 389▸

Below: **Eranthis hyemalis**
A ground-hugging plant with brilliant yellow flowers that look like buttercups and appear in midwinter if conditions are mild. It thrives in a heavy soil that is moist throughout the year. 387▸

Left: **Freesia 'Prince of Orange'**
A fine form of this perfumed flower that needs plenty of sun and shelter from the cold. It will thrive in a light sandy soil and bloom during the midsummer months. 390▸

Right: **Fritillaria imperialis**
A most unusual and impressive plant with drooping flowers and a crown of leaves on a tall stem. It needs a shady or partially shady situation and a well-drained soil to thrive. 390▸

Below: **Freesia 'Red Star'**
Although normally grown under glass, some varieties are available for outdoor use. All have highly coloured and scented flowers and sword-like leaves. Plant corms in spring. 390▸

Left: **Galtonia candicans**
In full sun and a moist soil, this plant will reward the grower with scented blooms throughout the summer. Reaching over 1m (39in) in height, the galtonia is suited to the back of the border. 392▸

Right: **Gladiolus byzantinus**
A small-flowered gladiolus that blooms much earlier than its large-flowered relations and does not need staking. Place in full sun in groups to make the most of the flowers. 392▸

Below: **Galanthus nivalis**
Normally flowering in midwinter, the low-growing snowdrop is often regarded as the herald of spring. It will grow best in light shade and a good soil that is moist and free-draining. Handle bulbs with care. 391▸

Above: **Gladiolus 'Spring Green'**
A small summer-flowering primulinus gladiolus with a slender and graceful form that is fine for cut flowers as well as the border. 409▸

Left: **Gladiolus 'Nanus Minetto'**
A miniature hybrid gladiolus with delicate form and finely marked blooms. These look well in flower arrangements and also in the garden border, ideally near the front. 410▸

Right: **Gladiolus 'Aristocrat'**
One of the large-flowered varieties available in brilliant colours. By staggering the planting you can have blooms throughout the summer. 409▸

Above:
Ipheion uniflorum 'Violaceum'
These spring-flowering plants have star-shaped scented blooms. 414▸

Far left: **Hyacinthus orientalis 'Anna Marie'**
These indoor bulbs are treated for forcing to give blooms in winter. 412▸

Left:
Hyacinthus orientalis 'Ostara'
A spring garden variety that will look good singly or en masse. 413▸

Right: **Hymenocallis × festalis**
A scented summer-flowering plant that has a narcissus-like trumpet and long slender petals. 413▸

Above: **Iris pumila 'Green Spot' (Pogoniris/Eupogon)**
A bearded iris with fine markings that thrives in a sunny border and blooms in early summer, after spring bulbs and before the summer flowers. 415▸

Gladiolus (Large-flowered)

- **Full sun**
- **Ordinary garden soil with added humus**
- **Plant 10-15cm (4-6in) deep**

The large-flowered gladiolus hybrids are half-hardy plants that need some protection against frost. The plants often reach 120cm (4ft) high. The flower spike is about 50cm (20in) long, and individual blooms are 17.5cm (7in) across. They flower in summer, in vivid shades of white, yellow, orange, red, purple, rust, pink and mauve, either with markings or plain.

These hybrids are easily grown from corms planted 10-15cm (4-6in) deep; in lighter soils plant at the greater depth. Put some sharp sand under the corms to aid drainage, and place in full sun. An ordinary garden soil with some manure added is ideal. As they mature, the plants may become top-heavy, so staking is useful. When the plant dies back after flowering, lift it and store the new corm in a frost-free place for the following year. Treat with pesticide and fungicide to keep plants healthy.

Take care

Protect against frost and excessive wetness. 405▸

Gladiolus (Primulinus hybrids)

- **Full sun**
- **Ordinary garden soil enriched with manure**
- **Plant 10-15cm (4-6in) deep**

These are not as vigorous or as big as the large-flowered gladiolus but they are free-flowering and decorative. The plants grow to a height of 45-90cm (18-36in), with the flower spike almost 40cm (16in) long; the flowers themselves, up to 7.5cm (3in) across, are placed alternately on the stem, and bloom after midsummer. A variety of colours is available, some with stripes and contrasting throats. The leaves are long, slender and sword-shaped.

The plant is half-hardy, surviving in some winters underground, but normally the corm is lifted in autumn. A new corm is found above the old one, which is discarded; store the young corm in a frost-free place during the winter. Grow in a well-drained soil, keeping it moist in the summer at flowering time. Treat with a fungicide to keep rot and fungus at bay.

Take care

Destroy diseased corms to prevent spread. 404▸

Gladiolus (Miniature hybrids)

- **Sunny position**
- **Good well-drained garden soil**
- **Plant 10-15cm (4-6in) deep**

These plants grow to 45-90cm (18-36in) tall, and the flower spikes are about 35cm (14in) long, with each flower about 5cm (2in) across. They bloom after midsummer, and flowers are often frilled or fluted. The colours are bright, and varied with blotches, spots and stripes.

These corms are best grown in a sunny part of the garden in a good well-drained soil; they should be planted 10-15cm (4-6in) deep, depending on the soil – plant deeper in light soil to give better anchorage. In heavy soil, add plenty of sharp sand under and around the corm to aid drainage, keep the young plant weeded, and water well once the flower spike starts to open. Lift the plant in autumn, remove the young corm and store it in a frost-free place for the following year. Keep the plant free from disease with a fungicide; if the plant wilts and turns yellow, destroy it to stop the virus disease spreading to others.

Take care

Do not grow in waterlogged soil. 404▸

Gladiolus (Butterfly hybrids)

- **Full sunshine**
- **Good garden soil**
- **Plant 10-15cm (4-6in) deep**

This plant is noted for the unusual markings on the throat of the blooms. They are 60-120cm (24-48in) tall, with flower spikes 45cm (18in) long; the alternating blooms, 10cm (4in) across, appear in summer. Flowers range from white through yellow, orange, or red to purple, with blotches, markings or edgings in contrasting colours.

They thrive in a sunny place in good well-drained soil. In light soils, plant corms 15cm (6in) deep, but in heavier soils this can be reduced to 10cm (4in). Plant out in spring, and start watering in early summer. The plant should be lifted in autumn when its leaves turn yellow. Leave it to dry for a few days, and the new corm will come away from the old one easily; store it through the winter in a frost-free place for the next year. Treat these plants with a fungicide.

Take care

Protect from frost.

Gloriosa rothschildiana

(Glory lily)

- **Light shade**
- **Balanced potting mixture**
- **Plant just under the surface**

These tender plants should be treated as greenhouse or pot plants unless you live in a very mild area. They have a climbing and trailing habit, and may reach 180cm (6ft) tall. The leaves are glossy, with a tendril at the leaf end which hooks onto supports. The striking flowers, 10cm (4in) across, have curved back petals of scarlet edged with golden yellow, and it blooms constantly through summer and autumn.

Plant the tuber in early spring in the greenhouse, at a temperature over 16°C (60°F). Use a 17.5cm (7in) pot. Water freely while it is growing, and give a liquid manure once a week until flowering has finished. The tuber should be kept dry through the winter in a cool but frost-free place. During summer provide a support, and shade it from direct sun. Seeds take up to four years to flower. Offsets taken in early spring and grown in pots will flower in two years.

Take care

If leaves fall early, allow the plant to almost dry before watering again.

Haemanthus natalensis coccineus

(Blood lily)

- **Sun or partial shade**
- **Balanced potting mixture**
- **Just cover with soil**

This tender greenhouse bulbous plant has long thick leaves that hug the ground and develop after the flowers have died. It forms a 5-7.5cm (2-3in) head of red blooms in late summer. The large bulb is 7.5cm (3in) in diameter, from which grows a plant only 20-30cm (8-12in) tall.

Plant the bulbs in a pot in spring. Leave them undisturbed for several years, but give them a liquid feed every two weeks throughout the summer. When the leaves dry off, put the pot in a cold place until growth starts again, early the following spring, when the soil should be moistened. Every few years take the bulb out and use fresh soil for repotting; offsets can be removed and potted up as separate bulbs, and should flower in two years' time. A 20cm (8in) pot of John Innes No. 2 potting mixture is ideal. Mealy bugs may attack the plant, leaving tufts of waxy wool; paint the areas with a systemic insecticide.

Take care

Do not disturb the root.

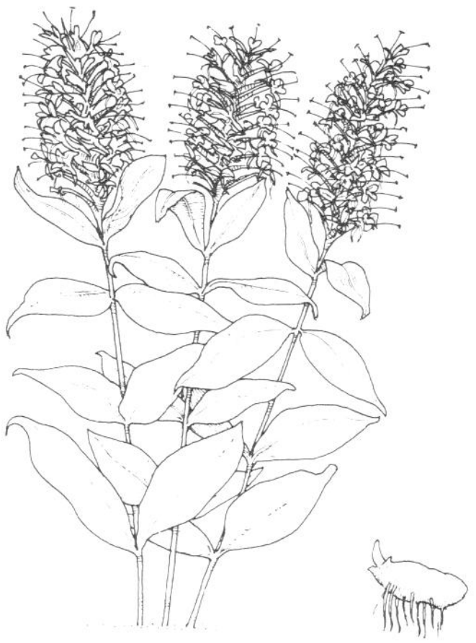

Hedychium gardnerianum

(Ginger-wort)

- **Sun or light shade**
- **Rich potting mixture**
- **Plant just below the surface**

This tender plant will grow outdoors only in very mild areas, and is usually grown as a pot plant. It is a perennial, 180cm (6ft) tall and 150cm (5ft) across; the leaves are often 30cm (12in) long and as broad. In summer it has spikes of scented yellow flowers 5cm (2in) wide, with brilliant scarlet stamens.

Due to its size, this plant needs a tub. Use John Innes No. 3 potting mixture supplemented with a liquid feed every two weeks during the growing period. In autumn the stems should be cut down almost to the rhizome. Let the plant rest in winter, keeping it dry. In early spring water it a little, increasing the amount as it grows. The plant can be repotted in spring when it starts to shoot; at this stage divide and replant the rhizomes to increase your stock. If grown outdoors, plant it in a sheltered place in summer and lift before the first frost.

Take care

Do not water during the winter.

Hyacinthus orientalis

(Dutch hyacinth)

- **Full light but not direct sun**
- **Bulb fibre**
- **Plant with tops showing through the surface**

This plant consists of a cluster of strap-like leaves around a central flower stem that bears a spike of scented bell-shaped blooms. The plant will reach 23cm (9in) tall and the flowerhead may be 15cm (6in) long. If potted in late summer the prepared bulb will bloom in winter; autumn planting gives spring bloom. The flowers may be white, yellow, pink, red, blue, purple or mauve, and some have double blooms.

Plant bulbs in a mixture of peat with shell and charcoal – this mix is known as bulb fibre. The fibre should be moist at all times, but keep the shoots dry – if they become wet they rot and die. Keep in a cool dark place for at least eight weeks to encourage root growth, then bring out into warmth and full light (but not direct sunlight) once the flower shoot has fully emerged from the bulb. Dutch hyacinths are usually trouble-free.

Take care

Keep bulb fibre moist, not wet. 406▸

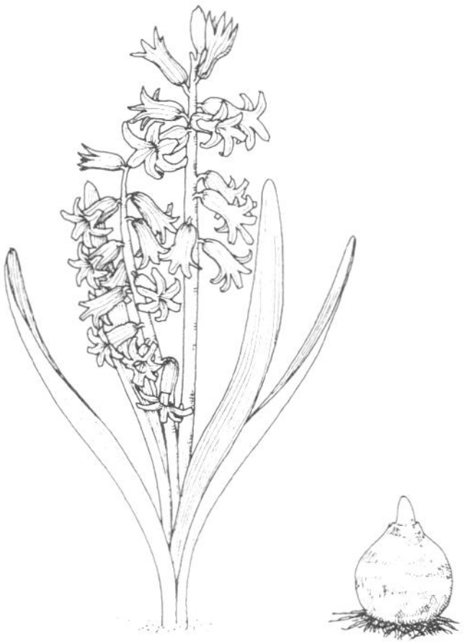

Hyacinthus orientalis

(Garden hyacinth)

- **Full sun or light shade**
- **Ordinary garden soil**
- **Plant 12.5-15cm (5-6in) deep**

These hyacinths flower in spring with bright scented blooms on a stem over 30cm (12in) long, and 15cm (6in) of the stem is covered in flowers. They are ideal bedding plants either in formal arrangements with other plants or in clumps to give patches of colour. They can be propagated from seed but may take six years to reach the flowering stage; it is far better to obtain specially prepared bulbs produced by professional bulb growers. These are planted in ordinary garden soil in autumn; choose a site in full sun or light shade. After flowering they can be lifted and moved to another part of the garden to recuperate, leaving space for other plants to provide summer colour. Treat the soil with a general pesticide to keep pests away. If disease occurs, with poor leaf and flower production, destroy the bulb to prevent spreading.

Take care

Buy bulbs from a good specialist. 406▶

Hymenocallis × festalis

- **Full sun, sheltered from frost**
- **Rich well-drained soil**
- **Plant with top just level with surface**

This plant is susceptible to frost; unless your garden has a near frost-free climate, treat it as a pot plant. The white scented flowers, 10cm (4in) across, have a centre not unlike a daffodil trumpet, but the outer petals are long and slender. The strap-like leaves are 30cm (12in) long. The plant grows to 45cm (18in) tall, and blooms in spring if grown as a pot plant; out of doors it flowers in summer.

When growing this as a pot plant use a medium or large pot with a general potting mixture. For early blooms keep it at 16°C (60°F), but for later flowers keep the greenhouse just frost-free. In spring give a mild liquid feed every two weeks. Keep it in shade, and water well in hot weather; repot every two or three years. For outdoors grow it in a pot and plant out in late spring in a well-drained soil in full sun. Generally this plant is trouble-free.

Take care

Protect from frost. 407▶

Ipheion uniflorum

- **Full sun**
- **Ordinary soil with good drainage**
- **Plant 5cm (2in) deep**

These bulbous plants are noted for their grass-like sea-green leaves and star-shaped flowers. The plants grow only 20cm (8in) tall, with spring flowers 5cm (2in) wide; the white to deep lavender-blue blooms are scented.

Bulbs should be planted in autumn. Plants should be kept weeded, and when leaves and flower stems die back in summer they should be removed. Position plants in full sun in well-drained soil. The bulbs are increased by bulblets, the plants should be lifted in autumn, divided, and replanted at once. Do this every two or three years to keep the plants free-flowering and healthy. Make sure bulbs do not dry out or become wet during transplanting, and keep the time out of the soil to the minimum. Ipheions are generally trouble-free provided the soil is kept free-draining.

Take care

Do not let bulbs dry out or get wet when planting or transplanting. **406-407▸**

Iris (Pogoniris/Arillate)

(Bearded irises)

- **Sunny position**
- **Rich light soil with some lime**
- **Plant 2.5-7.5cm (1-3in) below surface of soil**

Irises of the Pogoniris group have fleshy, hairy beards on the three outer petals (the *falls*). The three inner petals are called the *standards*, and between these are three strap-like petals known as the *style arms*. Within the Pogoniris section there are two groups: the first of these, the Arillate group, has a branching rhizome root that grows 2.5-7.5cm (1-3in) below the soil surface. Sword-like leaves sprout from the rhizome in a fan-like growth, and 12.5cm (5in) flowers are borne in early summer on a single stem up to 60cm (24in) tall. Colours are mainly white, blue and brown, with veining and markings. Rhizomes should be protected from excessive wetness. When foliage dies the plants may be lifted and divided. Use a pesticide and fungicide.

Take care

Do not let soil become too wet.

Iris (Pogoniris/Eupogon)

(Bearded irises)

- **Full sun**
- **Ordinary garden soil**
- **Plant with the top of the rhizome exposed**

Irises of this group are distinguished by the rhizomes that lie on the surface, by the scented flowers and by the blue-green sword-like leaves. Size varies from 7.5cm (3in) to 150cm (5ft) according to the variety; the dwarf members will thrive in rock gardens, and the taller varieties are suitable for the herbaceous border. Blooms appear from early to late spring in a wide range of colours and sizes. Many of the flowers are heavily veined, and up to 15cm (6in) across. These are delightful plants that help to fill the gap between spring and summer flowering plants.

Give them a sunny place with ordinary garden soil. Rhizomes should be planted either at midsummer or in early autumn. Keep them moist until established. Plants can be divided to increase stock. Use a pesticide and fungicide to keep plants healthy.

Take care

Cut leaves back in winter to stop slug attack. 408▸

Iris (Apogon/ Californicae)

(Beardless irises)

- **Sun or partial shade**
- **Acid or neutral garden soil**
- **Plant 2.5cm (1in) deep**

The leaves of these plants are slender, sword-shaped and normally evergreen. The flowers are up to 9cm (3.6in) across in late spring. Colours range from white through cream, yellow, orange and pale blue to deep purple; some have heavy marking on the falls and the three outer petals.

These irises are short-lived, but are easily grown from seed. This can be harvested from the plant and sown in autumn, in a temperature of about 10°C (50°F). Plant seedlings out when they are still very young to avoid later root disturbance; they should flower the following year. Rhizomes can be divided in autumn and replanted, but keep the roots moist until they are established. Poor-quality specimens should be thrown out to keep the rest healthy. Treat with a pesticide and fungicide, and destroy diseased plants.

Take care

Keep freshly planted rhizomes and young plants moist. 425▸

Iris (Apogon/Hexagona)

(Beardless irises)

- **Sun or light shade**
- **Moist rich soil**
- **Plant just below the surface**

This group has large six-ribbed seed pods, up to 10cm (4in) long. The leaves are narrow and evergreen. The flowers, up to 20cm (8in) wide, appear in midsummer; the zig-zag stems carry a flower bud and leaf at each change of direction.

The plants reach a height of 90cm (36in) and should be planted 40cm (16in) apart in a moist soil, with the rhizome just below the surface. Choose a site in either sun or light shade, and a rich soil that has a high humus content. In winter protect the plants with a layer of straw, compost or leaf-mould. There are a number of hybrids: of the named varieties, 'Wheelhorse' and 'Dixie Deb' have grown exceptionally well in temperate areas. Protect the plants with a general insecticide and fungicide; if plants become badly affected they should be lifted and destroyed to stop the trouble spreading.

Take care

Keep the rhizomes moist.

Iris (Apogon/Laevigatae)

(Beardless irises)

- **Full sun**
- **Grow in moist soil and water**
- **Just below surface of soil, or 7.5-15cm (3-6in) under water**

These irises thrive on the banks of streams, rivers, ponds and lakes. *I. laevigata, L. pseudacorus* and *I. versicolor* are water irises for the garden pool, but *I. kaempferi* should be planted in moist soil but not directly into water. The blooms of the kaempferi irises are particularly beautiful in both colouring and form. The flowers may grow up to 20cm (8in) across, in either single or double form. All these irises have the characteristic sword-shaped leaves, and all will grow up to 60cm (24in) tall except *I. pseudacorus,* which reaches 120cm (4ft) in water.

Plant rhizomes just under the soil, or between 7.5-15cm (3-6in) under water. Lift the plants every three years, and divide and replant. Treat the plant with a general pesticide and fungicide to keep trouble to a minimum. Take particular care to prevent chemicals entering the water.

Take care

Do not let plant or rhizome dry. 427▸

Iris (Apogon/Sibirica)

(Beardless irises)

- **Sunny position**
- **Moist garden soil**
- **Plant 2.5cm (1in) deep**

These irises grow well both in the border and by water. They are noted for their grass-like leaves, their hardiness and their summer flowers. Plants can reach 90cm (36in) tall, but most grow to only 60cm (24in). The flowers come in various colours and shadings and can measure 10cm (4in) across.

Hybrids are readily available from nurseries in autumn. Plant them in moist soil, but if next to water the rhizome must be at least 15cm (6in) above the water level to prevent rot. If the soil is dry, give it a good watering, and add humus to conserve moisture. Plant rhizomes 2.5cm (1in) deep in a sunny situation and avoid hoeing around the plant as the root system is very near the surface. Mulch well in spring to deter weed growth. The plants can be lifted in late autumn or early spring and divided and replanted; do this every four years or so.

Take care
Do not hoe around the root area.

Iris (Apogon/Spuria)

(Beardless irises)

- **Sunny situation**
- **Ordinary garden soil**
- **Plant 5cm (2in) deep**

These hardy irises have fibrous rhizomes, and double ridges on the seed pods. The leaves are sword-shaped, in some varieties growing to 90cm (36in) long; the leaves die down in winter leaving young fresh growth to last through to spring. The white, purple, yellow or deep blue flowers are up to 10cm (4in) wide, and some are scented.

Plant the rhizomes 5cm (2in) deep in good garden soil that has plenty of sun; water them well in and keep the surrounding soil moist. Once planted, in late autumn, they should be left alone; only dig them up if the flowers become small because they are too crowded. This should be done in late autumn; divide the root and replant with more space. It will take up to two years for them to start flowering again. Treat these irises with a pesticide and fungicide.

Take care
Do not disturb the plant unnecessarily.

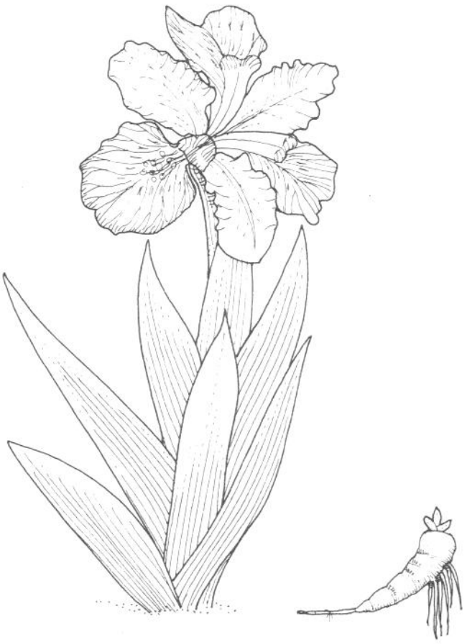

Iris (Crested section)

(Crested irises)

- **Partial shade**
- **Moist lime-free soil with humus**
- **Plant just below the surface**

These irises have orchid-like flowers with a cock's-comb crest instead of a beard. The smaller varieties are suitable for the rock garden as they grow only 15cm (6in) tall, with flowers over 5cm (2in) across; larger ones reach 45cm (18in) high, with flowers 7.5cm (3in) wide. The leaves are evergreen, broad, and glossy. The delicate blooms are white or lavender, with markings and spots.

The thin rhizomes should be planted in late spring, just under the surface; the soil should have a plentiful supply of humus – leaf-mould or peat – mixed with it. This should be topped up every spring with a mulch of extra humus. These irises can be lifted after flowering, divided and replanted with extra space around the rhizomes, but keep them moist until they are established. Shelter them from the sun in frosty weather so that they can thaw out gently. Protect them from slug and snail attacks with bait.

Take care

Keep moist in dry weather. 426▶

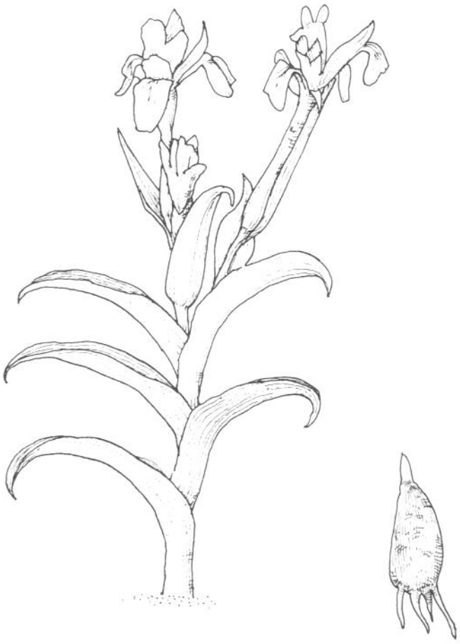

Iris (Juno/I. bucharica var.)

(Bulbous irises)

- **Sheltered site**
- **Light well-drained soil**
- **Plant 5cm (2in) deep**

These irises come from Turkestan and will grow to a height of 45cm (18in). Attached to the bulb are thick fleshy delicate roots, and if these are damaged the plant suffers. The leaves do not last long. Scented yellow and cream flowers appear in spring, over 5cm (2in) wide and up to seven blooms on each stem.

If you have an exposed site, grow these bulbs in pots and keep them protected until the weather is mild enough to plant them outside. Plant the bulbs in early autumn in a light well-drained soil that will keep dry in summer; if possible, position them among shrubs or under trees to provide shelter. After the leaves have died down, the plant can be lifted. Allow the roots to become limp and less fragile, tease out the bulbs, divide them and replant with more space around them. The plants should be treated with a pesticide and fungicide.

Take care

Avoid damaging the roots. 426▶

Iris (Reticulata/I. reticulata var.)

(Bulbous irises)

- **Light shade or sun**
- **Light well-drained limy soil**
- **Plant 5-7.5cm (2-3in) deep**

These hardy Asian bulbous plants have a net of fibres around the outside of the bulb and grass-like tubular leaves that are dark green with a paler tip. They are early flowering; some start at midwinter and others follow successively through to spring. The flowers are often 7.5cm (3in) wide, in lemon-yellow and blue. These plants are small, and ideal for the rock garden; they rarely grow more than 15cm (6in) tall.

Plant them in a light well-drained chalky soil; if the ground is heavy, the bulb may not shoot after the first year. Give each bulb a covering of 5-7.5cm (2-3in) of soil. They do best when planted in autumn. After flowering give a liquid feed every four weeks until the bulb dies back. If grown for indoor decoration, plant them in pots, keep in the cool until the flower buds show, then bring into the warm. Use a fungicide and pesticide to keep the plants healthy.

Take care

Do not plant in heavy moist soil. 429▸

Iris (Xiphium/I. xiphium var.)

(Bulbous irises)

- **Sunny site**
- **Good well-drained garden soil**
- **Plant 10-15cm (4-6in) deep**

In less temperate areas this iris is tender and short lived, but hybrids (known as Dutch, Spanish and English irises) are more vigorous and hardy. The English iris prefers a moist rich soil and should be left undisturbed; it flowers in summer with a range of colour that does not include yellow, the blooms reaching 12.5cm (5in) across, and it will grow to 60cm (24in) tall. The Dutch iris flowers from early summer and prefers a light soil, the 10cm (4in) wide blooms come in a wide range of colours, and grow to a height of 60cm (24in). The Spanish iris follows the Dutch flowering period, and is smaller, but the flowers have fine smoky shades; they enjoy a lighter, drier and warmer soil than the others.

Lift and ripen the bulbs by drying them in late summer and then replant in autumn where the soil is heavy. In warm light soils they can be left in the ground. Protect the plants with a pesticide and fungicide.

Take care

Soak in fungicide before planting.

Ixia viridiflora hybrids

(African corn lily)

- **Sunny situation**
- **Sandy soil**
- **Plant 7.5cm (3in) deep**

These plants are noted for their six-petalled star-shaped flowers in a variety of yellows, reds, purples or blues, up to 5cm (2in) wide. These flowers are borne on strong wiry stems up to 45cm (18in) tall, so they are good for cutting.

Ixias are not hardy, but will grow out of doors in milder parts of the temperate zone; otherwise they can be grown as pot plants. The corms should be planted during autumn in a sunny situation, in ordinary or sandy soil. To protect corms from frost, a good layer of ashes, bracken or compost should be spread over the area in late autumn before the frosts start. For pot growing, plant in the autumn and water in, then keep dry until the corms sprout; keep a temperature just above freezing but under 7°C (45°F). The plant can be lifted after flowering, and the offsets removed and replanted in autumn; seeds take up to three years to flower.

Take care

Protect from frost.

Ixiolirion pallasii

(Ixia lily)

- **Sheltered sunny position**
- **Well-drained soil**
- **Plant 7.5cm (3in) deep**

This elegant bulbous plant grows to 40cm (16in) tall, with long slender grey-green leaves. From spring to early summer it has fine displays of tubular flowers of a deep lavender blue, almost 5cm (2in) wide; these are popular for use as cut flowers.

The small bulbs should be planted in autumn, 7.5cm (3in) deep and 15cm (6in) apart, in a spot that is sheltered but sunny, in well-drained soil that has had plenty of leaf-mould added. For a good show of blooms these plants require a period of hot dry weather. The bulbs do best when they are left undisturbed; if they multiply and become overcrowded, the offsets can be removed in autumn when the leaves and flowers have died down, and planted in a nursery bed until they are mature enough to be planted out in their final flowering positions. To keep the plants healthy use a pesticide and fungicide.

Take care

The soil must not be too moist.

Lachenalia aloides/ tricolor

(Cape cowslips)

- **Maximum light**
- **Rich potting mixture**
- **Plant 2.5cm (1in) deep**

These are generally grown as indoor pot plants, although they can be used for hanging baskets, but as their flowering period is from midwinter to spring they are better for the conservatory rather than out of doors. They have pale strap-like leaves, sometimes spotted or marked with lavender, and will grow up to 30cm (12in) in height. The 2.5cm (1in) bell-shaped flowers are usually yellow in colour but often marked with orange or green.

The bulbs should be planted in a rich soil, six bulbs to a 15cm (6in) pot. Soak the soil after planting, leave it dry until the bulbs start to sprout, then water moderately until fully grown. Give a liquid feed then once a fortnight until the leaves turn yellow, allow the bulbs to dry off, and repot them into fresh soil in late summer. At this time small bulblets can be removed and grown separately in pots, and will reach flowering size in about two years.

Take care

Do not store bulbs over winter. 428▶

Leucojum aestivum 'Gravetye Giant'

(Snowflake)

- **Light shade**
- **Moist soil**
- **Plant 7.5cm (3in) deep**

These snowdrop-like plants have sword-like leaves. The large drooping bell flowers are produced in spring, 2.5cm (1in) long, in white with the petals tipped with green. 'Gravetye Giant' is an improved form, growing 50cm (20in) tall.

These plants prefer a moist soil, in which they should be planted 7.5cm (3in) deep and positioned so that they can enjoy some shade. They should be planted in late summer or early autumn, and left undisturbed for several years until they become too crowded, with too few blooms. Then, when the leaves have turned yellow they can be lifted, divided and replanted immediately, 20cm (8in) apart. This is a better way to increase your stock than by growing from seed, which can take six years to reach flowering size. These leucojums do not like drying off in summer so it is important to keep them moist. They are normally both pest- and disease-free.

Take care

Keep plants moist in droughts. 428▶

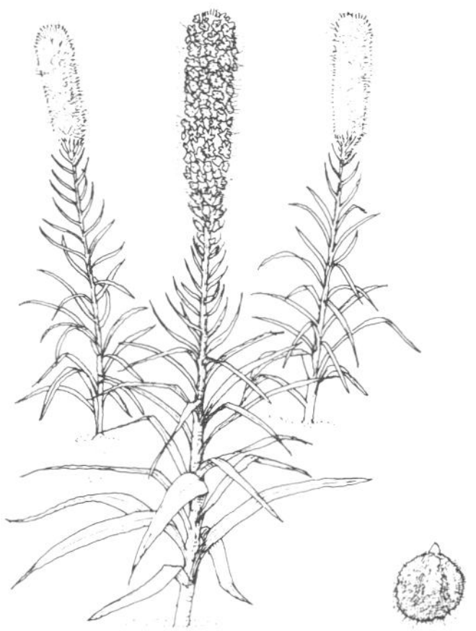

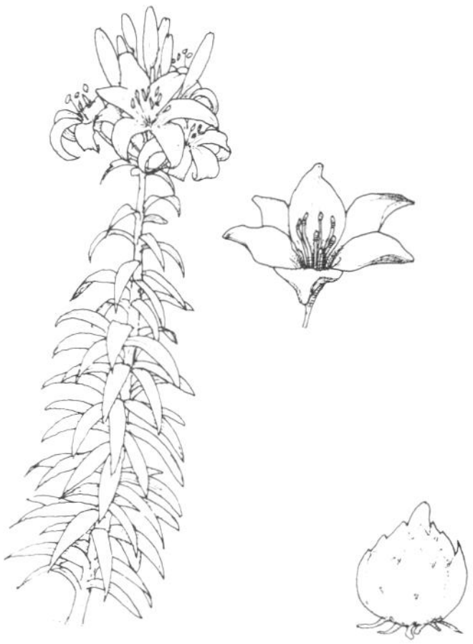

Liatris spicata

- **Open sunny site**
- **Heavy wet soil**
- **Plant 5cm (2in) deep**

This hardy tuberous plant grows to 90cm (36in) tall. It has a lily-like stem, which ends in a dense spike, 15-38cm (6-15in) long, of pinky purple flowers in early autumn.

These plants enjoy an open sunny place with plenty of moisture in the soil, even tolerating boggy sites. The tubers should be planted in early autumn or early spring, up to 45cm (18in) apart and 5cm (2in) deep, if the soil is moist; where soil is drier, plant deeper and add plenty of humus to retain moisture. A heavy mulch of compost or well-rotted manure will keep moisture from evaporating too quickly, and extra water should be given during dry periods. Remove dead flowers; and as the plant loses all its leaves, the spot must be marked to prevent damage through digging or hoeing during the winter. In spring the plant can be lifted, divided and replanted every few years to increase your stock; grown from seed it will take two years to flower.

Take care

Keep moist during droughts.

Lilium Asiatic cultivars (Division 1)

- **Full sun or semi-shade**
- **Well-drained garden soil**
- **Plant 10-15cm (4-6in) deep**

These are early-flowering lilies with blooms growing either singly or in groups springing from the same point on the stem. These cultivars grow up to 150cm (5ft) tall, with some flowers reaching 15cm (6in) across. Some forms have hanging flowers with petals curled back to form a 'Turk's cap'. Blooms appear at midsummer with a variety of colours, shapes and markings.

The bulbs should be planted 10-15cm (4-6in) deep in well-drained garden soil, in full sun or semi-shade, during the winter months. During the growing season they should be kept moist with plenty of water and mulching with peat, compost or leaf-mould. Every few years the plants can be lifted in the winter months, divided and replanted with more space around them. Seed will take up to three years to reach flowering. The plants should be treated with a general pesticide and fungicide.

Take care

Keep plants moist during the growing period. 430▸

Lilium Martagon hybrids (Division 2)

- **Partial shade or light woodland**
- **Well-drained garden soil**
- **Plant 10-15cm (4-6in) deep**

These hybrid lilies flower from late spring onwards. They are easily grown, and reach 150cm (5ft) tall, with flowers up to 7.5cm (3in) wide in white, cream, yellow, orange or deep red, with spots and markings on the petals.

They thrive in partial shade, tolerate lime, and require a good well-drained soil with plenty of leaf-mould, compost and well-rotted manure mixed into it to retain moisture in dry periods. The bulbs should be planted 10-15cm (4-6in) deep in the winter months, and left undisturbed for several years. During winter they can be lifted, divided and replanted with more space around them to increase stock; seeds take three years to mature to flowering size. Treat plants with a general pesticide and fungicide, and spread some slug bait on the soil.

Take care

Divide in rotation, as they take a year to recover.

Lilium candidum cultivars (Division 3)

- **Full sun**
- **Ordinary well-drained soil**
- **Plant 10cm (4in) deep**

These lilies grow to 180cm (6ft) tall, and in summer they have flowers 7.5cm (3in) long, with very curved petals. These blooms are scented, in yellow, orange and white with bright red pollen. The original parent, *L. candidum*, has been cultivated for over 3,500 years and revered by many civilizations.

Bulbs should be planted 10cm (4in) deep in autumn in a well-drained garden soil containing plenty of humus. To obtain a succession of flowers over the years, a few plants each year should be lifted, divided and replanted, as they take at least a year to recover. Seeds take up to three years to reach flowering size, so it is quicker to increase your stock by division. If weather conditions are bad for planting, put the bulbs in damp peat until the soil is ready, to stop them drying out. Lilies are attacked by a variety of ills; use a pesticide, a fungicide and slug bait.

Take care

Keep bulbs moist when transplanting, and be sure to stake mature plants.

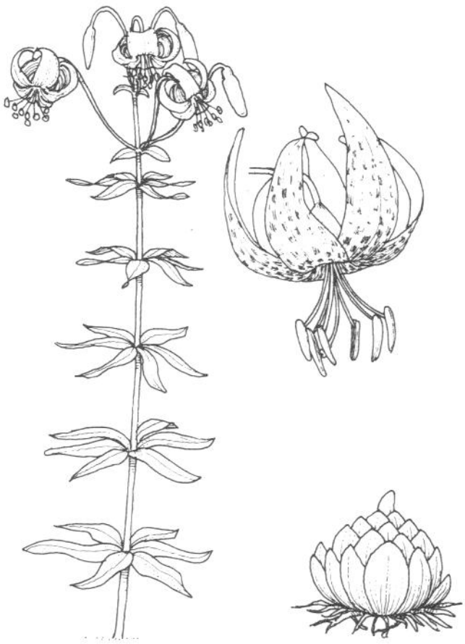

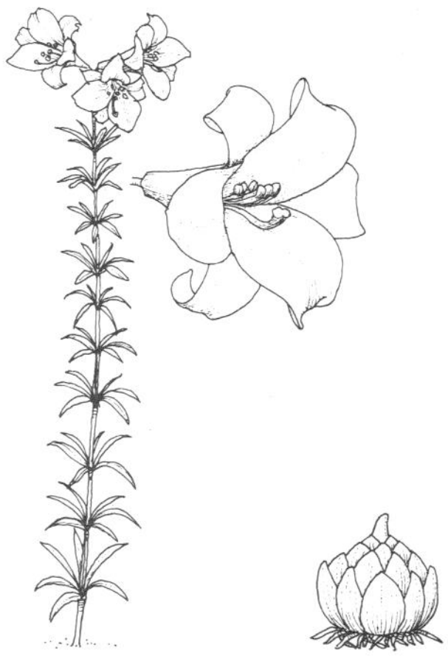

Lilium American cultivars (Division 4)

- **Light shade**
- **Well-drained acid soil**
- **Plant 15cm (6in) deep**

These varieties, grown from crossing American lilies, produce a range of plants that can reach 210cm (7ft), with 7.5cm (3in) blooms in yellow, orange and reds, some in two-colour forms with markings and spots.

Plant bulbs 15cm (6in) deep in a well-drained neutral to acid soil with plenty of peat, leaf-mould or compost. These cultivars give best results if grown in light shade. The bulbs should be left undisturbed, with a mulch of leaf-mould and bracken each winter. They can be lifted in late autumn, divided and replanted to give the bulbs more room, but treat only a few each year, as they take a season to recover. Give the plants a general pesticide and fungicide to keep them free from trouble. Use a slug bait to stop slug or snail damage to young shoots, but use the bait under a tile to prevent other animals reaching it.

Take care

Stake plants to prevent wind damage. 431▸

Lilium longiflorum cultivars (Division 5)

- **Full sun**
- **Limy soil**
- **Plant 10cm (4in) deep**

These plants are crosses of liles from Japan and Taiwan and are generally half-hardy and generally recommended as pot plants, although the variety 'Holland's Glory' is highly regarded for outdoor cultivation as well, with its large white strongly scented blooms. It grows to a height of 120cm (4ft).

The bulbs should be planted at a depth of 10cm (4in), in soil fortified with leaf-mould or compost to hold moisture during drought periods. They should be left undisturbed for several years; then they should be lifted in the autumn, divided and replanted with more space around each bulb. An autumn mulch of leaf-mould or compost is very beneficial, but do not use fresh manure because this will rot the roots. These lilies are prone to disease and care should be taken to treat them with a fungicide. If disease appears after treatment, lift the affected plant and destroy it. A pesticide will keep attacks from pests to a minimum.

Take care

Watch for disease.

Above: **Iris innominata (Apogon/Californicae)**
A beautiful beardless iris with evergreen leaves that thrives in a fibrous soil. It likes both sun and light shade and blooms in late spring. 415▸

Left: **Iris bucharica**
A Juno iris that is a bulbous plant and has scented yellow or white blooms in spring. It needs to be sheltered and kept on the dry side in summer. It can be grown as a pot plant but be sure to use a deep pot. 418▸

Right: **Iris kaempferi (Apogon/Laevigatae)**
A beardless iris that enjoys a moist soil. Developed in Japan to give a wide range of colours and forms, it flowers in early summer. 416▸

Below: **Iris gracilipes**
This small crested iris bears flowers in spring and is very suitable for planting in rock gardens provided it is sheltered and partially shaded. Ideally the soil should be acid and kept on the moist side. 418▸

Left: **Lachenalia aloides 'Van Tubergen'**
This is suitable as a pot plant, giving a good show of blooms through the winter provided the temperature does not drop too low. In summer it can be used in hanging baskets. 421▸

Right: **Leucojum aestivum 'Gravetye Giant'**
A late spring-flowering plant that likes a moist soil with some shade. Placed in a shrubbery or light woodland it will thrive and need little attention for several years. 421▸

Below: **Iris reticulata 'Jeanine'**
A bulbous iris that is very popular for the rock garden and border. It blooms in late winter and early spring and prefers a light chalky soil. Also suitable for growing indoors. 419▸

Above:
Lilium 'Cover Girl' (Division 1.)
An Asiatic lily with large wide open blooms that provide colour in a border in sun or semi-shade. 422♦

Below:
Lilium 'Enchantment' (Division 1)
A vigorous Asiatic lily with up to 16 outstanding cup-shaped flowers to a stem. Enjoys a sunny position. 422♦

Above:
Lilium 'Shuksan' (Division 4)
The petals on this American lily curl right back to form a 'Turk's cap'. The plant will grow as tall as a person and is ideal for the back of the border. 424▸

Above left:
Lilium 'Life' (Division 6)
A tall-growing Aurelian lily that makes a beautiful feature in a lightly shaded garden border. 441▸

Above: **Lilium 'Imperial Crimson' (Division 7)**
A scented Oriental lily with large blooms in the summer months. 441▸

Left: **Lilium regale**
A hardy and popular lily that enjoys full sun and ordinary soil. Scented flowers in midsummer. 442▸

Right: **Lilium tigrinum splendens**
Well known for its spotted petals and 'Turk's cap' form. 442▸

Left: **Narcissus cyclamineus**
An early spring-flowering dwarf narcissus that makes an ideal rock garden plant, where its unusual backward-facing petals and grass-like leaves can be appreciated. 443▶

Right:
Narcissus pseudonarcissus
A small narcissus that naturalizes well in light woodland or in grass, where its blooms can be enjoyed in spring. Plant in moist soil. 444▶

Below: **Muscari armeniacum**
The grape hyacinth prefers full sun and will thrive in rock gardens and borders, forming clumps of brilliant blue flowers in spring. It will thrive in ordinary garden soil. 443▶

Above: **Narcissus 'Fortune' (Division 2)**
A large-cupped narcissus that gives a fine display in the spring. The bulbs should be planted in a good moist soil in light shade. 445▸

Left: **Narcissus 'Rembrandt' (Division 1)**
A large trumpet narcissus that makes an outstanding show in the spring months. It can be forced for earlier blooming indoors. 445▸

Right: **Narcissus 'Ice Follies' (Division 2)**
Ideal for growing in the garden for spring flowers, this large-cupped narcissus needs light shade and moist soil. Can be forced in pots. 445▸

Above: **Narcissus 'Irene Copeland' (Division 4)**
A double narcissus that makes an effective contrast to the single form. It is particularly attractive as a cut flower in an arrangement. 446▶

Below: **Narcissus 'Grand Soleil d'Or' (Division 8)**
A bunch-flowering narcissus that produces an abundance of blooms to each bulb. An excellent pot plant for indoor flowers in early spring. 448▶

Above: **Narcissus 'Bartley' (Division 6)**
This delightful small narcissus has N. cyclamineus *as a parent, which shows in its swept back petals. Ideal for the front of borders.* 447▸

Above: **Narcissus 'Actaea' (Division 9)**
This well-known scented poeticus narcissus has white petals and a small flat frilled cup. It usually flowers after the other groups. 449▶

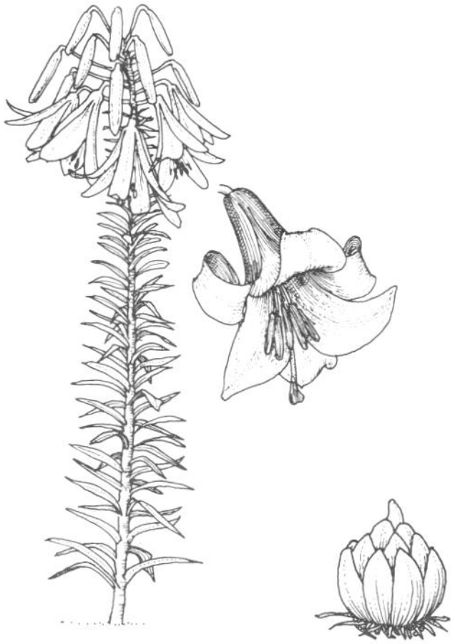

Lilium Trumpet and Aurelian cultivars

(Division 6)
- **Partial shade**
- **Rich well-drained soil**
- **Plant 15cm (6in) deep**

Grouped in this section are the funnel-shaped, bowl-shaped, pendent and star-like blooms that are mainly crosses from the Aurelian lilies. Some are lime-tolerant, but others are not. They grow to 210cm (7ft), and should be planted 30cm (12in) apart in a rich well-drained soil in partial shade at a depth of 15cm (6in). Most of this group are hardy, but a mulch of leaf-mould or compost spread over them in autumn will protect the less hardy from frost. The flowers, many of them scented, are often over 12.5cm (5in) across, and some reach 20cm (8in) wide. A wide range of colours is available; some have stripes, others are bicoloured or flushed with other shades. The flowering period is in late summer. The bulbs can be lifted in the winter months, divided and replanted, but make sure that they do not dry out. Use a pesticide and fungicide to keep the plants healthy.

Take care

Stake the taller lilies. 432▸

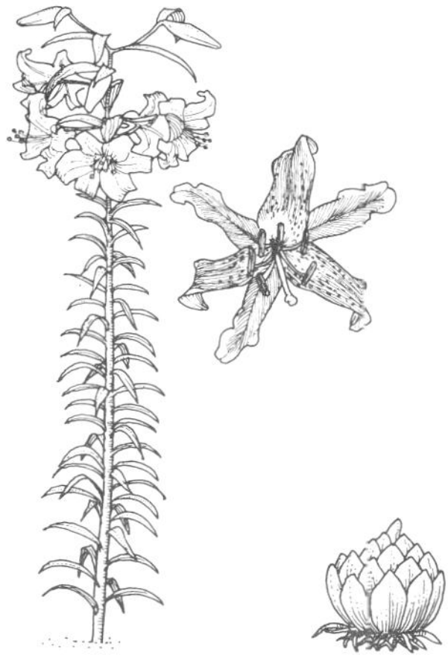

Lilium Oriental cultivars

(Division 7)
- **Full sun**
- **Rich well-drained gritty soil**
- **Plant 15cm (6in) deep**

These hybrid forms of Oriental lilies are often sub-divided into flower shapes: trumpet, bowl, star or flat and the very curved petal forms. The flowers appear in summer, and sometimes reach 25cm (10in) across; many are scented, and they have very decorative shapes in a wide range of colours, often marked, striped and spotted. The plants grow to a height of 210cm (7ft) and should be planted at a distance of 30cm (12in) apart and at a depth of 15cm (6in) in a rich, well-drained but gritty soil with plenty of humus.

Place them in full sun and as they grow stake them against being blown over. A mulch of humus in early spring is advisable. The bulbs can be lifted in the late autumn or winter months, divided and replanted with more space around them, but make sure that they do not lose moisture. Seeds take up to three years to flower.

Take care

Do not let the bulbs dry out when planting or replanting. 433▸

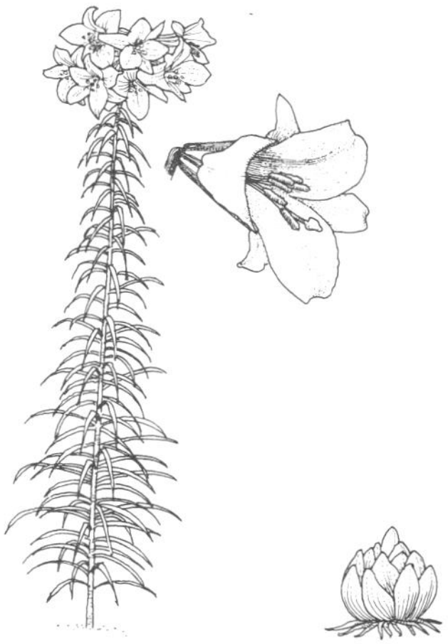

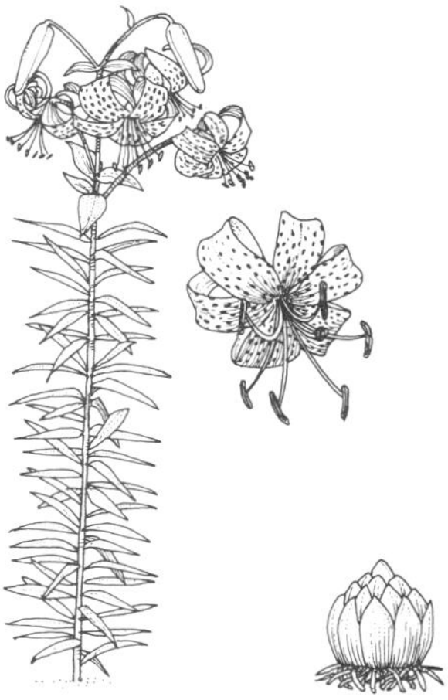

Lilium regale

(Regal lily)

- **Full sun**
- **Well-drained garden soil**
- **Plant just below the surface**

This lily originates from China, is very popular and is probably the best-known of all lilies, with its scented white funnel-shaped flowers up to 12.5cm (5in) long, blooming in summer. The centres of the flowers are brilliant yellow, and the backs of the petals have red-purple shading. These lilies can reach 180cm (6ft) but most grow to 120cm (4ft) tall.

Regal lilies require to be placed in full sun in a well-drained soil, with or without lime, and they will spread quickly. The bulbs should be planted just below the surface; some experts recommend planting as deep as 23cm (9in), but this is advisable only in a very light and free-draining soil. Bulbs can be lifted, divided and replanted during the winter months, without letting them dry out. Seeds take up to three years to reach maturity, and most people prefer to grow lilies from bulbs. In exposed areas they should be staked to prevent wind damage.

Take care

Keep the bulbs moist when planting or transplanting. 432▸

Lilium tigrinum

(Tiger lily)

- **Full sun**
- **Well-drained lime-free soil**
- **Plant 15cm (6in) deep**

This spectacular lily is a native of China, Korea and Japan and is grown for its very curved petals that give it a 'Turk's Cap' 10cm (4in) long in late summer. The bright orange or red-orange petals are spotted with black, and have dark red pollen on the anthers. There is a variety that has bright yellow blooms with purple spots, known as *L.trigrinum flaviflorum*. The plants can reach 180cm (6ft).

Bulbs should be planted at a depth of 15cm (6in) in a well-drained lime-free soil, 23cm (9in) apart. Grow this separate from other lilies, because it is prone to virus disease. Keep the soil moist throughout the growing season; it helps to add plenty of humus to the soil. Increase by picking off the *bulbils* – tiny bulbs that grow between the leaves and the stem at flowering time. They should come off easily. Plant them just under the soil surface in pots, keep for a year, then plant out. Watch for virus attack, and treat with pesticide.

Take care

Keep soil moist in droughts. 433▸

Muscari armeniacum

(Grape hyacinth)

- **Full sun**
- **Ordinary well-drained soil**
- **Plant 7.5cm (3in) deep**

The grape hyacinth has tight bell-like blue flowers grouped closely together like miniature inverted bunches of grapes on single stems in spring. The plants grow to a height of 25cm (10in), with an equal spread after the leaves separate at flowering time.

Plant the bulbs 7.5cm (3in) deep in a well-drained ordinary garden soil in full sun; shade will encourage leaf growth and less flowers. After a few years the bulbs will become congested and after the leaves turn yellow the plants need to be lifted, divided and replanted immediately. Sometimes the plants seed themselves; otherwise you can take the seed in summer, sow it in pans, and keep it cool in a cold frame. The seedlings can be transplanted the following year, and will come into flower in another year or so. The plants are normally pest-free, but occasionally the flowers are spoilt with smut, making black sooty areas; destroy plants to stop it spreading.

Take care

Plant in sun for good flowering. 434▸

Narcissus cyclamineus

- **Sun or partial shade**
- **Moist well-drained soil**
- **Plant 5cm (2in) deep**

Like all members of the narcissus and daffodil family, this species has the typical cup and petals, but the petals are turned back. The plant comes from Spain and Portugal, is small, only 20cm (8in) tall, and the trumpets are 5cm (2in) long. This dwarf habit makes it ideal for the rock garden, where its fine delicate form and dark green grass-like leaves keep it in scale with other low-growing plants. The yellow flowers bloom in early spring, and do equally well in the open or in partial shade provided the soil is moist.

Plant the bulbs 5cm (2in) deep and 5cm (2in) apart. They will seed themselves, or in late summer they can be lifted, divided and replanted to allow more space. Treat the plants with a pesticide and fungicide to keep troubles to a minimum, but if damage is bad it is better to destroy the plant.

Take care

Keep soil moist in dry periods. 434▸

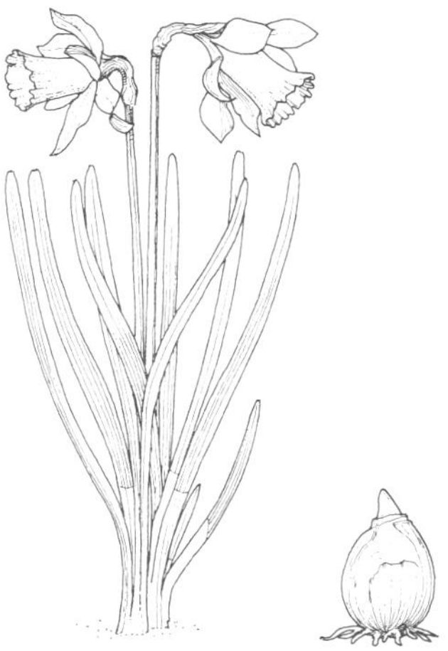

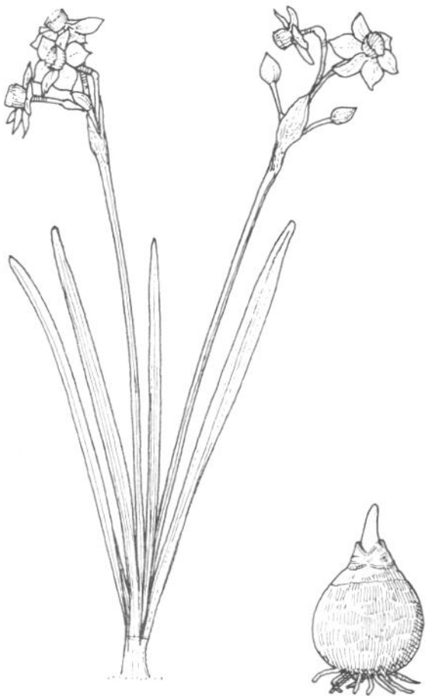

Narcissus pseudonarcissus

(Wild daffodil; Lent lily)

- **Sun or light shade**
- **Moist soil**
- **Plant 5cm (2in) deep**

This plant has strap-like leaves, and grows to a height of 30cm (12in). The flowers have bright lemon trumpets with very pale yellow petals 5cm (2in) across, and appear in spring. They thrive in a good moist soil, among low grass or in open woodland. They are good for naturalizing where a small daffodil will be in scale.

This species is easy to grow in a moist soil, and will be happy in either sun or light shade, where it should be planted at a depth of 5cm (2in). If the soil and the situation are to its liking, it will thrive and spread vigorously, forming clumps. After a few years it is advisable to lift the bulbs after the leaves have died back, divide them and replant with 7.5cm (3in) between bulbs. A more natural look is obtained by casting the bulbs over the area and planting them where they have fallen. Use a pesticide and fungicide to keep plants healthy.

Take care

Keep the plants moist, especially in hot weather. 435▸

Narcissus tazetta

(Bunch-flowered narcissus)

- **Sun or semi-shade**
- **Moist soil**
- **Plant 7.5-10cm (3-4in) deep**

This group of narcissi comes from a wide area spreading from the Canary Islands, through the Mediterranean, North India to China and Japan and is characterized by the bunch of blooms on the flower stem of a single flower. The leaves are strap-like, and the plant will grow to a height of between 30 and 45cm (12-18in). The blooms have white petals 3.8cm (1.5in) wide, with a shallow yellow cup. They have a strong perfume, and will flower in winter – among the earliest to bloom. They are often grown in pots, as some of the varieties are half-hardy.

The bulbs should be planted 7.5-10cm (3-4in) deep in a well-drained moist soil where there is either full sun or partial shade. Gently cast the bulbs over the ground and plant them where they fall, to give a natural random spacing. Every few years the clumps of plants should be lifted, divided and replanted with more space around them to grow.

Take care

Avoid waterlogged soil.

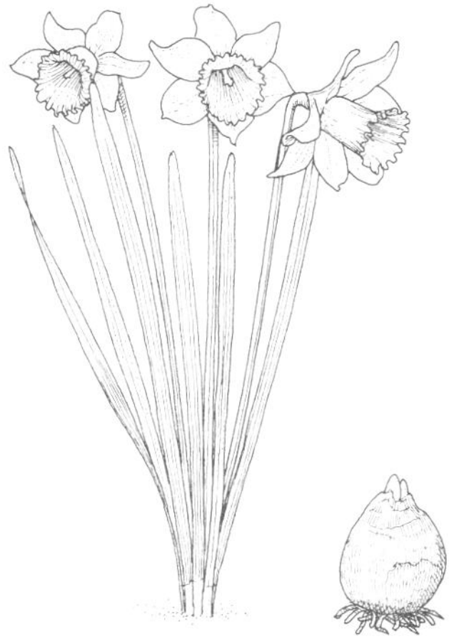

Narcissus Division 1

- **Light shade**
- **Moist well-drained soil**
- **Plant 7.5-10cm (3-4in) deep**

In this group the plants all have only one flower to a stem, and the trumpet or cup is longer than the petals. It has been further sub-divided into sections with trumpet and petals yellow, trumpet yellow and petals white, trumpet and petals white, and any other combination. These are all of garden origin, and will grow to 45cm (18in) tall. In this group are most of the popular daffodils, such as 'King Alfred' and 'Golden Harvest', with large blooms and fluted trumpets 7.5cm (3in) wide in spring.

These do equally well in the garden or forced in pots for earlier flowering. They should be planted in a good moist soil in late summer. Where they are grown in grass, do not use a mower until the leaves have turned yellow and the goodness of the soil has been taken up by the bulbs. Lift and divide the bulbs every few years to encourage large blooms and extra stock. Use a pesticide and fungicide.

Take care

Do not cut leaves until yellow. 436▶

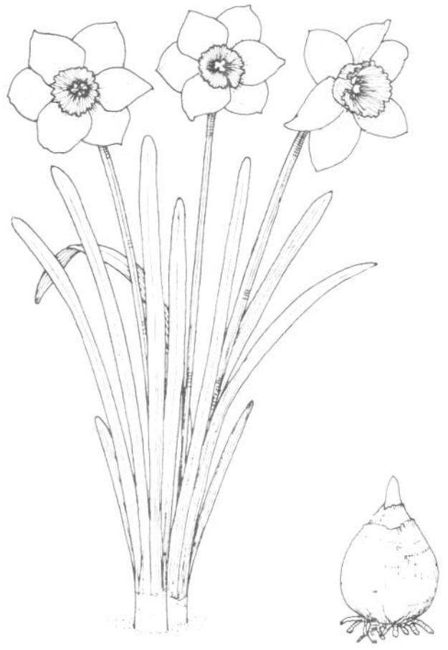

Narcissus Division 2

- **Light shade**
- **Well-drained moist soil**
- **Plant 7.5-10cm (3-4in) deep**

These are large-cupped narcissi with one flower to each stem, and the cup or trumpet is more than one third the length of the petals but no longer than them. The group has been sub-divided into sections with the cup darker than the petal colour; cup coloured and petals white, and cup and petals white. The cups may be frilled, serrated or plain, and the colours are white, yellow, orange pink or red. Among the highly prized varieties are 'Fortune', 'Carlton', 'Desdemona', 'Royal Orange', 'Ice Follies' and 'Tudor Minstrel', which has blooms of over 12.5cm (5in) across. Most of these grow to a height of 45cm (18in).

The mid-green strap-like leaves should be left to turn yellow and die back without tying them into knots, as this is the period when the bulb takes up nutrition for the next season. Increase by division in the autumn every few years. Use a pesticide and fungicide.

Take care

Keep moist in droughts. 436-437▶

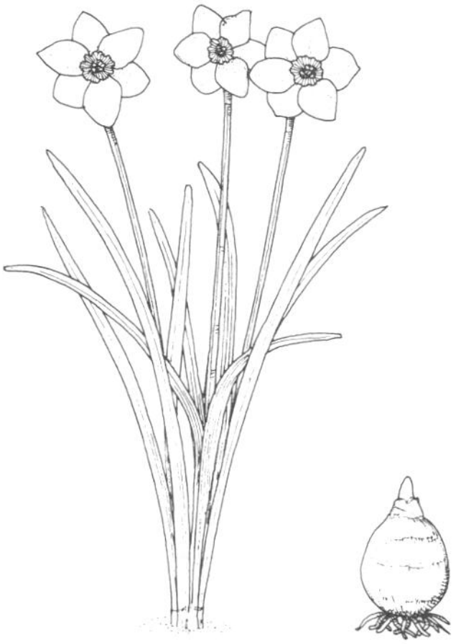

Narcissus Division 3

- **Semi-shade**
- **Rich well-drained moist soil**
- **Plant 7.5-10cm (3-4in) deep**

This group is of garden origin and has small cups with only one flower to each stem, and the cup is less than one third of the length of the petals – smaller than in Division 2. It has been sub-divided into sections with petals and cup coloured, petals white and cup coloured, and all white. Of these, 'Birma' has yellow petals and orange-scarlet cup; 'Enniskillen' has white petals and crimson-red cup; and 'Angel' has white petals and white cup, and is 12.5cms (5in) wide. These bloom in early spring and grow to a height of 45cm (18in), giving a splendid show in the garden especially where grown in clumps and drifts.

Plant in light shade in late summer, as soon as the bulbs become available. Leave them undisturbed for a few years before lifting and dividing to allow more space around them; this will encourage large blooms, provided the leaves have not been knotted or cut when they finish flowering. Use a pesticide and fungicide to keep down attacks.

Take care
Keep bulbs moist in droughts.

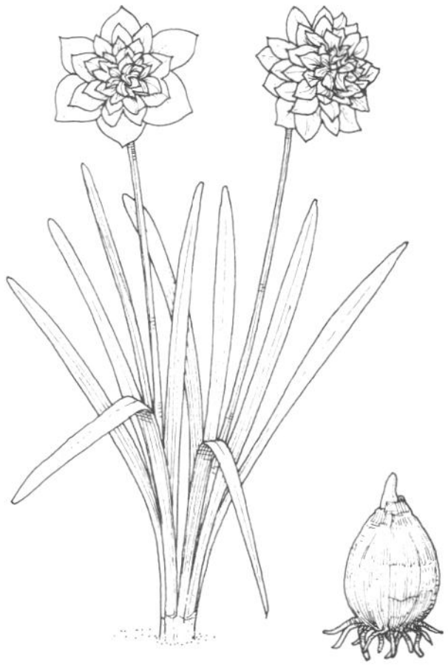

Narcissus Division 4

- **Light shade**
- **Rich well-drained soil**
- **Plant 7.5-10cm (3-4in) deep**

This group all have double flowers, one or more to each stem, and they grow 38-50cm (15-20in) tall. Some are scented, and others have dramatic flower forms: the well-known 'Irene Copeland', 'White Lion', and 'Golden Ducat' are all included in this section.

Bulbs should be planted in late summer, as soon as they become available in the shops, in a rich well-drained soil with 7.5-10cm (3-4in) of soil over them, and in semi-shade. Leave them for a few years before lifting and dividing the bulbs to increase your stock. This should be done after the leaves have turned yellow and died; they should not be touched before this as the plant uses this period to store food for the coming season. Grow them in clumps and drifts; for the best effect, cast the bulbs over the ground and plant them where they fall, which will give an informal spacing. The plants should be treated with a pesticide and fungicide to keep them healthy.

Take care
Keep moist during dry periods in spring and summer. 438▸

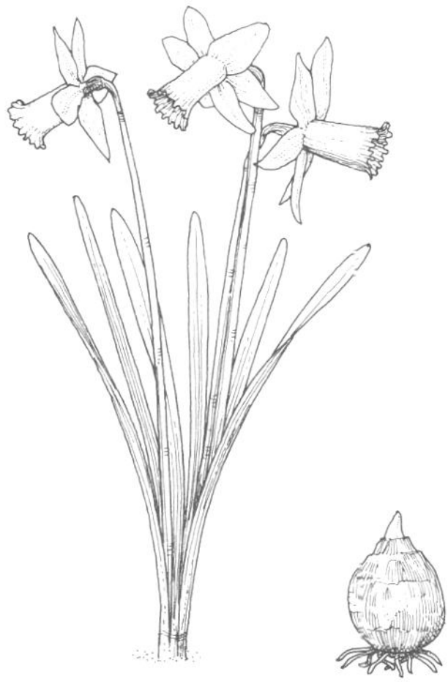

Narcissus Division 5

- **Partial shade**
- **Good well-drained soil**
- **Plant 5cm (2in) deep**

Some of the most delicate and graceful small narcissi are included in this group. Most have back-swept petals on their spring blooms. They are divided into two sub-sections: those that have the cup more than two-thirds of the length of the petals, and those that are less than this measurement. Within this group are *N. triandus albus* ('Angel's Tears'), with white flowers; and 'Tresamble', also white, with as many as six blooms to a stem. These are small plants, many less than 30cm (12in) tall but they make up in beauty what they lack in stature.

The bulbs should be planted 5cm (2in) deep in a well-drained but good garden soil, with partial shade to keep the soil moist in late spring and summer, when the plant stores up goodness for the following spring. After a few years the bulbs can be lifted in late summer, divided and replanted. They look well sited in rockeries and alpine gardens. Use a pesticide and fungicide to guard the plant against attack.

Take care

Keep the plants moist in droughts.

Narcissus Division 6

- **Light shade**
- **Good well-drained soil**
- **Plant 5-7.5 (2-3in) deep**

These cyclamineus narcissi are noted for their long trumpets and swept-back petals. The group is divided into those with the trumpet more, and those with it less, than two-thirds of the petal length. Of these plants there are some lovely small specimens that are ideal for the garden and for forcing to use indoors during the winter. In the garden their small stature, 20-38cm (8-15in), makes them suitable for rock gardens and the front of borders. The varieties 'February Gold', 'Peeping Tom' and 'Beryl' are representative of this section.

The bulbs should be planted in late summer when they become available, with 5-7.5cm (2-3in) of soil over them in a lightly shaded area with a good well-drained soil that has been enriched with leaf-mould and compost to improve its moisture-holding properties during drought periods. Lift and divide the bulbs every few years to increase stock. Treat plants with pesticide and fungicide to protect them.

Take care

Plant bulbs soon after purchase. 439▶

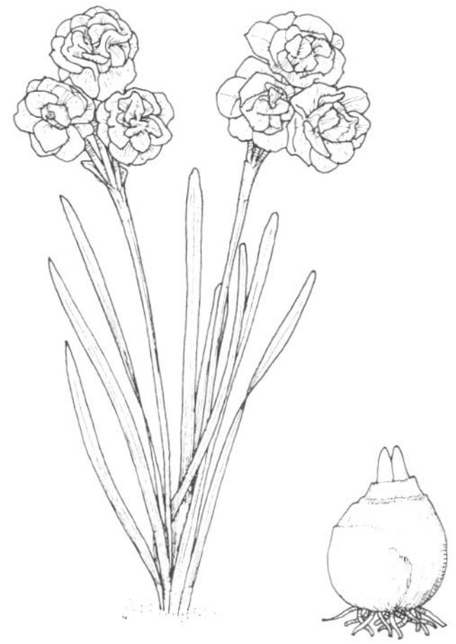

Narcissus Division 7

- **Partial shade**
- **Enriched garden soil**
- **Plant 5-7.5cm (2-3in) deep**

These are the jonquil narcissi, noted for their perfume, tubular leaves and yellow flowers up to 5cm (2in) across. Here again the division is grouped into those with large and small cups, with two-thirds of the petal length being the critical measurement. Most in this division will grow about 30cm (12in) tall, and some of the lovely single and double forms appear early: 'Waterperry' flowers in midwinter, and the beautiful 'Jonquilla Double' about a month later. These have dainty flowers and should be placed where their beauty can be seen properly, in containers, raised beds and on banks.

The bulbs should be planted 5-7.5cm (2-3in) deep in late summer, in an enriched garden soil with a high humus content but free-draining. After flowering the leaves should be left untouched; only when they die right back should they be removed. Every few years the plants can be lifted, divided and replanted to give space for development.

Take care
Avoid waterlogged soil.

Narcissus Division 8

- **Light shade**
- **Well-drained moist soil**
- **Plant 7.5-10cm (3-4in) deep**

These are descended from *N. tazetta* and have the same characteristic of bunch flowering. The majority of the hybrids are on the tender side, and should be grown for pot cultivation rather than for outdoors. Those that do thrive out of doors vary considerably, some blooming at midwinter, but others not till late spring. Generally they grow to about 40cm (16in) high, with sword-like leaves; the highly scented blooms are in a variety of colours, single and double. The best-known are 'Geranium', 'Winston Churchill', 'White Cheerfulness' and 'Yellow Cheerfulness'.

The bulbs enjoy a well-drained soil with plenty of humus, and a lightly shaded position, with 7.5-10cm (3-4in) of soil over them. Plant bulbs in late summer, as soon as you can obtain them; this is also the time for lifting, dividing and replanting. Use a pesticide and fungicide to keep the plants healthy.

Take care
Do not cut or remove the leaves until they die right down. 438▸

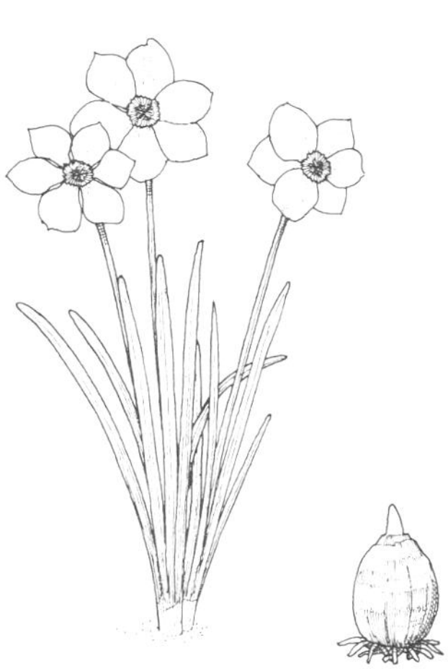

Narcissus Division 9

- **Semi-shade**
- **Well-drained rich soil**
- **Plant 7.5-10 (3-4in) deep**

These are the poeticus narcissi and are characterized by the white petals and the flat frilled bright red cup of the scented flowers; they usually appear after the other narcissi have finished blooming. The plants grow about 38cm (15in) tall, and the flowers reach 7.5cm (3in) across. The varieties best known are 'Actaea', 'Constable' and 'Old Pheasant Eye'.

Plant the bulbs in late summer as soon as they are available in the shops, 7.5-10cm (3-4in) deep, in rich well-drained soil that has plenty of humus added; the site needs to be lightly shaded. The leaves should be left untouched until they die right back, so that they can take up food for the coming season. When the bulbs become conjested, they should be lifted in late summer, divided and replanted with more space around them. Keep small bulbs in a nursery area until large enough to plant out. Keep pest and disease attack to a minimum with a pesticide and fungicide.

Take care

Keep moist during droughts. 440▸

Narcissus Division 10

- **Partial shade**
- **Good garden soil**
- **Plant 2.5-5cm (1-2in) deep**

In this section the Royal Horticultural Society has placed all the wild forms and wild hybrids, and all the miniature and less spectacular narcissi. These are ideal for rockeries, alpine gardens, containers and for naturalizing in the wilder parts of the garden. Some of these have curious forms and tiny blooms: among the noteworthy are *N. bulbocodium conspicuus* (Yellow hoop petticoat), 15cm (6in) high; *N. minimus*, the smallest of all trumpet daffodils, only 7.5cm (3in) tall; and *N. minor pumilis plenus*, a 15cm (6in) daffodil with double blooms.

The smaller bulbs need to be planted in late summer, with only 2.5cm (1in) of soil over them, but the larger bulbs can have double this amount. Position them in partial shade, in a good free-draining garden soil with plenty of humus. Spread the bulbs in a natural drift or series of clumps to give an informal look. They can be lifted in late summer, divided and replanted to increase stock.

Take care

Avoid waterlogged soil.

Nerine bowdenii

(Guernsey lily)

- **Sunny position**
- **Ordinary well-drained soil**
- **Plant just under the surface**

Nerine bowdenii, which comes from South Africa, is sufficiently hardy to withstand most winters in the temperate zone. It will grow to a height of 60cm (24in). The blooms open in autumn, with up to eight flowers in each cluster; the clusters are 15cm (6in) across, usually rose or deep pink, but there is also a white form. The mid-green leaves are narrow and strap-like.

The bulbs should be planted in either late summer or early spring, and in an ordinary well-drained soil and in a sunny position. The bulbs are placed just under the surface or, if the soil is light, they can be set deeper – as much as 10cm (4in). Where there are bulbs near the surface they should be covered with a thick layer of bracken, leaf-mould or compost to protect them against frost. They can be lifted in spring, divided and replanted to encourage larger blooms. Watch for mealy bugs and treat them with pesticide.

Take care

Keep moist when growing. 457▸

Nomocharis saluenensis varieties

- **Light shade**
- **Deep moist soil**
- **Plant 7.5-10 (3-4in) deep**

Nomocharis, a member of the lily family, grows to a height of 120cm (4ft). It has narrow leaves, and the saucer-shaped flowers are often 10cm (4in) across in summer; they are carried on a stem that will bear five or six white or pink blooms tinged with purple.

Plant them in early spring, in a soil that is deep and moist, and in the light shade. The bulbs should have 7.5cm (3in) of soil over them, but if the soil is light this can be increased to 10cm (4in). Cover the area each spring with a layer of compost, leaf-mould or peat. The bulbs are easily damaged: take care when planting, and avoid transplanting or digging around the roots. Increase your stock by taking seeds and sowing them in autumn or spring; grow in pots for a year, and plant out the following spring. Nomocharis plants are usually disease-free, but treat the surrounding soil with slug bait to deter slugs and snails.

Take care

Avoid damaging the roots.

Notholirion thomsonianum

- **Full sun**
- **Moist well-drained soil**
- **Plant 7.5cm (3in) deep**

This bulbous plant has its origins in the Western Himalayas, where it grows among rocks and in areas of stunted trees and shrubs. It can reach 80cm (32in) tall. It has highly perfumed blooms of white or rose, 5cm (2in) long, on flower stems not unlike a widely spaced hyacinth spur, in spring, with up to 20 bell-shaped flowers on the stem.

Plant the bulbs 7.5cm (3in) deep in full sun, if possible with some protection (such as a wall or fence) to keep off cold winds, in a well-drained soil that has had plenty of leaf-mould, peat or compost added to increase its moisture-retaining properties. The bulbs flower well if the plant is kept dry in summer, and this will encourage the bulb to ripen for the following season. Every few years, lift and remove offsets and grow them on separately in a nursery bed. Notholirions can also be grown as a pot plant in a cool greenhouse.

Take care

Keep the plants dry in summer.

Ornithogalum thyrsoides

(Chincherinchee)

- **Partial shade**
- **Good soil or potting mixture**
- **Plant 10cm (4in) deep**

This plant from South Africa has up to 30 white, cream or yellow star-like flowers grouped in a tight cluster at the top of the 45cm (18in) stem in summer. The mid-green leaves spring from the base of the plant and grow 30cm (12in) long. It is not hardy in the temperate zones where frosts occur, and should be grown in a pot.

Plant the bulbs in a 20cm (8in) pot of rich potting mixture in autumn and keep in a cool greenhouse for early spring flowering. In mild areas the bulbs can be planted out of doors in spring, with 10cm (4in) of soil over them; they should be well covered during the winter months with a thick mulch of bracken, leaf-mould or peat. Seeds can be sown but they will take up to four years to reach flowering size. Generally these are pest-free, but if sooty spots appear on the leaves, treat them with a fungicide, and if this has no effect, destroy the plant to stop the fungus spreading to other plants.

Take care

Protect against frost. 458▶

Ornithogalum umbellatum

(Star of Bethlehem)

- **Partial shade**
- **Ordinary well-drained soil**
- **Plant 7.5cm (3in) deep**

This plant grows to a height of 30cm (12in), with a spread of up to 20cm (8in). In spring, the flower stem carries a profusion of white star-like blooms with green stripes on the outside. The plant is hardy, and ideal for edgings and mass effects, even naturalizing in short grass or in shrubberies.

Plant the bulbs in autumn, in ordinary well-drained soil with 7.5cm (3in) of soil over them in an area where there is some shade; if possible, dig in a good quantity of peat, compost or leaf-mould beforehand. Once planted they need no attention and will continue to produce masses of blossom. To increase stock, lift the clumps of bulbs in late summer after the leaves have died down, divide them, and replant with more space. Seeds can be sown, but take up to four years to reach flowering size. Most ornithogalums are pest-free, but watch for fungus attack on leaves.

Take care

Keep plants moist in droughts.

Oxalis adenophylla

- **Full sun**
- **Sandy peaty soil**
- **Plant 5cm (2in) deep**

These 7.5cm (3in) tall bulbous plants are ideal for the rock garden and edges of borders. They have delicate cup-shaped lilac-pink flowers 2.5cm (1in) wide in midsummer, and small clusters of leaves that die down in winter.

The bulb-like rhizome should be planted in spring or autumn in a soil that is sandy but enriched with peat, leaf-mould or compost. Plant it 5cm (2in) deep in a sunny place, although it will stand partial shade. When the bulbs have finished flowering in summer, they can be lifted, divided and replanted with more space around them. This can also be grown as a decorative pot plant, using a 20-25cm (8-10in) pot and ordinary potting mixture such as John Innes No. 1. Keep it in the cool until ready to flower, and then bring it indoors. Every alternate year move it to a larger pot with fresh soil, or divide it and keep in the same size pot with new potting mixture.

Take care

Keep the plant moist during drought.

Pancratium maritimum

(Sea lily)

- **Sunny protected site**
- **Well-drained soil**
- **Plant 20cm (8in) deep**

These half-hardy bulbous plants grow out of doors only where there is shelter from frost; otherwise it is necessary to keep them in a frost-free greenhouse. The plant has narrow grey-green strap-like leaves and heavily scented white flowers in summer; they have an inner cup and six narrow petals with green stripes on the outside, and are 7.5cm (3in) wide. The plant grows 30cm (12in) tall and has a similar spread.

Place the bulbs 20cm (8in) deep in a well-drained soil, in a place sheltered from cold winds. They should be planted as soon as they become available in the autumn, and kept just moist during the winter. As the leaves grow increase the water until flowering finishes. In autumn the plant can be lifted, and offsets removed and grown on in pots until they are large enough to flower. Replant the parent bulbs and cover them with a thick layer of bracken, peat or leaf-mould.

Take care

Protect from frost.

Polianthes tuberosa 'The Pearl'

- **Full sun**
- **Well-drained soil or potting mixture**
- **Plant 2.5cm (1in) deep**

This tuberous-rooted plant is tender and should be grown as a pot plant unless your garden is frost-free. The mid-green leaves are strap-like and grow from ground level. The white flowers, like tubular stars, are arranged in terminal spikes up to 120cm (4ft) long. The blooms are among the most scented available and 'The Pearl' is a double variety flowering in late summer.

In autumn plant the bulb 2.5cm (1in) deep in a well-drained soil or a good potting mixture. In a 12.5cm (5in) pot, it can be kept in the greenhouse during winter, and brought indoors to bloom in late summer. Keep a series of plants at different stages by controlling the temperature, to produce flowers throughout the season. Keep in as light a place as possible to encourage sturdy growth, with just a little water until it is grown; then water freely. Purchase fresh tubers each year; offsets rarely flower.

Take care

Keep in a frost-free place.

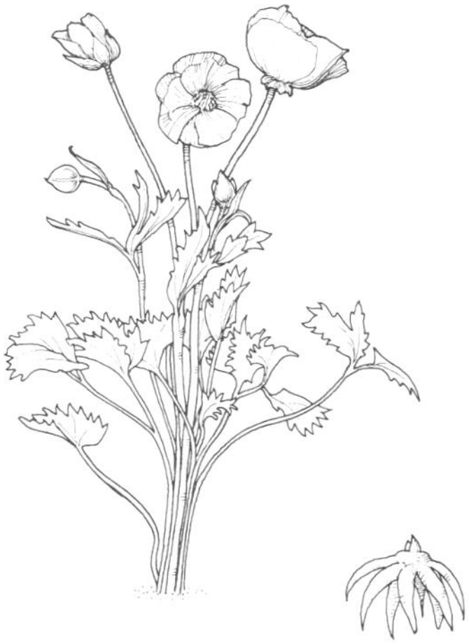

Puschkinia scilloides

(Striped quill)

- **Sun or partial shade**
- **Good sandy garden soil**
- **Plant 5cm (2in) deep**

This spring-flowering bulbous plant from Asia Minor is highly suitable for growing in low grass, in rockeries, or as a pot plant in a cool greenhouse. It grows to a height of 20cm (8in), with mid-green strap-like leaves and six-petalled bell-shaped flowers of silvery-blue, 1.25cm (0.5in) long, with a greenish blue stripe in the centre of each petal. There are up to six blooms on each stem.

In autumn, plant the bulbs 5cm (2in) deep in a good sandy garden soil, in either sun or partial shade, and leave them untouched unless you need to increase your stock. This can be done when the leaves have died down; lift the plants and remove offsets, dry them and then replant. This is far quicker than growing by seed, which can take up to four years to mature. Where possible leave the plants to form mats or carpets of flowers in drifts under mature trees or shrubs. The only pests that cause trouble are slugs, so lay slug bait.

Take care

Do not disturb the roots. 458▸

Ranunculus asiaticus

- **Sunny position**
- **Ordinary garden soil**
- **Plant 5cm (2in) deep**

These plants are hardy in milder areas, but in colder parts they should be kept in a frost-free place during winter. Most of these plants have deeply cut leaves of mid-green, and semi-double blooms up to 7.5cm (3in) wide that are fine as cut flowers because they last well.

At first sight they look a little like anemones, with flowers of crimson, pink, orange, gold or white.

They bloom in early summer, and should be placed in the sun in a good soil that has been well dug over with plenty of compost, peat or well-rotted manure added. The tubers should be planted at any time from midwinter to spring, 5cm (2in) deep, with the claw-like roots pointing downwards. In less mild areas the plant should be lifted when its leaves turn yellow; dry off the root system in the sun, and store in a frost-free place until replanting in spring. At this time the tubers can be divided to increase your stock.

Take care

The claw-like roots must point downwards. 459▸

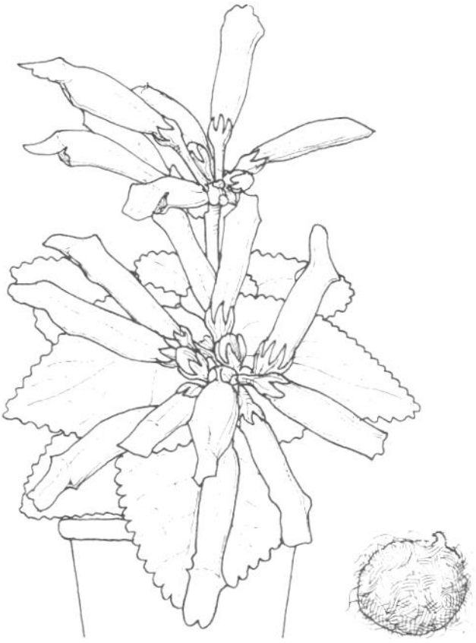

Rechsteineria cardinalis

- Shady site
- Good potting mixture
- Plant level with the surface

These tender plants from South Africa are grown as pot plants for their decorative foliage of green velvety leaves, and their scarlet tubular flowers, 5cm (2in) long. Usually they bloom in summer, but by staggering the sowing times the flowering season can be extended. They grow 23-45cm (9-18in) high.

The dormant tubers are started by putting them in moist peat at a temperature of 21°C (70°F). When the sprouts are almost 5cm (2in) long, put them into separate 15cm (6in) pots of John Innes No. 2, with the tops of the tubers level with the surface. Feed every two weeks with a liquid manure, and keep the temperature above 16°C (60°F). When they have finished flowering the leaves turn yellow. Leave off watering, remove dead growth and store for the winter in a frost-free place. In spring they should be potted up again. At this time the tubers can be divided so that each section has at least three shoots.

Take care
Do not bury tubers below surface.

Rhodohypoxis baurii

- Full sun
- Well-drained moist soil
- Plant just below the surface

These South African plants grow to only 7.5cm (3in) high, with a spread of 15cm (6in), and they have hairy pale sword-like leaves. The flowers have six petals, the three inner ones standing a fraction higher than the three outer ones; blooms vary from white to deep red, 3cm (1.25in) in diameter, and appear from spring to autumn.

Plant the corm-like rhizomes in autumn in a well-drained but moisture-retentive lime-free soil, with a good sunny position. In wet winters, put a cloche over the plants to keep them dry, and it will also give some protection against frost. Lift the plant in autumn to remove the offsets; replant these and they should flower the following year. Where excessive cold and damp occurs, treat them as pot plants. Grow them in 15cm (6in) pots of well-drained lime-free mixture, watering frequently until autumn; then repot, allow to almost dry and water as the plant begins shooting.

Take care
Avoid excessive wetness in winter.

Schizostylis coccinea

(Kaffir lily)

- **Sunny situation**
- **Moist soil**
- **Plant 2.5cm (1in) deep**

This elegant plant from South Africa grows to 90cm (36in). It has long slender leaves and spikes of up to ten star-shaped bright red or pink flowers almost 5cm (2in) across on each stem during autumn.

The rhizomes should be planted in spring in a moist place; they will even do well at the edge of water. Put them 2.5cm (1in) deep in a rich and fertile soil. A spring mulch of peat, compost or leaf-mould will help to keep the roots moist; if the soil dries out, water well. The growth remaining in late autumn should be cut down; cover the area with a layer of bracken to protect the roots against hard frost. As the plants are vigorous, they need lifting and dividing every few years, in spring. Make sure that each section of rhizome has several shoots, and plant them in their flowering positions. Treat with both a pesticide and a fungicide to keep them free from attack.

Take care

Keep the plants watered in summer and in droughts. 460▸

Scilla peruviana

(Cuban lily)

- **Warm sunny position**
- **Moist well-drained soil**
- **Plant 5cm (2in) deep**

This scilla is a bulbous plant from the Mediterranean with glossy strap-like leaves sometimes 30cm (12in) tall. The flowers vary from white through blue to dark purple, in late spring. The flowerheads have up to 100 star-shaped blooms, each about 2cm (0.8in) across.

The plants are easy to grow and need little after-care. They are recommended for rock and alpine gardens, growing in short grass or for indoor use in pots and containers. The bulbs should be planted 5cm (2in) deep in a moist but well-drained soil; add plenty of peat, leaf-mould or compost to improve the moisture-retention of the soil. The site should be warm and sunny. Put the bulbs out in late summer or early autumn, as soon as they become available. Scatter the bulbs over the area and plant them where they fall; this will give a casual and natural look. At this time offsets can be taken off mature plants and replanted to increase stock.

Take care

Keep moist during droughts.

Above: **Nerine bowdenii**
This fine showy plant bears lovely, deep pink flowers in the autumn. It enjoys a warm sunny border backed with a wall for protection against cold winds and frosts. 450▸

Above: **Ornithogalum thyrsoides**
This attractive, summer-flowering plant needs a sheltered position to grow well. If you live in a cold area treat it as a pot plant, it will then bloom in the early spring. 451▸

Right: **Ranunculus asiaticus**
An early summer-flowering plant that thrives in a sheltered sunny place and produces a succession of blooms that last well in water. The tubers increase in good soil. 454▸

Below: **Puschkinia scilloides**
This small plant produces its unusual blooms during the spring. It is ideal for rock gardens or as a pot plant and will tolerate full sun or partial shade. Leave it undisturbed. 454▸

Above:
Schizostylis coccinea 'Major'
A moisture-loving plant that flowers in autumn with red or pink blooms. These are vigorous and need to be divided every few years. 456▸

Above: **Scilla sibirica 'Atrocoerulea'**
These vivid blue spring flowers are best kept separate from other blue plants, which may look dull. 473▶

Below: **Scilla tubergeniana**
A much paler scilla that blooms as soon as it emerges from the soil in late winter. This low-growing plant is ideal for rock gardens. 473▶

Left: **Sinningia 'Orchidosena'**
The gloxinia produces brilliant blooms from its tuber and makes a fine outdoor container plant; if the night temperatures are right it will flower well. It can be used as an indoor plant but avoid direct sun. 474▸

Right: **Sprekelia formosissima**
A most unusual flower is produced by this half-hardy plant from Mexico. It enjoys full sun or light shade and a rich soil. It can be used for outdoor show, but give it some protection against cold winds and frost. 475▸

Below: **Sternbergia lutea**
An autumn-flowering plant that looks like a crocus and gives a show of brilliant yellow flowers. With its love of sun and its small stature it makes an ideal subject for the rockery. 475▸

Above: **Tigridia pavonia 'Rubra'**
A succession of vivid and unusual blooms adorns this plant in summer. The strange markings and spots amply justify its common name of tiger flower. Grow in full sun. 476▶

Left: **Tecophilaea cyanocrocus**
A low-growing rockery plant that thrives in a sandy soil in a sheltered place. Avoid too much wetness, especially in the winter, and protect against frost. Blooms in spring. 476▶

Right: **Tritonia crocata**
These delicate flowers appear in late spring in a wide range of colours. Use this plant as a container subject or as an indoor pot plant; in either situation it enjoys full sunshine. 478▶

Above: **Tulip 'Ida' (Division 4)**
A Triumph tulip that blooms in mid-season and thrives in full sun. Provide some lime in the soil. 480▸

Left: **Tulip 'Hadley' (Division 1)**
The large-flowered, single early bloom comes in the spring and makes a good formal plant. 478▸

Right: **Tulip 'Trance' (Division 3)**
A Mendel tulip that blooms in mid-spring. It prefers a sunny site where there is some lime in the soil. 479▸

Far right:
Tulip 'Montgomery' (Division 3)
These Mendel tulips, with striking margins, would grace any garden. 479▸

Above: **Tulip 'Golden Apeldoorn' (Division 5)**
A superb tall-growing and large-flowered Darwin hybrid. 480▸

Above right:
Tulip 'Aladdin' (Division 7)
A Lily-flowered tulip with typical waisted bloom and pointed petals. 481▸

Right:
Tulip 'Greenland' (Division 8)
The open bloom of this Cottage tulip appears in mid-season. 482▸

Below:
Tulip 'Orajezon' (Division 6)
These popular bedding Darwin tulips bloom in late spring. 481▸

Above: **Tulip 'Gold Medal' (Division 11)**
Enormous, double late blooms are characteristic of this group. 483▸

Left: **Tulip 'Flaming Parrot' (Division 10)**
These large, exotic Parrot flowers are heavily fringed. 483▸

Below left: **Tulip 'Allegretto' (Division 11)**
Flamboyant, double late flowers that are long lasting during the spring. 483▸

Below: **Tulip 'Giuseppe Verdi' (Division 12)**
These small Kaufmanniana blooms open out in sun like water-lilies. 484▸

Above: **Tulipa tarda**
A small plant that is ideal in a rock garden. The flowers open wide in sunshine and can have up to six blooms on each stem. 485▸

Below: **Tulip 'Yellow Empress' (Division 13)**
A Fosteriana variety with open long-lasting flowers of a medium size in mid-spring. Enjoys the sun. 484▸

Scilla sibirica 'Atrocoerulea'

- **Sun or partial shade**
- **Moist well-drained soil**
- **Plant 5cm (2in) deep**

The leaves of these scillas appear in early spring followed by the flower stems, of which there are three or four to each bulb; each stem bears up to five brilliant deep blue bell-shaped flowers, almost 2.5cm (1in) long, in spring. Plant these separate from other blue flowers, as the vivid blue of the scillas makes other blues look dull. The form 'Atrocoerulea' (also known as 'Spring Beauty') is a great improvement on the common form, with larger flowers and a more vigorous habit.

They will grow in any well-drained soil that holds moisture in drought periods. The bulbs should be planted in late summer or early autumn at a depth of 5cm (2in) in an area of sun or partial shade where they can be left undisturbed. Remove offsets from mature plants in autumn, and replant. Scatter the bulbs over the ground and plant where they fall to give a natural look. Use a pesticide and fungicide to keep plants healthy.

Take care

Plant as soon as the bulbs become available. 461▶

Scilla tubergeniana

- **Sun or semi-shade**
- **Moist well-drained soil**
- **Plant 5cm (2in) deep**

This scilla comes from the mountainous meadows and rocks of North-west Iran and grows to a height of 10cm (4in), with a similar spread. The flowers are pale blue or white, and open as soon as they emerge from the soil.

The bulbs should be planted as soon as they are purchased, in late summer or early autumn, in a sunny or half-shaded area of the garden where the soil is moist but well-drained. Cover the bulbs with 5cm (2in) of soil. For a casual effect the bulbs can be cast gently over the area and planted where they fall. To increase the moisture-holding properties of the soil dig in a good supply of leaf-mould, peat or compost before planting. Once planted the bulbs can be left untouched, but to increase stock, offsets can be taken from mature plants after the leaves have died down, and placed in a nursery bed to grow. Seed may take five years to reach flowering size.

Take care

Keep moist in dry weather. 46-▶

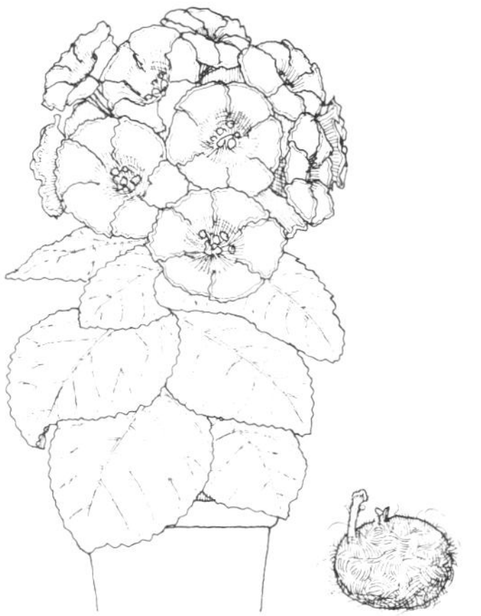

Sinningia speciosa

(Gloxinia)

- **Shade**
- **Fine peaty soil**
- **Plant with top level with soil**

Gloxinias, widely grown as pot plants, have the ability to flower from seed in five months provided the night temperatures are kept above 18°C (65°F). The leaves are velvety, fleshy and dark. The flowers are bell-shaped, with lobes around the open end, and up to 10cm (4in) long, in white, red, violet or purple, some with white edges. Both single and double forms are available. The plants grow to 25cm (10in) tall, with a spread of 30cm (12in).

Place tubers in moist peat in late winter, at a temperature of 21°C (70°F). As soon as the young shoots reach 5cm (2in), pot them in a peat-based mixture with the tuber top level with the surface; a 15cm (6in) pot to each tuber is adequate. Keep in a shaded greenhouse at above 18°C (65°F), and give a liquid feed every week while it is flowering. Cut down watering when the leaves turn yellow, and store until late winter. Gloxinias are generally trouble-free.

Take care

Keep the plants warm and moist. 462▸

Sparaxis tricolor

(Harlequin flower)

- **Warm sunny site**
- **Rich well-drained soil**
- **Plant 10cm (4in) deep**

This half-hardy plant is best grown as a pot plant unless you are in an area that is frost-free. It is noted for its flat blossoms, 5cm (2in) across, that appear in early summer. There are a number of flowers to each stem, in yellow, red; purple and white, sometimes with a number of colours on one bloom.

Plant corms in a well-drained but rich soil to a depth of 10cm (4in) in early winter, in a border that receives plenty of sun. The leaves will die down in summer, and the plant can be lifted, dried off and stored until early winter, when it can be planted again. When growing it in pots, put up to six corms in one 15cm (6in) pot, with a good potting mixture such as John Innes No. 2. Soak the pot well and then keep it dry until the leaves start to sprout; then water it until the leaves turn yellow, when it should be left to dry. Offsets can be taken at this time from a mature plant, and repotted immediately; they should flower in one year.

Take care

Protect against frost.

Sprekelia formosissima

- **Full light or light shade**
- **Rich potting mixture**
- **Plant with neck just above soil**

This Mexican half-hardy plant is grown as a pot plant for its funnel-shaped deep-red flowers. It grows 45cm (18in) tall with sparse strap-like leaves that appear after flowering has finished. The flower stems appear in spring, each stem bearing only one flower, 10cm (4in) wide.

Plant bulbs singly in 10cm (4in) pots of rich potting mixture such as John Innes No. 3 in late summer, with the neck of the bulb just above the surface. Keep the temperature over 8°C (45°F). Do not water until spring, then water with a liquid feed every two weeks from flowering until the leaves die back in summer. Repot in early autumn every few years, and at this time remove offsets and plant them in separate pots; they take up to four years to reach flowering. Look out for white tufts of waxy wool at the base of the leaves, caused by the mealy bug: use a systemic pesticide, painted on with a brush, to clear the attack.

Take care

Keep dry in autumn. 463▶

Sternbergia lutea

- **Full sun**
- **Well-drained soil**
- **Plant 10-15cm (4-6in) deep**

This plant from the Eastern Mediterranean and Iran looks like a crocus but flowers in autumn, with bright blooms up to 5cm (2in) long on a true stem. The strap-like leaves appear with the flower but remain small and immature until the following spring. The plant will reach a height of 15cm (6in), with a similar spread.

Plant the bulbs in late summer, 10-15cm (4-6in) deep in a well-drained soil, in a sunny part of the garden. Leave undisturbed until they become overcrowded, when they can be lifted in late summer, divided and replanted immediately to prevent drying out. The offsets can be removed and grown separately, and will mature and come into flower in one year. This plant can be grown with, or as an alternative to, autumn-flowering crocuses and will provide a show of brilliant yellow. Watch for mice eating bulbs; and if slugs attack the young growth, use a slug bait. Normally this plant is disease-free.

Take care

Leave undisturbed if possible. 462-463▶

Tecophilaea cyanocrocus

(Chilean crocus)

- **Warm sunny place**
- **Rich sandy soil**
- **Plant 5cm (2in) deep**

This plant has a few slender twisted leaves growing to a height of 12.5cm (5in). Its deep blue to purple petals have white throats. In their natural habitat in Chile these plants grow on stony well-drained slopes.

Plant them out of doors in a rich sandy soil that drains well, in a sunny and warm position with some protection from hard frost. In wet areas cover with a cloche to keep the plant dry during the winter months; this will stop the growth of the leaves, which are susceptible to low temperatures, and the plant will pick up in the spring. Plant the corms 5cm (2in) deep in mid-autumn. They can also be grown as pot plants in a cool greenhouse: place six corms in a 15cm (6in) pot of moist potting mixture, leave without water until the leaves shoot, then water until the leaves die. Allow the plants to dry out in the greenhouse, remove any offsets and grow on separately to flowering size.

Take care

Protect from frost damage. 464▸

Tigridia pavonia

(Tiger flower)

- **Sunny location**
- **Rich well-drained soil**
- **Plant 7.5-10cm (3-4in) deep**

These spectacular half-hardy plants from Mexico and Peru can reach 60cm (24in) tall, with long sword-shaped pleated leaves of mid-green. The flowers last only a day, but each stem produces a succession of up to eight blooms in summer. These are up to 10cm (4in) wide, and have three large petals with three small petals in between, surrounding a cup-shaped base; the larger petals are plain but the smaller ones are spotted in white, yellow or red, which gives them the common name of tiger flower.

Plant the corms in spring, 7.5-10cm (3-4in) deep in a rich well-drained soil, in a position where there is plenty of sun. Lift them in autumn and keep dry and frost-free until replanting time next spring. At this time cormlets can be removed and grown separately, to reach flowering size in a couple of years. During winter guard against mice eating the stored corms.

Take care

Keep moist in dry weather. 464-465▸

Trillium grandiflorum

- **Shady situation**
- **Moist well-drained soil**
- **Plant 10cm (4in) deep**

The trillium can grow to a height of 45cm (18in). It has pale to mid-green leaves, and large flowers 7.5cm (3in) across with the petals slightly turned back, blooming from mid-spring. The blooms are white on opening, gradually changing to pink; double varieties are available in white and pink.

Trilliums need a moist well-drained soil in a shady situation; added peat, leaf-mould or compost is beneficial. Rhizomes should be planted in late summer, as soon as they become available, at a depth of 10cm (4in). Planting in groups, with the bulbs 15cm (6in) apart, gives a massed effect. When leaves die down in late summer the plant can be lifted, and the rhizomes divided and replanted. Seeds can take up to six years to reach flowering size, so it is better to grow from rhizome sections, but make sure that each piece has a growing shoot on it.

Take care

Keep plants out of direct sun unless plenty of moisture is available.

Trillium sessile

- **Shady location**
- **Moist well-drained soil**
- **Plant 10cm (4in) deep**

This plant from central USA has deep green leaves marbled in grey, borne in a single group at the top of each stem. The stemless flowers have narrow, upright and partially twisted pointed petals that are often 7.5cm (3in) long; they are highly perfumed, and red to deep red in colour, blooming from mid-spring.

They thrive in a moist soil that is well-drained, with some leaf-mould, peat or compost mixed in to increase its moisture-holding qualities in hot weather. The plants can survive in direct sun if they have sufficient moisture, but most prefer cooler shady areas. The leaves die back in late summer, and at this time they can be lifted, divided and replanted, but each section of rhizome must have a growing shoot. Seeds are very slow to germinate, and can take up to six years to flower. Prevent slug attack with slug bait spread around the plants. Trilliums are usually disease-free.

Take care

Keep these plants moist.

Tritonia crocata

- **Full light**
- **Good potting mixture**
- **Plant 5cm (2in) deep**

This plant has fans of slender, sword-shaped mid-green leaves, and will grow to a height of 45cm (18in). In late spring it will produce a number of cup-shaped flowers up to 5cm (2in) wide, in white, yellow, pink, orange or copper.

Most of this group of plants are best grown as pot plants, although some can be used in late spring as container plants in the garden. Corms should be planted in moist potting mixture such as John Innes No. 2, five to a 15cm (6in) pot. After planting in early autumn, the pot should not be watered until the leaves start to shoot, unless the mixture dries right out. Keep a temperature of over 7°C (45°F) and put the plant in full light as much as possible. After flowering keep well watered until the leaves die back, then let the soil dry out in the greenhouse heat until early autumn, when it should be repotted. At this time offsets can be removed from the larger corms and grown on.

Take care

Support leggy plants with canes. 465▸

Tulip Division 1: Single Early

- **Full sun**
- **Slightly alkaline soil**
- **Plant 15cm (6in) deep at most**

Tulips were introduced into Europe from Turkey over 300 years ago and an industry for developing bulbs and hybrids has centred in Holland. In these pages, tulips have been split up into the official groups.

The single early is self-descriptive, single blooms in spring when grown out of doors, or in winter if forced under glass. The flowers grow to 12.5cm (5in) wide, and sometimes open flat in direct sunshine. A wide range of colours is available, in white, yellow, pink, red, orange, purple and mixtures. The plants, 15-38cm (6-15in) tall, are ideal for bedding or border planting.

Plant in late autumn in a slightly alkaline soil, in full sunlight, 15cm (6in) deep. When the petals fall, cut off the head to allow leaves and stem to feed the bulb for the following season. Offsets can be removed in late autumn and grown on. Use a pesticide and fungicide.

Take care

Dead-head the plants to build up the bulbs for next year. 466▸

Tulip Division 2: Double Early

- **Full sun**
- **Alkaline soil**
- **Plant 15cm (6in) deep at most**

This group of tulips has early-blooming flowers in spring, and if forced under glass can be in flower in late winter. The form is double, with blooms often reaching 10cm (4in) across. The plants grow to 30-38cm (12-15in), and leaves are often grey-green. A good example is 'Orange Nassau', a large blood-red tulip ideal for bedding out or forcing. The colours available are white, yellow, pink, orange, red, violet and purple, with many multicolours.

Plant out bulbs in late autumn in a slightly alkaline soil, 15cm (6in) deep. Tulips thrive in direct sunlight. When the petals fall, dead-head the plant but leave the stem and leaves to feed the bulb for the coming season. When the leaves turn yellow the plant can be lifted and stored for replanting in late autumn. Offsets can be taken at lifting time and grown on. Treat the plant with pesticide and fungicide.

Take care

Keep bulbs moist while growing.

Tulip Division 3: Mendel

- **Full sun**
- **Ordinary soil that is not acid**
- **Plant 15cm (6in) deep at most**

These tulips flower later than Divisions 1 and 2 and the blooms are more rounded, some 12.5cm (5in) across, and borne on slender stems. They flower in mid-spring, and colours include white, yellow, red and deep red. Representative of this division is 'Athleet', a lovely white tulip. Plants grow to a height of 50cm (20in), and the mid-green or blue-green leaves are shaped like a broad spear-head.

They enjoy an alkaline soil in full sun. Plant bulbs in late autumn at a depth of 15cm (6in), and water in well if the soil is dry. Keep moist during the growing period. When the petals fall, cut off the flowerhead to stop goodness concentrating on seed production to the detriment of the bulb. Bulbs can be lifted when the leaves turn yellow; remove offsets and grow on separately. The parent bulb can be dried and stored for replanting in late autumn. Treat the plants with a pesticide and fungicide to keep attacks to a minimum.

Take care

Keep moist while growing. 467▶

Tulip Division 4: Triumph

- **Sunny position**
- **Slightly alkaline soil**
- **Plant 15cm (6in) deep at most**

These tulips grow to 50cm (20in), and flower in mid-season, after the early singles and doubles but at the same time as the Mendel tulips in mid-spring. The blooms have an angular look and are carried on sturdy stems. The colours include white, yellow, orange, gold, pink, red and lilac. An example of this group is 'Garden Party', a white flower edged with pink.

These tulips thrive in a slightly alkaline soil in full sun. Bulbs should be planted at a depth of 15cm (6in) in late autumn; in light soils increase the depth to provide anchorage. Water in the bulbs and keep them moist during the growing period. After flowering cut the heads off to keep the nutrients feeding the bulb. When leaves turn yellow the plant can be lifted; remove offsets and grow on separately. Store the parent bulb in a dry place to ripen, before replanting in late autumn. Use a pesticide and fungicide to prevent attacks.

Take care

Keep dead-heading plants. 466-467▸

Tulip Division 5: Darwin Hybrids

- **Full sun**
- **Slightly alkaline soil**
- **Plant 15cm (6in) deep at most**

The tulips in this group are among the most brilliant and large-flowered. The leaves are grey-green and the plant grows over 60cm (24in) tall. Blooms reach 17.5cm (7in) wide when they open in mid-spring. The colours include yellow, orange, red and purple, with some spectacular multicoloured flowers. 'Golden Oxford' (a pure yellow), 'Big Chief' (one of the larger tulips grown, 65cm (26in) tall, with rose-coloured flowers) and 'Beauty of Apeldoorn' (a creamy yellow flushed with orange, with black base and anthers) are tulips that fall into this section.

These plants enjoy a slightly alkaline soil in full sun, and bulbs should be planted 15cm (6in) deep in late autumn. If the soil is dry, water well in and keep moist during the growing period. When the flowers have finished, cut off the heads to allow the stem and leaves to feed the bulb. Lift when the leaves turn yellow, remove offsets and plant separately.

Take care

In acid soils add lime or chalk. 468▸

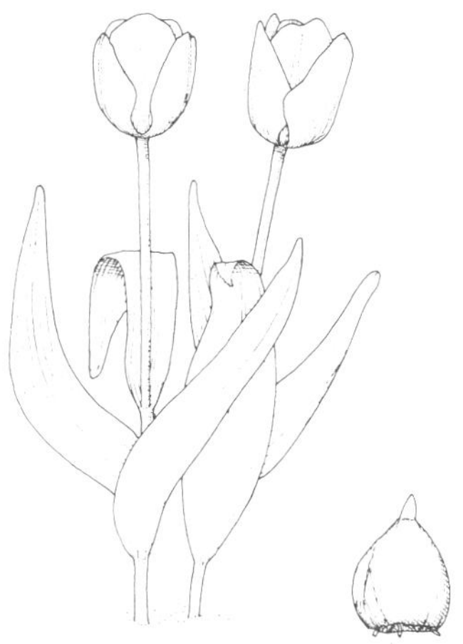

Tulip Division 6: Darwin

- **Full sun**
- **Good soil that is not acid**
- **Plant 15cm (6in) deep at most**

Within this group are the most popular bedding tulips, growing 75cm (30in) tall, with mid-green to blue-green leaves. The flowers are rounded and often reach 12.5cm (5in) across, blooming in late spring after the hybrids. Colours include white, yellow, orange, pink, red and purple, with a number of dramatic multicoloured varieties. Among many named tulips available are: 'Bleu Aimable' (lilac flushed with purple, and a blue base), 'Snowpeak' (pure white) and 'La Tulipe Noire' (deep purple-black).

These tulips thrive in good garden soil that is not acid; acid soil needs added lime or chalk to make it more alkaline. Choose a sunny position, with 15cm (6in) of soil over the bulbs, which should be planted in late autumn. Keep them moist during the growing period. When the flowers fade cut off the heads. When the leaves die lift the plant; remove offsets and replant them, storing the parent bulb until late autumn.

Take care

Keep moist while growing. 468▸

Tulip Division 7: Lily-flowered

- **Full sun**
- **Slightly alkaline soil**
- **Plant 15cm (6in) deep at most**

These tulips are noted for their flower shape, being slightly waisted with pointed petals that curl outwards. Blooms open in mid-spring and often reach 20cm (8in) wide. The leaves are green, some with a grey cast; the plants reach 60cm (24in) tall, and look very effective when massed. Colours include white, yellow, orange, red and multicoloured variations. Notable examples are 'Golden Duchess' (deep primrose yellow), 'Mariette' (deep rose, with a glorious texture to the petals), 'Picotee' (white, with a deep rose edging that increases in area as the plant ages) and 'White Triumphator' (a long white bloom).

These tulips enjoy full sun and a slightly alkaline soil. Plant 15cm (6in) deep in a sunny place in late autumn, and keep it moist while growing. Once the flower petals fall, cut off the heads. When leaves turn yellow, lift the plant, remove the offsets and grow them separately until mature. Use a pesticide and fungicide.

Take care

Add lime to an acid soil. 469▸

Tulip Division 8: Cottage

- **Full sun**
- **Ordinary slightly alkaline soil**
- **Plant 15cm (6in) deep at most**

This old group of tulips has oval or rounded flowers; petals occasionally have a hint of fringing, and are more loose and open than other forms. The flowers are up to 12.5cm (5in) across, in mid-spring. The plant is up to 90cm (36in) tall, with blue-green leaves. Flower colours include white, yellow, pink, red, lilac and green. Examples to note are 'Dillenburg' (a red-brown tulip that lasts well), 'Mrs John T. Scheepers' (with long oval yellow blooms) and 'Artist' (a strange mixture of green, pink and purple, with the petals partly fringed).

Plant cottage tulips in full sun, in an ordinary soil that is slightly alkaline. Bulbs should be planted in late autumn, 15cm (6in) deep. Keep the soil moist during the growing period. Dead-head the plants to stop seed production and when leaves have turned yellow they can be lifted; remove offsets to a nursery bed, and store parent bulbs for replanting in late autumn. Treat with a pesticide and fungicide to keep plants healthy.

Take care

Keep moist while growing. 469

Tulip Division 9: Rembrandt

- **Full sun**
- **Soil that is slightly alkaline**
- **Plant 15cm (6in) deep at most**

These are tulips with 'broken colours', usually Darwin types, which can be seen in old Dutch paintings. The rounded flowers open in mid-spring and are often 12.5cm (5in) wide, with vivid splashes of colour on the petals. The plants stand 75cm (30in) tall, with leaves sometimes having a blue-green cast. Blooms can be white, yellow, orange, red, pink, violet or brown. Two examples are 'May Blossom' (cream and purple) and 'Absalon' (dark coffee-brown and yellow).

Plant bulbs in late autumn, 15cm (6in) deep, in a good garden soil that is slightly alkaline, and in full sun. If the soil is dry at the time of planting, water it well, and leave until the plant starts growing; then keep moist until the leaves turn yellow. Once the flowers have finished, cut off the heads to allow the bulbs to take up food. When the leaves turn yellow, lift the plants, remove and replant the offsets, and store the parent bulbs for replanting in late autumn.

Take care

Dead-head plants after flowering.

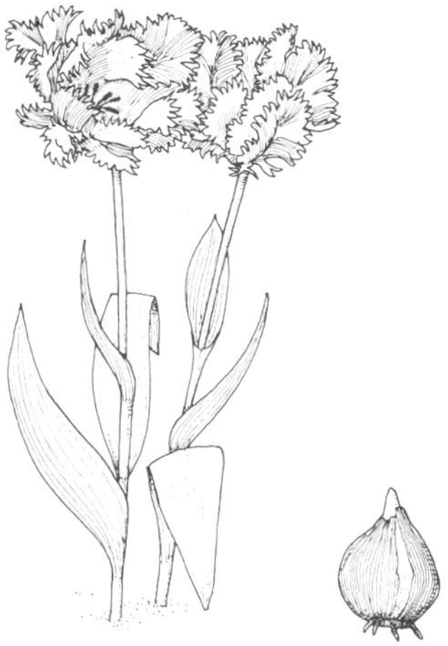

Tulip Division 10: Parrot

- **Full sun**
- **Good limy garden soil**
- **Plant 15cm (6in) deep at most**

Parrot tulips are easily recognized by their heavily fringed and feather-like petals. The blooms are large, reaching 20cm (8in) across, and appear in a range of brilliant white, yellow, pink, orange, red and purple in mid-spring. Plants grow to 60cm (24in) tall. Particularly noteworthy are 'Fantasy' (a soft rose, with pale stripes and featherings of green on the outer petals) and 'Gay Presto' (a brilliant showy bloom of white with scarlet markings).

Place bulbs in a sunny position, 15cm (6in) deep in an ordinary limy soil. Keep moist during the growing period, and when the petals fall off, dead-head the plants. When the leaves turn yellow, plants can be lifted and stored in a dry place until late autumn. Offsets can be removed and replanted in nursery beds to mature. Keep tulips free from attack with a pesticide and fungicide.

Take care

Dead-head to encourage flowering the following year. 470▸

Tulip Division 11: Double Late

- **Sunny position**
- **Limy soil**
- **Plant 15cm (6in) deep at most**

These tulips have huge double flowers that can reach 20cm (8in) wide, in a wide range of colours, and they remain in bloom for a long time. They grow to a height of 60cm (24in), and flowers are white, yellow, orange, pink, red or violets, many multicoloured, with stripes and edgings. Most notable of this group are 'Mount Tacoma' (white), 'Carnaval de Nice' (white with brilliant red stripes) and 'Orange Triumph' (orange with brown shading and yellow fringes, an enormous bloom that often reaches 20cm (8in) across).

Plant bulbs 15cm (6in) deep in a sunny position, although they can stand some shade. Keep the soil moist during the spring growing period, and when the flowers finish cut off the heads to allow the bulbs to take up nourishment for the coming season. When the leaves turn yellow, plants can be lifted, and offsets removed and replanted.

Take care

Watch for damage to blooms from wind or rain. 471▸

Tulip Division 12: Kaufmanniana varieties *(Water-lily tulip)*

- **Sunny sheltered site**
- **Well-drained soil**
- **Plant 15cm (6in) deep at most**

These small tulips have been developed from the parent plant *T. kaufmanniana*, which comes from Turkestan. They have fine pointed flowers that open out almost flat, which gives them the appearance of a water-lily. Some open early in spring and they grow to only 10-25cm (4-10in). They are sturdy, and some have attractively striped and mottled leaves. Most have two-coloured flowers almost 10cm (4in) long. These tulips are suitable for rock gardens, the front of borders or containers where they can be left undisturbed. Varieties to note are 'The First' (white with a golden base and red edges), 'Stresa' (red and yellow outside, yellow and brown inside) and 'Shakespeare' (a mixture of pinks and oranges with red shading, only 12.5cm/5 in tall).

Plant in well-drained soil in sunshine, at a depth of 15cm (6in). Keep them moist during spring, and dead-head after flowering.

Take care

Keep moist in spring. 471▶

Tulip Division 13: Fosteriana varieties

- **Full sun**
- **Slightly alkaline soil**
- **Plant 15cm (6in) deep at most**

These are derived from the parent plant *T. fosteriana*, which comes from Central Asia. They grow to a height of 45cm (18in), with large blunt-pointed flowers in reds and yellows in mid-spring, and grey-green leaves. There is only one white variety, 'White Emperor', with large long-lasting blooms. 'Red Emperor' has shiny brilliant red petals with a black base bordered with yellow; and 'Cantata', with orange-red flowers and apple-green leaves, grows only 23cm (9in) tall.

These bulbs thrive on a sunny site in a good garden soil with lime or chalk added. Cover the bulbs with 15cm (6in) of soil in late autumn and keep them moist during the growing season. When the flowers die, cut off their heads to build up the bulb for the following season. Plants may be left in the soil or lifted after the leaves turn yellow; at this time offsets can be removed, and grown on in nursery beds until mature.

Take care

Keep moist while growing. 472▶

Tulip Division 14: Greigii varieties

- Sunny site
- Add lime if soil is acid
- Plant 15cm (6in) deep at most

These hybrids are becoming popular for their decorative leaves and brilliant long-lasting flowers of red, yellow and near-white. The leaves are beautifully marked with stripes and mottles in browny purple, and the short sturdy growth helps plants to stand up to high winds, which makes them ideal for exposed sites. Generally growing to 25cm (10in), they flower in mid-spring. The petals reach 7.5cm (3in) long when the bloom opens fully in direct sunshine.

Where soil is acid, add some lime; where there is heavy clay, add plenty of sharp sand and fibrous material to help drainage. The bulbs should be planted in groups of up to a dozen to give a good display. Pick off the dead heads to build up the bulb for the next year.

Dust soil with an insecticide to deter pests. Most diseases are due to excessive moisture. If disease appears other than rot, destroy bulb.

Take care

Keep the area around the bulbs weed-free.

Tulipa tarda

- Sheltered and sunny position
- Well-drained soil with some lime
- Plant 15cm (6in) deep at most

This small plant from Central Asia is only 10cm (4in) tall and has up to six blooms on each stem; these are star-shaped, and the yellow petals, 5cm (2in) long, have prominent white tips and a green flush on the outside. When planted 7.5cm (3in) apart, they form a carpet of blooms in spring. The narrow leaves are mid-green in colour.

Plant the bulbs in late autumn, in a sunny sheltered position, 15cm (6in) deep in a good well-drained soil that has some lime in it. Plant them in groups of up to a dozen for good effect. During the growing season make sure that the soil does not dry out. After flowering cut off the dead heads to make the plant's strength go into the bulbs. The plants can be left in the soil, but when they become crowded, lift and divide to give them more room. These can also be grown in pots. To keep the plant healthy use a pesticide and fungicide.

Take care

Dead-head the plants to ensure future blooms. 472◆

Tulipa turkestanica

- **Sheltered, sunny situation**
- **Well-drained alkaline soil**
- **Plant 15cm (6in) deep at most**

This plant, a native of Central Asia and North-west China, has a simple six-petalled star-shaped bloom and slender grey-green leaves. The plant grows to a height of 20cm (8in). The flowers are white, with a green and bronze blush on the outside, and up to nine long-lasting blooms over 2.5cm (1in) long are carried by each flower stem in early spring.

Plant bulbs in late autumn in a well-drained soil that has some lime in it, 15cm (6in) deep, in an area where they can receive full sun. During the growing season keep them moist, but when flowers and leaves have faded they prefer to be kept dry. Dead-head the plants to keep the strength going into the bulb rather than for seed production. Plants can be left *in situ* to naturalize, but if they become congested they can be lifted after the leaves turn yellow; remove and replant offsets in a nursery bed, and give parent plants more room. Treat with a pesticide and fungicide.

Take care
Keep moist during spring droughts.

Zantedeschia aethiopica *(Arum lily)*

- **Sun or partial shade**
- **Deep moist soil**
- **Plant 10cm (4in) deep in soil, 30cm (12in) deep in water**

This half-hardy rhizomatous plant will grow out of doors in mild districts, but in less mild areas it should be treated as a pot plant. The leaves are 20cm (8in) long and over 10cm (4in) wide, arrow-shaped and glossy. The 90cm (36in) plant has unusual flowers: an irregular funnel has a central boss (or *spadix*) on which are borne the true flowers (the large cream-coloured funnel is not the actual flower but a *spathe*, or enlarged bud cover).

This is also an aquatic plant that can be grown as deep as 30cm (12in) below water. The deeper the rhizome is planted, the more hardy it seems; in soil, 10cm (4in) gives good protection in winter. Plant in spring in a deep moist soil, in sun or partial shade. To protect the root system during winter, cover plants with a thick layer of straw, bracken or ashes, to keep off the worst of the frosts. In late autumn the plant can be lifted, divided and replanted.

Take care
Guard against frost damage.

Picture Credits

The publishers wish to thank the following photographers and agencies who have supplied photographs for this book. Photographs have been credited by page number and position on the page: (B) Bottom, (T) Top, (C) Centre, (BL) Bottom Left, etc.

Line artwork
The drawings in this book have been prepared by Maureen Holt and David Papworth

Photographs
The majority of photographs in this book have been taken by Eric Crichton

Copyright in the following photographs belong to the suppliers:

Pat Brindley: 273(B), 274, 275(B), 276(B), 277, 342(B), 365(B), 408, 425, 426(B), 430(T), 432(B)

Brian Carter: endpapers, 1, 2-3, 5, 6

Erich Crichton: 17, 23(B), 44, 46-7(B), 78, 79(B), 81, 88(B), 108(TR), 111(BR), 112(TL), 113(TR,BR), 114-5(T), 118(B), 120, 149, 201, 203(B), 206(B), 209, 214(B), 215, 216, 233, 236-7(T), 240(T), 244(B), 246(T), 266(B), 269(B), 270-1(T), 270(B), 278, 279, 280, 303, 306(B), 308, 310(T), 312, 343(B), 397(B), 406(BR), 426(T), 428-9(B), 434-5(B), 458(TL), 462(T), 468(T), 472(T)

Ralph Gould: 23(T), 47(T), 52(T), 82(TL), 108(B), 117(T)

Harry Smith Photographic Collection: 337(R), 362(T), 364(T), 403(T), 427, 434(T), 435(T,B), 459, 465(B)

David Squire: 213(TR), 238(B), 248, 305(B)

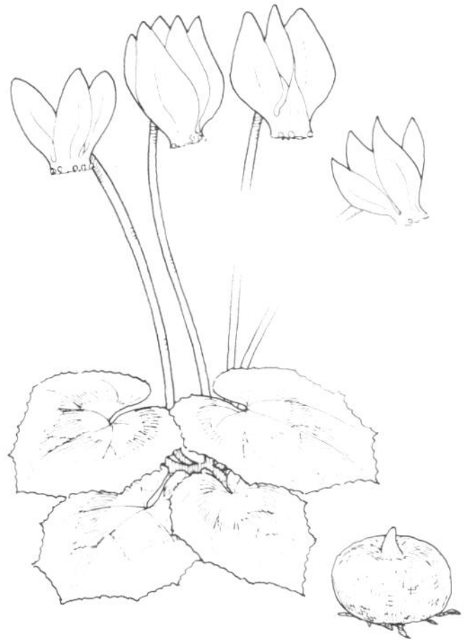

Cyclamen hederifolium

Gazania 'Sunbeam'